BITCOIN AND CRYPTOCURRENCY TECHNOLOGIES

BITCOIN AND CRYPTOCURRENCY TECHNOLOGIES

A Comprehensive Introduction

ARVIND NARAYANAN, JOSEPH BONNEAU, EDWARD FELTEN,
ANDREW MILLER, AND STEVEN GOLDFEDER

PRINCETON UNIVERSITY PRESS
Princeton and Oxford

Published by Princeton University Press, 41 William Street, Princeton, New Jersey 08540

In the United Kingdom: Princeton University Press, 6 Oxford Street, Woodstock, Oxfordshire OX20 1TR

press.princeton.edu

Cover image: Courtesy of Shutterstock

ISBN 978-0-691-17169-2

Library of Congress Cataloging-in-Publication Data

Names: Narayanan, Arvind, author.

Title: Bitcoin and cryptocurrency technologies : a comprehensive introduction / Arvind Narayanan, Joseph Bonneau, Edward Felten, Andrew Miller, and Steven Goldfeder.

Description: Princeton : Princeton University Press, [2016] | Includes bibliographical references and index.

Identifiers: LCCN 2016014802 | ISBN 9780691171692 (hardcover : alk. paper)

Subjects: LCSH: Bitcoin. | Electronic funds transfers. | Cryptography. | Money.

Classification: LCC HG1710 .N35 2016 | DDC 332.1/78—dc23 LC record available at https://lccn.loc.gov/2016014802

British Library Cataloging-in-Publication Data is available

This book has been composed in Charis

Printed on acid-free paper. ∞

Printed in the United States of America

5 7 9 10 8 6 4

Contents

Preface

There's a lot of excitement about Bitcoin and cryptocurrencies. Optimists claim that Bitcoin will fundamentally alter payments, economics, and even politics around the world. Pessimists claim Bitcoin is inherently broken and will suffer an inevitable and spectacular collapse.

Underlying these differing views is significant confusion about what Bitcoin is and how it works. We wrote this book to help cut through the hype and get to the core of what makes Bitcoin unique. To really understand what is special about Bitcoin, we need to understand how it works at a technical level. Bitcoin truly is a new technology, and we can only get so far by explaining it through simple analogies to past technologies.

We assume that you have a basic understanding of computer science—how computers work, data structures and algorithms, and some programming experience. If you're an undergraduate or graduate student of computer science, a software developer, an entrepreneur, or a technology hobbyist, this textbook is for you.

In this book, we address the important questions about Bitcoin. How does Bitcoin work? What makes it different? How secure are your bitcoins? How anonymous are Bitcoin users? What applications can we build using Bitcoin as a platform? Can cryptocurrencies be regulated? If we were designing a new cryptocurrency today, what would we change? What might the future hold?

After reading this book, you'll know everything you need to be able to separate fact from fiction when reading claims about Bitcoin and other cryptocurrencies. You'll have the conceptual foundations you need to engineer secure software that interacts with the Bitcoin network. And you'll be able to integrate ideas from Bitcoin into your own projects.

The online supplementary materials for this book include a series of homework questions to help you understand each chapter at a deeper level. In addition, there is a series of programming assignments in which you'll implement various components of Bitcoin in simplified models. Most of the material of this book is also available as a series of video lectures on Coursera. (A link to the supplementary materials can be found at http://press.princeton.edu/titles/10908.html.) You should also supplement your learning with information you can find online, including the Bitcoin wiki, forums, and research papers, and by interacting with your peers and the Bitcoin community.

Foreword
THE LONG ROAD TO BITCOIN

JEREMY CLARK

The path to Bitcoin is littered with the corpses of failed attempts. I've compiled a list of about a hundred cryptographic payment systems, both e-cash- and credit-card-based technologies, that are notable in some way (Table 0.1). Some are academic proposals that have been widely cited, while others are actual systems that were deployed and tested. Of all the names on this list, there's probably only one that you recognize—PayPal. And PayPal survived only because it quickly pivoted away from its original idea of cryptographic payments on handheld devices!

There's a lot to learn from this history. Where do the ideas in Bitcoin come from? Why do some technologies survive while many others die? What does it take for complex technical innovations to be successfully commercialized? If nothing else, this story will give you an appreciation of how remarkable it is that we finally have a real, working payment mechanism that's native to the Internet.

TRADITIONAL FINANCIAL ARRANGEMENTS

If you imagine a world without governments or currency, one system that could still work for acquiring goods is barter. Suppose Alice wants a tool, and Bob wants medicine. If each of them happen to have what the other person needs, then they can swap and both satisfy their needs.

But suppose Alice has food that she's willing to trade for a tool, while Bob, who has a tool, doesn't have any need for food. He wants medicine instead. Alice and Bob can't trade with each other, but if there's a third person, Carol, who has medicine that she's willing to trade for food, then it becomes possible to arrange a three-way swap where everyone gets what they need.

The drawback, of course, is coordination—arranging a group of people, whose needs and wants align, in the same place at the same time. Two systems emerged to solve coordination: credit and cash. Historians, anthropologists, and economists debate which of the two developed first, but that's immaterial for our purposes.

TABLE 0.1. NOTABLE ELECTRONIC PAYMENT SYSTEMS AND PROPOSALS

ACC	CyberCents	IKP	MPTP	Proton
Agora	CyberCoin	IMB-MP	Net900	Redi-Charge
AIMP	CyberGold	InterCoin	NetBill	S/PAY
Allopass	DigiGold	Ipin	NetCard	Sandia Lab E-Cash
b-money	Digital Silk Road	Javien	NetCash	Secure Courier
BankNet	e-Comm	Karma	NetCheque	Semopo
Bitbit	E-Gold	LotteryTickets	NetFare	SET
Bitgold	Ecash	Lucre	No3rd	SET2Go
Bitpass	eCharge	MagicMoney	One Click Charge	SubScrip
C-SET	eCoin	Mandate	PayMe	Trivnet
CAFÉ	Edd	MicroMint	PayNet	TUB
Checkfree	eVend	Micromoney	PayPal	Twitpay
ClickandBuy	First Virtual	MilliCent	PaySafeCard	VeriFone
ClickShare	FSTC Electronic Check	Mini-Pay	PayTrust	VisaCash
CommerceNet	Geldkarte	Minitix	PayWord	Wallie
CommercePOINT	Globe Left	MobileMoney	Peppercoin	Way2Pay
CommerceSTAGE	Hashcash	Mojo	PhoneTicks	WorldPay
Cybank	HINDE	Mollie	Playspan	X-Pay
CyberCash	iBill	Mondex	Polling	

In a credit-based system, Alice and Bob would be able to trade with each other in the example above. Bob would give Alice the tool, and Bob gets a favor that's owed to him. In other words, Alice has a debt that she needs to settle with Bob some time in the future. Alice's material needs are now satisfied, but she has a debt that she'd like to cancel, so that's her new "want." If Alice encounters Carol in the future, Alice can trade her food for Carol's medicine, then go back to Bob with the medicine and cancel the debt.

In contrast, in a cash-based system, Alice would buy the tool from Bob. Later, she might sell her food to Carol, and Carol can sell her medicine to Bob, completing the cycle. These trades can happen in any order, provided that the buyer in each transaction has cash on hand. In the end, of course, it's as if no money ever changed hands.

Neither system is clearly superior. A cash-based system needs to be bootstrapped with some initial allocation of cash, without which no trades can occur. A credit-based system doesn't need bootstrapping, but the drawback is that anyone who's owed a debt is taking on some risk. There's a chance that the other person never settles the debt.

Cash also allows us to be precise about how much something is worth. If you're bartering, it's hard to say whether a tool is worth more than medicine or medicine is worth more than food. Cash lets us use numbers to talk about value. That's why we use a blended system today—even when we're using credit, we measure debt in the amount of cash it would take to settle it.

These ideas come up in many contexts, especially in online systems, where users trade virtual goods of some kind. For example, peer-to-peer file-sharing networks must deal with the problem of freeloaders, that is, users who download files without sharing in turn. While swapping files might work, there is also the issue of coordination: finding the perfect person who has exactly the file you want and wants exactly the file you have. In projects like MojoNation and academic proposals like Karma, users are given some initial allocation of virtual cash that they must spend to receive a file and earn when they send a copy of a file to another user. A network of nodes (centralized for MojoNation and decentralized for Karma) keeps track of users' balances, and MojoNation explored implementing an exchange service between their internal currency and traditional currency. While MojoNation did not survive long enough to implement such an exchange, it became the intellectual ancestor of some protocols used today: BitTorrent and Tahoe-LAFS.

THE TROUBLE WITH CREDIT CARDS ONLINE

Credit and cash are fundamental ideas, to the point that we can sort the multitude of electronic payment methods into two piles. Bitcoin is obviously in the "cash" pile, but let's look at the other one first.

Credit card transactions are the dominant payment method used on the web today. If you've ever bought something from an online seller such as Amazon, you know how the arrangement goes. You type in your credit card details, you send it to Amazon, and then Amazon takes these credit card details and talks to a financial system involving processors, banks, credit card companies, and other intermediaries.

In contrast, if you use something like PayPal, what you see is an intermediary architecture. A company sits between you and the seller, so you send your credit card details to this intermediary, which approves the transaction and notifies the seller. The intermediary will settle its balance with the seller at the end of each day.

What you gain from this architecture is that you don't have to give the seller your credit card details, which can be a security risk. You might not even have to give the seller your identity, which would improve your privacy as well. The downside is that you lose the simplicity of interacting directly with the seller. Both you and the seller might have to have an account with the same intermediary.

Today most of us are comfortable with giving out our credit card information when shopping online, or at least we've grudgingly accepted it. We're also used to companies collecting data about our online shopping and browsing activities. But in the 1990s, the web was new, standards for protocol-level encryption were just emerging, and these concerns made consumers deeply uncertain and hesitant. In particular, it was considered crazy to hand over your credit card details to online vendors of unknown repute over an insecure channel. This environment generated a lot of interest in the intermediary architecture.

A company called FirstVirtual was an early payment intermediary, founded in 1994. Incidentally, they were one of the first companies to set up a purely virtual office with employees spread across the country and communicating over the Internet—hence the name.

FirstVirtual's proposed system was a little like PayPal's current system but preceded it by many years. As a user, you'd enroll with them and provide your credit card details. If you wanted to buy something from a seller, the seller would contact FirstVirtual with the details of the requested payment, FirstVirtual would confirm these details with you, and if you approved, your credit card would be billed. But two details are interesting. First, all of this communication happened over email; web browsers back in the day were just beginning to universally support encryption protocols like HTTPS, and the multiparty nature of payment protocol added other complexities. (Other intermediaries took the approach of encoding information into URLs or using a custom encryption protocol on top of HTTP.) Second, the customer would have 90 days to dispute the charge, and the merchant would receive the money only after those 3 months! With today's systems, the merchant does get paid immediately, but there still is the risk that the customer will file a chargeback or dispute the credit card statement. If that happens, the merchant will have to return the payment to the credit card company.

In the mid-1990s, a competing approach to the intermediary architecture was developed, which we'll call the SET architecture. SET also avoids the need for customers to send credit card information to merchants, but it additionally avoids the user having to enroll with the intermediary. In SET, when you are ready to make a purchase, your browser passes your view of the transaction details to a shopping application on your computer. The application encrypts it together with your credit card details in such a way that only the intermediary can decrypt it, and no one else can (including the seller). Having encrypted your data in this way, you can send it to the seller knowing that it's secure. The seller blindly forwards the encrypted data to the intermediary—along with their own view of the transaction details. The intermediary decrypts your data and approves the transaction only if your view matches the seller's view.

SET was a standard developed by Visa and MasterCard, together with many technology heavyweights of the day: Netscape, IBM, Microsoft, Verisign, and RSA. It was an umbrella specification that unified several existing proposals.

One company that implemented SET was CyberCash. It was an interesting company in many ways. In addition to credit card payment processing, they had a digital cash product called CyberCoin. This was a micropayment system—intended for small payments, such as paying a few cents to read an online newspaper article. That meant you'd probably never have more than $10 in your CyberCoin account at any time. Yet, amusingly, they were able to get U.S. government (FDIC) insurance for each account for up to $100,000.

There's more. Back when CyberCash operated, there was a misguided—and now abandoned—U.S. government restriction on the export of cryptography, which was considered a weapon. That meant software that incorporated meaningful encryption couldn't be offered for download to users in other countries. However, CyberCash was able to get a special exemption for their software from the Department of State. The government's argument was that extracting the encryption technology out of CyberCash's software would be harder than writing the crypto from scratch.

Finally, CyberCash has the dubious distinction of being one of the few companies affected by the Y2K bug—it caused their payment processing software to double-bill some customers. They later went bankrupt in 2001. Their intellectual property was acquired by Verisign, which then turned around and sold it to PayPal, where it lives today.

Why didn't SET work? The fundamental problem has to do with certificates. A certificate is a way to securely associate a cryptographic identity, that is, a public key, with a real-life identity. It's what a website needs to obtain—from companies like Verisign, which are called "certification authorities"—to be identified as secure in your browser (typically indicated by a lock icon). Putting security before usability, CyberCash and SET decided that not only would processors and merchants in their system have to get certificates, but all users also would have to get one as well. Obtaining a certificate is about as pleasant as doing your taxes, so the system was a disaster. Over the decades, mainstream users have given a firm and collective "no" to any system that requires end-user certificates, and such proposals have now been relegated to academic papers. Bitcoin deftly sidesteps this hairy problem by avoiding real-life identities altogether. In Bitcoin, public keys themselves are the identities by which users are known, as discussed in Chapter 1.

In the mid-1990s, when SET was being standardized, the World Wide Web Consortium was also looking at standardizing financial payments. They wanted to do it by extending the HTTP protocol instead, so that users wouldn't need extra software for transactions—they could just use their browsers. In fact, the Consortium had a very general proposal for how you might extend the protocol, and one of the use cases that they had was handling payments. This never happened—the whole extension framework was never deployed in any browsers. In 2015, almost two decades later, the Consortium announced that it wanted to take another crack at it, and that Bitcoin would be part of that standardization this time around. Given all the past failures, however, I won't be holding my breath.

FROM CREDIT TO (CRYPTO) CASH

Now let's turn to cash. I compared cash and credit earlier, and noted that a cash system needs to be bootstrapped, but the benefit is that it avoids the possibility of a buyer defaulting on her debt. Cash offers two additional advantages. The first is better anonymity. Since your credit card is issued in your name, the bank can track all your spending. But when you pay in cash, the bank doesn't come into the picture, and the other party doesn't need to know who you are. Second, cash can enable offline transactions where there's no need to phone home to a third party to get the transaction approved. Maybe the seller later uses a third party like a bank to deposit the cash, but that's much less of a hassle.

Bitcoin doesn't quite offer these two properties, but it comes close enough to be useful. Bitcoin is not anonymous to the same level as cash is. You don't need to use your real identity to pay in Bitcoin, but it's possible that your transactions can be tied together using clever algorithms based on the public ledger of transactions and then further linked to your identity if you're not careful. Chapter 6 gets into the messy but fascinating details behind Bitcoin anonymity.

Bitcoin doesn't work in a fully offline way either. The good news is it doesn't require a central server, instead relying on a peer-to-peer network, which is resilient in the way that the Internet itself is. Chapter 3 looks at tricks like "green addresses" and micropayments, which allow offline payments in certain situations or under certain assumptions.

The earliest ideas about applying cryptography to cash came from David Chaum in 1983. Consider this concept by means of a physical analogy. Let's say I start giving out pieces of paper that say: "The bearer of this note may redeem it for one dollar by presenting it to me" with my signature attached. If people trust that I'll keep my promise and consider my signature unforgeable, they can pass around these pieces of paper just like banknotes. In fact, banknotes themselves got their start as promissory notes issued by commercial banks. It's only in fairly recent history that governments stepped in to centralize the money supply and legally require banks to redeem notes.

I can do the same thing electronically with digital signatures, but that runs into the annoying "double-spending" problem—if you receive a piece of data representing a unit of virtual cash, you can make two (or more) copies of it and pass it on to different people. To stick with this analogy, let's stretch it a little bit and assume that people can make perfect copies and we have no way to tell copies from the original. Can we solve double spending in this world?

Here's a possible solution: I put unique serial numbers on each note I give out. When you receive such a note from someone, you check my signature, but you also call me on the phone to ask whether a note with that serial number has already been spent. Hopefully I'll say no, in which case you accept the note. I'll record the serial number as spent in my ledger, and if you try to spend that note, it won't work, because the recipient will call me and I'll tell them the note has already been spent. What you'll need to do instead is to periodically bring me all the notes you've received, and I'll issue you the same number of new notes with fresh serial numbers.

This works. It's cumbersome in real life, but straightforward digitally, provided I've set up a server to do the signing and recordkeeping of serial numbers. The only problem is that this isn't really cash anymore, because it's not anonymous—when I issue a note to you, I can record the serial number along with your identity, and I can do the same when someone else later redeems it. That means I can keep track of all the places where you're spending your money.

Here is where Chaum's innovation comes in. He figured out how to both keep the system anonymous and prevent double spending by inventing the digital equivalent of the following procedure: when I issue a new note to you, *you* pick the serial number. You write it down on the piece of paper, but cover it so that I can't see it. Then I'll sign it, still unable to see the serial number. This is called a "blind signature" in cryptography. It'll be in your interest to pick a long, random serial number to ensure that it will most likely be unique. I don't have to worry that you'll pick a serial number that's already been picked—you only shoot yourself in the foot by doing so and end up with a note that can't be spent.

This was the first serious digital cash proposal. It works, but it still requires a server run by a central authority, such as a bank, and for everyone to trust that entity. Moreover, every transaction needs the participation of this server to be completed. If the server goes down temporarily, payments grind to a halt. A few years later, in 1988, Chaum in collaboration with two other cryptographers, Amos Fiat and Moni Naor, proposed *offline* electronic cash. At first sight, this might seem impossible: if you try to spend the same digital note or coin at two different shops, how can they possibly stop this double spend unless they're both connected to the same payment network or central entity?

The clever idea is to stop worrying about preventing double spending and focus on detecting it, after the fact, when the merchant reconnects to the bank server. After all, this approach is why you're able to use your credit card on an airplane even if there is no network connection up in the skies. The transaction processing happens later, when the airline is able to reconnect to the network. If your card is denied, you'll owe the airline (or your bank) money. If you think about it, quite a bit of traditional finance is based on the idea of detecting an error or loss, followed by attempting to recover the money or punish the perpetrator. If you write someone a personal check, they have no guarantee that the money is actually in your account, but they can come after you if the check bounces. Conceivably, if an offline electronic cash system were widely adopted, the legal system would come to recognize double spending as a crime.

Chaum, Fiat, and Naor's idea for detecting double spending was an intricate cryptographic dance. At a high level, what it achieved was this: every digital coin issued to you encodes your identity, but in such a way that no one except you—not even the bank—can decode it. Every time you spend your coin, the recipient will require you to decode a random subset of the encoding, and they'll keep a record of this. This decoding isn't enough to allow them to determine your identity. But if you ever double spend a coin, eventually both recipients will go to the bank to redeem their notes, and when they do this, the bank can put the two pieces of information together to decode your identity completely, with an overwhelmingly high probability.

You might wonder whether someone can frame you as a double spender in this system. Suppose you spend a coin with me, and then I turn around and try to double spend it (without redeeming it with the bank and getting a new coin with my identity encoded). This won't work—the new recipient will ask me to decode a random subset, which will almost certainly not be the same as the subset you decoded for me, so I won't be able to comply with their decoding request.

Over the years, many cryptographers have looked at this construction and improved it in various ways. In the Chaum-Fiat-Naor scheme, if a coin is worth $100, and you wanted to buy something that cost only $75, say, there's no way to split that coin into $75 and $25 coins. All you could do is go back to the bank, cash in the $100 coin, and ask for a $75 coin and a $25 coin. But a 1991 paper by Tatsuaki Okamoto and Kazuo Ohta uses Merkle trees to create a system that does allow you to subdivide your coins. Merkle trees would show up in Bitcoin as well, and we'll meet them in Chapter 1. The Chaum-Fiat-Naor scheme also leaves a lot of room for improvements in efficiency. In particular, the application of something called "zero-knowledge proofs" to this scheme (most notably by Stefan Brands in the 1990s, and Jan Camenisch, Susan Hohenberger, and Anna Lysyanskaya in 2005) was very fruitful—zero-knowledge proofs have also been applied to Bitcoin, as discussed in Chapter 6.

But back to Chaum: he took his ideas and commercialized them. He formed a company in 1989 called "DigiCash," probably the earliest company that tried to solve the problem of online payments. They had about a 5-year head start on other companies like FirstVirtual and CyberCash, just discussed. The actual cash in DigiCash's system was called "ecash," and they had another system called "cyberbucks." Some banks actually implemented it—a few in the United States and at least one in Finland. This was in the 1990s, long before Bitcoin, which might come as a surprise to some Bitcoin enthusiasts who view banks as tech-phobic, anti-innovative behemoths.

Ecash is based on Chaum's protocols. Clients are anonymous, so banks can't trace how the former are spending their money. But merchants in ecash aren't anonymous. They have to return coins as soon as they receive them, so the bank knows how much they're making, at what times, and so on.

When you want to send money, you'd click on a link provided by the recipient that takes you to the DigiCash website. That would then open a reverse web connection back to your computer. That means your computer had to have the ability to accept incoming connections and act as a server. You'd have to have your own IP address, and your Internet service provider would have to allow incoming connections. If the connection was successful, then the ecash software would launch on your computer, and you'd be able to approve the transaction and send the money.

Chaum took out several patents on DigiCash technology, in particular on the blind-signature scheme that it used. His action was controversial, and it stopped other people from developing ecash systems that used the same protocol. But a group of cryptographers who hung out on what was called the "cypherpunks" mailing list wanted an alternative. Cypherpunks was the predecessor to the mailing list where Satoshi Nakamoto would later announce Bitcoin to the world, and this is no coincidence. The cypherpunk movement and the roots of Bitcoin are discussed in Chapter 7.

The cypherpunk cryptographers implemented a version of ecash called MagicMoney. It did violate the patents, but was billed as being only for experimental use. It was a fun piece of software to play with. The interface was all text based. You could send transactions by email. You would just copy and paste the transactions into your email and send it to another user. Hopefully, you'd use end-to-end email encryption software, such as PGP, to protect the transaction in transit.

Then there's Lucre, a proposal by Ben Laurie with contributions from many other people. Lucre tries to replace the blind-signature scheme in ecash with a nonpatent-encumbered alternative, and the rest of the system is largely the same.

Yet another proposal, by Ian Goldberg, tried to fix the problem of not being able to split your coins to make change. His idea was that the merchant could send you coins back if the merchant had some coins, so that you might overpay for the item if you didn't have exact change, and then you'd get some coins back. But notice that this practice introduces an anonymity problem. As we saw earlier, in ecash, senders are anonymous, but merchants aren't. When the merchant sends cash back, technically they're the sender, so they're anonymous. But you, as someone who has to return this cash to the bank, aren't anonymous. There's no way to design this system without breaking the anonymity of users trying to buy goods. So Goldberg came up with a proposal using different types of coins that would allow these transactions to occur, allow you to get change back, and still preserve your anonymity.

Why did DigiCash fail? The main problem was that it was hard to persuade banks and merchants to adopt it. Since there weren't many merchants that accepted ecash, users didn't want it either. Worse, it didn't support user-to-user transactions, or at least not very well. It was really centered on the user-to-merchant transaction. So if merchants weren't on board, there was no other way to bootstrap interest in the system. So at the end of the day, DigiCash lost, and the credit card companies won.

As a side note, Bitcoin allows user-to-merchant and user-to-user transactions. In fact, the protocol doesn't have a notion of merchant that's separate from the notion of user. The support for user-to-user transactions probably contributed to Bitcoin's success. There was something to do with your bitcoins right from the beginning: send them to other users, while the community tried to drum up support for Bitcoin and get merchants to accept it.

In the later years of the company, DigiCash also experimented with tamper-resistant hardware to try to prevent double spending rather than just detecting it. In this system, you'd get a small hardware device that was usually called a "wallet," or some sort of card. The device would keep track of your balance, which would decrease when you spent money and increase if you loaded the card with more money. The point of the device is that there should be no way to physically or digitally tamper with its counter. So if the counter hits zero, then the card stops being able to spend money until it's reloaded.

Many other companies had electronic cash systems based on tamper-resistant hardware. DigiCash later worked with Café, a company based in Europe. Another company based on this idea was called Mondex, and it was later acquired by MasterCard. Visa also had its own variant, VisaCash.

In Mondex, the user had a smart card and a "wallet unit," and could load either of them with cash. To do a user-to-user payment, the giver would first put their card into the wallet and move money off of the card onto the wallet. Then the receiver would stick their card in the wallet, and you'd move the money onto the second card. This was a way to exchange digital cash, and it was anonymous.

Mondex tested their technology in a bunch of communities. One community happened to be a city very close to where I grew up: Guelph, Ontario. You've probably already guessed that it didn't really catch on. A major problem with Mondex cards is that they're like cash—if you lost them or they were stolen, the money was gone. Worse, if the card malfunctioned—if the card reader wouldn't read it—it was impossible to determine whether that card had a balance on it. In these scenarios, Mondex would typically eat the cost. They'd assume that the card was loaded and reimburse the user for that lost money. Of course, that can cost a company a lot of money.

Furthermore, the wallet was slow and clunky. It was much faster to pay with a credit card or with cash. And retailers hated having several payment terminals; they wanted just one for credit cards. All these factors together did Mondex in.

However, these cards were smart cards, which means that they have small microcontrollers on them, and that technology has proved successful. In many countries today, including Canada, where I live, every single credit card and every single debit card now has smart card technology on it. It's used for a different purpose, though. It's not used to prevent double spending—the problem doesn't arise, since the technology is not cash based. The bank, rather than your card, keeps track of your balance or available credit. Instead, the chip is used for authentication, that is, to prove that you know the PIN associated with your account. But Mondex was using it long before this technology was adopted widely by the banking industry.

MINTING MONEY OUT OF THIN AIR

In the DigiCash system, if you have a digital cash object that's worth $100, what makes it actually worth $100? The answer is simple: to obtain ecash worth $100, you'd have to take $100 out of your bank account and give it to the bank that was issuing you the ecash. But many different proposals described how to do this, and different companies did it differently. One far-fetched possibility: what if the government of a particular country actually authorized services to mint digital money, creating new cash out of thin air? That was the idea behind NetCash, although it never got beyond the proposal stage. A different system, used by e-Gold, was to put a pile of gold in a vault and to issue digital cash only up to the value of the gold. Another company called Digigold wasn't fully backed by gold but had partial reserves.

All these ideas ultimately peg the value of digital cash to the dollar or a commodity. If the dollar's value goes up or down, the value of your digital money holdings will change along with it. A radically different possibility is to allow digital money to be its own currency, issued and valued independently of any other currency.

To create a free-floating digital currency that is likely to acquire real value, you need to have something that's scarce by design. In fact, scarcity is also the reason gold or diamonds have been used as a backing for money. In the digital realm, one way to achieve scarcity is to design the system so that minting money requires solving a computational problem (or "puzzle") that takes a while to crack. Bitcoin "mining," discussed in Chapter 5, implements this idea.

The basic idea—that solutions to computational puzzles could be digital objects that have some value—is pretty old. It was first proposed by cryptographers Cynthia Dwork and Moni Naor as a potential solution to reduce email spam back in 1992. What if, every time you sent an email, your computer would have to solve one of these puzzles that would take a few seconds to solve? To enforce this requirement, the recipient's email program would simply ignore your email if you didn't attach the solution to the computational puzzle. For the average user, it wouldn't be that much of a barrier to sending emails, because you're not sending emails very frequently. But if you're a spammer, you're trying to send out thousands or millions of emails all at once, and solving those computational puzzles could become prohibitive. A similar idea was later discovered independently by Adam Back in 1997 in a proposal called Hashcash.

These computational puzzles need to have some specific properties to be a useful spam deterrent. First, it should be impossible for a spammer to solve one puzzle and attach the solution to every email he sends. To ensure this, the puzzle should be specific to the email: it should depend on the sender and receiver, the contents of the email, and the approximate time at which it's sent. Second, the receiver should be able to easily check the puzzle solution without having to repeat the process of solving the puzzle. Third, each puzzle should be totally independent of the others, in the sense that solving one puzzle does not decrease the amount of time it takes to solve any other puzzle. Finally, since hardware improves with time and solving any given computational puzzle gets faster and cheaper, recipients should be able to adjust the difficulty of the puzzle solutions that they will accept. These properties can be achieved by using cryptographic hash functions to design the puzzles—see Chapter 1.

Bitcoin uses essentially the same computational puzzle as Hashcash, but with some minor improvements. Bitcoin does a lot more than Hashcash does, though—after all, it takes a whole book to explain Bitcoin! I only mention this because Hashcash inventor Adam Back has said, "Bitcoin is Hashcash extended with inflation control." I think that's overreaching a bit. It's sort of like saying "a Tesla is just a battery on wheels."

As with any good idea in cryptography, there are many variants of computational puzzles that aim to achieve slightly different properties. One proposal comes from Ron Rivest and Adi Shamir, the "R" and the "S" in the RSA cryptosystem. Observe that in Hashcash, your cost to solve a number of puzzles is simply the sum of the individual costs, by design. But this is different from the cost structure for a government to mint money. If you think about how anticounterfeiting technology works for a paper currency, there's a huge initial cost to acquire all the equipment, create the security features, and so on. But once the government has done all that, its costs go down, and the difference in costs is small for printing one bill or a hundred bills. In other words, minting paper money has a huge fixed cost but low marginal cost. Rivest and Shamir wanted to design computational puzzles that would mimic these properties, so that minting the first coin is massively computationally challenging, but minting subsequent coins is a lot cheaper. Their proposal also used hash functions, but in a different way. We won't get into the details of their solution, but the problem they were trying to solve is interesting at a high level.

Why did Hashcash never catch on for its intended purpose of preventing spam? Perhaps spam just wasn't a big enough problem to solve. For most people, spam is a nuisance but not something that they want to spend their computing cycles on combating. We have spam filters today that work pretty well at keeping spam out of our inboxes. It's also possible Hashcash wouldn't have actually stopped spammers. In particular, most spammers today send their spam using botnets (large groups of other people's computers that spammers take control of using malware). They might just as well use those computers to harvest Hashcash. That said, the idea of using computational puzzles to limit access to resources is still an idea that's kicking around. You can see it in some proposals for replacing network protocols, such as MinimaLT.

RECORDING EVERYTHING IN A LEDGER

Another key component of Bitcoin is the block chain: a ledger in which all Bitcoin transactions are securely recorded. The ideas behind the block chain are again quite old and trace back to a series of papers by Haber and Stornetta starting in 1991. Their proposal was a method for secure timestamping of digital documents rather than a digital money scheme. The goal of timestamping is to give an approximate idea of when a document came into existence. More importantly, timestamping accurately conveys the order of creation of these documents: if one came into existence before the other, the timestamps will reflect that. The security property requires that a document's timestamp can't be changed after the fact.

In Haber and Stornetta's scheme, there's a timestamping service to which clients send documents to timestamp. When the server receives a document, it signs the document together with the current time and a link or a pointer to the previous document, and issues a "certificate" with this information (Figure 0.1). The pointer in question is

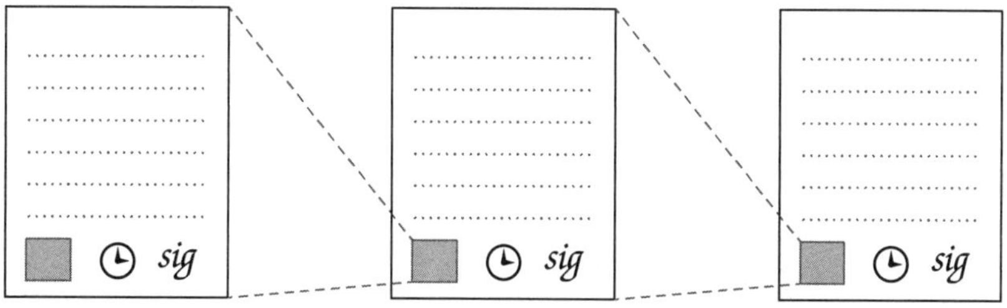

FIGURE 0.1. Linked timestamping. To create a certificate for a document, the timestamp server includes a hash pointer to the previous document's certificate and the current time, and it signs these three data elements together.

a special type of pointer that links to a piece of data instead of to a location. Then if the data in question changes, the pointer automatically becomes invalid. Chapter 1 discusses how to create such pointers using hash functions.

What this protocol achieves is that each document's certificate ensures the integrity of the contents of the previous document. In fact, you can apply this argument recursively: each certificate essentially fixes the entire history of documents and certificates up until that point. If we assume that each client in the system keeps track of at least a few certificates—their own documents' certificates, and those of the previous and following documents—then collectively the participants can ensure that the history cannot be changed after the fact. In particular, the relative ordering of documents is preserved.

A later paper proposed an efficiency improvement: instead of linking documents individually, we can collect them into blocks and link blocks together in a chain. In each block, the documents would again be linked together, but in a tree structure instead of linearly. This structure decreases the amount of checking needed to verify that a particular document appears at a particular point in the history of the system. This hybrid scheme is shown in Figure 0.2.

This data structure forms the skeleton of Bitcoin's block chain, as discussed in Chapter 3. Bitcoin refines it in a subtle but important way: a Hashcash-esque protocol is used to delay how fast new blocks are added to the chain. This modification has profound and favorable consequences for Bitcoin's security model. There is no longer the need for

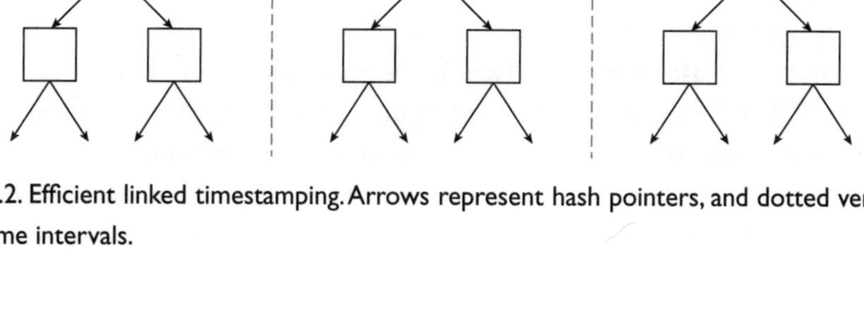

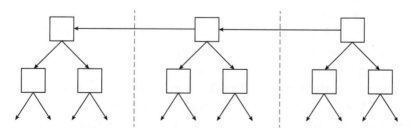

FIGURE 0.2. Efficient linked timestamping. Arrows represent hash pointers, and dotted vertical lines indicate time intervals.

trusted servers; instead, events are recorded by a collection of untrusted nodes called "miners." Every miner keeps track of blocks, rather than having to rely on regular users to do it. Anyone can become a miner by solving computational puzzles to create blocks. Bitcoin also eliminates the need for signatures, relying only on hash pointers to ensure the integrity of the data structure. Finally, the actual timestamps aren't of much importance in Bitcoin, and the point of the system is to record the relative ordering of transactions in a tamper-resistant way. In fact, Bitcoin blocks aren't created in a fixed schedule. The system ensures that a new one is created every 10 minutes on average, but there's considerable variation in the time between successive blocks.

In essence, Bitcoin combines the idea of using computational puzzles to regulate the creation of new currency units with the idea of secure timestamping to record a ledger of transactions and prevent double spending. There were earlier, less sophisticated, proposals that combined these two ideas. The first is called b-money, proposed by Wei Dai in 1998. In b-money, anyone can create money using a Hashcash-like system. It has a peer-to-peer network, sort of like the one in Bitcoin. Each node maintains a ledger, but it's not a global ledger as in the Bitcoin block chain. Each node has its own ledger of what it thinks everyone's balance is.

Another similar proposal, by Nick Szabo, is called Bitgold. Szabo says he had the idea for Bitgold as early as 1998, but didn't get around to blogging about it until 2005. The reason I mention this is that there's a minor conspiracy theory popularized by Nathaniel Popper, a *New York Times* reporter who wrote a very good book on the history of Bitcoin. Popper notes that the blog post's timestamps were changed after Satoshi posted the Bitcoin white paper, so that the Bitgold proposal looks like it was written up about two months after Bitcoin was released. Popper believes, like many other observers, that Szabo could be Satoshi, even though Szabo denies it. Popper cites the timestamp change as evidence of Szabo/Satoshi trying to obscure the link by covering up the fact that he invented a predecessor of Bitcoin (i.e., by making it look like Bitgold didn't precede Bitcoin).

The problem with this explanation is that if you actually read the contents of the blog posts, Szabo is clear about having had this idea in 1998, and he doesn't try to change those dates. So a more reasonable explanation is that he just bumped the post to the top of his blog after Bitcoin popularized similar ideas, to make sure that people were aware of his prior proposal.

Bitcoin has several important differences from b-money and Bitgold. First, in the latter two proposals, computational puzzles are used directly to mint currency. Anyone can solve a puzzle, and the solution is a unit of money itself. In Bitcoin, puzzle solutions themselves don't constitute money. They are used to secure the block chain and only indirectly lead to minting money. Second, b-money and Bitgold rely on timestamping services that sign off on the creation or transfer of money. Bitcoin, as we've seen, doesn't require trusted timestamping and merely tries to preserve the relative order of blocks and transactions.

Finally, in b-money and Bitgold, if disagreement arises about the ledger among the servers or nodes, there is no clear way to resolve it. Letting the majority decide seems to be implicit in both authors' writings. But since anyone can set up a node—or a hundred of them, hiding behind different identities—these mechanisms aren't very secure, unless a centralized gatekeeper controls entry into the network. In Bitcoin, in contrast, for an attacker to change history, they must solve computational puzzles at a faster rate than the rest of the participants combined. This is not only more secure, it allows us to quantify the security of the system.

B-money and Bitgold were informal proposals—b-money was a post on a mailing list, and Bitgold was a series of blog posts. Neither took off, or was even implemented directly. Unlike the Bitcoin white paper, no full specification or any code was supplied for Bitgold or b-money. The proposals gloss over issues that may or may not be solvable. The first, as we've already mentioned, is how to resolve disagreements about the ledger. Another problem is determining how hard the computational puzzle should be to mint a unit of currency. Since hardware tends to get dramatically cheaper over time for a fixed amount of computing power, Bitcoin incorporates a mechanism to automatically adjust the difficulty of the puzzles periodically. B-money and Bitgold don't include such a mechanism, which can result in problems, since coins may lose their value if it become trivially easy to create new ones.

HINTS ABOUT SATOSHI

You may know that Satoshi Nakamoto is the pseudonym adopted by the creator of Bitcoin. While his identity remains a mystery, he communicated extensively in Bitcoin's early days. Let's use these communications to dig a little bit into questions like when he started working on Bitcoin, to what extent he was influenced by the prior ideas we've looked at, and what motivated him.

Satoshi says he started coding Bitcoin around May 2007. I'll take him at his word; the fact that he's anonymous is not a reason to think he'd lie about things like that. He registered the domain bitcoin.org in August 2008. And at that time, he started sending private emails to a few people he thought might be interested in the proposal. A little later, in October 2008, he publicly released a white paper that described the protocol, and soon after, he released the initial code for Bitcoin as well. Then he stuck around for about 2 years, during which he posted lots of messages on forums, corresponded by email with many people, and responded to people's concerns. On the programming side, he submitted patches to the code. He maintained the source code in conjunction with other developers, fixing issues as they arose. By December 2010, others had slowly taken over the maintenance of the project, and he stopped communicating with them.

I've been referring to Satoshi Nakamoto as a "he," but I have no particular reason to believe Satoshi is a man and not a woman. I'm just using the male pronoun, since Satoshi is a male name. I've also been referring to him as a single individual. There is a theory that Satoshi Nakamoto might be a collection of individuals. I don't buy this theory—I think Satoshi is probably just one person. If we look at the entirety of the online interactions undertaken under the Satoshi pseudonym, if we think about the 2 years that Satoshi spent replying to emails and patching code, it's hard to imagine that this effort could be the result of multiple people sharing user accounts and passwords, responding in a similar style and a similar voice, and making sure they didn't contradict one another. It just seems a much simpler explanation that at least this portion of Satoshi's activity was done by a single individual.

Furthermore, it's clear from his writings and patches that this individual understood the full code base of Bitcoin and all its design aspects. So it's reasonable to assume that the same individual wrote the original code base and the white paper as well. Finally, it's possible that Satoshi had help with the original design. However, after Bitcoin's release, Satoshi was quick to attribute any help he received from other contributors. It would be out of character for him to mislead us about inventing something by himself if he had had help from other people.

What did Satoshi know about the history of ecash? To understand this better, we can start by looking at what he cites in his white paper as well as the references that existed on early versions of the Bitcoin website. In the white paper, he cites some papers on basic cryptography and probability theory. He also cites the timestamping work that I mentioned earlier, and it's natural to think that he based the design of the block chain on these references, since the similarities are so apparent. He also cites the Hashcash proposal, whose computational puzzle is similar to the one used in Bitcoin. And he references b-money. Later, on the website, he added references to Bitgold and to a scheme by Hal Finney for reusing computational puzzle solutions.

But if we look at the email exchanges that were made public by people who corresponded with Satoshi Nakamoto in the early days, we find that the b-money proposal was actually added after the fact, at the suggestion of Adam Back. Satoshi then emailed Wei Dai, who created b-money, and apparently, Dai was the one who told him about Bitgold. So these proposals probably weren't inspirations for the original design. He later corresponded a lot with Hal Finney, and that's quite a reasonable explanation for why he cites Finney's work, at least on the website.

Based on this information, it seems plausible that when creating Bitcoin, Hashcash and timestamping were the only things from the history of ecash that Satoshi knew about or thought were relevant. After he came to know of b-money and Bitgold, however, he seems to have appreciated their relevance. In mid-2010, the Wikipedia article on Bitcoin was flagged for deletion by Wikipedia's editors, because they thought it wasn't noteworthy. So there was some discussion between Satoshi and others about how to word the article so that Wikipedia would accept it. To that end, Satoshi suggested this description of Bitcoin: "Bitcoin is an implementation of Wei Dai's b-money proposal on Cypherpunks in 1998 and Nick Szabo's Bitgold proposal." So Satoshi, by this point, did see positioning Bitcoin as an extension of these two ideas or an implementation of these two prior systems as a good explanation of how it worked.

But what about the other proposals—the Chaumian ecash schemes and the credit card proposals that we looked at? Did Satoshi know any of that history when designing Bitcoin? It's hard to tell. He didn't give any indication of knowing that history, but it's just as likely that he didn't reference the history because it wasn't relevant to Bitcoin. Bitcoin uses a completely different decentralized model, so there's no compelling reason to dwell on old centralized systems that failed.

Satoshi himself makes this point, by mentioning Chaumian ecash in passing, in one of his posts to the Bitcoin forums. Writing about another proposal called opencoin.org, he notes that they seem to be "talking about the old Chaumian central mint stuff, but maybe only because that was the only thing available. Maybe they would be interested in a new direction. A lot of people automatically dismiss e-currency as a lost cause because of all the companies that failed since the 1990s. I hope it's obvious it was only the centrally controlled nature of those systems that doomed them. I think this is the first time we're trying a decentralized, non-trust-based system." This is a good indication of what Satoshi thought of the earlier proposals, and specifically how he thought Bitcoin differed from them. Bitcoin's decentralization is indeed a defining feature that sets it apart from almost everything we've looked at.

Another interesting quote from Satoshi suggests that he might not be an academic. Most academic researchers think about ideas and write them down immediately, before they build the system. Satoshi says that he took an opposite approach: "I actually did Bitcoin kind of backwards. I had to write all the code before I could convince myself that I could solve every problem, then I wrote the paper. I think I will be able to release the code sooner than I could write a detailed specification."

Since a bit of myth surrounds Satoshi, it's worth mentioning that he made mistakes like everyone else and wasn't a perfect oracle of the future. There are bugs and questionable design choices in the original Bitcoin code. For example, a feature to send bitcoins to IP addresses never caught on and, in retrospect, was a bad idea. When he described what Bitcoin was useful for, his scenarios were centered on the idea of using it across the Internet. That use case is central to Bitcoin, of course, but it's not the only one. He didn't indicate a vision of going into a coffee shop and being able to pay for your coffee with Bitcoin, for example.

Why does Satoshi maintain his anonymity? There are many possible reasons. To begin with, it might be just for fun. Many people write novels anonymously, and some graffiti artists, like Banksy, maintain their anonymity. In fact, in the community that Satoshi was involved in at that time—the cypherpunk community and the cryptography mailing list—it was common practice for people to post anonymously.

Or legal worries might have influenced Satoshi's choice. Two U.S. companies, Liberty Reserve and e-Gold, ran into legal trouble for money laundering. In 2006, one of the founders of Liberty Reserve fled the United States, fearing that he would be indicted on money laundering charges. In contrast, e-Gold's founders stayed in the United States, and one was actually indicted and eventually pled guilty to the charges. This guilty plea was registered just before Satoshi set up the Bitcoin website and started emailing people about his proposal. That said, numerous people have invented ecash systems, and nobody else was scared of the legal implications or has chosen to remain anonymous. So legal concerns may or may not have been the reason.

It's also worth recalling that certain aspects of ecash were patented, and that members of the cypherpunk movement were concerned about implementing ecash systems due to these patents. In fact, one post to the cypherpunks mailing list proposed that a group of anonymous coders implement ecash, so that if someone were to sue, they wouldn't be able to find the coders. While it is difficult to think that Bitcoin would violate the ecash patents, given how different its design is, perhaps Satoshi was being very cautious. Or maybe he was just inspired by the idea of an anonymous coder from the cypherpunk community.

A final reason that's often cited is personal security. We know that Satoshi has a lot of bitcoins from his mining in the early days, and due to Bitcoin's success, these coins are now worth a lot of money. I think this reason is plausible. After all, choosing to be anonymous isn't a decision you make once, it's something that you do on a continual basis. That said, it probably wasn't Satoshi's original reason. The first time Satoshi used the name Satoshi Nakamoto, he hadn't even released the white paper or the codebase for Bitcoin, and it's hard to imagine that he had any idea that it would be as successful as it was. In fact, at many points in its early history, Satoshi was optimistic but cautious about Bitcoin's prospects. He seems to have understood that many previous efforts had failed and that Bitcoin might fail as well.

CONCLUDING REMARKS

The success of Bitcoin is quite remarkable if you consider all the ventures that failed trying to do what it does. Bitcoin has several notable innovations, including the block chain and a decentralized model that supports user-to-user transactions. It provides a practically useful but less-than-perfect level of anonymity for users (Chapter 6 takes a detailed look at anonymity in Bitcoin). In one sense it's weaker than the strong anonymity in DigiCash, but in another sense it's stronger. That's because in DigiCash, it was only the senders of the money that maintained their anonymity and not the merchants. Bitcoin gives both senders and receivers (whether users or merchants) the same level of anonymity.

Let me conclude with some lessons to be learned from Bitcoin through the lens of the previous systems that we've looked at. The first is to not give up on a problem. Just because people failed for 20 years to develop digital cash doesn't mean that a system out there will not work. The second is to be willing to compromise. If you want perfect anonymity or perfect decentralization, you'll probably need to degrade other areas of your design. Bitcoin, in retrospect, seems to have made the right compromises. It scales back anonymity a bit and requires participants to be online and connected to the peer-to-peer network, which turned out to be acceptable to users.

A final lesson is success through numbers. Bitcoin was able to build up a community of passionate users as well as developers willing to contribute to the open-source technology. This approach differs markedly from previous attempts at digital cash, which were typically developed by a company, with the only advocates for the technology being the employees of the company itself. Bitcoin's current success is due in large part to the vibrant supporting community who pushed the technology, got people to use it, and persuaded merchants to adopt it.

Jeremy Clark
Concordia University

FURTHER READING

This accessible overview of digital cash schemes focuses on practical issues:

P. Wayner. *Digital Cash: Commerce on the Net*, second edition. Waltham, MA: Morgan Kaufmann, 1997.

A cryptographically oriented overview of e-cash systems (Chapter 1) and micropayments (Chapter 7) is:

B. Rosenberg, ed. *Handbook of Financial Cryptography and Security*. Boca Raton, FL: CRC Press, 2011.

Although not Chaum's earliest paper on e-cash, this is arguably the most innovative, and it formed a template used by many other papers:

D. Chaum, A. Fiat, and M. Naor. "Untraceable Electronic Cash." In *CRYPTO 88: Proceedings of the 8th Annual International Cryptology Conference on Advances in Cryptology*. London: Springer Verlag, 1990.

Many papers improved the efficiency of Chaum-Fiat-Naor using modern cryptographic techniques, but arguably the most significant is:

J. Camenisch, S. Hohenberger, and A. Lysyanskaya. "Compact E-cash: Theory and Applications of Cryptographic Techniques," 2005.

Some practical security observations on the financial industry and proposals, including Mondex, can be found in:

R. Anderson. *Security Engineering*, second edition. Hoboken, NJ: Wiley, 2008.

An overview of the implementation of Chaum's ecash proposal is:

B. Schoenmakers. "Security Aspects of the Ecash Payment System." In *State of the Art in Applied Cryptography*. New York: Springer, 1997.

Two papers cited by Satoshi Nakamoto in the Bitcoin white paper are integral to Bitcoin's design:

A. Back. "Hashcash—A Denial of Service Counter-Measure," 2002. Available at hashcash.org/papers/hashcash.pdf.

S. Haber and W. S. Stornetta. "Secure Names for Bitstrings." CCS, 1997.

BITCOIN AND CRYPTOCURRENCY TECHNOLOGIES

CHAPTER 1

Introduction to Cryptography and Cryptocurrencies

All currencies need some way to control supply and enforce various security properties to prevent cheating. In fiat currencies, organizations like central banks control the money supply and add anticounterfeiting features to physical currency. These security features raise the bar for an attacker, but they don't make money impossible to counterfeit. Ultimately, law enforcement is necessary for stopping people from breaking the rules of the system.

Cryptocurrencies too must have security measures that prevent people from tampering with the state of the system and from equivocating (that is, making mutually inconsistent statements to different people). If Alice convinces Bob that she paid him a digital coin, for example, she should not be able to convince Carol that she paid her that same coin. But unlike fiat currencies, the security rules of cryptocurrencies need to be enforced purely technologically and without relying on a central authority.

As the word suggests, cryptocurrencies make heavy use of cryptography. Cryptography provides a mechanism for securely encoding the rules of a cryptocurrency system in the system itself. We can use it to prevent tampering and equivocation, as well as to encode, in a mathematical protocol, the rules for creation of new units of the currency. Thus, before we can properly understand cryptocurrencies, we need to delve into the cryptographic foundations that they rely on.

Cryptography is a deep academic research field using many advanced mathematical techniques that are notoriously subtle and complicated. Fortunately, Bitcoin relies on only a handful of relatively simple and well-known cryptographic constructions. In this chapter, we specifically study cryptographic hashes and digital signatures, two primitives that prove to be useful for building cryptocurrencies. Later chapters introduce more complicated cryptographic schemes, such as zero-knowledge proofs, that are used in proposed extensions and modifications to Bitcoin.

Once the necessary cryptographic primitives have been introduced, we'll discuss some of the ways in which they are used to build cryptocurrencies. We'll complete this chapter with examples of simple cryptocurrencies that illustrate some of the design challenges that need to be dealt with.

1.1. CRYPTOGRAPHIC HASH FUNCTIONS

The first cryptographic primitive that we need to understand is a *cryptographic hash function*. A *hash function* is a mathematical function with the following three properties:

- Its input can be any string of any size.
- It produces a fixed-sized output. For the purpose of making the discussion in this chapter concrete, we will assume a 256-bit output size. However, our discussion holds true for any output size, as long as it is sufficiently large.
- It is efficiently computable. Intuitively this means that for a given input string, you can figure out what the output of the hash function is in a reasonable amount of time. More technically, computing the hash of an n-bit string should have a running time that is $O(n)$.

These properties define a general hash function, one that could be used to build a data structure, such as a hash table. We're going to focus exclusively on *cryptographic* hash functions. For a hash function to be cryptographically secure, we require that it has the following three additional properties: (1) collision resistance, (2) hiding, and (3) puzzle friendliness.

We'll look more closely at each of these properties to gain an understanding of why it's useful to have a function that satisfies them. The reader who has studied cryptography should be aware that the treatment of hash functions in this book is a bit different from that in a standard cryptography textbook. The puzzle-friendliness property, in particular, is not a general requirement for cryptographic hash functions, but one that will be useful for cryptocurrencies specifically.

Property 1: Collision Resistance

The first property that we need from a cryptographic hash function is that it is collision resistant. A collision occurs when two distinct inputs produce the same output. A hash function $H(\cdot)$ is collision resistant if nobody can find a collision (Figure 1.1). Formally:

Collision resistance. A hash function H is said to be collision resistant if it is infeasible to find two values, x and y, such that $x \neq y$, yet $H(x) = H(y)$.

Notice that we said "nobody can find" a collision, but we did not say that no collisions exist. Actually, collisions exist for any hash function, and we can prove this by a simple counting argument. The input space to the hash function contains all strings of all lengths, yet the output space contains only strings of a specific fixed length. Because the input space is larger than the output space (indeed, the input space is infinite, while the output space is finite), there must be input strings that map to the same output

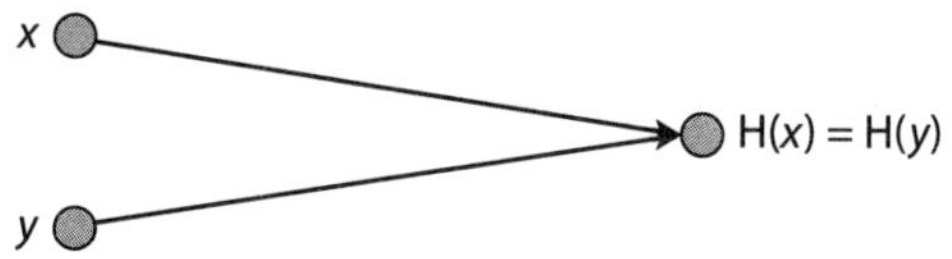

FIGURE 1.1. A hash collision. *x* and *y* are distinct values, yet when input into hash function *H*, they produce the same output.

string. In fact, there will be some outputs to which an infinite number of possible inputs will map (Figure 1.2).

Now, to make things even worse, we said that it has to be impossible to find a collision. Yet there are methods that are guaranteed to find a collision. Consider the following simple method for finding a collision for a hash function with a 256-bit output size: pick $2^{256} + 1$ distinct values, compute the hashes of each of them, and check whether any two outputs are equal. Since we picked more inputs than possible outputs, some pair of them must collide when you apply the hash function.

The method above is guaranteed to find a collision. But if we pick random inputs and compute the hash values, we'll find a collision with high probability long before examining $2^{256} + 1$ inputs. In fact, if we randomly choose just $2^{130} + 1$ inputs, it turns out there's a 99.8 percent chance that at least two of them are going to collide. That we can find a collision by examining only roughly the square root of the number of possible outputs results from a phenomenon in probability known as the *birthday paradox*. In the homework questions (see the online supplementary material for this book, which can be found at http://press.princeton.edu/titles/10908.html), we examine this in more detail.

This collision-detection algorithm works for every hash function. But, of course, the problem is that it takes a very long time to do. For a hash function with a 256-bit output, you would have to compute the hash function $2^{256} + 1$ times in the worst case, and about 2^{128} times on average. That's of course an astronomically large number—if a computer calculates 10,000 hashes per second, it would take more than one octillion

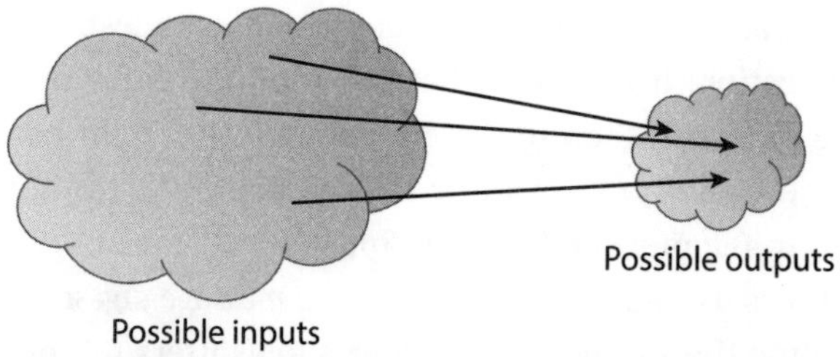

FIGURE 1.2. Inevitability of collisions. Because the number of inputs exceeds the number of outputs, we are guaranteed that there must be at least one output to which the hash function maps more than one input.

(10^{27}) years to calculate 2^{128} hashes! For another way of thinking about this, we can say that if every computer ever made by humanity had been computing since the beginning of the universe, the odds that they would have found a collision by now are still infinitesimally small. So small that it's far less than the odds that the Earth will be destroyed by a giant meteor in the next two seconds.

We have thus found a general but impractical algorithm to find a collision for *any* hash function. A more difficult question is: Is there some other method that could be used on a particular hash function to find a collision? In other words, although the generic collision detection algorithm is not feasible to use, there may be some other algorithm that can efficiently find a collision for a specific hash function.

Consider, for example, the following hash function:

$$H(x) = x \bmod 2^{256}$$

This function meets our requirements of a hash function as it accepts inputs of any length, returns a fixed-sized output (256 bits), and is efficiently computable. But this function also has an efficient method for finding a collision. Notice that this function just returns the last 256 bits of the input. One collision, then, would be the values 3 and $3 + 2^{256}$. This simple example illustrates that even though our generic collision detection method is not usable in practice, there are at least some hash functions for which an efficient collision detection method does exist.

Yet for other hash functions, we don't know whether such methods exist. We suspect that they are collision resistant. However, no hash functions have been *proven* to be collision resistant. The cryptographic hash functions that we rely on in practice are just functions for which people have tried really, really hard to find collisions and haven't yet succeeded. And so we choose to believe that those are collision resistant. (In some cases, such as the hash function known as MD5, collisions were eventually found after years of work, resulting in the function being deprecated and phased out of practical use.)

APPLICATION: MESSAGE DIGESTS

Now that we know what collision resistance is, the logical question is: What is it useful for? Here's one application: If we know that two inputs x and y to a collision-resistant hash function H are different, then it's safe to assume that their hashes $H(x)$ and $H(y)$ are different—if someone knew an x and y that were different but had the same hash, that would violate our assumption that H is collision resistant.

This argument allows us to use hash outputs as a *message digest*. Consider SecureBox, an authenticated online file storage system that allows users to upload files and to ensure their integrity when they download them. Suppose that Alice uploads really large files, and she wants to be able to verify later that the file she downloads is the same as the one she uploaded. One way to do that would be to save the whole big file locally, and directly compare it to the file she downloads. While this works, it largely defeats the purpose of uploading it in the first place; if Alice needs to have access to a local copy of the file to ensure its integrity, she can just use the local copy directly.

Collision-resistant hashes provide an elegant and efficient solution to this problem. Alice just needs to remember the hash of the original file. When she later downloads the file from SecureBox, she computes the hash of the downloaded file and compares it to the one she stored. If the hashes are the same, then she can conclude that the file is indeed the same one she uploaded, but if they are different, then Alice can conclude that the file has been tampered with. Remembering the hash thus allows her to detect not only accidental corruption of the file during transmission or on SecureBox's servers but also intentional modification of the file by the server. Such guarantees in the face of potentially malicious behavior by other entities are at the core of what cryptography gives us.

The hash serves as a fixed-length digest, or unambiguous summary, of a message. This gives us a very efficient way to remember things we've seen before and to recognize them again. Whereas the entire file might have been gigabytes long, the hash is of fixed length—256 bits for the hash function in our example. This greatly reduces our storage requirement. Later in this chapter and throughout the book, we'll see applications for which it's useful to use a hash as a message digest.

Property 2: Hiding

The second property that we want from our hash functions is that it is *hiding*. The hiding property asserts that if we're given the output of the hash function $y = H(x)$, there's no feasible way to figure out what the input, x, was. The problem is that this property can't be true in the form stated. Consider the following simple example: we're going to do an experiment where we flip a coin. If the result of the coin flip was heads, we're going to announce the hash of the string "heads." If the result was tails, we're going to announce the hash of the string "tails."

We then ask someone, an adversary, who didn't see the coin flip, but only saw this hash output, to figure out what the string was that was hashed (we'll soon see why we might want to play games like this). In response, they would simply compute both the hash of the string "heads" and the hash of the string "tails," and they could see which one they were given. And so, in just a couple steps, they can figure out what the input was.

The adversary was able to guess what the string was because only two values of x were possible, and it was easy for the adversary to just try both of them. To be able to achieve the hiding property, there must be no value of x that is particularly likely. That is, x has to be chosen from a set that is, in some sense, very spread out. If x is chosen from such a set, this method of trying a few values of x that are especially likely will not work.

The big question is: Can we achieve the hiding property when the values that we want do not come from a spread-out set as in our "heads" and "tails" experiment? Fortunately, the answer is yes! We can hide even an input that's not spread out by concatenating it with another input that *is* spread out. We can now be slightly more precise about what we mean by hiding (the double vertical bar $\|$ denotes concatenation).

Hiding. A hash function H is said to be hiding if when a secret value r is chosen from a probability distribution that has *high min-entropy*, then, given $H(r \| x)$, it is infeasible to find x.

In information theory, *min-entropy* is a measure of how predictable an outcome is, and high min-entropy captures the intuitive idea that the distribution (i.e., of a random variable) is very spread out. What that means specifically is that when we sample from the distribution, there's no particular value that's likely to occur. So, for a concrete example, if r is chosen uniformly from among all strings that are 256 bits long, then any particular string is chosen with probability $1/2^{256}$, which is an infinitesimally small value.

APPLICATION: COMMITMENTS

Now let's look at an application of the hiding property. In particular, what we want to do is something called a *commitment.* A commitment is the digital analog of taking a value, sealing it in an envelope, and putting that envelope out on the table where everyone can see it. When you do that, you've committed yourself to what's inside the envelope. But you haven't opened it, so even though you've committed to a value, the value remains a secret from everyone else. Later, you can open the envelope and reveal the value that you committed to earlier.

Commitment scheme. A commitment scheme consists of two algorithms:

- *com* := commit(*msg*, *nonce*) The commit function takes a message and secret random value, called a *nonce*, as input and returns a commitment.
- verify(*com*, *msg*, *nonce*) The verify function takes a commitment, nonce, and message as input. It returns true if *com* == commit(*msg*, *nonce*) and false otherwise.

We require that the following two security properties hold:

- *Hiding*: Given *com*, it is infeasible to find *msg*.
- *Binding*: It is infeasible to find two pairs (*msg*, *nonce*) and (*msg′*, *nonce′*) such that *msg* ≠ *msg′* and commit(*msg*, *nonce*) == commit(*msg′*, *nonce′*).

To use a commitment scheme, we first need to generate a random *nonce*. We then apply the *commit* function to this nonce together with *msg*, the value being committed to, and we publish the commitment *com*. This stage is analogous to putting the sealed envelope on the table. At a later point, if we want to reveal the value that we committed to earlier, we publish the random nonce that we used to create this commitment, and the message, *msg*. Now anybody can verify that *msg* was indeed the message committed to earlier. This stage is analogous to opening the envelope.

Every time you commit to a value, it is important that you choose a new random value *nonce*. In cryptography, the term *nonce* is used to refer to a value that can only be used once.

The two security properties dictate that the algorithms actually behave like sealing and opening an envelope. First, given *com*, the commitment, someone looking at the envelope can't figure out what the message is. The second property is that it's binding. This ensures that when you commit to what's in the envelope, you can't change your mind later. That is, it's infeasible to find two different messages, such that you can commit to one message and then later claim that you committed to another.

So how do we know that these two properties hold? Before we can answer this, we need to discuss how we're going to actually implement a commitment scheme. We can do so using a cryptographic hash function. Consider the following commitment scheme:

$$\text{commit}(msg, nonce) := H(nonce \parallel msg),$$
$$\text{where } nonce \text{ is a random 256-bit value}$$

To commit to a message, we generate a random 256-bit nonce. Then we concatenate the nonce and the message and return the hash of this concatenated value as the commitment. To verify, someone will compute this same hash of the nonce they were given concatenated with the message. And they will check whether the result is equal to the commitment that they saw.

Take another look at the two properties required of our commitment schemes. If we substitute the instantiation of *commit* and *verify* as well as $H(nonce \parallel msg)$ for *com*, then these properties become:

- *Hiding*: Given $H(nonce \parallel msg)$, it is infeasible to find *msg*.
- *Binding*: It is infeasible to find two pairs $(msg, nonce)$ and $(msg', nonce')$ such that $msg \neq msg'$ and $H(nonce \parallel msg) == (nonce' \parallel msg')$.

The hiding property of commitments is exactly the hiding property that we required for our hash functions. If *key* was chosen as a random 256-bit value, then the hiding property says that if we hash the concatenation of *key* and the message, then it's infeasible to recover the message from the hash output. And it turns out that the binding property is implied by the collision-resistant property of the underlying hash function. If the hash function is collision resistant, then it will be infeasible to find distinct values *msg* and *msg′* such that $H(nonce \,\|\, msg) = H(nonce' \,\|\, msg')$, since such values would indeed be a collision. (Note that the reverse implications do not hold. That is, it's possible that you can find collisions, but none of them are of the form $H(nonce \,\|\, msg) == H(nonce' \,\|\, msg')$. For example, if you can only find a collision in which two distinct nonces generate the same commitment for the same message, then the commitment scheme is still binding, but the underlying hash function is not collision resistant.)

Therefore, if H is a hash function that is both collision resistant and hiding, this commitment scheme will work, in the sense that it will have the necessary security properties.

Property 3: Puzzle Friendliness

The third security property we're going to need from hash functions is that they are puzzle friendly. This property is a bit complicated. We first explain what the technical requirements of this property are and then give an application that illustrates why this property is useful.

Puzzle friendliness. A hash function H is said to be puzzle friendly if for every possible n-bit output value y, if k is chosen from a distribution with high min-entropy, then it is infeasible to find x such that $H(k \,\|\, x) = y$ in time significantly less than 2^n.

Intuitively, if someone wants to target the hash function to have some particular output value y, and if part of the input has been chosen in a suitably randomized way, then it's very difficult to find another value that hits exactly that target.

APPLICATION: SEARCH PUZZLE

Let's consider an application that illustrates the usefulness of this property. In this application, we're going to build a *search puzzle*, a mathematical problem that requires searching a very large space to find the solution. In particular, a search puzzle has no shortcuts. That is, there's no way to find a valid solution other than searching that large space.

Search puzzle. A search puzzle consists of

- a hash function, H,
- a value, *id* (which we call the *puzzle-ID*), chosen from a high min-entropy distribution, and
- a target set Y.

A solution to this puzzle is a value, x, such that

$$H(id \parallel x) \in Y.$$

The intuition is this: if H has an n-bit output, then it can take any of 2^n values. Solving the puzzle requires finding an input such that the output falls within the set Y, which is typically much smaller than the set of all outputs. The size of Y determines how hard the puzzle is. If Y is the set of all n-bit strings, then the puzzle is trivial, whereas if Y has only one element, then the puzzle is maximally hard. That the puzzle ID has high min-entropy ensures that there are no shortcuts. On the contrary, if a particular value of the ID were likely, then someone could cheat, say, by precomputing a solution to the puzzle with that ID.

If a hash funtion is puzzle friendly, then there's no solving strategy for this puzzle that is much better than just trying random values of x. And so, if we want to pose a puzzle that's difficult to solve, we can do it this way as long as we can generate puzzle-IDs in a suitably random way. We're going to use this idea later, when we talk about Bitcoin mining, starting in Chapter 2—mining is a sort of computational puzzle.

SHA-256

We've discussed three properties of hash functions and one application of each of these properties. Now let's discuss a particular hash function that we're going to use a lot in this book. Many hash functions exist, but this is the one Bitcoin uses primarily, and it's a pretty good one to use. It's called *SHA-256.*

Recall that we require that our hash functions work on inputs of arbitrary length. Luckily, as long as we can build a hash function that works on fixed-length inputs, there's a generic method to convert it into a hash function that works on arbitrary-length inputs. It's called the *Merkle-Damgård transform.* SHA-256 is one of a number of commonly used hash functions that make use of this method. In common terminology, the underlying fixed-length collision-resistant hash function is called the *compression function.* It has been proven that if the underlying compression function is collision resistant, then the overall hash function is collision resistant as well.

The Merkle-Damgård transform is quite simple. Suppose that the compression function takes inputs of length m and produces an output of a smaller length n. The input to the hash function, which can be of any size, is divided into *blocks* of length $m - n$. The construction works as follows: pass each block together with the output of the previous block into the compression function. Notice that input length will then be $(m - n) + n = m$, which is the input length to the compression function. For the first block, to which there is no previous block output, we instead use an *initialization vector* (IV in Figure 1.3). This number is reused for every call to the hash function, and in practice you can just look it up in a standards document. The last block's output is the result that you return.

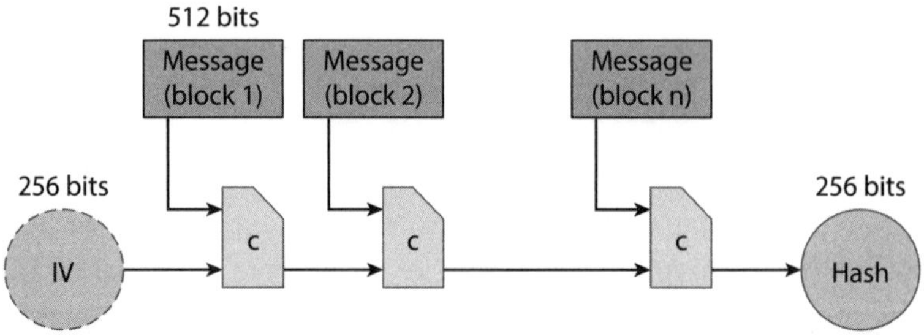

FIGURE 1.3. SHA-256 hash function (simplified). SHA-256 uses the Merkle-Damgård transform to turn a fixed-length collision-resistant compression function into a hash function that accepts arbitrary-length inputs. The input is padded, so that its length is a multiple of 512 bits. IV stands for initialization vector.

Modeling Hash Functions

Hash functions are the Swiss Army knife of cryptography: they find a place in a spectacular variety of applications. The flip side to this versatility is that different applications require slightly different properties of hash functions to ensure security. It has proven notoriously hard to pin down a list of hash function properties that would result in provable security across the board.

In this text, we've selected three properties that are crucial to the way that hash functions are used in Bitcoin and other cryptocurrencies. Even in this space, not all of these properties are necessary for every use of hash functions. For example, puzzle friendliness is only important in Bitcoin mining, as we'll see.

Designers of secure systems often throw in the towel and model hash functions as functions that output an independent random value for every possible input. The use of this "random oracle model" for proving security remains controversial in cryptography. Regardless of one's position on this debate, reasoning about how to reduce the security properties that we want in our applications to fundamental properties of the underlying primitives is a valuable intellectual exercise for building secure systems. Our presentation in this chapter is designed to help you learn this skill.

SHA-256 uses a compression function that takes 768-bit input and produces 256-bit outputs. The block size is 512 bits. See Figure 1.3 for a graphical depiction of how SHA-256 works.

We've talked about hash functions, cryptographic hash functions with special properties, applications of those properties, and a specific hash function that we use in Bitcoin. In the next section, we discuss ways of using hash functions to build more complicated data structures that are used in distributed systems like Bitcoin.

1.2. HASH POINTERS AND DATA STRUCTURES

In this section, we discuss *hash pointers* and their applications. A hash pointer is a data structure that turns out to be useful in many of the systems that we consider. A hash

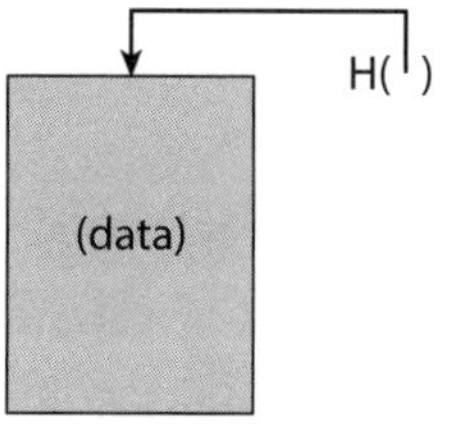

FIGURE 1.4. Hash pointer. A hash pointer is a pointer to where data is stored together with a cryptographic hash of the value of this data at some fixed point in time.

pointer is simply a pointer to where some information is stored together with a cryptographic hash of the information. Whereas a regular pointer gives you a way to retrieve the information, a hash pointer also allows you to verify that the information hasn't been changed (Figure 1.4).

We can use hash pointers to build all kinds of data structures. Intuitively, we can take a familiar data structure that uses pointers, such as a linked list or a binary search tree, and implement it with hash pointers instead of ordinary pointers, as we normally would.

Block Chain

Figure 1.5 shows a linked list using hash pointers. We call this data structure a *block chain*. In a regular linked list where you have a series of blocks, each block has data as well as a pointer to the previous block in the list. But in a block chain, the previous-block pointer will be replaced with a hash pointer. So each block not only tells us where the value of the previous block was, but it also contains a digest of that value, which allows us to verify that the value hasn't been changed. We store the head of the list, which is just a regular hash-pointer that points to the most recent data block.

A use case for a block chain is a *tamper-evident log*. That is, we want to build a log data structure that stores data and allows us to append data to the end of the log. But if somebody alters data that appears earlier in the log, we're going to detect the change.

To understand why a block chain achieves this tamper-evident property, let's ask what happens if an adversary wants to tamper with data in the middle of the chain.

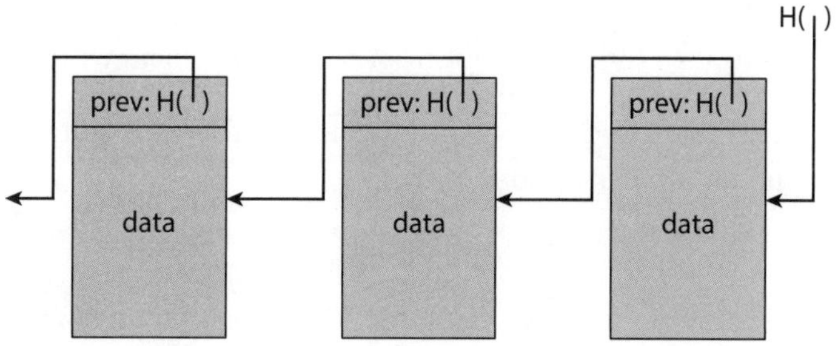

FIGURE 1.5. Block chain. A block chain is a linked list that is built with hash pointers instead of pointers.

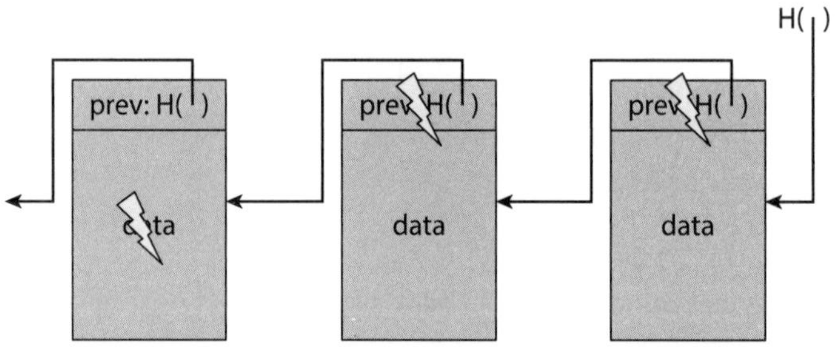

FIGURE 1.6. Tamper-evident log. If an adversary modifies data anywhere in the block chain, it will result in the hash pointer in the following block being incorrect. If we store the head of the list, then even if an adversary modifies all pointers to be consistent with the modified data, the head pointer will be incorrect, and we can detect the tampering.

Specifically, the adversary's goal is to do it in such a way that someone who remembers only the hash pointer at the head of the block chain won't be able to detect the tampering. To achieve this goal, the adversary changes the data of some block k. Since the data has been changed, the hash in block $k + 1$, which is a hash of the entire block k, is not going to match up. Remember that we are statistically guaranteed that the new hash will not match the altered content, since the hash function is collision resistant. And so we will detect the inconsistency between the new data in block k and the hash pointer in block $k + 1$. Of course, the adversary can continue to try and cover up this change by changing the next block's hash as well. The adversary can continue doing this, but this strategy will fail when she reaches the head of the list. Specifically, as long as we store the hash pointer at the head of the list in a place where the adversary cannot change it, she will be unable to change any block without being detected (Figure 1.6).

The upshot is that if the adversary wants to tamper with data anywhere in this entire chain, to keep the story consistent, she's going to have to tamper with the hash pointers all the way to the end. And she's ultimately going to run into a roadblock, because she won't be able to tamper with the head of the list. Thus, by remembering just this single hash pointer, we've essentially determined a tamper-evident hash of the entire list. So we can build a block chain like this containing as many blocks as we want, going back to some special block at the beginning of the list, which we will call the *genesis block*.

You may have noticed that the block chain construction is similar to the Merkle-Damgård construction discussed in Section 1.1. Indeed, they are quite similar, and the same security argument applies to both of them.

Merkle Trees

Another useful data structure that we can build using hash pointers is a binary tree. A binary tree with hash pointers is known as a *Merkle tree* (Figure 1.7), after its inventor, Ralph Merkle. Suppose we have some blocks containing data. These blocks make up the

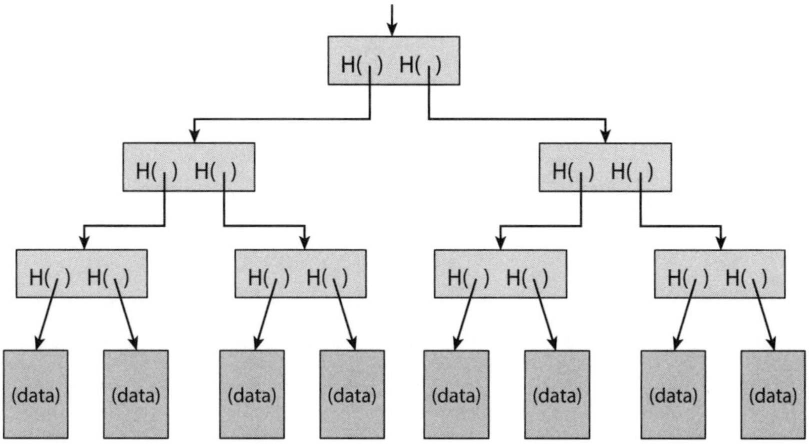

FIGURE 1.7. Merkle tree. In a Merkle tree, data blocks are grouped in pairs, and the hash of each of these blocks is stored in a parent node. The parent nodes are in turn grouped in pairs, and their hashes stored one level up the tree. This pattern continues up the tree until we reach the root node.

leaves of our tree. We group these data blocks into pairs of two, and then for each pair we build a data structure that has two hash pointers, one to each of the blocks. These data structures make up the next level of the tree. We in turn group these into groups of two, and for each pair create a new data structure that contains the hash of each. We continue doing this until we reach a single block, the root of the tree.

As before, we remember just one hash pointer: in this case, the one at the root of the tree. We now have the ability to traverse through the hash pointers to any point in the list. This allows us to make sure that the data has not been tampered with because, just as we saw for the block chain, if an adversary tampers with some data block at the bottom of the tree, his change will cause the hash pointer one level up to not match, and even if he continues to tamper with other blocks farther up the tree, the change will eventually propagate to the top, where he won't be able to tamper with the hash pointer that we've stored. So again, any attempt to tamper with any piece of data will be detected by just remembering the hash pointer at the top.

Proof of Membership

Another nice feature of Merkle trees is that, unlike the block chain that we built before, they allow a concise *proof of membership*. Suppose that someone wants to prove that a certain data block is a member of the Merkle tree. As usual, we remember just the root. Then they need to show us this data block, and the blocks on the path from the data block to the root. We can ignore the rest of the tree, as the blocks on this path are enough to allow us to verify the hashes all the way up to the root of the tree. See Figure 1.8 for a graphical depiction of how this works.

If there are n nodes in the tree, only about $\log(n)$ items need to be shown. And since each step just requires computing the hash of the child block, it takes about $\log(n)$ time

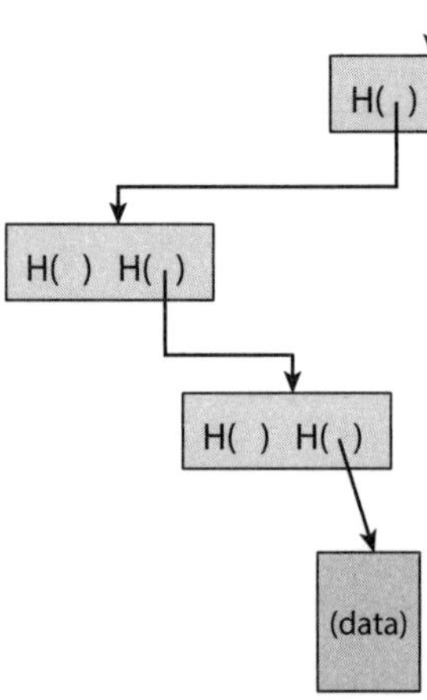

FIGURE 1.8. Proof of membership. To prove that a data block is included in the tree only requires showing the blocks in the path from that data block to the root.

for us to verify it. And so even if the Merkle tree contains a large number of blocks, we can still prove membership in a relatively short time. Verification thus runs in time and space that's logarithmic in the number of nodes in the tree.

A *sorted Merkle tree* is just a Merkle tree where we take the blocks at the bottom and sort them using some ordering function. This can be alphabetical order, lexicographical order, numerical order, or some other agreed-on ordering.

Proof of Nonmembership

Using a sorted Merkle tree, it becomes possible to verify nonmembership in logarithmic time and space. That is, we can prove that a particular block is not in the Merkle tree. And the way we do that is simply by showing a path to the item just before where the item in question would be and showing the path to the item just after where it would be. If these two items are consecutive in the tree, then this serves as proof that the item in question is not included—because if it were included, it would need to be between the two items shown, but there is no space between them, as they are consecutive.

We've discussed using hash pointers in linked lists and binary trees, but more generally, it turns out that we can use hash pointers in any pointer-based data structure as long as the data structure doesn't have cycles. If there are cycles in the data structure, then we won't be able to make all the hashes match up. If you think about it, in an acyclic data structure we can start near the leaves, or near the things that don't have any pointers coming out of them, compute the hashes of those, and then work our way back toward the beginning. But in a structure with cycles, there's no end that we can start with and compute back from.

To consider another example, we can build a directed acyclic graph out of hash pointers, and we'll be able to verify membership in that graph very efficiently. It also will be easy to compute. Using hash pointers in this manner is a general trick that you'll see time and again in the context of distributed data structures and in the algorithms that we discuss later in this chapter (Section 1.5) and throughout the book.

1.3. DIGITAL SIGNATURES

In this section, we look at *digital signatures*. This is the second cryptographic primitive, along with hash functions, that we need as building blocks for the cryptocurrency discussion in Section 1.5. A digital signature is supposed to be the digital analog to a handwritten signature on paper. We desire two properties from digital signatures that correspond well to the handwritten signature analogy. First, only you can make your signature, but anyone who sees it can verify that it's valid. Second, we want the signature to be tied to a particular document, so that the signature cannot be used to indicate your agreement or endorsement of a different document. For handwritten signatures, this latter property is analogous to ensuring that somebody can't take your signature and snip it off one document and glue it to the bottom of another one.

How can we build this in a digital form using cryptography? First, let's make the above intuitive discussion slightly more concrete. This will allow us to reason better about digital signature schemes and discuss their security properties.

Digital signature scheme. A digital signature scheme consists of the following three algorithms:

- (*sk*, *pk*) := generateKeys(*keysize*) The generateKeys method takes a key size and generates a key pair. The secret key *sk* is kept privately and used to sign messages. *pk* is the public verification key that you give to everybody. Anyone with this key can verify your signature.
- sig := sign(*sk*, *message*) The sign method takes a message and a secret key, *sk*, as input and outputs a signature for *message* under *sk*.
- isValid := verify(*pk*, *message*, *sig*) The verify method takes a message, a signature, and a public key as input. It returns a boolean value, *isValid*, that will be true if *sig* is a valid signature for *message* under public key *pk*, and false otherwise.

We require that the following two properties hold:

- Valid signatures must verify:
  verify(*pk*, *message*, sign(*sk*, *message*)) == true.
- Signatures are *existentially unforgeable*.

We note that generateKeys and sign can be randomized algorithms. Indeed, generateKeys had better be randomized, because it ought to be generating different keys for different people. In contrast, verify will always be deterministic.

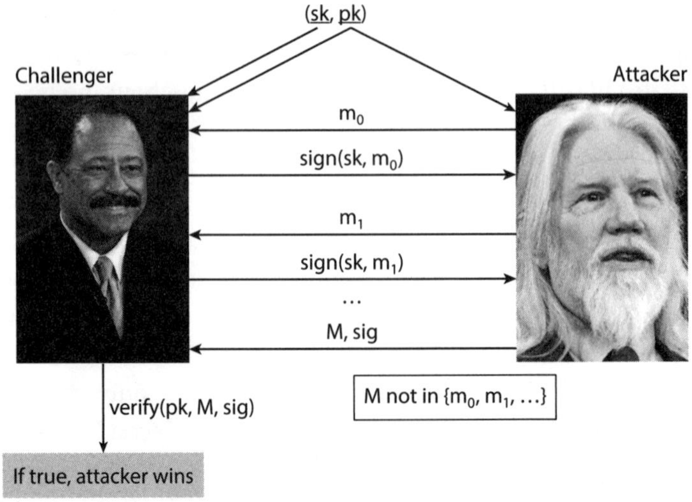

FIGURE 1.9. Unforgeability game. The attacker and the challenger play the unforgeability game. If the attacker is able to successfully output a signature on a message that he has not previously seen, he wins. If he is unable to do so, the challenger wins, and the digital signature scheme is unforgeable. Photograph of Whit Diffie (right), cropped, © Kevin Bocek. Licensed under Creative Commons CC BY 2.0.

Let us now examine the two properties that we require of a digital signature scheme in more detail. The first property is straightforward—that valid signatures must be verifiable. If I sign a message with *sk*, my secret key, and someone later tries to validate that signature over that same message using my public key, *pk*, the signature must validate correctly. This property is a basic requirement for signatures to be useful at all.

Unforgeability. The second requirement is that it's computationally infeasible to forge signatures. That is, an adversary who knows your public key and sees your signatures on some other messages can't forge your signature on some message for which he has not seen your signature. This unforgeability property is generally formalized in terms of a game that we play with an adversary. The use of games is quite common in cryptographic security proofs.

In the unforgeability game, an adversary claims that he can forge signatures, and a challenger tests this claim (Figure 1.9). The first thing we do is use generateKeys to generate a secret signing key and a corresponding public verification key. We give the secret key to the challenger, and we give the public key to both the challenger and the adversary. So the adversary only knows information that's public, and his mission is to try to forge a message. The challenger knows the secret key. So he can make signatures.

Intuitively, the setup of this game matches real-world conditions. A real attacker would likely be able to see valid signatures from his would-be victim on different documents. And the attacker might even be able to manipulate the victim into signing innocuous-looking documents if that's useful to the attacker.

To model this in our game, we allow the adversary to get signatures on some documents of his choice, for as long as he wants, as long as the number of guesses is plausible. To give an intuitive idea of what we mean by a plausible number of guesses, we would allow the adversary to try 1 million guesses, but not 2^{80} guesses. In asymptotic terms, we allow the adversary to try a number of guesses that is a polynomial function of the key size, but no more (e.g., he cannot try exponentially many guesses).

Once the adversary is satisfied that he's seen enough signatures, then he picks some message, M, that he will attempt to forge a signature on. The only restriction on M is that it must be a message for which the adversary has not previously seen a signature (because then he can obviously send back a signature that he has been given). The challenger runs the verify algorithm to determine whether the signature produced by the attacker is a valid signature on M under the public verification key. If it successfully verifies, the adversary wins the game.

We say that the signature scheme is unforgeable if and only if, no matter what algorithm the adversary is using, his chance of successfully forging a message is extremely small—so small that we can assume it will never happen in practice.

Practical Concerns

Several practical things must be done to turn the algorithmic idea into a digital signature mechanism that can be implemented. For example, many signature algorithms are randomized (in particular, the one used in Bitcoin), and we therefore need a good source of randomness. The importance of this requirement can't be overestimated, as bad randomness will make your otherwise-secure algorithm insecure.

Another practical concern is the message size. In practice, there's a limit on the message size that you're able to sign, because real schemes are going to operate on bit strings of limited length. There's an easy way around this limitation: sign the hash of the message, rather than the message itself. If we use a cryptographic hash function with a 256-bit output, then we can effectively sign a message of any length as long as our signature scheme can sign 256-bit messages. As we have discussed, it's safe to use the hash of the message as a message digest in this manner, since the hash function is collision resistant.

Another trick that we will use later is that you can sign a hash pointer. If you sign a hash pointer, then the signature covers, or protects, the whole structure—not just the hash pointer itself, but everything the chain of hash pointers points to. For example, if you were to sign the hash pointer located at the end of a block chain, the result is that you would effectively be digitally signing the entire block chain.

ECDSA

Now let's get into the nuts and bolts. Bitcoin uses a particular digital signature scheme known as the *Elliptic Curve Digital Signature Algorithm* (ECDSA). ECDSA is a U.S. government standard, an update of the earlier DSA algorithm adapted to use elliptic curves.

These algorithms have received considerable cryptographic analysis over the years and are generally believed to be secure.

More specifically, Bitcoin uses ECDSA over the standard elliptic curve secp256k1, which is estimated to provide 128 bits of security (i.e., it is as difficult to break this algorithm as it is to perform 2^{128} symmetric-key cryptographic operations, such as invoking a hash function). Although this curve is a published standard, it is rarely used outside Bitcoin; other applications using ECDSA (such as key exchange in the TLS protocol for secure web browsing) typically use the more common secp256r1 curve. This is just a quirk of Bitcoin, as it was chosen by Satoshi (see the Foreword) in the early specification of the system and is now difficult to change.

We won't go into all the details of how ECDSA works, as some complicated math is involved and understanding it is not necessary for the rest of this book. If you're interested in the details, refer to our Further Reading section at the end of this chapter. It might be useful to have an idea of the sizes of various quantities, however:

Private key:	256 bits
Public key, uncompressed:	512 bits
Public key, compressed:	257 bits
Message to be signed:	256 bits
Signature:	512 bits

Note that even though ECDSA can technically only sign messages 256 bits long, this is not a problem: messages are always hashed before being signed, so effectively any size message can be efficiently signed.

With ECDSA, a good source of randomness is essential, because a bad source will likely leak your key. It makes intuitive sense that if you use bad randomness when generating a key, then the key you generate will likely not be secure. But it's a quirk of ECDSA that, even if you use bad randomness only when making a signature and you use your perfectly good key, the bad signature will also leak your private key. (For those familiar with DSA, this is a general quirk in DSA and is not specific to the elliptic-curve variant.) And then it's game over: if you leak your private key, an adversary can forge your signature. We thus need to be especially careful about using good randomness in practice. Using a bad source of randomness is a common pitfall of otherwise secure systems.

This completes our discussion of digital signatures as a cryptographic primitive. In the next section, we discuss some applications of digital signatures that will turn out to be useful for building cryptocurrencies.

1.4. PUBLIC KEYS AS IDENTITIES

Let's look at a nice trick that goes along with digital signatures. The idea is to take a public key, one of those public verification keys from a digital signature scheme, and

Cryptocurrencies and Encryption

If you've been waiting to find out which encryption algorithm is used in Bitcoin, we're sorry to disappoint you. There is no encryption in Bitcoin, because nothing needs to be encrypted, as we'll see. Encryption is only one of a rich suite of techniques made possible by modern cryptography. Many of them, such as commitment schemes, involve hiding information in some way, but they are distinct from encryption.

equate it to an identity of a person or an actor in a system. If you see a message with a signature that verifies correctly under a public key, *pk*, then you can think of this as *pk* stating the message. You can literally think of a public key as being like an actor, or a party in a system, who can make statements by signing those statements. From this viewpoint, the public key is an identity. For someone to speak for the identity *pk*, he must know the corresponding secret key, *sk*.

A consequence of treating public keys as identities is that you can make a new identity whenever you want—you simply create a new fresh key pair, *sk* and *pk*, via the *generateKeys* operation in our digital signature scheme. This *pk* is the new public identity that you can use, and *sk* is the corresponding secret key that only you know and that lets you speak on behalf of the identity *pk*. In practice, you may use the hash of *pk* as your identity, since public keys are large. If you do that, then to verify that a message comes from your identity, one will have to check that (1) *pk* indeed hashes to your identity, and (2) the message verifies under public key *pk*.

Moreover, by default, your public key *pk* will basically look random, and nobody will be able to uncover your real-world identity by examining *pk*. (Of course, once you start making statements using this identity, these statements may leak information that allows others to connect *pk* to your real-world identity. We discuss this in more detail shortly.) You can generate a fresh identity that looks random, like a face in the crowd, and is controlled only by you.

Decentralized Identity Management

This brings us to the idea of decentralized identity management. Rather than having a central authority for registering users in a system, you can register as a user by yourself. You don't need to be issued a username, nor do you need to inform someone that you're going to be using a particular name. If you want a new identity, you can just generate one at any time, and you can create as many as you want. If you prefer to be known by five different names, no problem! Just make five identities. If you want to be somewhat anonymous for a while, you can create a new identity, use it for just a little while, and then throw it away. All these things are possible with decentralized identity management, and this is the way Bitcoin, in fact, handles identity. These identities are called *addresses*, in Bitcoin jargon. You'll frequently hear the term "address" used in the context of Bitcoin and cryptocurrencies, and it's really just a hash of a public key. It's an

> **Security and Randomness**
>
> The idea that you can generate an identity without a centralized authority may seem counterintuitive. After all, if someone else gets lucky and generates the same key as you, can't they steal your bitcoins?
>
> The answer is that the probability of someone else generating the same 256-bit key as you is so small that we don't have to worry about it in practice. For all intents and purposes, we are guaranteed that it will never happen.
>
> More generally, in contrast to beginners' intuition that probabilistic systems are unpredictable and hard to reason about, often the opposite is true—the theory of statistics allows us to precisely quantify the chances of events we're interested in and to make confident assertions about the behavior of such systems.
>
> But there's a subtlety: the probabilistic guarantee is true only when keys are generated at random. The generation of randomness is often a weak point in real systems. If two users' computers use the same source of randomness or use predictable randomness, then the theoretical guarantees no longer apply. So to ensure that practical guarantees match the theoretical ones, it is crucial to use a good source of randomness when generating keys.

identity that someone made up out of thin air, as part of this decentralized identity management scheme.

At first glance, it may seem that decentralized identity management leads to great anonymity and privacy. After all, you can create a random-looking identity all by yourself without telling anyone your real-world identity. But it's not that simple. Over time, the identity that you create makes a series of statements. People see these statements and thus know that whoever owns this identity has done a certain series of actions. They can start to connect the dots, using this series of actions to make inferences about your real-world identity. An observer can link together these observations over time and make inferences that lead to such conclusions as, "Gee, this person is acting a lot like Joe. Maybe this person is Joe."

In other words, in Bitcoin you don't need to explicitly register or reveal your real-world identity, but the pattern of your behavior might itself be identifying. This is the fundamental privacy question in a cryptocurrency like Bitcoin, and indeed we'll devote Chapter 6 to it.

1.5. TWO SIMPLE CRYPTOCURRENCIES

Now let's move from cryptography to cryptocurrencies. Eating our cryptographic vegetables will start to pay off here, and we'll gradually see how the pieces fit together and why cryptographic operations like hash functions and digital signatures are actually useful. In this section we discuss two very simple cryptocurrencies. Of course, much of the rest of the book is needed to spell out all the details of how Bitcoin itself works.

Goofycoin

The first of the two is *Goofycoin*, which is about the simplest cryptocurrency we can imagine. There are just two rules of Goofycoin. The first rule is that a designated entity, Goofy, can create new coins whenever he wants and these newly created coins belong to him.

To create a coin, Goofy generates a unique coin ID `uniqueCoinID` that he's never generated before and constructs the string `CreateCoin [uniqueCoinID]`. He then computes the digital signature of this string with his secret signing key. The string, together with Goofy's signature, is a coin. Anyone can verify that the coin contains Goofy's valid signature of a `CreateCoin` statement and is therefore a valid coin.

The second rule of Goofycoin is that whoever owns a coin can transfer it to someone else. Transferring a coin is not simply a matter of sending the coin data structure to the recipient—it's done using cryptographic operations.

Let's say Goofy wants to transfer a coin that he created to Alice. To do this, he creates a new statement that says "Pay this to Alice" where "this" is a hash pointer that references the coin in question. And as we saw earlier, identities are really just public keys, so "Alice" refers to Alice's public key. Finally, Goofy signs the string representing the statement. Since Goofy is the one who originally owned that coin, he has to sign any transaction that spends the coin. Once this data structure representing Goofy's transaction is signed by him, Alice owns the coin. She can prove to anyone that she owns the coin, because she can present the data structure with Goofy's valid signature. Furthermore, it points to a valid coin that was owned by Goofy. So the validity and ownership of coins are self-evident in the system.

Once Alice owns the coin, she can spend it in turn. To do this, she creates a statement that says, "Pay this to Bob's public key" where "this" is a hash pointer to the coin that was owned by her. And of course, Alice signs this statement. Anyone, when presented with this coin, can verify that Bob is the owner. They can follow the chain of hash pointers back to the coin's creation and verify that at each step, the rightful owner signed a statement that says "pay this coin to [new owner]" (Figure 1.10).

To summarize, the rules of Goofycoin are:

- Goofy can create new coins by simply signing a statement that he's making a new coin with a unique coin ID.
- Whoever owns a coin can pass it on to someone else by signing a statement that says, "Pass on this coin to X" (where X is specified as a public key).
- Anyone can verify the validity of a coin by following the chain of hash pointers back to its creation by Goofy, verifying all signatures along the way.

Of course, there's a fundamental security problem with Goofycoin. Let's say Alice passed her coin on to Bob by sending her signed statement to Bob but didn't tell anyone else. She could create another signed statement that pays the same coin to Chuck. To

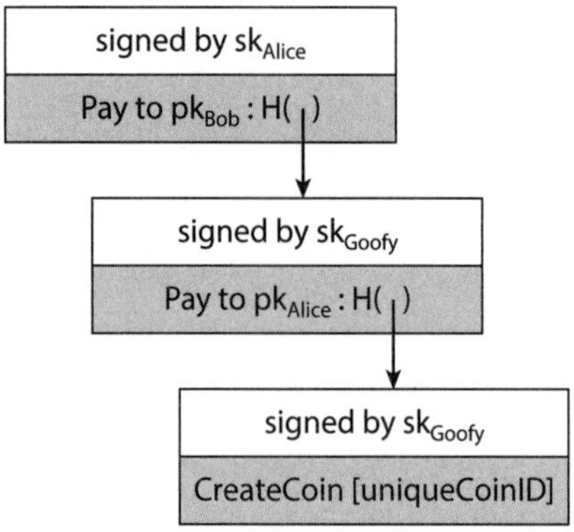

FIGURE 1.10. Goofycoin coin. Shown here is a coin that's been created (bottom) and spent twice (middle and top).

Chuck, it would appear that it is a perfectly valid transaction, and now he's the owner of the coin. Bob and Chuck would both have valid-looking claims to be the owner of this coin. This is called a *double-spending attack*—Alice is spending the same coin twice. Intuitively, we know coins are not supposed to work that way.

In fact, double-spending attacks are one of the key problems that any cryptocurrency has to solve. Goofycoin does not solve the double-spending attack, and therefore it's not secure. Goofycoin is simple, and its mechanism for transferring coins is actually similar to that of Bitcoin, but because it is insecure, it is inadequate as a cryptocurrency.

Scroogecoin

To solve the double-spending problem, we'll design another cryptocurrency, called *Scroogecoin*. Scroogecoin is built off of Goofycoin, but it's a bit more complicated in terms of data structures.

The first key idea is that a designated entity called Scrooge publishes an *append-only ledger* containing the history of all transactions. The append-only property ensures that any data written to this ledger will remain forever in the ledger. If the ledger is truly append only, we can use it to defend against double spending by requiring all transactions to be written in the ledger before they are accepted. That way, it will be publicly documented if coins were previously sent to a different owner.

To implement this append-only functionality, Scrooge can build a block chain (the data structure discussed in Section 1.2), which he will digitally sign. It consists of a series of data blocks, each with one transaction in it (in practice, as an optimization, we'd really put multiple transactions in the same block, as Bitcoin does.) Each block has the ID of a transaction, the transaction's contents, and a hash pointer to the previous block. Scrooge digitally signs the final hash pointer, which binds all the data in this entire structure, and he publishes the signature along with the block chain (Figure 1.11).

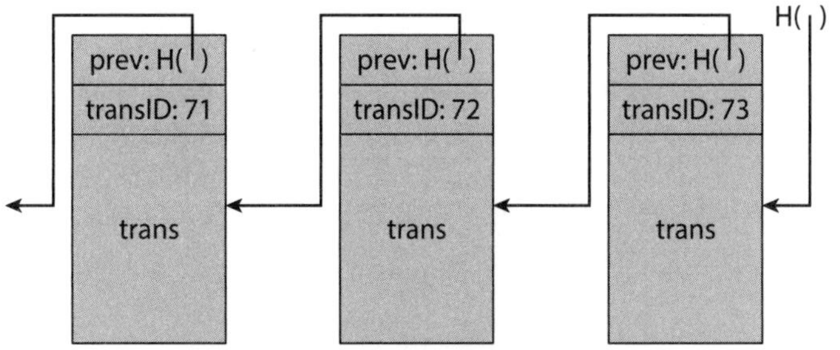

FIGURE 1.11. Scroogecoin block chain.

In Scroogecoin, a transaction only counts if it is in the block chain signed by Scrooge. Anybody can verify that a transaction was endorsed by Scrooge by checking Scrooge's signature on the block that records the transaction. Scrooge makes sure that he doesn't endorse a transaction that attempts to double spend an already spent coin.

Why do we need a block chain with hash pointers in addition to having Scrooge sign each block? This ensures the append-only property. If Scrooge tries to add or remove a transaction, or to change an existing transaction, it will affect all following blocks because of the hash pointers. As long as someone is monitoring the latest hash pointer published by Scrooge, the change will be obvious and easy to catch. In a system where Scrooge signed blocks individually, you'd have to keep track of every single signature Scrooge ever issued. A block chain makes it easy for any two individuals to verify that they have observed the same history of transactions signed by Scrooge.

In Scroogecoin, there are two kinds of transactions. The first kind is `CreateCoins`, which is just like the operation Goofy could do in Goofycoin to make a new coin. With Scroogecoin, we'll extend the semantics a bit to allow multiple coins to be created in one transaction (Figure 1.12).

transID: 73		type:CreateCoins	
coins created			
num	*value*	*recipient*	
0	3.2	0x...	← coinID 73(0)
1	1.4	0x...	← coinID 73(1)
2	7.1	0x...	← coinID 73(2)

FIGURE 1.12. `CreateCoins` transaction. This `CreateCoins` transaction creates multiple coins. Each coin has a serial number in the transaction. Each coin also has a value; it's worth a certain number of scroogecoins. Finally, each coin has a recipient, which is a public key that gets the coin when it's created. So `CreateCoins` creates multiple new coins with different values and assigns them to people as initial owners. We refer to coins by CoinIDs. A CoinID is a combination of a transaction ID and the coin's serial number in that transaction.

transID: 73		type:PayCoins
consumed coinIDs: 68(1), 42(0), 72(3)		
coins created		
num	*value*	*recipient*
0	3.2	0x...
1	1.4	0x...
2	7.1	0x...
signatures		

FIGURE 1.13. A PayCoins transaction.

By definition, a CreateCoins transaction is always valid if it is signed by Scrooge. We won't worry about when or how many coins Scrooge is entitled to create, just like we didn't worry in Goofycoin about how Goofy was chosen as the entity allowed to create coins.

The second kind of transaction is PayCoins. It consumes some coins (i.e., destroys them) and creates new coins of the same total value. The new coins might belong to different people (public keys). This transaction has to be signed by everyone who's paying in a coin. So if you're the owner of one of the coins that's going to be consumed in this transaction, then you need to digitally sign the transaction to say that you're OK with spending this coin.

The rules of Scroogecoin say that the PayCoins transaction is valid if it satisfies four conditions:

- The consumed coins are valid, that is, they were created in previous transactions.
- The consumed coins have not already been consumed in some previous transaction. That is, this is not a double-spend transaction.
- The total value of the coins that come out of this transaction is equal to the total value of the coins that went in. That is, only Scrooge can create new value.
- The transaction is validly signed by the owners of all coins consumed in the transaction.

If these conditions are met, then this PayCoins transaction is valid, and Scrooge will accept it (Figure 1.13). He'll write it into the ledger by appending it to the block chain, after which everyone can see that this transaction has happened. It is only at this point that the participants can accept that the transaction has actually occurred. Until it is published, it might be preempted by a double-spending transaction even if it is otherwise validated by the first three conditions.

Coins in this system are immutable—they are never changed, subdivided, or combined. Each coin is created, once, in one transaction and then later consumed in another transaction. But we can get the same effect as being able to subdivide or combine coins by using transactions. For example, to subdivide a coin, Alice creates a new transaction that consumes that one coin and then produces two new coins of the same total value. Those two new coins could be assigned back to her. So although coins are immutable in this system, it has all the flexibility of a system that doesn't have immutable coins.

Now we come to the core problem with Scroogecoin. Scroogecoin will work in the sense that people can see which coins are valid. It prevents double spending, because everyone can look into the block chain and see that all transactions are valid and that every coin is consumed only once. But the problem is Scrooge—he has too much influence. He can't create fake transactions, because he can't forge other people's signatures. But he could stop endorsing transactions from some users, denying them service and making their coins unspendable. If Scrooge is greedy (as his novella namesake suggests), he could refuse to publish transactions unless they transfer some mandated transaction fee to him. Scrooge can also of course create as many new coins for himself as he wants. Or Scrooge could get bored of the whole system and stop updating the block chain completely.

The problem here is centralization. Although Scrooge is happy with this system, we, as users of it, might not be. While Scroogecoin may seem like an unrealistic proposal, much of the early research on cryptosystems assumed there would indeed be some central trusted authority, typically referred to as a *bank*. After all, most real-world currencies do have a trusted issuer (typically a government mint) responsible for creating currency and determining which notes are valid. However, cryptocurrencies with a central authority largely failed to take off in practice. There are many reasons for this, but in hindsight it appears that it's difficult to get people to accept a cryptocurrency with a centralized authority.

Therefore, the central technical challenge that we need to solve to improve on Scroogecoin and create a workable system is: Can we de-Scrooge-ify the system? That is, can we get rid of that centralized Scrooge figure? Can we have a cryptocurrency that operates like Scroogecoin in many ways but doesn't have any central trusted authority?

To do that, we need to figure out how all users can agree on a single published block chain as the authoritative history of all transactions. They must all agree on which transactions are valid, and which transactions have actually occurred. They also need to be able to assign IDs in a decentralized way. Finally, the minting of new coins also needs to be decentralized. If we can solve these problems, then we can build a currency that would be like Scroogecoin but without a centralized party. In fact, this would be a system much like Bitcoin.

FURTHER READING

Steven Levy's *Crypto* is an enjoyable nontechnical look at the development of modern cryptography and the people behind it:

Levy, Steven. *Crypto: How the Code Rebels Beat the Government—Saving Privacy in the Digital Age.* London: Penguin, 2001.

Modern cryptography is a rather theoretical field. Cryptographers use mathematics to define primitives, protocols, and their desired security properties in a formal way and to prove them secure based on widely accepted assumptions about the computational hardness of specific mathematical tasks. In this chapter we've used intuitive language to discuss hash functions and digital signatures. For the reader interested in exploring these and other cryptographic concepts in a more mathematical way and in greater detail, see:

Katz, Jonathan, and Yehuda Lindell. *Introduction to Modern Cryptography*, second edition. Boca Raton, FL: CRC Press, 2014.

For an introduction to applied cryptography, see:

Ferguson, Niels, Bruce Schneier, and Tadayoshi Kohno. *Cryptography Engineering: Design Principles and Practical Applications*. Hoboken, NJ: John Wiley & Sons, 2012.

Perusing the National Institute of Standards and Technology (NIST) standard that defines SHA-256 is a good way to develop an intuition for what cryptographic standards look like:

NIST. "Secure Hash Standards, Federal Information Processing Standards Publication." FIPS PUB 180-4. Information Technology Laboratory, NIST, Gaithersburg, MD, 2008.

Finally, here's the paper describing the standardized version of the ECDSA signature algorithm:

Johnson, Don, Alfred Menezes, and Scott Vanstone. "The Elliptic Curve Digital Signature Algorithm (ECDSA)." *International Journal of Information Security* 1(1), 2001: 36–63.

CHAPTER 2

How Bitcoin Achieves Decentralization

In this chapter, we discuss decentralization in Bitcoin. In Chapter 1, we looked at the crypto basics that underlie Bitcoin and ended with the description of a simple currency called Scroogecoin. Scroogecoin achieves a lot of what we want in a ledger-based cryptocurrency, but it has one glaring problem—it relies on a centralized authority (Scrooge). We ended with the question of how to decentralize, or de-Scrooge-ify, this currency. Answering that question is the focus of this chapter.

As you read through this chapter, note that the mechanism by which Bitcoin achieves decentralization is not purely technical—it is a combination of technical methods and clever incentive engineering. By the end of this chapter, you should have a really good appreciation for how this decentralization is achieved, and, more generally, how Bitcoin works and why it is secure.

2.1. CENTRALIZATION VERSUS DECENTRALIZATION

Decentralization is an important concept that is not unique to Bitcoin. The notion of competing paradigms of centralization versus decentralization arises in a variety of different digital technologies. To best understand how it plays out in Bitcoin, it is useful to understand the central conflict—the tension between these two paradigms—in a variety of other contexts.

On one hand we have the Internet, a famously decentralized system that has historically competed with and prevailed against "walled-garden" alternatives like AOL's and CompuServe's information services. Then there's email, which at its core is a decentralized system based on the Simple Mail Transfer Protocol (SMTP), an open standard. Although it does have competition from proprietary messaging systems like Facebook or LinkedIn mail, email has managed to remain the default for person-to-person communications online. In the case of instant messaging and text messaging, we have a hybrid model that can't be categorically described as centralized or decentralized. Finally there's social networking: despite numerous concerted efforts by hobbyists, developers, and entrepreneurs to create alternatives to the dominant centralized model, centralized systems like Facebook and LinkedIn still dominate this space. In fact, this conflict long predates the digital era—we see a similar struggle between the two models in the history of telephony, radio, television, and film.

Decentralization is not all or nothing; almost no system is purely decentralized or purely centralized. For example, email is fundamentally a decentralized system based on a standardized protocol, SMTP, and anyone who wishes can operate an email server of their own. Yet what has happened in the market is that a small number of centralized webmail providers have become dominant. Similarly, even though the Bitcoin protocol is decentralized, services like Bitcoin exchanges, where you can convert bitcoins into other currencies, and wallet software (software that allows people to manage their bitcoins) may be centralized or decentralized to varying degrees.

With this in mind, let's break down the question of how the Bitcoin protocol achieves decentralization into five more specific questions:

1. Who maintains the ledger of transactions?
2. Who has authority over which transactions are valid?
3. Who creates new bitcoins?
4. Who determines how the rules of the system change?
5. How do bitcoins acquire exchange value?

The first three questions reflect the technical details of the Bitcoin protocol—these three questions are the focus of this chapter.

Different aspects of Bitcoin fall on different points on the centralization/decentralization spectrum. First, the peer-to-peer network is close to purely decentralized, since anybody can run a Bitcoin node, and the entry barrier is fairly low. You can go online and easily download a Bitcoin client and run a node on your laptop or your desktop. Currently there are several thousand such nodes. Second, Bitcoin *mining*, which we study in Section 2.4, is technically also open to anyone, but it requires a high capital cost. As a result, the Bitcoin mining ecosystem has a high degree of centralization or concentration of power. Many in the Bitcoin community see this as quite undesirable. Third, Bitcoin nodes run updates to the software, which has a bearing on how and when the rules of the system change. One can imagine that there are numerous interoperable implementations of the protocol, as with email. But in practice, most nodes run the reference implementation, and its developers are trusted by the community and have a lot of power.

2.2. DISTRIBUTED CONSENSUS

We've discussed, in a generic manner, centralization and decentralization. Let's now examine decentralization in Bitcoin at a more technical level. A key term that comes up throughout this discussion is *consensus*, specifically, *distributed consensus*. The key technical problem to solve in building a distributed e-cash system is achieving distributed consensus. Intuitively, you can think of our goal as decentralizing Scroogecoin, the hypothetical currency discussed in Chapter 1.

Distributed consensus has various applications, and it has been studied for decades in computer science. The traditional motivating application is reliability in distributed systems. Imagine you're in charge of the backend for a large social networking company, such as Facebook. Systems of this sort typically have thousands or even millions of servers, which together form a massive distributed database that records all actions that happen in the system. Each piece of information must be recorded on several different nodes in this backend, and the nodes must be in sync about the overall state of the system.

The implications of having a distributed consensus protocol reach far beyond this traditional application. If we had such a protocol, we could use it to build a massive, distributed key-value store that maps arbitrary keys, or names, to arbitrary values. A distributed key-value store, in turn, would enable many applications. For example, we could use it to build a distributed domain name system, which is simply a mapping between humanly intelligible domain names and IP addresses. We could build a public key directory, which is a mapping between email addresses (or some other form of real-world identity) and public keys.

That's the intuition of what distributed consensus is, but it is useful to provide a technical definition, as this will help us determine whether a given protocol meets the requirements.

Distributed consensus protocol. There are n nodes that each have an input value. Some of these nodes are faulty or malicious. A distributed consensus protocol has the following two properties:

- It must terminate with all honest nodes in agreement on the value.
- The value must have been generated by an honest node.

What does this mean in the context of Bitcoin? To understand how distributed consensus works in Bitcoin, remember that Bitcoin is a peer-to-peer system. When Alice wants to pay Bob, what she actually does is broadcast a transaction to all Bitcoin nodes that make up the peer-to-peer network (Figure 2.1).

Incidentally, you may have noticed that Alice broadcasts the transaction to all Bitcoin peer-to-peer nodes, but Bob's computer is nowhere in this picture. It's of course possible that Bob is running one of the nodes in the peer-to-peer network. In fact, if he wants to be notified that this transaction did in fact happen and that he has been paid, running a node might be a good idea. Nevertheless, there is no requirement that Bob be listening on the network; running a node is not necessary for Bob to receive the funds. The bitcoins will be his regardless of whether he's operating a node on the network.

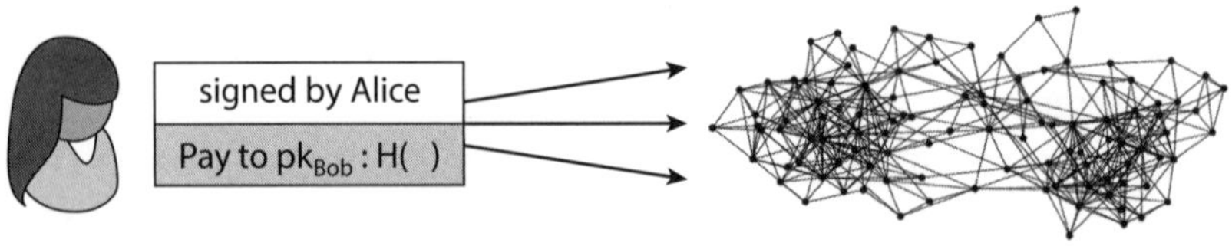

FIGURE 2.1. Broadcasting a transaction. To pay Bob, Alice broadcasts the transaction to the entire Bitcoin peer-to-peer network.

What exactly is it that the nodes might want to reach consensus on in the Bitcoin network? Given that a variety of users are broadcasting these transactions to the network, the nodes must agree on exactly which transactions were broadcast and the order in which these transactions occurred. This will result in a single, global ledger for the system. Recall that in Scroogecoin, for optimization, we put transactions into blocks (see Section 1.5). Similarly, in Bitcoin, consensus takes place on a block-by-block basis.

So at any given point, all nodes in the peer-to-peer network have a ledger consisting of a sequence of blocks, each containing a list of transactions that they have reached consensus on. Additionally, each node has a pool of outstanding transactions that it has heard about but that have not yet been included in the block chain. For these transactions, consensus has not yet happened, and so by definition, each node might have a slightly different version of the outstanding transaction pool. In practice, this occurs because the peer-to-peer network is not perfect, so some nodes may have heard about a transaction that other nodes have not yet heard about.

How exactly do nodes come to consensus on a block? One way to do this is as follows. At regular intervals (e.g., every 10 minutes), every node in the system proposes its own outstanding transaction pool to be included in the next block. Then the nodes execute some consensus protocol, where each node's input is its own proposed block. Now, some nodes may be malicious and put invalid transactions into their blocks, but we can assume that other nodes are honest. If the consensus protocol succeeds, a valid block will be selected as the output. Even if the selected block was proposed by only one node, it's a valid output as long as the block is valid. Now there may be some valid outstanding transaction that did not get included in the block, but this is not a problem. If some transaction somehow didn't make it into this particular block, it could just wait and get into the next block.

This approach bears some resemblence to how Bitcoin works, but it's not quite how it works. This approach has several technical problems. First, consensus in general is a hard problem, since nodes might crash or be outright malicious. Second, and specifically in the Bitcoin context, the network is highly imperfect. It's a peer-to-peer system, and not all pairs of nodes are connected to each other. There could be faults in the network because of poor Internet connectivity, for example, and thus running a consensus protocol in which all nodes must participate is not really possible. Finally, there's a lot of latency in the system, because it's distributed over the Internet.

Latency and Global Time

The Bitcoin protocol must reach consensus in the face of two types of obstacles: imperfections in the network (e.g., latency and nodes crashing) and deliberate attempts by some nodes to subvert the process.

One particular consequence of this high latency is that there is no notion of global time. As a result, not all nodes can agree on a common ordering of events based simply on observing timestamps. So the consensus protocol cannot contain instructions of the form, "The node that sent the first message in step 1 must do x in step 2." This simply will not work, because not all nodes will agree on which message was sent first in step 1 of the protocol.

Impossibility Results

The lack of global time heavily constrains the set of algorithms that can be used in the consensus protocols. In fact, because of these constraints, much of the literature on distributed consensus is somewhat pessimistic, and many impossibility results have been proven. One famous impossibility result concerns the *Byzantine Generals Problem.* In this classic problem, the Byzantine army is separated into divisions, each commanded by a general. The generals communicate by messenger to devise a joint plan of action. Some generals may be traitors and may intentionally try to subvert the process so that the loyal generals cannot arrive at a unified plan. The goal of this problem is for all loyal generals to arrive at the same plan without the traitorous generals being able to cause them to adopt a bad plan. It has been proven that this is impossible to achieve if one-third or more of the generals are traitors.

A much more subtle impossibility result, known by the names of the authors who first proved it, is the *Fischer-Lynch-Paterson* impossibility result. Under some conditions, which include the nodes acting in a deterministic manner, they proved that consensus is impossible with even a single faulty process.

Despite these impossibility results, there are some consensus protocols in the literature. One of the better known among these protocols is *Paxos*. Paxos makes certain compromises. On the one hand, it never produces an inconsistent result. On the other hand, it accepts the trade-off that under certain conditions, albeit rare ones, the protocol can fail to make any progress.

Breaking Traditional Assumptions

But there's good news: these impossibility results were proven for a specific model. They were intended to study distributed databases, and this model doesn't carry over very well to the Bitcoin setting, because Bitcoin violates many of the assumptions built into the models. In a way, the results tell us more about the model than they do about the problem of distributed consensus.

Ironically, with the current state of research, consensus in Bitcoin works better in practice than in theory. That is, we observe consensus working but have not developed the theory to fully explain why it works. But developing such a theory is important, as it can help us predict unforeseen attacks and problems, and only when we have a strong theoretical understanding of how Bitcoin consensus works will we have strong guarantees of Bitcoin's security and stability.

What are the assumptions in traditional models for consensus that Bitcoin violates? First, it introduces the idea of incentives, which is novel for a distributed consensus protocol. This is only possible in Bitcoin because it is a currency and therefore has a natural mechanism to incentivize participants to act honestly. So Bitcoin doesn't quite solve the distributed consensus problem in a general sense, but it solves it in the specific context of a currency system.

Second, Bitcoin embraces the notion of randomness. As we shall see in the next two sections, Bitcoin's consensus algorithm relies heavily on randomization. Also, it does away with the notion of a specific starting point and ending point for consensus. Instead, consensus takes place over a long time, about an hour in the practical system. But even at the end of that time, nodes can't be certain that any particular transaction or a block has made it into the ledger. Instead, as time goes on, the probability increases that your view of any block will match the eventual consensus view, and the probability that the views will diverge goes down exponentially. These differences in the model are key to how Bitcoin gets around the traditional impossibility results for distributed consensus protocols.

2.3. CONSENSUS WITHOUT IDENTITY USING A BLOCK CHAIN

In this section we study the technical details of Bitcoin's consensus algorithm. Recall that Bitcoin nodes do not have persistent, long-term identities. This is another difference from traditional distributed consensus algorithms. One reason for this lack of persistent identities is that in a peer-to-peer system, there is no central authority to assign identities to participants and verify that they're not creating new nodes at will. The technical term for this is a *Sybil attack*. Sybils are just copies of nodes that a malicious adversary can create to make it look like there are a lot of different participants, when in fact all those pseudo-participants are really controlled by the same adversary. The other reason is that pseudonymity is inherently a goal of Bitcoin. Even if it were possible or easy to establish identities for all nodes or all participants, we wouldn't necessarily want to do that. Although Bitcoin doesn't give strong anonymity guarantees in that the different transactions that one makes can often be linked together, it does have the property that nobody is forced to reveal their real-life identity (e.g., their name or IP address) to participate. And that's an important property and a central feature of Bitcoin's design.

If nodes did have identities, the design would be easier. First, identities would allow us to put in the protocol instructions of the form, "Now the node with the lowest numerical ID should take some step." Without identities, the set of possible instructions is more constrained. But a second, much more serious, reason for nodes to have identities is for security. If nodes were identified and it weren't trivial to create new node identities, then we could make assumptions about the number of nodes that are malicious, and we could derive security properties based on those numbers. For both of these reasons, the lack of identities introduces difficulties for the consensus protocol in Bitcoin.

We can compensate for the lack of identities by making a weaker assumption. Suppose there is somehow an ability to pick a random node in the system. A good motivating analogy for this is a lottery or a raffle, or any number of real-life systems where it's hard to track people, give them identities, and verify those identities. What we do in those contexts is to give out tokens, tickets, or something similar. That enables us to later pick a random token ID and call on the owner of that ID. So for the moment, take a leap of faith and assume that it is possible to pick a random node from the Bitcoin network in this manner. Further assume, for the moment, that this algorithm for token generation and distribution is sufficiently smart so that if the adversary tries to create a lot of Sybil nodes, all those Sybils together will obtain only one token. Thus, the adversary is not able to multiply his power by creating new nodes. If you think this is a lot to assume, don't worry. In Section 2.4, we remove these assumptions and show in detail how properties equivalent to these are realized in Bitcoin.

Implicit Consensus

This assumption of random node selection makes possible something that we call *implicit consensus*. There are multiple rounds in our protocol, each corresponding to a different block in the block chain. In each round, a random node is somehow selected, and this node gets to propose the next block in the chain. There is no consensus algorithm for selecting the block, and no voting of any kind. The chosen node unilaterally proposes what the next block in the block chain will be. But what if that node is malicious? Well, a process exists for handling that, but it is an implicit one. Other nodes will implicitly accept or reject that block by choosing whether or not to build on top of it. If they accept that block, they will signal their acceptance by extending the block chain and including the accepted block. In contrast, if they reject that block, they will extend the chain by ignoring that block and building on the previous block that they accepted. Recall that each block contains a hash of the block that it extends. This is the technical mechanism that allows nodes to signal which block it is that they are extending.

Bitcoin consensus algorithm (simplified). This algorithm is simplified in that it assumes the ability to select a random node in a manner that is not vulnerable to Sybil attacks.

1. New transactions are broadcast to all nodes.

2. Each node collects new transactions into a block.
3. In each round, a *random* node gets to broadcast its block.
4. Other nodes accept the block only if all transactions in it are valid (unspent, valid signatures).
5. Nodes express their acceptance of the block by including its hash in the next block they create.

Let's now analyze why this consensus algorithm works. To do this, consider how a malicious adversary—call her Alice—may be able to subvert this process.

STEALING BITCOINS

Can Alice simply steal bitcoins belonging to another user at an address she doesn't control? No. Even if it is Alice's turn to propose the next block in the chain, she cannot steal other users' bitcoins. Doing so would require Alice to create a valid transaction that spends that coin. This would require Alice to forge the owners' signatures, which she cannot do if a secure digital signature scheme is used. So as long as the underlying cryptography is solid, she's not able to simply steal bitcoins.

DENIAL-OF-SERVICE ATTACK

Let's consider another attack. Suppose that Alice really dislikes some other user Bob. Alice can then decide that she will not include any transactions originating from Bob's address in any block that she proposes to put in the block chain. In other words, she's denying service to Bob. Even though this is a valid attack that Alice can try to mount, luckily it's nothing more than a minor annoyance. If Bob's transaction doesn't make it into the next block that Alice proposes, he will just wait until an honest node has the chance to propose a block, and then his transaction will get into that block. So that's not really a good attack either.

DOUBLE-SPEND ATTACK

Alice may try to launch a double-spend attack. To understand how that works, let's assume that Alice is a customer of some online merchant or website run by Bob, who provides some online service in exchange for payment in bitcoins. Let's say Bob's service allows the download of some software. So here's how a double-spend attack might work. Alice adds an item to her shopping cart on Bob's website, and the server requests payment. Then Alice creates a Bitcoin transaction from her address to Bob's and broadcasts it to the network. Let's say that some honest node creates the next block, and includes this transaction in that block. So there is now a block that was created by an honest node that contains a transaction that represents a payment from Alice to the merchant Bob.

Recall that a transaction is a data structure that contains Alice's signature, an instruction to pay to Bob's public key, and a hash. This hash represents a pointer to a previous transaction output that Alice received and is now spending. That pointer must reference a transaction that was included in some previous block in the consensus chain.

Note, by the way, that there are two different types of hash pointers here that can easily be confused. Blocks include a hash pointer to the previous block that they're extending. Transactions include one or more hash pointers to previous transaction outputs that are being redeemed.

Let's return to how Alice can launch a double-spend attack. The latest block was generated by an honest node and includes a transaction in which Alice pays Bob for the software download. On seeing this transaction included in the block chain, Bob concludes that Alice has paid him and allows Alice to download the software. Suppose the next random node that is selected in the next round happens to be controlled by Alice. Since Alice gets to propose the next block, she could propose one that ignores the block that contains the payment to Bob and instead contains a pointer to the previous block. Furthermore, in the block that she proposes, Alice includes a transaction that transfers the very coins that she was sending to Bob to a different address that she herself controls. This is a classic double-spend pattern. Since the two transactions spend the same coins, only one of them can be included in the block chain. If Alice succeeds in including the payment to her own address in the block chain, then the transaction in which she pays Bob is useless, because it can never be included later in the block chain (Figure 2.2).

How do we know whether this double-spend attempt is going to succeed or not? Well, that depends on which block will ultimately end up on the long-term consensus chain—the one with the Alice → Bob transaction or the one with the Alice → Alice

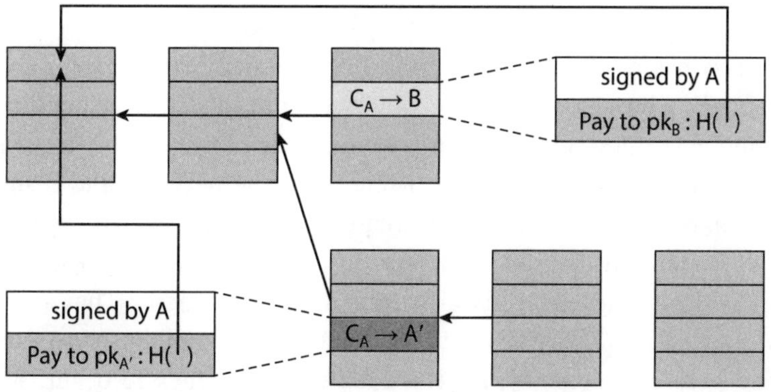

FIGURE 2.2. A double-spend attempt. Alice creates two transactions: one in which she sends Bob bitcoins, and a second in which she double spends those bitcoins by sending them to a different address, which she controls. As they spend the same bitcoins, only one of these transactions can be included in the block chain. The arrows between blocks are pointers from one block to the previous block that it extends by including a hash of that previous block within its own contents. C_A is used to denote a coin owned by Alice.

transaction. What determines which block will be included? Honest nodes follow the policy of extending the longest valid branch, so which branch will they extend? There is no right answer! At this point, the two branches are the same length—they only differ in the last block, and both of these blocks are valid. The node that chooses the next block then may decide to build on either one of them, and this choice will largely determine whether the double-spend attack succeeds.

A subtle point: from a moral point of view, there is a clear difference between the block containing the transaction that pays Bob and that containing the transaction in which Alice double spends those coins to her own address. But this distinction is only based on our knowledge of the story that Alice first paid Bob and then attempted to double spend. From a technological point of view, however, these two transactions are identical, and both blocks are equally valid. The nodes that are looking at this really have no way to tell which is the morally legitimate transaction.

In practice, nodes often follow a heuristic of extending the block that they first detected on the peer-to-peer network. But it's not a solid rule. And in any case, because of network latency, it could easily be that the block that a node first detected is actually the one that was created second. So there is at least some chance that the next node chosen to propose a block will extend the block containing the double spend. Alice could further try to increase the likelihood of this happening by bribing the next node to do so. If the next node does build on the double-spend block for whatever reason, then this chain will now be longer than the one that includes the transaction to Bob. At this point, the next honest node is much more likely to continue to build on this chain, since it is longer. This process will continue, and it will become increasingly likely that the block containing the double spend will be part of the long-term consensus chain. In contrast, the block containing the transaction to Bob is completely ignored by the network—it is now called a stale block or an *orphan block*.

Let's now reconsider this situation from Bob-the-merchant's point of view (Figure 2.3). Understanding how Bob can protect himself from this double-spending attack is a key part of understanding Bitcoin security. When Alice broadcasts the transaction that represents her payment to Bob, Bob is listening on the network and hears about this transaction even before the next block is created. If Bob were even more foolhardy than we previously described, he can complete the checkout process on the website and allow Alice to download the software right at that moment. That's called a *zero-confirmation transaction*. This leads to an even more basic double-spend attack than the one described before. Previously, for the double-spend attack to occur, we had to assume that a malicious actor controls the node that proposes the next block. But if Bob allows Alice to download the software before the transaction receives even a single confirmation on the block chain, then Alice can immediately broadcast a double-spend transaction, and an honest node may include it in the next block instead of the transaction that pays Bob.

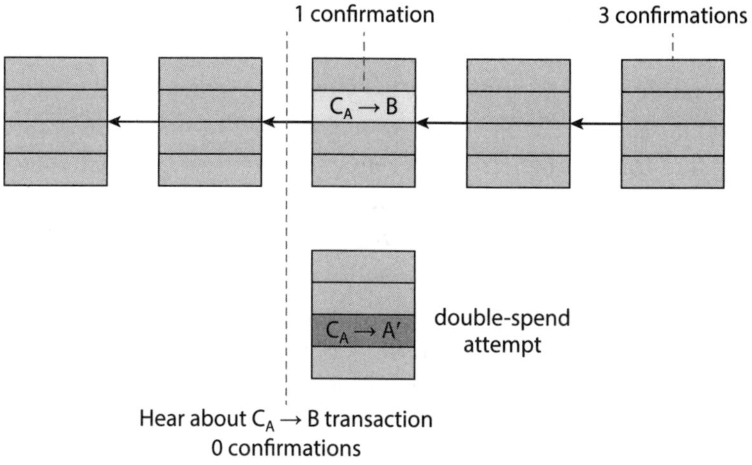

FIGURE 2.3. Bob the Merchant's point of view. This is what Alice's double-spend attempt looks like from Bob's viewpoint. To protect himself from this attack, Bob should wait to release the merchandise until the transaction with which Alice pays him is included in the block chain and has several confirmations.

However, a cautious merchant would not release the software to Alice even after the transaction was included in one block; he would continue to wait. If Bob sees that Alice successfully launches a double-spend attack, he realizes that the block containing Alice's payment to him has been orphaned. He should abandon the transaction and not let Alice download the software. Instead, if it happens that despite the double-spend attempt, the next several nodes build on the block with the Alice → Bob transaction, then Bob gains confidence that this transaction will be on the long-term consensus chain.

In general, the more confirmations a transaction gets, the higher the probability that it is going to end up on the long-term consensus chain. Recall that honest nodes always extend the longest valid branch that they find. The chance that the shorter branch with the double spend will catch up to the longer branch becomes increasingly tiny as the latter grows longer than any other branch. This is especially true if only a minority of the nodes are malicious—for a shorter branch to catch up, several malicious nodes would have to be picked in close succession.

In fact, the double-spend probability decreases exponentially with the number of confirmations. So, if the transaction that you're interested in has received k confirmations, then the probability that a double-spend transaction will end up on the long-term consensus chain goes down exponentially as a function of k. The most common heuristic that's used in the Bitcoin ecosystem is to wait for six confirmations. There is nothing really special about the number six. It's just a good trade-off between the amount of time you have to wait and your guarantee that the transaction you're interested in ends up on the consensus block chain.

To recap, protection against invalid transactions is entirely cryptographic. But it is enforced by consensus, which means that if a node does attempt to include a cryptographically invalid transaction, then the only reason that transaction won't end up in the long-term consensus chain is because a majority of the nodes are honest and won't include an invalid transaction in the block chain. In contrast, protection against double spending is purely by consensus. Cryptography has nothing to say about this, and two transactions that represent a double-spend attempt are both valid from a cryptographic perspective. But it's the consensus that determines which one will end up on the long-term consensus chain. And finally, you're never 100 percent sure that a transaction you're interested in is on the consensus branch. But this exponential probability guarantee is rather good. After about six transactions, there's virtually no chance that you're going to be deceived.

2.4. INCENTIVES AND PROOF OF WORK

In the previous section, we took a basic look at Bitcoin's consensus algorithm and developed a good intuition for why we believe that it's secure. But recall from the beginning of the chapter that Bitcoin's decentralization is partly a technical mechanism and partly clever incentive engineering. So far we've mostly looked at the technical mechanism. Now let's talk about the incentive engineering built into Bitcoin.

We asked you to take a leap of faith earlier in assuming that we're able to pick a random node and, perhaps more problematically, that at least 50 percent of the time, this process will pick an honest node. This assumption of honesty is particularly problematic if there are financial incentives for participants to subvert the process, in which case we can't really assume that a node will be honest. The question then becomes: Can we give nodes an incentive for behaving honestly?

Consider again the double-spend attempt after one confirmation (see Figure 2.2). Can we somehow penalize the node that created the block with the double-spend transaction? Well, not really. As mentioned earlier, it's hard to know which is the morally legitimate transaction. But even if we did, it's still hard to punish nodes, since they don't have identities. So instead, let's flip the question around and ask: Can we reward each of the nodes that created the blocks that did end up on the long-term consensus chain? Well, again, since those nodes don't reveal their real-world identities, we can't quite mail them cash to their home addresses. If only there were some sort of digital currency that we could use instead . . . you can probably see where this is going. We're going to use bitcoins to incentivize the nodes that created these blocks.

Let's pause for a moment. Everything described so far is just an abstract algorithm for achieving distributed consensus and is not specific to the application. Now we're going to use the fact that the application we're building through this distributed consensus process is in fact a currency. Specifically, we're going to incentivize nodes to behave honestly by paying them in units of this currency.

Block Reward

How is this done? Two separate incentive mechanisms are used in Bitcoin. The first is the *block reward*. According to the rules of Bitcoin, the node that creates a block gets to include a special transaction in that block. This transaction is a coin-creation transaction, analogous to `CreateCoins` in Scroogecoin, and the node can also choose the recipient address of this transaction. Of course that node will typically choose an address belonging to itself. You can think of this as a payment to the node in exchange for the service of creating a block on the consensus chain.

As of 2015, the value of the block reward is fixed at 25 bitcoins. But it actually halves with every 210,000 blocks created. Based on the rate of block creation, the rate halves roughly every four years. We're now in the second period. For the first four years of Bitcoin's existence, the block reward was 50 bitcoins; now it's 25. And it's going to keep halving. This has some interesting consequences, which we address below.

You may be wondering why the block reward incentivizes honest behavior. It may appear, based on what we've said so far, that this node gets the block reward regardless of whether it proposes a valid block or behaves maliciously. But this is not true! Think about it—how will this node collect its reward? That will only happen if the block in question ends up on the long-term consensus branch, because just like every other transaction, the coin-creation transaction will only be accepted by other nodes if it ends up on the consensus chain. That's the key idea behind this incentive mechanism. It's a subtle but powerful trick. It incentivizes nodes to behave in whatever way they believe will get other nodes to extend their blocks. So if most of the network is following the longest-valid-branch rule, it incentivizes all nodes to continue to follow that rule. That's Bitcoin's first incentive mechanism.

We mentioned that every 210,000 blocks (or approximately four years), the block reward is cut in half. In Figure 2.4, the slope of this curve is going to keep halving. This is a geometric series, and you might know that it means that there is a finite sum of bitcoins created by this mechanism. It works out to a total of 21 million bitcoins.

Note that this is the only way in which new bitcoins can be created. There is no other coin-generation mechanism, which is why 21 million is a final and total number (as the rules stand now, at least) for how many bitcoins there can ever be. This block reward will run out in 2140, as things stand now. Does that mean that the system will stop working in 2140 and become insecure, because nodes no longer have the incentive to behave honestly? Not quite. The block reward is only the first of two incentive mechanisms in Bitcoin.

Transaction Fees

The second incentive mechanism is the *transaction fee*. The creator of any transaction can choose to make the total value of the transaction outputs less than the total value of its inputs. Whoever creates the block that first puts that transaction into the block

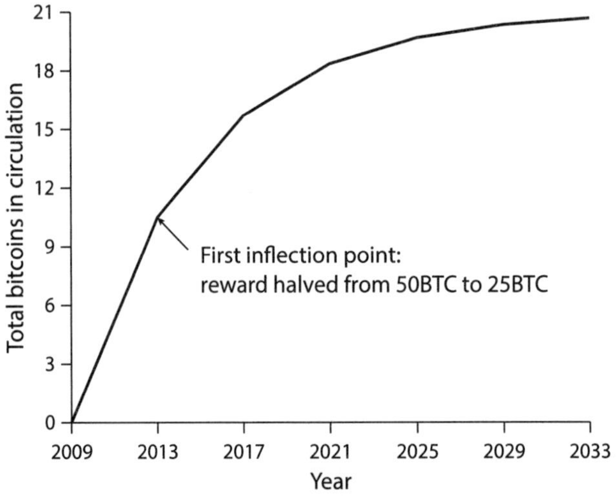

FIGURE 2.4. Total supply of bitcoins with time. The block reward is cut in half every 4 years, limiting the total supply of bitcoins to 21 million. This is a simplified model and the actual curve looks slightly different, but it has the same 21 million limit.

chain gets to collect the difference, which acts a transaction fee. So if you're a node that is creating a block containing, say, 200 transactions, then the sum of those 200 transaction fees is paid to the address that you put into that block. The transaction fee is purely voluntary, but we expect, based on our understanding of the system, that as the block reward starts to run out, it will become more and more important, almost mandatory, for users to include transaction fees to maintain a reasonable quality of service. To a certain degree, this is already starting to happen now. But it is currently unclear precisely how the system will evolve; it really depends on a lot of game theory, which hasn't been fully worked out yet. This is an interesting area of open research in Bitcoin.

A few problems still remain with the consensus mechanism as described here. The first major one is the leap of faith that we asked you to take that somehow we can pick a random node. Second, we've created a new problem by giving nodes these incentives for participation. The system can become unstable as the incentives cause a free-for-all, where everybody wants to run a Bitcoin node in the hope of capturing some of these rewards. And a third one is an even trickier version of this problem: an adversary might create a large number of Sybil nodes to try and subvert the consensus process.

Mining and Proof of Work

All these problems are related, and all have the same solution, which is called *proof of work*. The key idea behind proof of work is that we approximate the selection of a random node by instead selecting nodes in proportion to a resource that we hope that nobody can monopolize. If, for example, that resource is computing power, then it's a proof-of-work system. Alternately, it could be in proportion to ownership of the currency, which is known as *proof of stake*. Although it's not used in Bitcoin, proof of stake is a legitimate alternate model that is used in other cryptocurrencies. We'll see more about proof of stake and other proof-of-work variants in Chapter 8.

But back to proof of work. Let's clarify what it means to select nodes in proportion to their computing power. This can be thought of as allowing nodes to compete with one another by using their computing power, which will result in nodes automatically being picked in proportion to that capacity. Yet another view of proof of work is that we're making it moderately hard to create new identities. It's a sort of tax on identity creation and therefore on the Sybil attack. This might all appear a bit vague, so let's look at the details of the proof-of-work system used in Bitcoin, which should clarify the concept.

Bitcoin achieves proof of work using *hash puzzles*. To create a block, the node that proposes that block is required to find a number (a nonce; see Section 1.1), such that when you concatenate the nonce, the previous hash, and the list of transactions that make up the block and then take the hash of this whole string, then that hash output should be a number that falls in a target space that is quite small in relation to the much larger output space of that hash function. We can define such a target space as any value falling below a certain target value. In this case, the nonce will have to satisfy the following inequality:

$$H(nonce \parallel prev\_hash \parallel tx \parallel tx \parallel \ldots \parallel tx) < target$$

As we have seen, normally a block contains a series of transactions that a node is proposing. In addition, a block also contains a hash pointer to the previous block. (We are using the term "hash pointer" loosely. The pointer is just a string in this context, as it need not tell us where to find this block. We can find the block by asking other peers on the network for it. The important part is the hash that both acts as an ID when requesting other peers for the block and lets us validate the block once we have obtained it.) In addition, we're now requiring that a block also contain a nonce. The idea is that we want to make it moderately difficult to find a nonce that satisfies this required property, which is that hashing the whole block together, including that nonce, is going to result in a particular type of output. If the hash function satisfies the puzzle-friendliness property from Chapter 1, then the only way to succeed in solving this hash puzzle is to just try enough nonces one by one until you get lucky. So specifically, if this target space were just 1 percent of the overall output space, you would have to try about 100 nonces before you are likely to get lucky. In reality, the size of this target space is not nearly as high as 1 percent of the output space. It's much, much smaller than that, as we will see shortly.

This notion of hash puzzles and proof of work completely does away with the requirement to magically pick a random node. Instead, nodes are simply independently competing to solve these hash puzzles all the time. Once in a while, one of them will find a random nonce that satisfies this property. That lucky node then gets to propose the next block. By this means, the system is completely decentralized. Nobody is deciding which node gets to propose the next block.

Difficult to Compute

There are three important properties of hash puzzles. The first is that they need to be quite difficult to compute. We said moderately difficult, but you'll see why this actually varies with time. As of 2015, the difficulty level is over 10^{20} hashes per block. In other words, the size of the target space is less than $1/10^{20}$ of the size of the output space of the hash function. Searching the output space thus involves a lot of computation—it's out of the realm of possibility for a commodity laptop, for example. Because of this, only some nodes even bother to compete in this block creation process. This process of repeatedly trying and solving these hash puzzles is known as *Bitcoin mining*, and the participating nodes are called *miners*. Even though technically anybody can be a miner, power has become concentrated in the mining ecosystem due to the high cost of mining.

Parameterizable Cost

The second property we want is that the cost should be parameterizable rather than fixed for all time. This is accomplished by having all the nodes in the Bitcoin peer-to-peer network automatically recalculate the target (i.e., the size of the target space as a fraction of the output space) every 2,016 blocks. They recalculate the target in such a way that the average time between successive blocks produced in the Bitcoin network is about 10 minutes. With a 10-minute average time between blocks, 2,016 blocks works out to two weeks. In other words, the recalculation of the target happens roughly every two weeks.

Consider what this means. Suppose you are a miner, and you've invested a certain fixed amount of hardware into Bitcoin mining. But the overall mining ecosystem is growing, more miners are coming in, or they're deploying faster and faster hardware, which means that over a two-week period, slightly more blocks are going to be found than expected. So nodes will automatically readjust the target, and the amount of work that you have to do to find a block will increase. So if you invest a fixed amount in hardware, the rate at which you find blocks actually depends on what other miners are doing. A very nice formula captures this: the probability that any given miner, Alice, is going to win the next block is equivalent to the fraction of global hash power that she controls. So if Alice has mining hardware that's about 0.1 percent of total hash power, she will find roughly one in every 1,000 blocks.

What is the purpose of this readjustment? Why do we want to maintain this 10-minute invariant? The reason is quite simple. If blocks were to come very close together, then there would be a lot of inefficiency, and we would lose the optimization benefits of being able to put many transactions in a single block. There is nothing magical about the number 10, and if you changed from 10 minutes to 5 minutes, the system would probably work just fine. There's been a lot of discussion about the ideal block latency

Two Models of Miner Behavior

In the research fields of distributed systems and computer security, it is common to assume that some percentage of nodes are honest and to show that the system works as intended even if the other nodes behave arbitrarily. That's basically the approach we've taken here, except that we weight nodes by hash power when computing the majority. The original Bitcoin white paper contains this type of analysis as well.

But the field of game theory provides an entirely different—and arguably more sophisticated and realistic—way to determine how a system will behave. In this view, we don't split nodes into honest and malicious. Instead, we assume that *every* node acts according to its incentives. Each node picks a (randomized) strategy to maximize its payoff, taking into account other nodes' potential strategies. If the protocol and incentives are designed well, then most nodes will follow the rules most of the time. "Honest" behavior is then just one strategy among many, and we attach no particular moral salience to it.

In the game-theoretic view, the big question is whether the default miner behavior is a *Nash equilibrium*, that is, whether it represents a stable situation in which no miner can realize a higher payoff by deviating from honest behavior. This question is still contentious and is an active area of research.

that *altcoins* (alternative cryptocurrencies) should have. But despite some disagreements about the ideal latency, everybody agrees that it should be a fixed amount. It cannot be allowed to go down without limit. That's why Bitcoin features automatic target recalculation.

The way that this cost function and proof of work is set up allows us to reformulate our security assumption. Here's where we finally depart from the last leap of faith that we asked you to take earlier. Instead of assuming that somehow the majority of nodes are honest in a context where nodes don't even have identities and not being clear about what "honesty" means, we can now state crisply that many attacks on Bitcoin are infeasible if the majority of miners, weighted by hash power, are following the protocol—that is, are honest. This is true because if most miners, weighted by hash power, are honest, then competition for proposing the next block will automatically ensure at least a 50 percent chance that the next block to be proposed at any point is coming from an honest node.

Solving hash puzzles is probabilistic, because nobody can predict which nonce is going to solve the hash puzzle. The only way to solve the puzzle is to try nonces one by one and hope that one succeeds. Mathematically, this process is called a *Bernoulli trial*. A Bernoulli trial is an experiment with two possible outcomes, and the probability of each outcome occurring is fixed between successive trials. Here, the two outcomes are (1) the hash falls in the target, and (2) it does not. Assuming that the hash function behaves like a random function, the probability of those two outcomes is fixed. Typically, nodes try so many nonces that Bernoulli trials, a discrete probability process, can be well approximated by a continuous probability process known as a *Poisson process*,

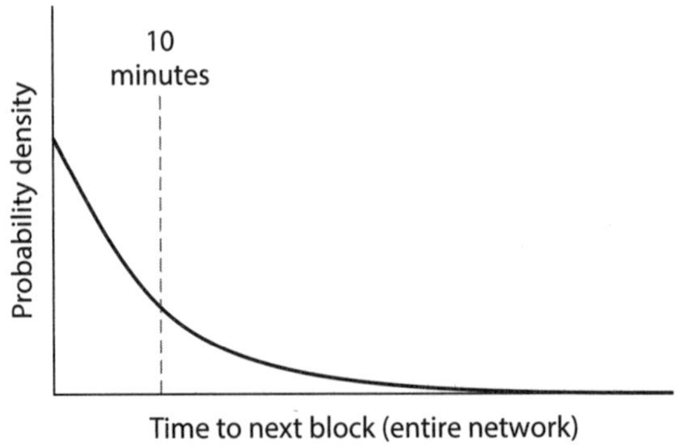

FIGURE 2.5. Probability density function of the time until the next block is found.

one in which events occur independently at a constant average rate. The end result is that the probability density function showing the relative likelihood of the time until the next block is found looks like the graph in Figure 2.5.

This is known as an *exponential distribution.* Some small probability exists that if a block has been found now, the next block is going to be found very soon, say, within a few seconds or a minute. And there is also some small probability that it will take a long time, say, an hour, to find the next block. But overall, the network automatically adjusts the difficulty so that the inter-block time is maintained at an average, long term, of 10 minutes. Notice that Figure 2.5 shows how frequently blocks are going to be created by the entire network, regardless of which miner actually finds the block.

If you're a miner, you're probably interested in how long it will take you to find a block. What does this probability density function look like? It will have the same shape but a different scale on the *x*-axis. Again, it can be represented by a nice equation.

For a specific miner:

$$\text{mean time to next block} = \frac{\text{10 minutes}}{\text{fraction of hash power}}$$

If you have 0.1 percent of the total network hash power, this equation states that you're going to find blocks once every 10,000 minutes, which is just about a week. Not only is your mean time between blocks going to be high, but the variance of the time between blocks found by you is also going to be high. This has some important consequences that are discussed in Chapter 5.

Trivial to Verify

Now we turn to the third important property of this proof-of-work function: it is trivial to verify that a node has computed proof of work correctly. Even if it takes a node, on average, 10^{20} tries to find a nonce that makes the block hash fall below the target, that nonce must be published as part of the block. It is thus trivial for any other node to look at the block contents, hash them all together, and verify that the output is less than the target. This is quite an important property, because, once again, it allows us to get rid of centralization. We don't need any centralized authority verifying that miners are doing their job correctly. Any node or any miner can instantly verify that a block found by another miner satisfies this proof-of-work property.

2.5. PUTTING IT ALL TOGETHER

Cost of Mining

Let's now look at mining economics. We mentioned that it is quite expensive to operate as a miner. At the current difficulty level, finding a single block takes computing about 10^{20} hashes, and the block reward is about 25 bitcoins, which is a sizable amount of money at the current exchange rate. These numbers allow for an easy calculation of whether it's profitable for one to mine, and we can capture this decision with a simple statement:

If

mining reward > *mining cost*

then the miner makes a profit

where

mining reward = *block reward* + *tx fees*

mining cost = *hardware cost* + *operating costs (electricity, cooling, etc.)*

Fundamentally, the miner obtains her mining rewards from block rewards and transaction fees. The miner asks herself how these rewards compare to the total expenditure, which is the hardware and electricity cost.

But there are some complications to this simple equation. The first is that, as you may have noticed, the hardware cost is a fixed cost, whereas the electricity is a variable cost that is incurred over time. Another complication is that the reward obtained by miners depends on the rate at which they find blocks, which depends on not only the power of their hardware, but also on the ratio of their hash rate to the total global hash rate. A third complication is that the costs that the miner incurs are typically denominated in dollars or some other traditional currency, but their reward is denominated in bitcoins. So this equation has a hidden dependence on Bitcoin's exchange rate at any given time. And finally, so far we've assumed that the miner is interested in honestly following the protocol. But the miner might choose to use some other mining strategy instead of always attempting to extend the longest valid branch. So this equation doesn't capture all the nuances of the different strategies that the miner can employ. Actually analyzing whether it makes sense to mine is a complicated game theory problem that's not easily answered.

There Is No Such Thing as One Bitcoin

Bitcoin doesn't have fixed denominations like U.S. dollar bills, and in particular, there is no special designation of "1 bitcoin." Bitcoins are just transaction outputs, and in the current rules, they can have an arbitrary value to eight decimal places of precision. The smallest possible value is 0.00000001 BTC (bitcoins), which is called 1 *satoshi*.

At this point, we have a pretty good picture of how Bitcoin achieves decentralization. We now recap the major points and put it all together for an even better understanding.

Let's start with identities. As we've learned, real-world identities are not required to participate in the Bitcoin protocol. Any user can create any number of pseudonymous key pairs at any moment. When Alice wants to pay Bob in bitcoins, the Bitcoin protocol does not specify how Alice learns Bob's address. Given these pseudonymous key pairs as identities, transactions are basically messages broadcast to the Bitcoin peer-to-peer network that are instructions to transfer coins from one address to another. Bitcoins are just transaction outputs, and we will discuss this in much more detail in Chapter 3.

The goal of the Bitcoin peer-to-peer network is to propagate all new transactions and new blocks to all Bitcoin peer nodes. But the network is highly imperfect and does a best-effort attempt to relay this information. The security of the system doesn't come from the perfection of the peer-to-peer network. Instead, the security comes from the block chain and the consensus protocol that we devoted much of this chapter to studying.

When we say that a transaction is included in the block chain, what we really mean is that the transaction has achieved numerous confirmations. No fixed number of confirmations is necessary before we are sufficiently convinced of the transaction's inclusion, but six is a commonly used heuristic. The more confirmations a transaction has received, the more certain you can be that this transaction is part of the consensus chain. Orphan blocks (blocks that don't make it into the consensus chain) often arise. Various reasons can lead to a block being orphaned. The block may contain an invalid transaction, or a double-spend attempt. Orphaning can also just be a result of network latency. That is, two miners may simply end up finding new blocks within just a few seconds of each other. So both of these blocks were broadcast nearly simultaneously on the network, and one of them will inevitably be orphaned.

We next looked at hash puzzles and mining. Miners are special types of nodes that decide to compete in this game of creating new blocks. They're rewarded for their effort in terms of both newly minted bitcoins (the block reward) and existing bitcoins (transaction fees), provided that other miners build on their blocks. A subtle but crucial point: say that Alice and Bob are two different miners, and Alice has 100 times as much computing power as Bob. This does not mean that Alice will always win the race against Bob to find the next block. Instead, Alice and Bob have a probability ratio of finding the next block of 100 to 1. In the long term, Bob will find, on average, 1 percent of the number of blocks that Alice finds.

We expect that miners will typically be somewhere close to the economic equilibrium in the sense that the expenditure they incur in terms of hardware and electricity will be roughly equal to the rewards they obtain. The reason is that if a miner is consistently making a loss, she will probably stop mining. In contrast, if mining is very profitable given typical hardware and electricity costs, then more mining hardware would enter the network. The increased hash rate would lead to an increase in the difficulty, and each miner's expected reward would drop.

This notion of distributed consensus permeates Bitcoin. In a traditional (fiat) currency, consensus does come into play to a limited extent. Specifically, a consensus process determines the exchange rate of the currency. That is certainly true in Bitcoin as well. We need consensus about the value of bitcoins. But in Bitcoin, additionally, we need consensus on the state of the ledger, which is what the block chain accomplishes. In other words, even the accounting of how many bitcoins you own is subject to consensus. When we say that Alice owns a certain amount or number of bitcoins, what we actually mean is that the Bitcoin peer-to-peer network, as recorded in the block chain, considers the sum total of all Alice's addresses to own that number of bitcoins. That is the ultimate nature of truth in Bitcoin: ownership of bitcoins is nothing more than other nodes agreeing that a given party owns those bitcoins.

Finally, we need consensus about the rules of the system, because occasionally these rules have to change. Two types of changes are made to the rules of Bitcoin, known respectively as *soft forks* and *hard forks*. We defer a detailed discussion of the differences to Chapters 3 and 7.

Getting a Cryptocurrency off the Ground

Another subtle concept is that of *bootstrapping*. A tricky interplay takes place among three different ideas in Bitcoin: the security of the block chain, the health of the mining ecosystem, and the value of the currency. We obviously want the block chain to be secure for Bitcoin to be a viable currency. For the block chain to be secure, an adversary must not be able to overwhelm the consensus process. This in turn means that an adversary cannot create a lot of mining nodes and assume 50 percent or more of the new block creation.

But when will these conditions be met? A prerequisite is having a healthy mining ecosystem made up of largely honest, protocol-following nodes. But what's a prerequisite for that—when can we be sure that a lot of miners will put a lot of computing power into participating in this hash-puzzle-solving competition? They're only going to make the effort if the exchange rate of bitcoins is pretty high, because the rewards miners receive are denominated in bitcoins, whereas their expenditures are in dollars. So the higher the value of the currency, the more incentivized these miners are going to be.

But what ensures a high and stable value of the currency? That can only happen if users in general trust the security of the block chain. If they believe that the network could be overwhelmed at any moment by an attacker, then Bitcoin will not have much value as a currency. So you have an interlocking interdependence among the security of the block chain, a healthy mining ecosystem, and the exchange rate.

Because of the cyclical nature of this three-way dependence, the existence of each of these is predicated on the existence of the others. When Bitcoin was first created, none of these three conditions was met. There were no miners other than Nakamoto himself running the mining software (see the Foreword). Bitcoin didn't have a lot of value as a currency. And the block chain was, in fact, insecure, because not much mining was going on, and anybody could have easily overwhelmed this process.

There's no simple explanation for how Bitcoin went from not having any of these properties to having all three of them. Media attention was part of the story—the more people hear about Bitcoin, the more they become interested in mining. And the more they get interested in mining, the more confidence people will have in the security of the block chain, because then more mining activity is going on, and so forth. Incidentally, every new altcoin that wants to succeed also has to somehow solve this problem of pulling itself up by its bootstraps.

The 51 Percent Attack

Finally, let's consider what would happen if consensus failed and there was in fact a *51 percent attacker* (one who controls a majority of the mining power in the Bitcoin network). We'll consider a variety of possible attacks and see which ones can actually be carried out by such an attacker.

First of all, can this attacker steal coins from an existing address? As you may have guessed, the answer is no, because stealing from an existing address is not possible unless you subvert the cryptography. It's not enough to subvert the consensus process. This is not completely obvious. Let's say the 51 percent attacker creates an invalid block that contains an invalid transaction that tries to steal bitcoins from an existing address that the attacker doesn't control and transfer them to his own address. The attacker can pretend that it's a valid transaction and keep building on this block. He may even succeed in making this block part of the longest branch. But the other, honest nodes are simply not going to accept this block with an invalid transaction and are going to keep mining based on the last valid block that they found in the network. So a fork in the chain will occur.

Now imagine this from the point of view of the attacker, who is trying to spend these invalid coins and sends them to some merchant Bob as payment for goods or services. Bob is presumably running a Bitcoin node himself, and it will be an honest node. Bob's node will reject that branch as invalid, because it contains an invalid transaction. It has been determined to be invalid, because the signatures don't check out. So Bob's node will simply ignore the longest branch, because it's an invalid branch. And because of that, subverting consensus is not enough. You have to subvert cryptography to steal bitcoins. So we conclude that this attack is not possible for a 51 percent attacker.

Note that this is only a thought experiment. If there were, in fact, actual signs of a 51 percent attack, what would probably happen is that the developers would notice it and react. They would update the Bitcoin software, and we might expect that the rules of the system, including the peer-to-peer network, might change to make it more difficult for this attack to succeed. But we can't quite predict that. So we're working in a simplified model, where a 51 percent attack happens, but no changes or tweaks are made to the rules of the system.

Let's consider another attack. Can the 51 percent attacker suppress some transactions? Let's say there is some user, Carol, whom the attacker really doesn't like. The attacker knows some of Carol's addresses and wants to make sure that no coins belonging to any of those addresses can be spent. Is that possible? Since he controls the consensus process of the block chain, the attacker can simply refuse to create any new blocks that contain transactions from one of Carol's addresses. The attacker can further refuse to build on blocks that contain such transactions. However, he can't prevent these transactions from being broadcast to the peer-to-peer network, because the network doesn't depend on the block chain or on consensus, and we're assuming that the attacker doesn't fully control the network. The attacker cannot stop the transactions from reaching the majority of nodes, so even if the attack succeeds, it will at least be apparent that the attack is happening.

Can the attacker change the block reward? That is, can the attacker start pretending that the block reward is, instead of 25 bitcoins, say, 100 bitcoins? This is a change to the rules of the system, and because the attacker doesn't control the copies of the Bitcoin software that all honest nodes are running, this is also not possible. The reason is similar to that explaining why the attacker cannot include invalid transactions. Other nodes will simply not recognize the increase in the block reward, and the attacker will thus be unable to spend them.

Finally, can the attacker somehow destroy confidence in Bitcoin? Well, let's imagine what would happen. If there were a variety of double-spend attempts, situations in which nodes did not extend the longest valid branch, and other attempted attacks, then people likely would decide that Bitcoin is no longer acting as a decentralized ledger that they can trust. They would lose confidence in the currency, and we might expect that the exchange rate of Bitcoin would plummet. In fact, if it were known that a party controls 51 percent of the hash power, then it's possible that people would lose confidence in Bitcoin even if the attacker is not necessarily trying to launch any attacks. So it is not only possible, but in fact likely, that a 51 percent attacker of any sort will destroy confidence in the currency. Indeed, this is the main practical threat if a 51 percent attack were ever to materialize. Considering the amount of expenditure that the adversary would have to put into attacking Bitcoin and achieving a 51 percent majority, none of the other attacks that we described really make sense from a financial point of view.

Hopefully, at this point you understand how decentralization is achieved in Bitcoin. You should have a good command of how identities work in Bitcoin, how transactions are propagated and validated, the role of the peer-to-peer network in Bitcoin, how the block chain is used to achieve consensus, and how hash puzzles and mining work. These concepts provide a solid foundation and a good launching point for understanding a lot of the more subtle details and nuances of Bitcoin, which we're going to see in subsequent chapters.

FURTHER READING

The Bitcoin white paper is:

Nakamoto, Satoshi. "Bitcoin: A Peer-to-Peer Electronic Cash System." 2008. Available at https://bitcoin.org/bitcoin.pdf.

The original application of proof of work is:

Back, Adam. "Hashcash—A Denial of Service Counter-measure." 2002. Available at http://www.hashcash.org/papers/hashcash.pdf.

The Paxos algorithm for consensus is:

Lamport, Leslie. "Paxos Made Simple." *ACM Sigact News* 32(4), 2001: 18–25.

CHAPTER 3

Mechanics of Bitcoin

This chapter is about the mechanics of Bitcoin. Whereas the discussion in the first two chapters was relatively generalized, we now delve into the details. We'll look at real data structures, real scripts, and learn the details and language of Bitcoin in a precise way to set up the discussion in the rest of this book. This chapter is challenging, because it is detail oriented and we cover a lot of ground. You'll learn the specifics and the quirks that make Bitcoin what it is.

To recap where we left off in Chapter 2, the Bitcoin consensus mechanism gives us an append-only ledger, a data structure that we can only write to. Once data is written to it, it's there forever. A decentralized protocol establishes consensus about the value of that ledger, and miners use the protocol and validate transactions. The protocol and miners together make sure that transactions are well formed, that the the bitcoins involved aren't already spent, and that the ledger and network can function as a currency. At the same time, we assumed that a currency existed to motivate these miners. In this chapter we look at the details of how that currency is engineered to motivate the miners who make this whole process happen.

3.1. BITCOIN TRANSACTIONS

Let's start with transactions, Bitcoin's fundamental building block. We use a simplified model of a ledger for the moment. Instead of blocks, let's suppose individual transactions are added to the ledger one at a time.

How can we build a currency based on such a ledger? The first model you might think of, which is actually the mental model many people have of how Bitcoin works, is an account-based system. You can add some transactions that create new coins and credit them to somebody. And then later you can transfer the coins. A transaction would be something like "move 17 coins from Alice to Bob," and it would be signed by Alice. That's all the information in the ledger about the transaction. In Figure 3.1, after Alice receives 25 coins in the first transaction and then transfers 17 coins to Bob in the second, she'd have 8 bitcoins left in her account.

The downside to this way of doing things is that anyone who wants to determine

Create 25 coins and credit to Alice$_{\text{ASSERTED BY MINERS}}$
Transfer 17 coins from Alice to Bob$_{\text{SIGNED(Alice)}}$
Transfer 8 coins from Bob to Carol$_{\text{SIGNED(Bob)}}$
Transfer 5 coins from Carol to Alice$_{\text{SIGNED(Carol)}}$
Transfer 15 coins from Alice to David$_{\text{SIGNED(Alice)}}$

FIGURE 3.1. An account-based ledger.

whether a transaction is valid will have to keep track of these account balances. Take another look at Figure 3.1. Does Alice have the 15 coins that she's trying to transfer to David? To figure this out, you'd have to track every transaction affecting Alice back in time to determine whether her net balance when she tries to transfer 15 coins to David is greater than 15 coins. Of course we can make this a bit more efficient with some data structures that track Alice's balance after each transaction. But that's going to require a lot of extra housekeeping besides the ledger itself.

Because of these drawbacks, Bitcoin doesn't use an account-based model. Instead, Bitcoin uses a ledger that just keeps track of transactions, similar to Scroogecoin in Section 1.5.

Transactions specify a number of inputs and a number of outputs (recall PayCoins in Scroogecoin). You can think of the inputs as coins being consumed (created in a previous transaction) and the outputs as coins being created. For transactions in which new currency is being minted, no coins are being consumed (recall CreateCoins in Scroogecoin). Each transaction has a unique identifier. Outputs are indexed beginning with 0, so we refer to the first output as "output 0."

Let's now work our way through Figure 3.2. Transaction 1 has no inputs, because this transaction is creating new coins, and it has an output of 25 coins going to Alice. Also, since this is a transaction where new coins are being created, no signature is required. Now suppose that Alice wants to send some of those coins to Bob. To do so, she creates a new transaction, transaction 2 in our example. In the transaction, she has to explicitly refer to the previous transaction where these coins are coming from. Here, she refers to output 0 of transaction 1 (indeed the only output of transaction 1), which assigned 25 bitcoins to Alice. She also must specify the output addresses in the transaction. In this example, Alice specifies two outputs, 17 coins to Bob and 8 coins to Alice. And, of course, the entire content of the transaction is signed by Alice, so that we know that Alice actually authorizes it.

Change addresses. Why does Alice have to send money to herself in this example? Just as coins in Scroogecoin are immutable, in Bitcoin, either all or none of a transaction output must be consumed by another transaction. Alice only wants to pay 17 bitcoins to Bob, but the output that she owns is worth 25 bitcoins. So she needs to create a new output, where 8 bitcoins are sent back to herself. It could be a different address from

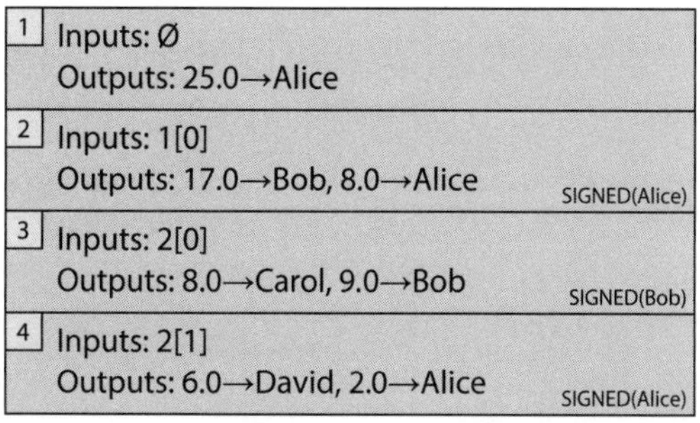

FIGURE 3.2. A transaction-based ledger. This is the type of ledger used by Bitcoin.

the one that owned the 25 bitcoins, but it would have to be owned by her. This is called a *change address*.

Efficient verification. When a new transaction is added to the ledger, how easy is it to check whether it is valid? In this example, we need to look up the transaction output that Alice referenced, make sure that it has a value of 25 bitcoins, and that it hasn't already been spent. Looking up the transaction output is easy, since we're using hash pointers. To ensure it hasn't been spent, we need to scan the block chain between the referenced transaction and the latest block. We don't need to go all the way back to the beginning of the block chain, and it doesn't require keeping any additional data structures (although, as we'll see, additional data structures will speed things up).

Consolidating funds. As in Scroogecoin, since transactions can have many inputs and many outputs, splitting and merging value is easy. For example, suppose Bob received money in two different transactions—17 bitcoins in one, and 2 in another. Bob might want to have a single transaction output available for later, so that he can spend all 19 bitcoins he controls. That's easy—he creates a transaction using the two inputs and one output, with the output address being one that he owns. That lets him consolidate those two transactions.

Joint payments. Similarly, joint payments are also easy to do. Suppose Carol and Bob both want to pay David. They can create a transaction with two inputs and one output, but with the two inputs owned by two different people. And the only difference from the previous example is that since the two outputs from prior transactions that are being claimed here are from different addresses, the transaction needs two separate signatures—one by Carol and one by Bob.

Transaction syntax. Conceptually that's really all there is to a Bitcoin transaction. Now let's see how it's represented at a low level in Bitcoin. Ultimately, every data structure that's sent on the network is a string of bits. What's shown in Figure 3.3 is low level, but this is further compiled down to a compact binary format that's not human-readable.

As you can see in Figure 3.3, a transaction consists of three parts: some metadata, a series of inputs, and a series of outputs:

```
              {
                "hash":"5a42590fbe0a90ee8e8747244d6c84f0db1a3a24e8f1b95b10c9e050990b8b6b",
                "ver":1,
                "vin_sz":2,
metadata        "vout_sz":1,
                "lock_time":0,
                "size":404,
                "in":[
                 {
                    "prev_out":{
                    "hash":"3be4ac9728a0823cf5e2deb2e86fc0bd2aa503a91d307b42ba76117d79280260",
                    "n":0
                   },
                     "scriptSig":"30440..."
input(s)         },
                 {
                    "prev_out":{
                    "hash":"7508e6ab259b4df0fd5147bab0c949d81473db4518f81afc5c3f52f91ff6b34e",
                    "n":0
                   },
                   "scriptSig":"3f3a4..."
                  }
                 ],
                 "out":[
                  {
                    "value":"10.12287097",
output(s)           "scriptPubKey":"OP_DUP OP_HASH160 69e02e18b5705a05dd6b28ed517716c894b3d42e
                          OP_EQUALVERIFY OP_CHECKSIG"
                  }
                 ]
              }
```

FIGURE 3.3. The contents of an actual Bitcoin transaction.

- *Metadata.* Some housekeeping information is present—the size of the transaction, the number of inputs, and the number of outputs. The hash of the entire transaction is supplied, which serves as a unique ID for the transaction. That's what allows us to use hash pointers to reference transactions. And a `lock_time` field is supplied, which we'll come back to later.
- *Inputs.* The transaction inputs form an array, and each input has the same form. An input specifies a previous transaction, so it contains a hash of that transaction, which acts as a hash pointer to it. The input also contains the index of the previous transaction's outputs that are being claimed. And then there's a signature. Remember that we have to sign to show that we actually have the ability to claim those previous transaction outputs.
- *Outputs.* The outputs are again an array. Each output has just two fields. They each have a value, and the sum of all the output values has to be less than or equal to the sum of all the input values. If the sum of the output values is less than the sum of the input values, the difference is a transaction fee that goes to the miner who publishes this transaction.

And then there's a funny line that looks like what we want to be the recipient address. Each output is supposed to go to a specific public key, and indeed, something is in that field that looks like it's the hash of a public key. But there's also other information that looks like a set of commands. Indeed, this field is a script, and we discuss scripts next.

3.2. BITCOIN SCRIPTS

Each transaction output doesn't just specify a public key. It actually specifies a script. What is a script, and why do we use them? In this section, we study the Bitcoin scripting language and come to understand why a script is used instead of simply assigning a public key.

The most common type of transaction in Bitcoin is to redeem a previous transaction output by signing with the correct key. In this case, we want the transaction output to specify, "this can be redeemed by a signature from the owner of address X." Recall that an address is a hash of a public key. So merely specifying the address X doesn't tell us what the public key is, and it doesn't give us a way to check the signature! So instead the transaction output must state: "this can be redeemed by a public key that hashes to X, along with a signature from the owner of that public key." As we'll see, this is exactly what the most common type of script in Bitcoin specifies (Figure 3.4).

But what happens to this script? Who runs it, and how exactly does this sequence of instructions enforce the above statement? The secret is that the inputs also contain scripts instead of signatures. To confirm that a transaction redeems a previous transaction output correctly, we combine the new transaction's input script and the earlier transaction's output script. We simply concatenate them, and the resulting script must run successfully for the transaction to be valid. These two scripts are *scriptPubKey* and *scriptSig*, because in the simplest case, the output script just specifies a public key (or an address to which the public key hashes), and the input script specifies a signature with that public key. The combined script can be seen in Figure 3.5.

Bitcoin Scripting Language

The scripting language was built specifically for Bitcoin and is just called "Script" or "the Bitcoin scripting language." It has many similarities to a language called "Forth," which is an old, simple, stack-based programming language. But you don't need to understand Forth to understand Bitcoin scripting. The key design goals for Script were to have something simple and compact, yet with native support for cryptographic

```
OP_DUP
OP_HASH160
69e02e18...
OP_EQUALVERIFY
OP_CHECKSIG
```

FIGURE 3.4. An example Pay-to-PubkeyHash script, the most common type of output script in Bitcoin.

```
<sig>
<pubKey>
--------------
OP_DUP
OP_HASH160
<pubKeyHash?>
OP_EQUALVERIFY
OP_CHECKSIG
```

FIGURE 3.5. Combining scriptPubKey and scriptSig. To check whether a transaction correctly redeems an output, we create a combined script by appending the scriptPubKey of the referenced output transaction (bottom) to the scriptSig of the redeeming transaction (top). Notice that <pubKeyHash?> contains a "?." We use this notation to indicate that we will later check to confirm that this is equal to the hash of the public key provided in the redeeming script.

operations. So, for example, there are special-purpose instructions to compute hash functions and to compute and verify signatures.

The scripting language is stack-based. This means that every instruction is executed exactly once, in a linear manner. In particular, there are no loops in the Bitcoin scripting language. So the number of instructions in the script gives us an upper bound on how long it might take to run and how much memory it could use. The language is not Turing complete, which means that it doesn't have the ability to compute arbitrarily powerful functions. And this is by design—miners have to run these scripts, which are submitted by arbitrary participants in the network. They should not have the power to submit a script that might have an infinite loop.

Only two possible outcomes can result when a Bitcoin script is executed. It either executes successfully with no errors, in which case the transaction is valid. Or, if there's any error while the script is executing, the whole transaction will be invalid and shouldn't be accepted into the block chain.

The Bitcoin scripting language is very small. There's only room for 256 instructions, because each one is represented by one byte. Of those 256, 15 are currently disabled, and 75 are reserved. The reserved instruction codes haven't been assigned any specific meaning yet, but might be used for instructions that are added at a later time.

Many basic instructions are those you'd expect to be in any programming language. There's basic arithmetic, basic logic (e.g., "if" and "then" statements), throwing errors, not throwing errors, and returning early. Finally, there are crypto instructions, which include hash functions, instructions for signature verification, as well as a special and important instruction called `CHECKMULTISIG` that lets you check multiple signatures with one instruction. Table 3.1 lists some of the most common instructions in the Bitcoin scripting language.

The `CHECKMULTISIG` instruction requires specifying *n* public keys and a parameter *t* for a threshold. For this instruction to execute successfully, at least *t* signatures from *t* out of *n* of those public keys must be present and valid. We'll show some examples of

TABLE 3.1. COMMON SCRIPT INSTRUCTIONS AND THEIR FUNCTION

Name	Function
OP_DUP	Duplicates the top item on the stack.
OP_HASH160	Hashes twice: first using SHA-256 and then a different hash function called RIPEMD-160.
OP_EQUALVERIFY	Returns true if the inputs are equal. Returns false and marks the transaction as invalid if they are unequal.
OP_CHECKSIG	Checks that the input signature is valid using the input public key for the hash of the current transaction.
OP_CHECKMULTISIG	Checks that the *t* signatures on the transaction are valid signatures from *t* of the specified public keys.

the use of multisignatures in Section 3.3, but it should be immediately clear that this is quite a powerful primitive. We can use it to express in a compact way the concept that *t* out of *n* specified entities must sign for the transaction to be valid.

Incidentally, there's a bug in the multisignature implementation. The `CHECKMULTISIG` instruction pops an extra data value off the stack and ignores it. This is just a quirk of the Bitcoin language, and one has to deal with it by putting an extra dummy variable onto the stack. The bug was in the original implementation, and the costs of fixing it are much higher than the damage it causes, as we discuss in Section 3.6. At this point, this bug is considered a feature in Bitcoin, in that it's not going away.

Executing a Script

To execute a script in a stack-based programming language, all we need is a stack that we can push data to and pop data from. We won't need any other memory or variables. That's what makes the language so computationally simple. There are two types of instructions: data instructions and opcodes. When a data instruction appears in a script, that data is simply pushed onto the top of the stack. In contrast, opcodes perform some function, often taking as input data on top of the stack.

Now let's look at how the Bitcoin script in Figure 3.5 is executed. Refer to Figure 3.6, which shows the state of the stack after each instruction. The first two instructions in this script are data instructions—the signature and the public key used to verify that signature—specified in the scriptSig component of a transaction input in the redeeming transaction. As mentioned, a data instruction is just pushed onto the stack. The rest of the script was specified in the scriptPubKey component of a transaction output in the referenced transaction.

First we have the duplicate instruction, OP_DUP, so we just push a copy of the public key onto the top of the stack. The next instruction is OP_HASH160, which tells us to pop the top stack value, compute its cryptographic hash, and push the result onto the top of the stack. When this instruction finishes executing, we will have replaced the public key on the top of the stack with its hash.

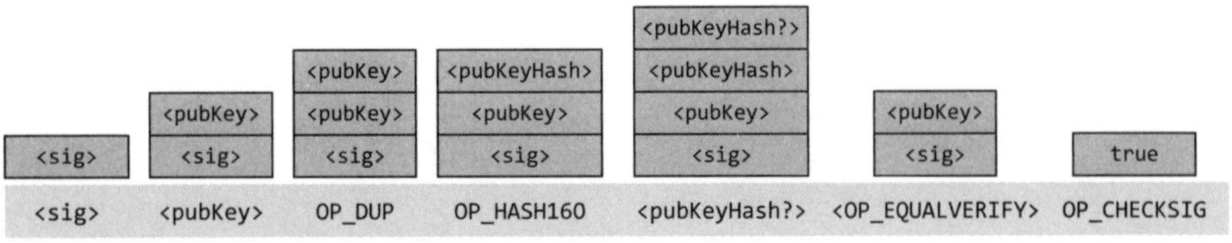

FIGURE 3.6. Execution of a Bitcoin script. On the bottom, we show the instruction in the script. Data instructions are denoted with surrounding angle brackets, whereas opcodes begin with "OP_." On the top, we show the stack just after the instruction listed under it has been executed.

Next, we do one more push of data onto the stack. Recall that this data was specified by the sender of the referenced transaction. It is the hash of a public key that the sender specified; the corresponding private key must be used to generate the signature to redeem these coins. At this point, two values are at the top of the stack: the hash of the public key (as specified by the sender) and the hash of the public key that was used by the recipient when trying to claim the coins.

At this point, the EQUALVERIFY command executes, which checks that the two values at the top of the stack are equal. If they aren't, an error is thrown, and the script stops executing. But in our example, we'll assume that they're equal; that is, the recipient of the coins used the correct public key. That instruction will consume those two data items at the top of the stack, and the stack now contains two items—a signature and the public key.

We've already checked that this public key is in fact the public key that the referenced transaction specified, and now we have to check whether the signature is valid. This is a great example of how the Bitcoin scripting language is built with cryptography in mind. Even though it's a fairly simple language in terms of logic, it has some quite powerful instructions, such as OP_CHECKSIG. This single instruction both pops those two values off of the stack and does the entire signature verification.

But what is this a signature of? What is the input to the signature function? It turns out you can only sign one thing in Bitcoin—an entire transaction. So the CHECKSIG instruction pops the two values (the public key and signature) off the stack and verifies that the signature is valid for the entire transaction using that public key. Now we've executed every instruction in the script, and nothing is left on the stack. Provided no errors occurred, the output of this script will simply be `true`, indicating that the transaction is valid.

What's Used in Practice

In theory, Script lets us specify, in some sense, arbitrary conditions that must be met to spend coins. But as of 2015, this flexibility isn't used much. If we look at the scripts that have actually been used in the history of Bitcoin, nearly all are identical to the script used in our example. This script just specifies one public key and requires a signature for that public key to spend the coins.

A few other instructions are also used. MULTISIG is used a little bit, as is a special type of script, Pay-to-Script-Hash, which we discuss shortly. But other than that, there hasn't been much diversity in the scripts used. This is because Bitcoin nodes, by default, have a whitelist of standard scripts, and they refuse to accept scripts that are not on the list. This doesn't mean that those scripts can't be used at all; it just makes them harder to use. In fact this distinction is a subtle point, which we return to when discussing the Bitcoin peer-to-peer network.

Proof of Burn

A proof of burn is a script that can never be redeemed. Sending coins to a proof-of-burn script establishes that they have been destroyed, since there's no possible way for them to be spent. One use of proof of burn is to bootstrap an alternative to Bitcoin by forcing people to destroy bitcoins to gain coins in the new system. We discuss this use in more detail in Chapter 10. Proof of burn is quite simple to implement: the OP_RETURN opcode throws an error if it's ever reached. No matter what values you put before OP_RETURN, that instruction will eventually be executed, in which case this script will return `false`.

Because the error is thrown, the data in the script that comes after OP_RETURN will not be processed. So this is an opportunity for users to put arbitrary data in a script, and hence into the block chain. If, for some reason, you want to write your name, or if you want to timestamp and prove that you knew some data at a specific time, you can create a low-value Bitcoin transaction. You can destroy a very small amount of currency, but you can then write whatever you want into the block chain, which should be retained for the life of the Bitcoin system.

Pay-to-Script-Hash

One consequence of the way Bitcoin scripts work is that the sender of coins has to specify the script exactly. But this can sometimes be quite a strange way of doing things. For example, suppose that you are shopping online, and you're about to order something and are ready to pay. You ask for the address to which your coins should be sent. Now suppose that the company you're ordering from is using MULTISIG addresses. Then, since the one spending the coins has to specify this, the retailer says to you, "Oh, well, we're doing something fancy now. We're using MULTISIG. Send the coins to some complicated script." You might say, "I don't know how to do that. That's too complicated. As a consumer, I just want to send to a simple address."

Bitcoin has a clever solution to this problem, and it applies not only to multisignature addresses but also to any complicated condition governing when coins can be spent. Instead of telling the sender "send your coins to the hash of this public key," the receiver can instead tell the sender "send your coins to the hash of this *script*. Impose the condition that to redeem those coins, it is necessary to reveal the script that has the given hash, and further, provide data that will make the script evaluate to true." The sender achieves this by using the Pay-to-Script-Hash (P2SH) transaction type, which has the above semantics.

Specifically, the P2SH script simply hashes the top value on the stack, checks whether it matches the provided hash value, and then executes a special second step of validation: that top data value from the stack is reinterpreted as a sequence of instructions and is executed a second time as a script, with the rest of the stack as input.

Getting support for P2SH was quite complicated, since it wasn't part of Bitcoin's initial design specification. It was added after the fact. This is probably the most notable feature that's been added to Bitcoin after its original specification. And it solves a couple of important problems. It removes the need for a complex response from the sender, because the recipient can just specify a hash that the sender sends money to. In our example above, Alice need not worry that Bob is using MULTISIG; she just sends to Bob's P2SH address, and it is Bob's responsibility to specify the fancy script when he wants to redeem the coins.

P2SH also has a nice efficiency gain. Miners have to track the set of output scripts that haven't been redeemed yet, and with P2SH outputs, the output scripts are now much smaller, as they only specify a hash. All of the complexity is pushed to the input scripts.

3.3. APPLICATIONS OF BITCOIN SCRIPTS

Now that you understand how Bitcoin scripts work, let's take a look at some of the powerful applications that can be realized with this scripting language. It turns out we can do many neat things that justify the complexity of having the scripting language instead of just specifying public keys.

Escrow Transactions

Suppose that Alice and Bob want to do business with each other—Alice wants to pay Bob in bitcoins for Bob to send some physical goods to Alice. The problem is that Alice doesn't want to pay until after she's received the goods, but Bob doesn't want to send the goods until after he has been paid. What can we do about that? A nice solution in Bitcoin is to introduce a third party and use an escrow transaction.

Escrow transactions can be implemented quite simply using MULTISIG. Alice doesn't send the money directly to Bob, but instead creates a MULTISIG transaction that requires two of three people to sign to redeem the coins. And those three people are going to be Alice, Bob, and some third-party arbitrator, Judy, who will come into play in case there's any dispute. So Alice creates a 2-out-of-3 MULTISIG transaction that sends some coins she owns and specifies that they can be spent if any two of Alice, Bob, and Judy sign. This transaction is included in the block chain, and at this point, these coins are held in escrow among Alice, Bob, and Judy, such that any two of them can specify where the coins should go. At this point, Bob is convinced that it's safe to send the goods over to Alice, so he'll mail or deliver them physically. Now in the normal case, Alice and Bob are both honest. So, Bob will send over the goods that Alice is expecting, and when Alice receives the goods, Alice and Bob both sign a transaction redeeming the funds from escrow and sending them to Bob. Notice that in this case where both Alice and Bob are honest, Judy never had to get involved at all. There was no dispute, and Alice's and Bob's signatures met the 2-out-of-3 requirement of the MULTISIG transaction. So in the normal case, this isn't that much less efficient than Alice just sending Bob the money. It requires just one extra transaction on the block chain.

But what would happen if Bob didn't actually send the goods or they got lost in the mail? Or if the goods were not what Alice ordered? Alice now doesn't want to pay Bob, because she thinks she has been cheated, and she wants her money back. So Alice is definitely not going to sign a transaction that releases the money to Bob. But Bob may deny any wrongdoing and refuse to sign a transaction that releases the money back to Alice. This is when Judy needs to be involved. Judy has to decide which of these two people deserves the money. If Judy decides that Bob cheated, Judy will be willing to sign a transaction along with Alice, sending the money from escrow back to Alice. Alice's and Judy's signatures meet the 2-out-of-3 requirement of the MULTISIG transaction, and Alice will get her money back. And, of course, if Judy thinks that Alice is at fault here, and Alice is simply refusing to pay when she should, Judy can sign a transaction along with Bob, sending the money to Bob. So Judy decides between the two possible outcomes. But the advantage of this method is that she won't have to be involved unless there's a dispute.

Green Addresses

Another cool application is what are called *green addresses*. Suppose Alice wants to pay Bob, and Bob is offline. Since he's offline, Bob can't look at the block chain to see whether a transaction that Alice is sending is there. It's also possible that Bob is online, but doesn't have the time to look at the block chain and wait for the transactions to be confirmed. Remember that normally we want a transaction to be in the block chain and be confirmed by six blocks, which takes up to an hour, before we trust that it's really in the block chain. But for some merchandise, such as food, Bob can't wait an hour before delivering. If Bob were a street vendor selling hot dogs, it's unlikely that Alice would wait around for an hour to receive her food. Or maybe for some other reason Bob doesn't have any connection to the Internet and is thus not able to check the block chain.

To solve this problem of being able to send money using Bitcoin without the recipient accessing the block chain, we have to introduce another third party, which we'll call the bank (in practice it could be an exchange or any other financial intermediary). Alice talks to her bank: "Hey, it's me, Alice. I'm your loyal customer. Here's my card or my identification. And I'd really like to pay Bob here, could you help me out?" And the bank answers "Sure. I'm going to deduct some money out of your account. And draw up a transaction transferring money from one of my green addresses to Bob."

Notice that this money is coming directly from the bank to Bob. Some of the money, of course, might be in a change address going back to the bank. But essentially, the bank is paying Bob from a bank-controlled address, which we call a "green address." Moreover, the bank guarantees that it will not double spend this money. So as soon as Bob sees that this transaction is signed by the bank, if he trusts the bank's guarantee not to double spend the money, he can accept that the money will eventually be his when it's confirmed in the block chain.

This is a real-world guarantee, not a Bitcoin-enforced guarantee. For this system to work, Bob has to trust that the bank, in the real world, cares about its reputation and so won't double spend. And the bank will be able to say, "You can look at my history. I've been using this green address for a long time, and I've never double spent. Therefore, I'm very unlikely to do so in the future." Thus Bob no longer has to trust Alice, whom he may know nothing about. Instead, he places his trust in the bank to not double spend the money that it sent him.

Of course, if the bank ever does double spend, people will stop trusting its green address(es). In fact, the two most prominent online services that implemented green addresses were Instawallet and Mt. Gox, and both ended up collapsing. Today, green addresses aren't used much. When the idea was first proposed, it generated much excitement as a way to make payments more quickly and without accessing the block chain. Now, however, people have become quite nervous about the idea and are worried that it puts too much trust in the bank.

Efficient Micropayments

Our third example of Bitcoin scripts is one that makes micropayments efficient. Suppose that Alice is a customer who wants to continually pay Bob small amounts of money for some service that Bob provides. For example, Bob may be Alice's wireless service provider and requires her to pay a small fee for every minute that she talks on her phone.

Creating a Bitcoin transaction for every minute that Alice speaks on the phone won't work. That will create too many transactions, and the transaction fees add up. If the value of each transaction is on the order of what the transaction fee is, Alice will pay quite a high cost to do this.

We want to combine all these small payments into one big payment at the end. It turns out that there's a neat way to do this. We start with a MULTISIG transaction that pays the maximum amount Alice would ever need to spend to an output requiring both Alice and Bob to sign to release the coins. Now, after the first minute that Alice has used the service (or the first time she needs to make a micropayment), she signs a transaction spending the coins sent to the MULTISIG address, sending one unit of payment to Bob and returning the rest to Alice. After the next minute of using the service, Alice signs another transaction, this time paying two units to Bob and sending the rest to herself. Notice these are signed only by Alice and haven't been signed by Bob yet, nor are they being published to the block chain. Alice will keep sending these transactions to Bob every minute that she uses the service. Eventually, Alice will finish using the service and tells Bob, "I'm done, please cut off my service." At this point Alice will stop signing additional transactions. On hearing this, Bob will disconnect her service, sign the last transaction that Alice sent, and publish it to the block chain.

Since each transaction was paying Bob a bit more, and Alice a bit less, the final transaction that Bob redeems pays him in full for the service that he provided and returns the rest of the money to Alice. All those transactions that Alice signed along the way won't make it to the block chain. Bob doesn't have to sign them. They'll just be discarded.

Technically, all these intermediate transactions are double spends. So unlike the case for green addresses, where we were specifically trying to avoid double spends by using a strong guarantee, with this micropayment protocol, we're actually generating a huge number of potential double spends. In practice, however, if both parties are operating normally, Bob will never sign any transaction but the last one, in which case the block chain won't detect any attempt at a double spend.

There's one other tricky detail: what if Bob never signs the last transaction? He may just say, "I'm happy to let the coins sit there in escrow forever," in which case, maybe the coins won't move, but Alice will lose the full value that she paid at the beginning. There's a very clever way to avoid this problem using a feature that we mentioned briefly earlier and will explain now.

Lock Time

To avoid this problem, before the micropayment protocol can even start, Alice and Bob will both sign a transaction that refunds all of Alice's money to her, but the refund is "locked" until some time in the future. So after Alice signs, but before she broadcasts, the first MULTISIG transaction that puts her funds into escrow, she'll want to get this refund transaction from Bob and hold on to it. That guarantees that if she makes it to time *t* and Bob hasn't signed any of the small transactions that Alice has sent, Alice can publish this transaction, which refunds all the money directly to her.

What does it mean that the refund is locked until time *t*? Recall that the metadata in Bitcoin transactions includes a lock_time parameter, which was not explained in Section 3.2. If you specify any value other than zero for the lock time, it tells miners not to publish the transaction until the specified time. The transaction will be invalid before a specific block number. So this is a way of preparing a transaction that can only be spent at some future time—provided the coin it's trying to spend hasn't already been spent by then in some other transaction. It works quite nicely in the micropayment protocol as a safety valve to reassure Alice that if Bob never signs, eventually she'll be able to get her money back.

These examples show some of the neat things we can do with Bitcoin scripts. We discussed three simple and practical examples, but many others have been researched. One of them is the multiplayer lottery, a complicated multistep protocol with lots of transactions having different lock times and escrows in case people cheat. Some neat protocols use the Bitcoin scripting language to allow different people to combine their coins in such a way that it's hard to trace who owns which coin. We discuss this protocol in detail in Chapter 6.

Smart Contracts

The general term for contracts like the ones discussed in this section is "smart contracts." These are contracts for which we have some degree of technical enforcement in Bitcoin, whereas traditionally they are enforced through laws or courts of arbitration. A really cool feature of Bitcoin is that we can use scripts, miners, and transaction validation to realize the escrow protocol or the micropayment protocol without resorting to a centralized authority.

Research into smart contracts goes far beyond the applications discussed in this section. There are many types of smart contracts that people want to enforce but that aren't supported by the Bitcoin scripting language today. Or at least, nobody has come up with a creative way to implement them. As we have seen, with a bit of creativity, you can do quite a lot with the Bitcoin script as it currently stands.

3.4. BITCOIN BLOCKS

So far in this chapter we've looked at how individual transactions are constructed and redeemed. But as described in Chapter 2, transactions are grouped together into blocks. Why is this? Basically, grouping them is an optimization. If miners had to reach consensus on each transaction individually, the rate at which new transactions could be accepted by the system would be much lower. Also, a hash chain of blocks is much shorter than a hash chain of transactions would be, since a large number of transactions can be put into each block. This makes it more efficient to verify the block chain data structure.

The block chain is a clever combination of two different hash-based data structures. The first is a hash chain of blocks. Each block has a block header, a hash pointer to some transaction data, and a hash pointer to the previous block in the sequence. The second data structure is a per-block tree of all transactions included in that block. This structure is a Merkle tree and allows us to have an efficient digest of all transactions in the block. As discussed in Chapter 1, to prove that a transaction is included in a specific block, we can provide a path through the tree whose length is logarithmic in the number of transactions in the block. To recap, a block consists of header data followed by a list of transactions arranged in a tree structure (Figure 3.7).

The header mostly contains information related to the mining puzzle, which we

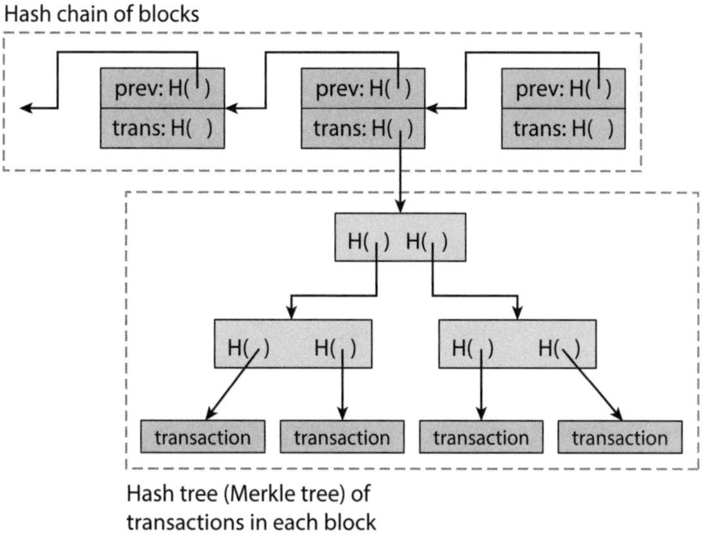

FIGURE 3.7. Bitcoin block chain. The Bitcoin block chain contains two different hash structures. The first is a hash chain of blocks that links the different blocks to one another. The second is internal to each block and is a Merkle tree of transactions in the block.

briefly discussed in Chapter 2 and revisit in Chapter 5. Recall that the hash of the block header has to start with a large number of zeros for the block to be valid. The header also contains a nonce that miners can change, a timestamp, and bits (an indication of how difficult this block was to find). Only the header is hashed during mining. So to verify a chain of blocks, all we need to do is look at the headers. The only transaction data included in the header is the root of the transaction tree—the `mrkl_root` field.

Another interesting thing about blocks is that they have a special transaction in the Merkle tree called the *coinbase transaction* (Figure 3.8). It is analogous to CreateCoins in Scroogecoin. New coins are created in Bitcoin with this transaction. It differs in several ways from an ordinary transaction:

1. It always has a single input and a single output.
2. The input doesn't redeem a previous output and thus contains a null hash pointer, since the transaction is minting new bitcoins and not spending existing coins.
3. The value of the output is currently a little more than 25 BTC. The output value is the miner's revenue from the block. This revenue consists of two components: a flat mining reward, which is set by the system and which halves every 210,000 blocks (about 4 years), and the transaction fees collected from every transaction included in the block.
4. It has a special "coinbase" parameter, which is completely arbitrary—miners can put whatever they want in it.

```
"in":[
        {
          "prev_out":{
            "hash":“000000.....0000000",
            "n":4294967295
          },
          "coinbase":"..."
      },
      [
"out":[
       {
         "value":"25.03371419",
         "scriptPubKey":"OPDUP OPHASH160 ... ”
       }
      ]
```

FIGURE 3.8. Coinbase transaction. A coinbase transaction creates new coins. It does not redeem a previous output, and it has a null hash pointer indicating this. It has a coinbase parameter, which can contain arbitrary data. The value of the coinbase transaction is the block reward plus all transaction fees included in the block.

Famously, in the first block ever mined in Bitcoin, the coinbase parameter referenced a story in the *Times of London* newspaper involving the chancellor bailing out banks. This reference has been interpreted as political commentary on the motivation for starting Bitcoin. It also serves as a sort of proof that the first block was mined after the story came out on January 3, 2009. One way in which the coinbase parameter has since been used is to signal support by miners for different new features.

The best way to familiarize yourself with the block format and transaction format is to explore the block chain yourself. Many websites make these data accessible, such as blockchain.info. You can look at the graph of transactions, see which transactions redeem which other transactions, look for transactions with complicated scripts, and examine the block structure and see how blocks refer to other blocks. Since the block chain is a public data structure, developers have built pretty wrappers to explore it graphically.

3.5. THE BITCOIN NETWORK

So far we have discussed the ability of participants to publish a transaction and insert it into the block chain as if this happens by magic. In fact it happens through the Bitcoin network, which is a peer-to-peer network inheriting many ideas from other peer-to-peer networks that have been proposed for all sorts of other purposes. In the Bitcoin network, all nodes are equal. There is no hierarchy—no special nodes or master nodes. It runs over TCP and has a random topology, where each node peers with other random nodes. New nodes can join at any time. In fact, you can download a Bitcoin client today, spin up your computer as a node, and it will have rights and capabilities equal to those of every other node on the Bitcoin network.

The network changes over time and is quite dynamic, because nodes enter and leave it. There is no explicit way to leave the network. Instead, if a node hasn't been active in a while—3 hours is the duration hardcoded into common clients—other nodes start to forget it. In this way, the network gracefully handles nodes going offline.

Recall that nodes connect to random peers, and no geographic topology of any sort exists. Suppose you launch a new node and want to join the network. You start with a simple message to one node that you know about. This is usually called your *seed node*, and there are a few different ways you can look up lists of seed nodes to try connecting to. You send a special message, saying, "Tell me the addresses of all the other nodes in the network that you know about." You can repeat the process with the new nodes you learn about as many times as you want. Then you can choose which ones to peer with, and you'll be a fully functioning member of the Bitcoin network. Several initialization steps involve randomness, and the ideal outcome is that you're peered with a random set of nodes. To join the network, all you need to know is how to contact one node that's already on the network.

What is the network good for? To maintain the block chain, of course. So to publish a transaction, we want the entire network to hear about it. This happens through a simple *flooding* algorithm, sometimes called a *gossip protocol*. If Alice wants to pay Bob some money, her client creates and her node sends this transaction to all the nodes it's peered with. Each of those nodes executes a series of checks to determine whether to accept and relay the transaction. If the checks pass, the accepting node in turn sends it to all its peer nodes. Nodes that hear about a transaction put it in a pool of transactions that they've heard about but that are not yet on the block chain. If a node hears about a transaction that's already in its pool, it doesn't further broadcast it. This ensures that the flooding protocol terminates and transactions don't loop around the network forever. Remember that every transaction is identified uniquely by its hash, so it's easy to look up a transaction in the pool.

When nodes hear about a new transaction, how do they decide whether they should propagate it? There are four checks. The first and most important check is transaction validation—the transaction must be valid with the current block chain. Nodes run the script for each previous output being redeemed and ensure that the scripts return `true`. Second, they check that the outputs being redeemed haven't already been spent. Third, they won't relay an already-seen transaction, as mentioned earlier. Fourth, by default, nodes only accept and relay standard scripts based on a small whitelist of scripts.

All these checks are just sanity checks. Well-behaving nodes all implement these to try to keep the network healthy and running properly, but no rule says that nodes have to follow these specific steps. Since it's a peer-to-peer network and anybody can join, there's always the possibility that a node might forward double spends, nonstandard transactions, or outright invalid transactions. That's why every node must do the checking for itself.

Since the network has latency, it's possible that nodes will end up with different versions of the pending transaction pool. This becomes particularly interesting and important when a double spend is attempted. Suppose Alice attempts to pay the same bitcoin to both Bob and Charlie, and she sends out two transactions at roughly the same time. Some nodes will hear about the Alice → Bob transaction first, while others will hear about the Alice → Charlie transaction first. When a node hears about either transaction, it adds the transaction to its transaction pool. If it hears about the other one later, the node will detect a double spend. The node then drops the latter transaction and won't relay or add it to its transaction pool. As a result, the nodes will temporarily disagree on which transactions should be put in the next block. This is called a "race condition."

The good news is that this situation is easily handled. Whoever mines the next block will essentially break the tie and decide which of those two pending transactions should be put permanently into a block. Let's say the Alice → Charlie transaction makes it into the block. When nodes with the Alice → Bob transaction hear about this block, they'll drop the transaction from their memory pools, because it is a double spend. When nodes with the Alice → Charlie transaction hear about this block, they'll drop that transaction from their memory pools, because it's already in the block chain. So there will be no more disagreement once this block propagates through the network.

Since the default behavior is for nodes to retain whatever they hear first, network position matters. If two conflicting transactions or blocks are announced at two different positions in the network, they both begin to flood throughout the network; which transaction a node sees first will depend on where it is in the network.

Of course this assumes that every node implements this logic that it keeps what it hears about first. But no central authority is enforcing this behavior, and nodes are free to implement any other logic they want for choosing which transactions to keep and whether to forward a transaction. We'll look more closely at miner incentives in Chapter 5.

So far we've been mostly discussing propagation of transactions. The logic for announcing a new block, when a miner finds one, is almost exactly the same as propagating a new transaction, and it is subject to the same race conditions. If two valid blocks are mined at the same time, only one of these can be included in the long-term consensus chain. Ultimately, which of these blocks will be included depends on which blocks the other nodes build on, and the block that does not make it into the consensus chain will be orphaned.

Validating a block is more complex than validating transactions. In addition to validating the header and making sure that the hash value is in the acceptable range, nodes must validate every transaction included in the block. Finally, a node will forward a

Zero-Confirmation Transactions and Replace-by-Fee

In Chapter 2 we looked at zero-confirmation transactions, where the recipient accepts the transaction as soon as it is broadcast on the network. This isn't designed to be secure against double spends. But as we saw, the default behavior for miners in the case of conflicting transactions is to include the transaction they received first, which makes double spending against zero-confirmation transactions moderately hard. As a result, and due to their convenience, zero-confirmation transactions have become common.

Since 2013, some participants have shown an interest in changing the default policy to *replace-by-fee*, whereby nodes replace a pending transaction in their pool if they hear of a conflicting transaction that includes a higher fee. This is the rational behavior for miners, at least in a short-term sense, as it ensures a better fee for them. However, replace-by-fee would make double spending against zero-confirmation attacks far easier in practice.

Replace-by-fee has therefore attracted controversy, both in terms of the technical question of whether it is possible to prevent or deter double spending in a replace-by-fee world, and the philosophical question of whether Bitcoin should try to support zero-confirmation as best it can, or abandon it. We won't dive into the long-running controversy here, but Bitcoin has recently adopted "opt-in" replace-by-fee, whereby transactions can mark themselves (using the sequence-number field) as eligible for replacement by higher-fee transactions.

block only if it builds on the longest branch, based on its perspective of what the block chain (which is really a tree of blocks) looks like. This avoids forks building up. But just as with transactions, nodes can implement different logic—they might relay blocks that aren't valid or blocks that build off of an earlier point in the block chain. The latter action results in a fork, but the protocol is designed to withstand small forks.

What is the latency of the flooding algorithm? Figure 3.9 shows the average time for new blocks to propagate to every node in the network. The three lines show the 25th, the 50th, and the 75th percentile block propagation times. As you can see, propagation time is basically proportional to the size of the block. This is because network bandwidth is the bottleneck. The larger blocks take more than 30 seconds to propagate to most nodes in the network. So the protocol isn't particularly efficient. On the Internet, 30 seconds is a pretty long time. In Bitcoin's design, having a simple network with little structure and in which nodes are equal and can come and go at any time took priority over efficiency. So a block may need to go through many nodes before it reaches the most distant nodes in the network. If the network were instead designed top-down for efficiency, it would ensure that the path between any two nodes is short.

Size of the Network

It is difficult to measure how big the network is, since it is dynamic and has no central authority. Some researchers have come up with size estimates. On the high end, some

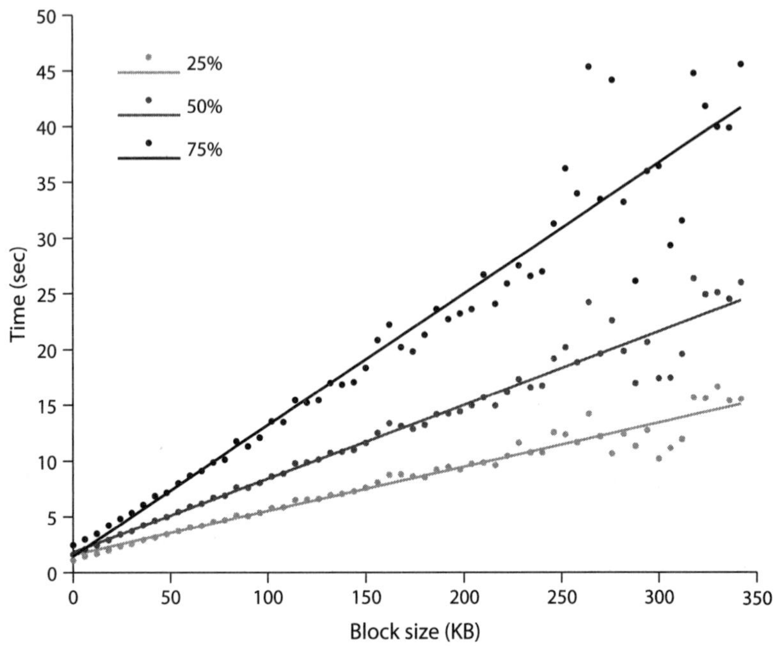

FIGURE 3.9. Block propagation time. This graph shows the average time it takes a block to reach various percentages of the nodes in the network. Source: Yonatan Sompolinsky and Aviv Zohar, "Accelerating Bitcoin's Transaction Processing," 2014. Available at https://eprint.iacr.org/2013/881. Data courtesy of Yonatan Sompolinsky and Aviv Zohar.

estimate that more than 1 million IP addresses in a given month will act at some point (at least temporarily) as a Bitcoin node. In contrast, only about 5,000 to 10,000 nodes seem to be permanently connected and fully validate every transaction they hear. This may seem like a surprisingly low number, but as of 2015, no evidence indicates that the number of fully validating nodes is going up, and it may in fact be dropping.

Storage Requirements

Fully validating nodes must stay permanently connected so as to hear about all Bitcoin transactions. The longer a node is offline, the more catching up it will have to do when it rejoins the network. Such nodes also have to store the entire block chain and need a good network connection to be able to hear every new transaction and forward it to peers. The storage requirement is currently in the tens of gigabytes (see Figure 3.10), well within the abilities of a single commodity desktop machine.

Finally, fully validating nodes must maintain the entire set of unspent transaction outputs, which are the coins available to be spent. Ideally this should be stored in memory rather than on disk, so that on hearing a new proposed transaction on the network, the node can quickly look up the transaction outputs that it's attempting to claim, run the scripts, see whether the signatures are valid, and add the transaction to the

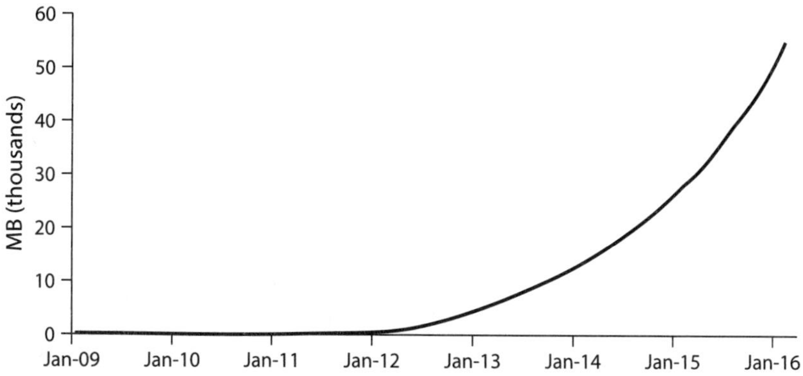

FIGURE 3.10. Size of the block chain. Fully validating nodes must store the entire block chain, which, as of the end of 2015, is more than 50 gigabytes.

transaction pool. As of mid-2014, more than 44 million transactions were on the block chain, of which 12 million were unspent. Fortunately, that's still small enough to fit in less than a gigabyte of memory in an efficient data structure.

Lightweight Nodes

In contrast to fully validating nodes, there are lightweight nodes, also called "thin" clients or "Simplified Payment Verification" (SPV) clients. In fact, nearly all nodes on the Bitcoin network are lightweight nodes. These differ from fully validating nodes in that they don't store the entire block chain. They only store the pieces that they need to verify specific transactions that concern them. If you use a wallet program, it typically incorporates an SPV node. The node downloads the block headers and transactions that represent payments to your addresses.

An SPV node doesn't have the security level of a fully validating node. Since the node has block headers, it can check that the blocks were difficult to mine, but it can't check to see whether every transaction included in a block is actually valid, because it doesn't have the transaction history and doesn't know the set of unspent transaction outputs. SPV nodes can only validate transactions that actually affect them. So they're essentially trusting the fully validating nodes to have validated all the other transactions that are out there. This isn't a bad security trade-off. The SPV nodes assume that fully validating nodes exist and are doing the hard work, and that if miners went through the trouble to mine this block (which is a really expensive process), they probably also did some validation to make sure that the block wouldn't be rejected.

The cost savings of being an SPV node are huge. The block headers are only about 1/1,000 the size of the block chain. So instead of storing a few tens of gigabytes, it's only a few tens of megabytes. Even a smartphone can easily act as an SPV node in the Bitcoin network.

Since Bitcoin rests on an open protocol, ideally many different implementations would interact with one another seamlessly. That way if there's a bad bug in one, it's not likely to bring down the entire network. The good news is that the protocol has been successfully reimplemented from scratch. The bad news is that most nodes on the network are running the bitcoind library, written in C+ + and maintained as part of Bitcoin Core, the reference implementation of Bitcoin.

3.6. LIMITATIONS AND IMPROVEMENTS

Here we discuss some built-in limitations to the Bitcoin protocol, and why it's challenging to improve them. Many constraints are hardcoded into the Bitcoin protocol. These constraints were chosen when Bitcoin was proposed in 2009, before anyone had any idea that it might grow into a globally important currency. Among the constraints are the limits on the average time per block, the size of blocks, the number of signature operations in a block, the divisibility of the currency, the total number of bitcoins, and the block reward structure.

The limitations on the total number of bitcoins in existence, as well as the structure of the mining rewards, will very likely never change, because the economic implications of changing them are too great. Miners and investors have made big bets on the system, assuming that the Bitcoin reward structure and the limited supply of bitcoins will remain as initially planned. If that changes, it will have significant financial implications for some individuals. So the community has basically agreed that those aspects, whether or not they were wisely chosen, will not change.

Some other changes would seem to make everybody better off, because with hindsight it seems that some initial design choices were not optimal. Chief among these are limits that affect the throughput of the system. How many transactions can the Bitcoin network process per second? This limitation comes from the hardcoded limit on the size of blocks. Each block is limited to a megabyte, or about 1 million bytes. Each transaction is at least 250 bytes. Dividing 1 million by 250, we see that each block has a limit of 4,000 transactions, and given that blocks are found about every 10 minutes, we're left with about 7 transactions per second, which is all that the Bitcoin network can handle. It may seem that changing these limits would be a matter of tweaking a constant in a source code file somewhere. However, such a change is hard to implement in practice, for reasons discussed later in the section.

So how does 7 transactions per second compare to other networks? It's quite low compared to the throughput of any major credit card processor. Visa's network is said to handle about 2,000 transactions per second around the world on average and is capable of handling 10,000 transactions per second during busy periods. Even PayPal, which is newer and smaller than Visa, can handle 100 transactions per second at peak times. That's an order of magnitude more than Bitcoin can manage.

Another limitation that is potentially problematic in the long term is that the choices of cryptographic algorithms in Bitcoin are fixed. Only a couple of hash algorithms are available, and only one signature algorithm can be used—ECDSA, over the specific elliptic curve called secp256k1 (see Chapter 1). There's some concern that over the lifetime of Bitcoin—which users hope will be very long—this algorithm might be broken. Cryptographers might come up with a clever new attack that makes the algorithm insecure. The same is true of the hash functions; in fact, in the past decade, we've seen steady progress in the cryptanalysis of hash functions. SHA-1, a hash function that is included in Bitcoin as an alternative to SHA-256, has already been shown to have some cryptographic weaknesses, albeit not fatal ones. To be resilient against advances in cryptanalysis, the Bitcoin scripting language would have to be extended to support new cryptographic algorithms.

Changing the Protocol

How can we go about introducing new features into the Bitcoin protocol? You might think that this is simple—just release a new version of the software, and tell all nodes to upgrade. In reality, though, it is quite complicated. In practice, it's impossible to assume that every node would upgrade. Some nodes in the network would fail to get the new software or fail to get it in time. The implications of having most nodes upgrade while some nodes are running the old version depends very much on the nature of the changes in the software. We can differentiate between two types of changes: those that would cause a *hard fork* and those that would cause a *soft fork*.

HARD FORKS

One type of change that we can make introduces new features that were previously considered invalid. That is, the new version of the software would recognize blocks as valid that the old software would reject. Now consider what happens when most nodes have upgraded, but some have not. Soon the longest branch will contain blocks that are considered invalid by the old nodes. So the old nodes will work on a branch of the block chain that excludes blocks with the new feature. Until they upgrade their software, they'll consider their own (shorter) branch to be the longest valid branch.

This type of change is called a "hard-forking" change, because it makes the block chain split. Every node in the network will be on one or the other side of the fork based on which version of the protocol it's running. Of course, the branches will never join together again. This is considered unacceptable by the community, since old nodes would effectively be cut out of the Bitcoin network if they don't upgrade their software.

SOFT FORKS

A second type of change that we can make to Bitcoin is to add features that make validation rules stricter. That is, they restrict the set of valid transactions (or the set of valid blocks) such that the old version would accept all the blocks, whereas the new version would reject some of the blocks accepted by the old version. This type of change is called a "soft fork," and it can avoid the permanent split that a hard fork introduces.

Consider what happens when introducing a new version of the software with a soft-forking change. The nodes running the new software will be enforcing some new, tighter set of rules. Provided that the majority of nodes switch over to the new software, these nodes will be able to enforce the new rules. Introducing a soft fork requires enough nodes to switch to the new version of the protocol that they'll be able to enforce the new rules, even though the old nodes won't be able to enforce the new rules (because they haven't heard of them yet).

There is a risk that old miners might mine invalid blocks, because they include some transactions that are invalid under the new, stricter rules. But the old miners will at least figure out that some of their blocks are being rejected, even if they don't understand the reason. This might prompt their operators to upgrade their software. Furthermore, if their branch is overtaken by the new miners, the old miners will switch to it. That's because blocks considered valid by new miners are also considered valid by old miners. Thus, no hard fork occurs; instead, there will be many small, temporary forks.

The classic example of a change that was made via soft fork is Pay-to-Script-Hash (P2SH), discussed in Section 3.2. P2SH was not present in the first version of the Bitcoin protocol. Its introduction caused a soft fork, because for old nodes, a valid P2SH transaction would still verify correctly. As interpreted by the old nodes, the script is simple—it hashes one data value and checks whether the hash matches the value specified in the output script. Old nodes don't carry out the (now required) additional step of running that value itself to see whether it is a valid script. We rely on new nodes to enforce the new rules (i.e., that the script actually redeems this transaction).

So what changes could we possibly add with a soft fork? P2SH was successful. It's also possible that new cryptographic schemes could be added by a soft fork. We could also add some extra metadata in the coinbase parameter that has some agreed-on meaning. Today, any value is accepted in the coinbase parameter. But we could, in the future, require that the coinbase have some specific format. One proposed idea is that, in each new block, the coinbase includes the Merkle root of a tree containing the entire set of unspent transactions. It would only result in a soft fork, because old nodes might mine a block that didn't have the required new coinbase parameter, so that block would be rejected by the network, but the old node would catch up and join the main chain that the network is mining.

Other changes might require a hard fork. Examples include adding new opcodes to Bitcoin, changing the limits on block or transactions size, or fixing various bugs. Fixing the bug discussed in Section 3.2, where the MULTISIG instruction pops an extra value off the stack, would also require a hard fork. That explains why, even though it's an annoying bug, it's much easier to leave it in the protocol and work around it rather than have a hard-forking change to Bitcoin. Changes that would result in a hard fork, even though some of them would be nice, are highly unlikely to be implemented within the current climate of Bitcoin. But many of these ideas have been tested and proved to be

Bitcoin's Block-Size Conundrum

Because of Bitcoin's growing popularity, as of early 2016, it has become common for the 1-megabyte space in blocks to be filled up before another block has been mined (especially when, by chance, a block takes longer than 10 minutes to find), resulting in some transactions having to wait one or more additional blocks to make their way into the block chain. But increasing the block-size limit would require a hard fork.

The question of whether and how to address the block chain's limited bandwidth for transactions has gripped the Bitcoin community. The discussion started years ago, but with little progress toward consensus, it has gradually become more acrimonious, escalating to a circus. We discuss Bitcoin's community, politics, and governance in Chapter 7.

Depending on the resolution of the block-size problem, some details in this chapter might become slightly out of date. The technical details of increasing Bitcoin's transaction-processing capacity are interesting, and we encourage you to read more online.

successful in alternative cryptocurrencies, which start from scratch. We discuss these alternatives in a lot more detail in Chapter 10.

At this point, you should be familiar with the technical mechanics of Bitcoin and how a Bitcoin node operates. But human beings aren't Bitcoin nodes, and you're never going to run a Bitcoin node in your head. So how do you, as a human, actually interact with this network to make it useful as a currency? How do you find a node to inform about your transaction? How do you obtain bitcoins in exchange for cash? How do you store your bitcoins? All these questions are crucial for building a currency that actually works for people, as opposed to just software. We answer these questions in the next chapter.

FURTHER READING

This chapter covers a lot of technical details, and you may find it difficult to absorb them all at once. To supplement the material in this chapter, it's useful to go online and see some of the things we discussed in practice. Numerous websites allow you to examine blocks and transactions and see what they look like. One such "blockchain explorer" is the website blockchain.info.

A developer-focused book on Bitcoin that covers the technical details well (see especially Chapters 5–7) is:

Antonopoulos, Andreas M. *Mastering Bitcoin: Unlocking Digital Cryptocurrencies*. Newton, MA: O'Reilly Media, 2014.

CHAPTER 4

How to Store and Use Bitcoins

4.1. SIMPLE LOCAL STORAGE

Let's begin with the simplest way of storing bitcoins: simply putting them on a local device. As a recap, to spend a bitcoin, you need to know some public information and some secret information. The public information is what goes on the block chain—the identity of the coin, how much it's worth, and so on. The secret information is the secret key of the owner of the bitcoin (presumably, you). You don't need to worry too much about how to store the public information, because you can always retrieve it when needed. But the secret signing key is something you'd better keep track of. So in practice, storing your bitcoins is all about storing and managing your keys.

Storing bitcoins is all about storing and managing Bitcoin secret keys.

When figuring out how to store and manage keys, three goals should be kept in mind. The first is availability: being able to actually spend your coins when you want to. The second is security: making sure that nobody else can spend your coins. If someone gets the power to spend your coins, they could send your coins to themselves, and then you no longer have the coins. The third goal is convenience: managing your keys should be relatively easy. As you can imagine, achieving all three simultaneously can be a challenge.

Different approaches to key management offer different trade-offs between availability, security, and convenience.

The simplest key management method is to store them in a file on your own local device: your computer, phone, or some other kind of gadget that you carry, own, or control. This is great for convenience: having a smartphone app that allows spending coins with the push of a few buttons is hard to beat. But this option isn't great for availability or security—if you lose the device, if the device crashes and you have to wipe the disk, or if your file gets corrupted, your keys are lost, and so are your coins. Similarly for security: if someone steals or breaks into your device, or infects it with malware, she can copy your keys and then send all your coins to herself.

In other words, storing your private keys on a local device, especially a mobile device, is a lot like carrying around money in your wallet or in your purse. It's useful to have some spending money, but you don't want to carry around your life savings, because you might lose it, or somebody might steal it. So what you typically do is store a little bit of information—a little bit of money—in your wallet and keep most of your money somewhere else.

Wallets

If storing your bitcoins locally, you'd typically use *wallet software*, which is software that keeps track of your coins, manages the details of your keys, and makes things convenient with a nice user interface. If you want to send $4.25 worth of bitcoins to your local coffee shop, the wallet software would give you some easy way to do that. Wallet software is especially useful because you typically want to use a lot of different addresses with different keys associated with them. Recall that creating a new public/private key pair is easy, and you can use this to improve your anonymity or privacy. Wallet software gives you a simple interface that tells you how much is in your wallet. When you want to spend bitcoins, it handles the details of which keys to use, how to generate new addresses, and so on.

Encoding Keys: Base 58 and QR Codes

To spend or receive bitcoins, you also need a way to exchange an address with the other party—the address to which bitcoins are to be sent. Two main methods are used to encode addresses so that they can be communicated from receiver to spender: as a text string or as a QR code.

To encode an address as a text string, we take the bits of the key and convert them from a binary number to a base-58 number. Then we use a set of 58 characters to encode each digit as a character; this is called "base-58 notation." Why 58? Because that's the total number of available uppercase letters, lowercase letters, and digits that can be used as characters (minus a few that might be confusing or look like another character). For example, capital letter "O" and zero are both taken out, because they look too much alike. This allows encoded addresses to be read out over the phone or read from printed paper and typed in, should that be necessary. Ideally, such manual methods of communicating addresses can be avoided through such methods as QR codes, which we now discuss.

`1A1zP1eP5QGefi2DMPTfTL5SLmv7DivfNa`

The address that received the very first Bitcoin block reward in the genesis block, base-58 encoded.

The second method for encoding a Bitcoin address is as a QR code, a simple kind of two-dimensional barcode (Figure 4.1). The advantage of a QR code is that you can take

FIGURE 4.1. QR code representing an actual Bitcoin address. Feel free to send us some bitcoins.

a picture of it with a smartphone, and wallet software can automatically turn the barcode into a sequence of bits that represents the corresponding Bitcoin address. This is useful in a store, for example: the checkout system might display a QR code, and you can pay with your phone by scanning the code and sending coins to that address. It is also useful for phone-to-phone transfers.

Vanity Addresses

Some individuals or merchants like to have an address that starts with some humanly meaningful text. For example, the gambling website Satoshi Bones has users send money to addresses containing the string "bones" in positions 2–6, such as `1bonesEeTcABPjLzAb1VkFgySY6Zqu3sX` (all regular addresses begin with the character 1, indicating Pay-to-PubkeyHash.)

Addresses are outputs of a hash function, which produces random-looking data, so how did the string "bones" get in there? If Satoshi Bones were simply making up these addresses, lacking the ability to invert hash functions, they wouldn't know the corresponding private keys and hence wouldn't actually control those addresses. Instead, they repeatedly generated private keys until they got lucky and found one that hashed

Speeding Up Vanity Address Generation

In Bitcoin, if we call the private key x, the public key is g^x. The exponentiation represents what's called "scalar multiplication in an elliptic curve group." The address is $H(g^x)$, the hash of the public key. We won't get into the details here, but exponentiation is the time-consuming step in address generation.

The naive way to generate vanity addresses would be to pick a pseudorandom x, compute $H(g^x)$, and repeat if the resulting address doesn't work. A much faster approach is to try $x + 1$ if the first x fails and continue incrementing instead of picking a fresh x each time. That's because $g^{x+1} = g\, g^x$, and we've already computed g^x, so we only need a multiplication operation for each address instead of exponentiation, and that's much faster. In fact, it speeds up vanity address generation by more than two orders of magnitude.

to this pattern. Such addresses are called *vanity addresses*, and there are tools to generate them.

How much work does this take? Since there are 58 possibilities for every character, if you want to find an address that starts with a specific k-character string, you'll need to generate 58^k addresses on average until you get lucky. So finding an address starting with "bones" would have required generating more than 600 million addresses! Such a search can be done on an ordinary laptop today. But the search becomes exponentially harder with each extra character in the desired name. Finding a 15-character prefix would require an infeasible amount of computation and (without finding a break in the underlying hash function) should be impossible.

4.2. HOT AND COLD STORAGE

As just mentioned, storing bitcoins on your computer is like carrying money around in your wallet or your purse. This is called *hot storage*. It's convenient but also somewhat risky. In contrast, *cold storage* is offline. It's locked away somewhere, it's not connected to the Internet, and it's archival. So cold storage is safer and more secure, but of course not as convenient as hot storage. This is analogous to carrying some money on your person but putting your life's savings somewhere safer.

To have separate hot and cold storage, obviously you need to have separate secret keys for each—otherwise, the coins in cold storage would be vulnerable if the hot storage is compromised. You'll want to move coins back and forth between the hot side and the cold side, so each side will need to know the other's addresses, or public keys.

Cold storage is not online, and so the hot storage and the cold storage won't be able to connect to each other across any network. But the good news is that cold storage doesn't have to be online to receive coins—since the hot storage knows the cold storage addresses, it can send coins to cold storage at any time. At any time if the amount of money in your hot wallet becomes uncomfortably large, you can transfer a chunk of it to cold storage, without putting your cold storage at risk by connecting to the network. Next time the cold storage connects, it will be able to receive from the block chain information about those transfers to it, and then the cold storage will be able to manipulate those coins.

But there's a little problem with managing cold storage addresses. As mentioned earlier, for privacy and other reasons, we want to be able to receive each coin at a separate address with different secret keys. So when we transfer a coin from the hot side to the cold side, we'd like to use a fresh cold address for that purpose. But because the cold side is not online, we must have some way for the hot side to find out about those addresses.

The blunt solution is for the cold side to generate a big batch of addresses all at once and send them over for the hot side to use up one by one. The drawback is that we have to periodically reconnect the cold side to transfer more addresses.

Hierarchical Deterministic Wallets

A more effective solution is to use a *hierarchical deterministic wallet.* It allows the cold side to use an essentially unbounded number of addresses and the hot side to know about these addresses, but with only a short, one-time communication between the two sides. But it requires a bit of cryptographic trickery.

When discussing key generation and digital signatures in Chapter 1, we looked at a function generateKeys that generates a public key (which acts as an address) and a secret key. In a hierarchical deterministic wallet, key generation works differently. Instead of generating a single address, we generate what we call "address generation info," and rather than a private key, we generate what we call "private key generation info." Given the address generation info, we can generate a sequence of addresses: we apply an address generation function that takes as input the address generation info and any integer i and generates the ith address in the sequence. Similarly, we can generate a sequence of private keys using the private key generation info.

The cryptographic magic that makes this useful is that for every i, the ith address and ith secret key match up—that is, the ith secret key controls, and can be used to spend, bitcoins from the ith address, just as if the pair were generated the old-fashioned way. So it's as though we have a sequence of regular key pairs.

The other important cryptographic property here is security: the address generation info doesn't leak any information about the private keys. Thus it's safe to give the address generation info to anybody, so that anybody can generate the ith key.

Not all digital signature schemes can be modified to support hierarchical deterministic key generation. Some can and some can't, but the good news is that the digital signature scheme used by Bitcoin, ECDSA, does support hierarchical deterministic key generation. That is, the cold side generates arbitrarily many keys, and the hot side generates the corresponding addresses (Figure 4.2).

Here's how it works. Recall that normally an ECDSA private key is a random number x, and the corresponding public key is g^x. For hierarchical deterministic key generation, we'll need two other random values k and y:

private key generation info: k, x, y
ith private key: $x_i = y + H(k \| i)$
address generation info: k, g^y
ith public key: $g^{x_i} = g^{H(k\|i)} \cdot g^y$
ith address: $H(g^{x_i})$

This scheme has all the properties we want: each side is able to generate its sequence of keys, and the corresponding keys match up (because the public key corresponding to a private key x is g^x). It has one other property that we haven't talked about: when you give out the public keys, those keys won't be linkable to one another—that is, it won't be possible to infer that they come from the same wallet. The straw-man solution of having the cold side generate a big batch of addresses does have this property, but we

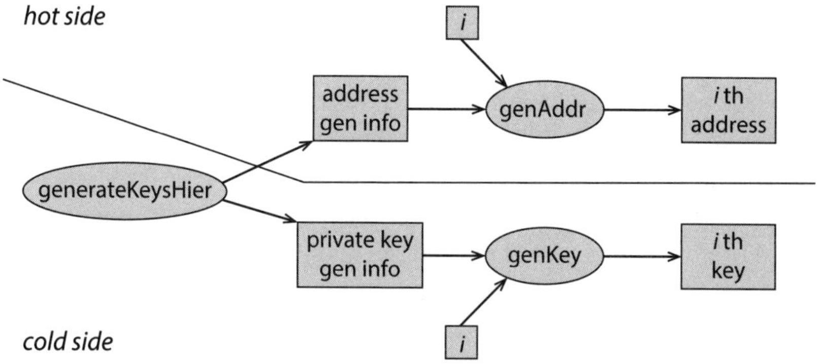

FIGURE 4.2. Schema of a hierarchical deterministic wallet. The cold side creates and saves private key generation information and address generation information. It does a one-time transfer of the latter to the hot side. The hot side generates a new address sequentially every time it sends coins to the cold side. When the cold side reconnects, it generates addresses sequentially and checks the block chain for transfers to those addresses until it reaches an address that hasn't received any coins. It can also generate private keys sequentially if it sends some coins back to the hot side or spends them some other way.

had to take care to preserve it in the new technique, because the keys aren't in fact independently generated. This property is important for privacy and anonymity, which are the topics of Chapter 6.

Here we have two levels of security, with the hot side being at a lower level. If the hot side is compromised, the unlinkability property just discussed will be lost, but the private keys (and the bitcoins) are still safe. In general, this scheme supports arbitrarily many security levels—hence the term "hierarchical"—although we haven't discussed the details. This can be useful, for instance, when there are multiple levels of delegation in a company.

Now let's discuss the different ways in which cold information—whether one or more keys, or key generation info—can be stored. The first way is to store it in some kind of device and put that device in a safe. It might be a laptop computer, a mobile phone or tablet, or a thumb drive. The important thing is to turn the device off and lock it up, so that if somebody wants to steal it, they have to break into the locked storage.

Brain Wallet

The second method we can use is called a *brain wallet*. This method controls access to bitcoins using nothing but a secret passphrase. It avoids the need for hard drives, paper, or any other long-term storage mechanism. This property can be particularly useful in situations where you have poor physical security (e.g., perhaps when traveling abroad).

The key trick behind a brain wallet is to have a predictable algorithm for turning a passphrase into a public and a private key. For example, you could hash the passphrase with a suitable hash function to derive the private key, and given the private key, the public key can be derived in a standard way. Further, combining this with the deterministic wallet technique discussed earlier, we can generate an entire sequence of addresses and private keys from a passphrase, thus enabling a complete wallet.

However, an adversary can also obtain all private keys in a brain wallet if he can guess the passphrase. As always in computer security, we must assume that the adversary knows the procedure you used to generate keys, and only your passphrase provides security. So the adversary can try various passphrases and generate addresses using them; if he finds any unspent transactions on the block chain at any of those addresses, he can immediately transfer them to himself. The adversary may never know (or care) who the coins belonged to, and the attack doesn't require breaking into any machines. Guessing brain wallet passphrases is not directed toward specific users, and it leaves no trace.

Furthermore, unlike the task of guessing your email password, which can be rate-limited by your email server (called *online guessing*), with brain wallets, the attacker can download the list of addresses with unredeemed coins and try as many potential passphrases as he has the computational capacity to check. Note that the attacker doesn't need to know which addresses correspond to brain wallets. This is called *offline guessing* or *password cracking*. It is much more challenging to come up with passphrases that are easy to memorize and yet won't be vulnerable to guessing in this manner. One secure way to generate a passphrase is to have an automatic procedure for picking a random 80-bit number and turning that number into a passphrase in such a way that different numbers result in different passphrases.

In practice, it is also wise to use a deliberately slow function to derive the private key from the passphrase to ensure it takes as long as possible for the attacker to try all possibilities. This is known as *key stretching*. To create a deliberately slow key-derivation function, we can take a fast cryptographic hash function like SHA-256 and compute, say, 2^{20} iterations of it, multiplying the attacker's workload by a factor of 2^{20}. Of course, if we make it too slow, it will start to become annoying to the users, as their devices must recompute this function any time they want to spend coins from their brain wallets.

If a brain wallet passphrase is inaccessible—it's been forgotten, hasn't been written down, and can't be guessed—then the coins are lost forever.

Generating Memorable Passphrases

One passphrase-generation procedure that gives about 80 bits of entropy is to pick a random sequence of six words from among the 10,000 most common English words ($6 \cdot \log_2(10000)$ is roughly 80). Many people find these easier to memorize than a random string of characters. Here are a couple of passphrases generated by this method:

```
worn till alloy focusing okay reducing
earth dutch fake tired dot occasions
```

FIGURE 4.3. Bitcoin paper wallet with the public key encoded both as a two-dimensional barcode and in base-58 notation.

Paper Wallet

The third option is called a *paper wallet* (Figure 4.3). We can print the key material to paper and then put that paper in a safe or other secure place. Obviously, the security of this method is just as good or bad as the physical security of the paper that we're using. Typical paper wallets encode both the public and private keys in two ways: as a two-dimensional barcode and in base-58 notation. Just as with a brain wallet, storing a small amount of key material is sufficient to re-create a wallet.

Tamper-Resistant Device

The fourth way that we can store offline information is to put it in some kind of *tamper-resistant device*. Either we put the key into the device or the device generates the key; either way, the device is designed so that there's no way it will output or divulge the key. The device instead signs statements with the key, and does so when we, say, press a button or give it some kind of password. One advantage is that if the device is lost or stolen we'll know it, and the only way the key can be stolen is if the device is stolen. This is different from storing your key on a laptop.

In general, people might use some combination of these four methods to secure their keys. For hot storage, and especially for hot storage holding large numbers of bitcoins, people are willing to work hard to devise novel security schemes for protection. We discuss one of these more advanced schemes in the next section.

4.3. SPLITTING AND SHARING KEYS

Up to now we've looked at different ways of storing and managing the secret keys that control bitcoins, but we've always put the key in one place—whether locked in a safe, or in software, or on paper. This leaves us with a single point of failure. If something goes wrong with that single storage place, then we're in trouble. We could create and store backups of the key material, but although this decreases the risk of the key getting lost or corrupted (availability), it increases the risk of theft (security). This trade-off seems fundamental. Can we take a piece of data and store it in such a way that availability and security increase at the same time? Remarkably, the answer is yes, and it is once again a trick that uses cryptography, called *secret sharing*.

Here's the idea: we want to divide our secret key into some number N of pieces. We want to do it in such a way that if given any K of those pieces, then we can reconstruct the original secret, but given fewer than K pieces, we won't be able to learn anything about the original secret.

Given this stringent requirement, simply cutting up the secret into pieces won't work, because even a single piece gives some information about the secret. We need something cleverer. And since we're not cutting up the secret, we call the individual components "shares" instead of pieces.

Suppose we have $N = 2$ and $K = 2$. That means we're generating two shares based on the secret, and we need both shares to be able to reconstruct the secret. Let's call our secret S, which is just a big (e.g., 128-bit) number. We could generate a 128-bit random number R and make the two shares be R and S ⊕ R. (⊕ represents bitwise XOR). Essentially, we've encrypted S with a one-time pad, and we store the key (R) and the ciphertext (S ⊕ R) in separate places. Neither the key nor the ciphertext by itself tells us anything about the secret. But given the two shares, we simply XOR them together to reconstruct the secret.

This trick works as long as N and K are the same—we just generate $N - 1$ different random numbers for the first $N - 1$ shares, and the final share would be the secret XOR'd with all other $N - 1$ shares. But if N is larger than K, this doesn't work anymore, and we need some algebra.

Take a look at Figure 4.4. First we generate the point $(0, S)$ on the y-axis, and then draw a line with a random slope through that point. Next we generate points on that line, as many as we want. It turns out that this is a secret sharing of S, with N being the number of points we generated, and $K = 2$.

Why does this method work? First, given two of the points generated, you can draw a line through them and see where it intercepts the y-axis. That gives you S. But if you're given only a single point, it tells you nothing about S, because the slope of the line is randomly generated. Every line through your point is equally likely, and they would all intersect the y-axis at different points.

There's only one other subtlety: to make the math work, we have to do all our arithmetic modulo a large prime number P. It doesn't need to be secret, just really big. And the secret S has to be between 0 and $P - 1$ inclusive. So by "generate points on the line," what we mean is that we generate a random value R, also between 0 and $P - 1$, and the points we generate are

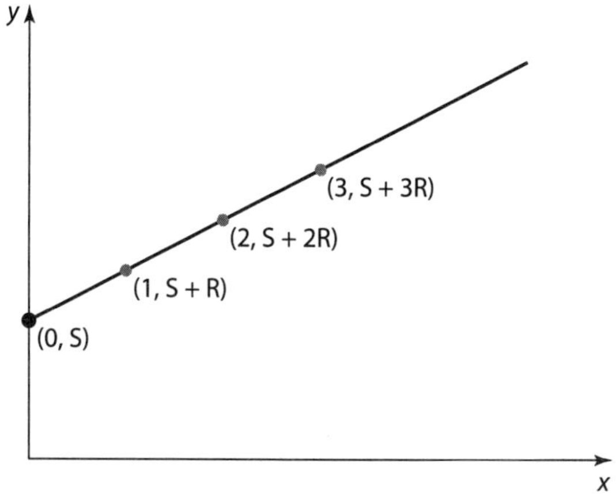

FIGURE 4.4. Geometric illustration of 2-out-of-*N* secret sharing. *S* represents the secret, encoded as a (large) integer. The line has a slope chosen at random. The points off the *y*-axis (specifically, their *y*-coordinates $S + R, S + 2R, \ldots$) correspond to shares. Any two such points are sufficient to reconstruct the point on the *y*-axis, and hence the secret. All arithmetic is done modulo a large prime number.

$$x = 1, y = (S + R) \bmod P$$
$$x = 2, y = (S + 2R) \bmod P$$
$$x = 3, y = (S + 3R) \bmod P$$

and so on. The secret corresponds to the point $x = 0, y = (S + 0 \cdot R) \bmod P$, which is just $x = 0, y = S$.

This method shares a secret with $K = 2$ and any value of N. It is already pretty good—for instance, if $N = 4$, you can divide your secret key into four shares and put them on four different devices, so that if someone steals any one of those devices, they learn nothing about your key. However, even if two of those devices are destroyed in a fire, you can reconstruct the key using the other two. So as promised, we've increased both availability and security.

But we can do better: we can secret-share with any N and K as long as K is no more than N. To see how, look again at Figure 4.4. We used a line instead of some other shape, because a line is a polynomial of degree 1. So to reconstruct a line, we need two points and no fewer than two. If we wanted $K = 3$, we would have used a parabola, which is a quadratic polynomial, or a polynomial of degree 2. Exactly three points are needed to construct a quadratic function. Table 4.1 illustrates the procedure.

There is a formula called *Lagrange interpolation* that allows you to reconstruct a polynomial of degree $K - 1$ from any K points on the polynomial's curve. This method is an algebraic version (and a generalization) of the geometric intuition of drawing a straight line through two points with a ruler. As a result, we have a way to store any secret as N shares such that we're safe even if an adversary learns up to $K - 1$ of them, and at the same time we can tolerate the loss of up to $N - K$ of them.

TABLE 4.1. THE MATH BEHIND SECRET SHARING

Equation	Degree	Shape	Random parameters	Number of points (K) needed to recover S
$(S + RX) \bmod P$	1	Line	R	2
$(S + R_1X + R_2X^2) \bmod P$	2	Parabola	R_1, R_2	3
$(S + R_1X + R_2X^2 + R_3X^3) \bmod P$	3	Cubic	R_1, R_2, R_3	4

Note: Representing a secret via a series of points on a random polynomial curve of degree $K - 1$ allows the secret to be reconstructed if, and only if, at least K of the points ("shares") are available.

None of this is specific to Bitcoin, by the way. You can secret-share your passwords right now and give shares to your friends or put them on different devices. But no one really does this with secrets like passwords. Convenience is one reason; another is that there are other security mechanisms available for important online accounts, such as two-factor security using SMS (text message) verification. But with Bitcoin, if you're storing your keys locally, you don't have those security options. There's no way to make the control of a Bitcoin address dependent on receipt of an SMS message. The situation is different with online wallets, which we examine in the next section. But not too different—it just shifts the problem to a different place. After all, the online wallet provider will need some way to avoid a single point of failure when storing *their* keys.

Threshold Cryptography

But there's still a problem with secret sharing: if we take a key and split it up in this way, and we then want to use the key to sign something, we still need to bring the shares together and recalculate the initial secret to be able to sign with that key. The point where we bring all the shares together is still a single point of vulnerability where an adversary might be able to steal the key.

Cryptography can solve this problem as well: if the shares are stored on different devices, we can produce Bitcoin signatures in a decentralized fashion without ever reconstructing the private key on any single device. This is called a *threshold signature*. The best use-case is a wallet with two-factor security, which corresponds to the case $N = 2$ and $K = 2$. Suppose that you configured your wallet to split its key material between your desktop and your phone. Then you might initiate a payment on your desktop, which would create a partial signature and send it to your phone. Your phone would then alert you with the payment details—recipient, amount, and so forth—and request your confirmation. If the details check out, you'd confirm, and your phone would complete the signature using its share of the private key and then broadcast the transaction to the block chain. If there were malware on your desktop that tried to steal your bitcoins, it might initiate a transaction that sent the funds to the hacker's address, but then you'd get an alert on your phone for a transaction you didn't authorize, and you'd know something was wrong. The mathematical details behind threshold signatures are complex, and we won't discuss them here.

Threshold Signatures

Threshold signatures are a cryptographic technique to take a single key, split it into shares, store them separately, and sign transactions without reconstructing the key. Multisignatures are a feature of Bitcoin script by which you can specify that control of an address is split among multiple independent keys. Although there are some differences between the two techniques, they both increase security by avoiding single points of failure.

Multisignatures

An entirely different option is available for avoiding a single point of failure: multisignatures, which we mentioned in Chapter 3. Instead of taking a single key and splitting it, Bitcoin script directly allows you to stipulate that control over an address be split among different keys. These keys can then be stored in different locations, and the signatures produced separately. Of course, the completed, signed transaction will be constructed on some device, but even if the adversary controls this device, all she can do is to prevent it from being broadcast to the network. She can't produce valid multisignatures of some other transaction without the involvement of the other devices.

As an example, suppose that Andrew, Arvind, Ed, Joseph, and Steven, the authors of this book, are cofounders of a company, and the company has a lot of bitcoins. We might use multisignatures to protect our large store of bitcoins. Each of the five of us will generate a key pair, and we'll protect our cold storage using 3-out-of-5 multisignatures, which means that three of us must sign to create a valid transaction.

As a result, we know that we're relatively secure if the five of us keep our keys separately and secure them differently. An adversary would have to compromise three out of the five keys. If one or even two of us go rogue, they can't steal the company's coins, because you need at least three keys to do that. At the same time, if one of us loses our key or gets run over by a bus and our brain wallet is lost, the others can still get the coins back and transfer them to a new address and resecure the keys. In other words, multisignatures help you to manage large amounts of cold-stored coins in a way that's relatively secure and requires action by multiple people before anything drastic happens.

Here we have motivated threshold signatures by explaining how the technique can help achieve two-factor (or multifactor) security, and multisignatures technique by explaining how it can help a set of individuals share control over jointly held funds. But either technology is applicable to either situation.

4.4. ONLINE WALLETS AND EXCHANGES

So far we've talked about how you can store and manage your bitcoins yourself. Now we discuss ways you can use other people's services to help you do that. The first thing you could do is use an online wallet.

Online Wallets

An *online wallet* is like a local wallet that you manage yourself, except the information is stored in the cloud, and you access it using a web interface on a computer or an app on a smartphone. Some online wallet services that are popular in 2015 are Coinbase and blockchain.info.

What's crucial from the point of view of security is that the site delivers the code that runs on your browser or the app, and it also stores your keys. At a minimum it will have the ability to access your keys. Ideally, the site will encrypt those keys under a password that only you know, but of course you have to trust them to do that. You have to trust their code to not leak your keys or your password.

An online wallet has certain trade-offs compared to doing things yourself. A big advantage is that it's convenient. You don't have to install anything on your computer to be able to use an online wallet in your browser. On your phone you may have to install an app just once, and it won't need to download the block chain. It will work across multiple devices—you can have a single wallet that you access on your desktop and phone, and it will work, because the real wallet lives in the cloud.

However, there are security worries. If the site or the people who operate it turn out to be malicious or are compromised somehow, your bitcoins are in trouble, because the site supplies the code that has its grubby fingers on your bitcoins.

Ideally, the site or the service is run by security professionals who are better trained, or perhaps more diligent than you in maintaining security. So you might hope that they do a better job and that your coins are actually more secure than if you stored them yourself. But at the end of the day, you have to trust them and you have to rely on them not being compromised.

Bitcoin Exchanges

To understand *Bitcoin exchanges*, let's first talk about how banks or bank-like services operate in the traditional economy. You give the bank some money—a deposit—and the bank promises to give you back that money later. Of course, crucially, the bank doesn't actually just take your money and put it in a box in the back room. All the bank does is promise that if you ask for the money, they'll give it back. The bank typically puts the money somewhere else, that is, invests it. The bank probably keeps some money in reserve to make sure that it can pay out the demand for withdrawals on a typical day, or maybe even an unusual day. Many banks typically use something called *fractional reserve*: they keep a certain fraction of all demand deposits on reserve just in case.

Bitcoin exchanges are businesses that—at least from the user interface standpoint—function in a similar way to banks. They accept deposits of bitcoins and will, just like a bank, promise to give them back on demand later. You can also transfer fiat currency—traditional currency like dollars and euros—into an exchange by transferring from your bank account. The exchange promises to pay back either or both types of currency on demand. The exchange lets you do various banking-like activities. You can make and receive Bitcoin payments. That is, you can direct the exchange to pay out some bitcoins to a particular party, or you can ask someone else to deposit funds into the particular exchange on your behalf—put the coins into your account. You can also exchange bitcoins for fiat currency or vice versa. Typically, Bitcoin exchanges make the exchange by finding some customer who wants to buy bitcoins with dollars and another customer who wants to sell bitcoins for dollars, and matching them up. In other words, they try to find customers willing to take opposite positions in a transaction. If there's a mutually acceptable price, they will consummate that transaction.

Suppose your account at some exchange holds $5,000 and 3 BTC, and you use the exchange to place an order to buy 2 BTC for $580 each. The exchange finds someone who is willing to take the other side of that transaction, and the transaction takes place. Now you have 5 BTC in your account instead of 3 BTC, and $3,840 instead of $5,000.

The important thing to note here is that when this transaction happened involving you and another customer of the same exchange, no transaction actually happened on the Bitcoin block chain. The exchange doesn't need to go to the block chain to transfer bitcoins or dollars from one account to another. All that happens in this transaction is that the exchange is now making a different promise to you than they were making before. Before they said, "we'll give you $5,000 and 3 BTC," and now they're saying "we'll give you $3,840 and 5 BTC." It's just a change in their promise—no actual movement of money takes place through the dollar economy or through the block chain. Of course, the other participant in the transaction has had the promises made to him change in the opposite way.

There are pros and cons to using exchanges. One of the big advantages is that exchanges help connect the Bitcoin economy and the flows of bitcoins with the fiat currency economy, so that it's easy to transfer value back and forth.

The disadvantage is risk. You have the same kinds of risk that you face with banks. Those risks fall into three categories.

Three Types of Risks

The first risk is the risk of a *bank run*. A run occurs when many people show up at the same time and demand their money back. Since the bank maintains only fractional reserves, it might be unable to cope with the simultaneous withdrawals. The danger stems from panic behavior: once the rumor starts to circulate that a bank or exchange might be in trouble and might start refusing to honor withdrawals, then people stampede in to try to withdraw their money ahead of the crowd, and an avalanche of demand results.

The second risk is that the owners of the banks might just be crooks running a Ponzi scheme. This is a scheme where someone gets people to give them money in exchange for profits in the future, but then actually takes their money and uses it to pay out the profits to people who bought previously. Such a scheme is doomed to eventually fail and cause a lot of people to lose a lot of money. Bernie Madoff most famously pulled this off in recent memory.

The third risk is that of a hack: the risk that someone—perhaps even an employee of the exchange—will manage to penetrate the security of the exchange. Since exchanges store key information that controls large numbers of bitcoins, they need to be careful about their software security and their procedures—how they manage their cold and hot storage and all of that. If something goes wrong, your money could get stolen from the exchange.

All these things have happened. We have seen exchanges that failed due to the equivalent of a bank run. We've seen exchanges fail because the operators of the exchange were crooks, and we've seen exchanges fail because of break-ins. In fact, the statistics are not encouraging. A study in 2013 found that 18 of 40 Bitcoin exchanges closed because of a failure or some inability to pay out the money that the exchange had promised to pay out.

The most famous example of this is of course Mt. Gox. Mt. Gox was at one time the largest Bitcoin exchange, and it eventually became insolvent, unable to pay out the money that it owed. Mt. Gox was a Japanese company, and it ended up declaring bankruptcy and leaving a lot of people wondering where their money had gone. As of 2014, the bankruptcy of Mt. Gox is working through the Japanese and American courts, and it's going to be a while before we know exactly where the money went. The one thing we know is that a lot of money is involved, and Mt. Gox doesn't have it anymore. So this is a cautionary tale about the use of exchanges.

Connecting this back to banks, we don't see a 45 percent failure rate for banks in most developed countries, which is partly due to regulation. Governments regulate traditional banks in various ways.

Bank Regulation

Governments often impose a minimum reserve requirement on banks. In the United States, the fraction of demand deposits that banks are required to have in liquid form is typically 3–10 percent, so that the bank can handle a surge of withdrawals if necessary. Governments also often regulate the types of investments and money management methods that banks can use. The goal is to ensure that the banks' assets are invested in places that are relatively low risk, because their assets are really those of the depositors in some sense.

In exchange for these forms of regulation, governments typically do things to help banks or help their depositors. First, governments issue deposit insurance. That is, the government promises depositors that if a bank that follows these rules goes under, the government will make good on at least part of those deposits. Governments also sometimes act as a "lender of last resort." If a bank experiences difficulty but is basically solvent, the government may step in and loan the bank money to tide it over until it can move money around as necessary to get itself out of the woods.

So traditional banks are regulated in this way. Bitcoin exchanges are not. The question of whether or how Bitcoin exchanges or other Bitcoin businesses should be regulated is a topic that we come back to in Chapter 7.

Proof of Reserve

A Bitcoin exchange or someone else who holds bitcoins can use a cryptographic trick called a "proof of reserve" to reassure customers about the safety of the money they deposited. The goal is for the exchange or business holding bitcoins to prove that it has a fractional reserve—that they retain control of perhaps 25 percent or maybe even 100 percent of the deposits that people have made.

We can break the proof-of-reserve problem into two pieces. The first is to prove how much reserve the exchange is holding—the relatively easy part. The company simply publishes a valid payment-to-self transaction of the claimed reserve amount. That is, if they claim to have 100,000 bitcoins, they create a transaction in which they pay 100,000 bitcoins to themselves and show that the transaction is valid. Then they sign a challenge string—a random string of bits generated by some impartial party—with the same private key that was used to sign the payment-to-self transaction. This proves that someone who knew that private key participated in the proof of reserve.

We should note two caveats. Strictly speaking, this process is not a proof that the party claiming to own the reserve in fact owns it, but only that whoever does own those 100,000 bitcoins is willing to cooperate in this process. Nonetheless, it looks like a proof that somebody controls or knows someone who controls the given amount of money. Also, note that you could always underclaim: the organization might have 150,000 bitcoins but choose to make a payment-to-self of only 100,000. So this proof of reserve establishes the minimum that the company has, not the maximum.

Proof of Liabilities

The second piece is to prove how many demand deposits a company holds, which is the hard part. If the exchange can prove its reserves and demand deposits, then anyone can simply divide those two numbers to determine its fractional reserve. We'll present a scheme that allows the exchange to over-claim, but not under-claim, its demand deposits. So if the company can prove that its reserves are at least a certain amount and its liabilities are at most a certain amount, taken together, it has proved a lower bound on its fractional reserve.

If the exchange didn't care at all about the privacy of its users, it could simply publish its records—specifically, the username and amount of every customer with a demand deposit. Now anyone can calculate the exchange's total liabilities, and if it omitted any customers or lied about the value of their deposits, it runs the risk that those customers would expose the fraud. The company could make up fake users, but it can only increase the value of its claimed total liabilities this way. So as long as there aren't customer complaints, publication lets the company prove a lower bound on its deposits.

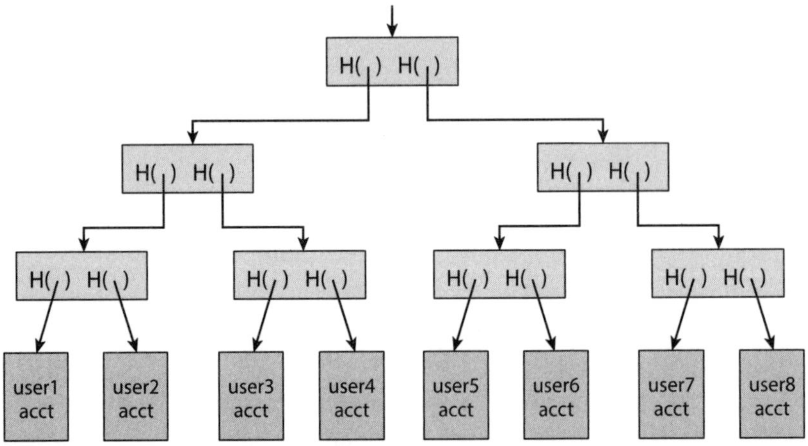

FIGURE 4.5. Proof of liabilities. The exchange publishes the root of a Merkle tree that contains all users at the leaves, including deposit amounts. Any user can request a proof of inclusion in the tree and verify that the deposit sums are propagated correctly to the root of the tree.

The trick, of course, is to prove this lower bound while respecting the privacy of its users.

To do this, the exchange can use Merkle trees, discussed in Chapter 1. Recall that a Merkle tree is a binary tree built with hash pointers, so that each pointer indicates not only where we can get a piece of information but also what the cryptographic hash of that information is. The exchange executes the proof by constructing a Merkle tree in which each leaf corresponds to a user and by publishing its root hash (Figure 4.5). Similar to the naive protocol discussed in the previous paragraph, each user is responsible for ensuring that she is included in the tree. In addition, there's a way for users to collectively check the claimed total of deposits. Let's delve into the details now.

We're going to add to each one of these hash pointers another field, or attribute. This attribute is a number that represents the total monetary value in bitcoins of all deposits that are in the subtree beneath that hash pointer in the tree. For this to be true, the value corresponding to each hash pointer should be the sum of the values of the two hash pointers beneath it.

The exchange constructs this tree, cryptographically signs the root pointer along with the root attribute value, and publishes it. The root value is of course the total liabilities, the number we're interested in. The exchange is making the claim that all users are represented in the leaves of the tree, that their deposit values are represented correctly, and that the values are propagated correctly up the tree, so that the root value is the sum of all users' deposit amounts.

Now each customer can go to the organization and ask for proof of correct inclusion. The exchange must then show the customer the partial tree from that user's leaf up to the root, as shown in Figure 4.6. The customer then verifies that:

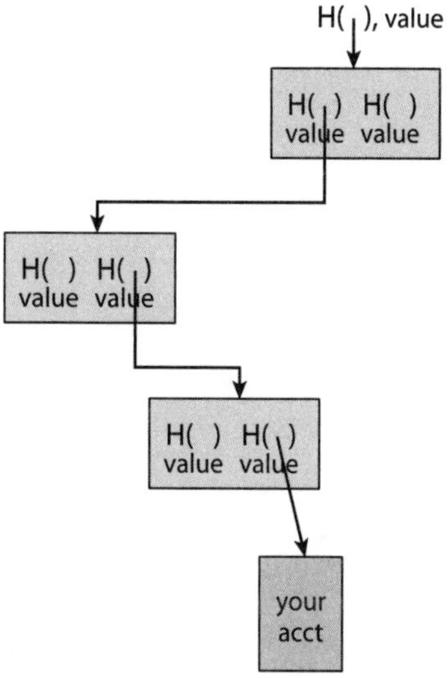

FIGURE 4.6. Proof of inclusion in a Merkle tree. The leaf node is revealed, as well as the siblings of the nodes on the path from the leaf to the root.

1. The root hash pointer and root value are the same as what the exchange signed and published.
2. The hash pointers are consistent all the way down; that is, each hash value is indeed the cryptographic hash of the node it points to.
3. The leaf contains the correct user account information (e.g., username/user ID and deposit amount).
4. Each value is the sum of the values of the two values beneath it.
5. Neither of the values is a negative number.

The good news is that if every customer does this, then every branch of this tree will be explored, and someone will verify that for every hash pointer, its associated value equals the sum of the values of its two children. Crucially, the exchange cannot present different values in any part of the tree to different customers. That's because doing so would either imply the ability to find a hash collision, or presenting different root values to different customers, which we assume is impossible.

Let's recap. First, the exchange proves that they have at least X amount of reserve currency by doing a self-transaction of that amount. Then they prove that their customers have at most an amount Y deposited. This shows that their reserve fraction is at least X/Y. What that means is that if a Bitcoin exchange wants to prove that they hold 25 percent (or 100 percent) of reserves on all deposits, they can do it in a way that's independently verifiable by anybody, and no central regulator is required.

You might notice that the two proofs presented here (the proof of reserves by signing a challenge string and the proof of liabilities via a Merkle tree) reveal a lot of private information. Specifically, they reveal all addresses being used by the exchange, the total value of the reserves and liabilities, and even some information about the individual customer balances. Real exchanges are hesitant to publish this information, and as a result, cryptographic proofs of reserve have been rare.

A recently proposed protocol called "Provisions" enables the same proof of solvency, but without revealing the total liabilities or reserves or the addresses in use. This protocol uses more advanced cryptography, and we won't cover it here, but it's another example showing how cryptography can be used to ensure privacy.

Solvency is one aspect of regulation that Bitcoin exchanges can prove voluntarily, but other aspects of regulation are harder to guarantee, as we discuss in Chapter 7.

4.5. PAYMENT SERVICES

So far we've talked about how you can store and manage your bitcoins. Now let's consider how a merchant—whether an online merchant or a local retailer—can accept payments in bitcoins in a practical way. Merchants who support Bitcoin payments generally do so because their customers want to be able to pay with bitcoins. Merchants may not want to hold on to bitcoins, but simply receive dollars or whatever is the local fiat currency at the end of the day. They want an easy way to do this without worrying too much about technology, changing their websites, or building some type of point-of-sale technology.

Merchants also want low risk. Various risks are possible: using new technology may cause their websites to go down, costing them money. There's the security risk of handling bitcoins—someone might break into their hot wallets, or some employee could make off with their bitcoins. Finally there's the exchange rate risk: the value of bitcoins in dollars might fluctuate from time to time. The merchant who might want to sell a pizza for $12 wants to know that she's going to get $12 or something close to it, and that the value of the bitcoins received in exchange for that pizza won't drop drastically before she can exchange those bitcoins for dollars.

Payment services exist to allow both the customer and the merchant to get what they want, bridging the gap between these different desires.

The process of receiving Bitcoin payments through a payment service might look like this to the merchant:

1. The merchant goes to a payment service website and fills out a form describing the item, price, and presentation of the payment widget, and so on. Figure 4.7 shows an example of a form from Coinbase.
2. The payment service generates HTML code that the merchant can drop into her website.
3. When the customer clicks the payment button, various things happen in the background and eventually the merchant gets a confirmation saying, "a payment was made by customer [customer-id] for item [item-id] in amount [value]."

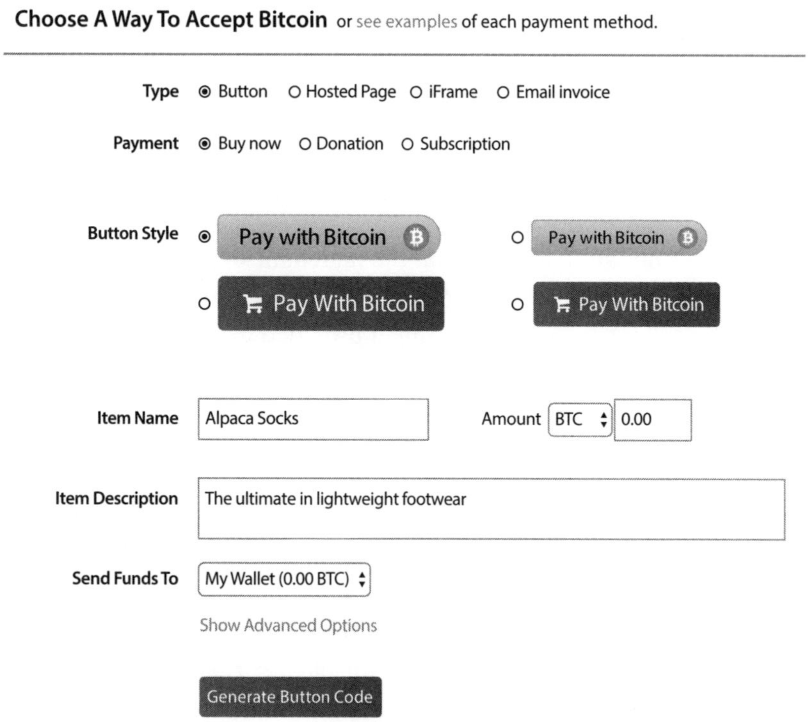

FIGURE 4.7. Example payment service interface for generating a pay-with-Bitcoin button. A merchant can use this interface to generate an HTML snippet to embed on her website.

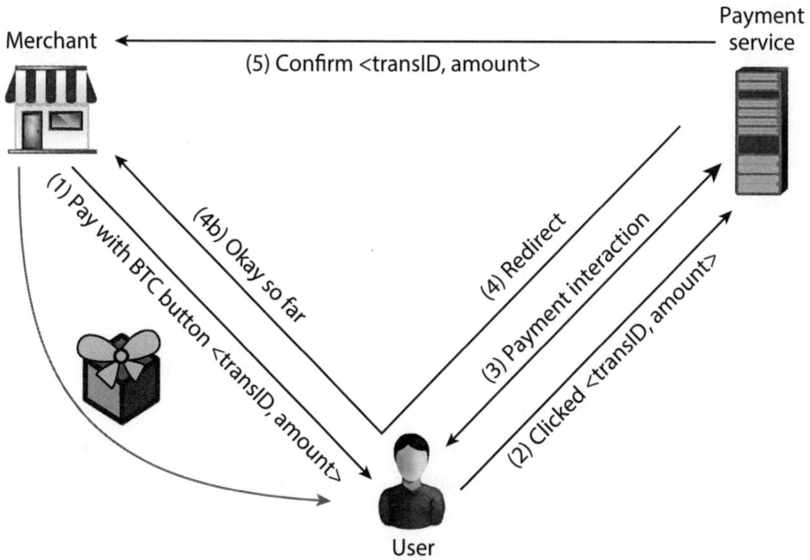

FIGURE 4.8. Payment process involving a user, merchant, and payment service.

While this manual process makes sense for a small site selling one or two items, or a site wishing to receive donations, copy-pasting HTML code for thousands of items is of course infeasible. So payment services also provide programmatic interfaces for adding a payment button to dynamically generated web pages.

Now let's look at the payment process in more detail to see what happens when the customer makes a purchase with Bitcoin (the steps below are illustrated in Figure 4.8):

1. The user picks out an item to buy on the merchant website, and when it comes time to pay, the merchant delivers a webpage that contains the "Pay with Bitcoin" button, which is the HTML snippet provided by the payment service. The page also contains a transaction ID—an identifier that's meaningful to the merchant and allows her to locate a record in her own accounting system—along with an amount the merchant wants to be paid.
2. If the user wants to pay with bitcoins, he clicks that button. That will trigger an HTTPS request to the payment service saying that the button was clicked and passing on the identity of the merchant, the merchant's transaction ID, and the amount.
3. Now the payment service knows that this customer—whoever he is—wants to pay a certain amount in bitcoins, and so the payment service pops up some kind of box or initiates some interaction with the user. This gives the user information about how to pay, and the user will then initiate a Bitcoin transfer to the payment service through his preferred wallet.
4. Once the user has created the payment, the payment service will redirect the browser to the merchant, passing on the message from the payment service that it looks okay so far. This might mean, for example, that the payment service has observed the transaction broadcast to the peer-to-peer network, but the transaction hasn't received enough (or any) confirmations so far. This completes the payment as far as the user is concerned, with the merchant's shipment of goods pending a final confirmation from the payment service.
5. The payment service later directly sends a confirmation to the merchant containing the transaction ID and amount. By doing this, the payment service tells the merchant that the service owes the merchant money at the end of the day. The merchant then ships the goods to the user.

The final step is the one where the payment service actually sends money to the merchant, in dollars or some fiat currency, via a deposit to the merchant's bank account. This happens at the end of fixed settlement periods, perhaps once a day, rather than once for each purchase. The payment service keeps a small percentage as a fee; that's how these services make their revenue. Some of these details might vary depending on the payment service, but this is the general scheme of things.

To recap, at the end of this process, the customer pays bitcoins, and the merchant gets dollars, minus a small percentage, and everyone is happy. Recall that the merchant wants to sell items for a particular number of dollars (or whatever the local fiat currency is). The payment service handles everything else—receiving bitcoins from customers and making deposits at the end of the day.

Crucially, the payment service absorbs all the risk. It absorbs the security risk, so it needs to have good security procedures to manage its bitcoins. It absorbs the exchange rate risk, because it's receiving bitcoins and paying out dollars. If the price of dollars against bitcoins fluctuates wildly, the payment service might lose money. But then if it fluctuates wildly in the other direction the service might earn money, but it's a risk. Absorbing those risks is part of the payment service's business.

Note that the payment service probably operates on a large scale, so it receives large numbers of bitcoins and pays out large numbers of dollars. It will have a constant need to exchange the bitcoins it's receiving for more dollars, so that it can keep the cycle going. Therefore, a payment service has to be an active participant in the exchange markets that link together fiat currencies and the Bitcoin economy. So the service needs to worry about not only what the exchange rate is, but also how to exchange currency in large volumes.

That said, if it can solve these problems, the fee that the service receives on every transaction makes it a potentially lucrative business, because it solves the mismatch between customers' desire to pay bitcoins and merchants' desire to obtain dollars and concentrate on selling goods.

4.6. TRANSACTION FEES

The topic of transaction fees has come up in previous chapters and will come up again in later chapters. Here we discuss the practical details of how transaction fees are set in Bitcoin today.

When a transaction is put into the Bitcoin block chain, that transaction might include a transaction fee. Recall that a transaction fee is just defined to be the difference between the total value of coins that go into a transaction minus the total value of coins that come out. The inputs always have to be at least as big as the outputs, because a regular transaction can't create coins, but if the inputs are bigger than the outputs, then the difference is deemed to be a transaction fee, and that fee goes to the miner who made the block that includes this transaction.

Why do transaction fees exist at all? The reason is that there is some cost that someone has to incur to relay your transaction. The Bitcoin nodes need to relay your transaction, and ultimately, a miner has to build your transaction into a block, and it costs them a little bit to do that. For example, if a miner's block is slightly larger because it contains your transaction, it will take slightly longer to propagate to the rest of the network, and there's a slightly higher chance that the block will be orphaned if another block was found nearly simultaneously by another miner.

So, there is a cost—both to the peer-to-peer network and to the miners—of incorporating your transaction. The idea of a transaction fee is to compensate miners for those costs they incur to process your transaction. Nodes don't receive monetary compensation in the current system, although running a node is of course far less expensive than being a miner. Generally you're free to set the transaction fee to whatever you want it to be. You can pay no fee, or you can set the fee quite high. In general, if you pay a higher transaction fee, your transaction will be relayed and recorded more quickly and reliably.

To get an idea of how miners set transaction fees, we now look at the transaction fees in the reference implementation. But we note a few caveats. First, the specifics discussed here are current as of version 0.10.0, released in 2015, and may be different in later versions. Second, the rationale behind the default policy is in large part to prevent "pollution" of the block chain by large numbers of low-value transactions. It isn't an attempt to accurately model miners' transaction-processing costs.

Of course, miners are free to deviate from the default policy. As of 2015, transaction fees account for 1 percent or less of miner revenues, so miners by and large stick with the default. But as the block reward dwindles and transaction fees start to constitute a greater proportion of miners' revenues, we can expect to see more variation in transaction-fee requirements.

The default transaction fees are as follows. No fee is charged if a transaction meets all three of these conditions:

1. the transaction is less than 1000 bytes in size,
2. all outputs are 0.01 BTC or larger, and
3. the priority is high enough.

Priority is defined as (sum of [input age · input value])/(transaction size). In other words, consider all inputs to the transaction, and for each one, compute the product of that input's age and its value in bitcoins, and add up all those products. Note that the longer a transaction output sits unspent, the more it ages, and the more it will contribute to priority when it is finally spent.

If you meet these three requirements, then your transaction will be relayed and recorded in the block chain without a fee. Otherwise a fee is charged. That fee is about 0.0001 BTC per 1,000 bytes, and as of 2015, that's a fraction of a U.S. penny per 1,000 bytes. The approximate size of a transaction is 148 bytes for each input plus 34 bytes for each output and 10 bytes for other information. So a transaction with two inputs and two outputs would be about 400 bytes.

If you make a transaction that doesn't meet the fee requirements, it will probably find its way into the block chain, but to get your transaction recorded more quickly and reliably generally requires paying the standard fee. Thus most wallet software and payment services include the standard fee structure in the payments they process, and so you'll see a bit of money raked off for transaction fees when you engage in everyday Bitcoin business.

4.7. CURRENCY EXCHANGE MARKETS

By currency exchange we mean trading bitcoins for fiat currencies like dollars and euros. In Section 4.4 we discussed currency exchange services, but here we consider them as a market—its size and extent, how it operates, and a little bit about the economics of this market.

In many ways it operates like the market between two fiat currencies, such as dollars and euros. The price will fluctuate depending on how badly people want to buy euros versus how badly people want to buy dollars on a particular day. In the Bitcoin world websites like bitcoincharts.com show the bitcoin exchange rate for various fiat currencies on different exchanges.

As you'll see if you explore the site, trading is heavy, and the prices move in real time as trades are made. It's a liquid market with plenty of sites that you can go to to buy or sell bitcoins. In March 2015 the volume on Bitfinex, the largest Bitcoin–dollar exchange, was about 70,000 BTC or about $21 million over a 24-hour period.

Another option is to meet people to trade bitcoins in real life. There are sites that help you do this. On localbitcoins.com, for example, you can specify your location and that you wish to buy bitcoins with cash. The site then lists people who at the time of your search are willing to sell bitcoins at that location, and in each case it tells you what price and how many bitcoins they're offering. You can then contact any of them and arrange to meet somewhere (e.g., at a coffee shop or in a park), give them dollars and receive bitcoins in exchange. For small transactions, it may be sufficient to wait for only one or two confirmations on the block chain before completing the exchange.

Finally, some places have regular meet-ups where people go to trade bitcoins. You can go to a certain park or street corner or café at a scheduled day and time to do business with a group of people wanting to buy or sell bitcoins. One reason someone might prefer obtaining bitcoins in person over doing so online is that it's anonymous, to the extent that a transaction in a public place can be considered anonymous. However, opening an account with an exchange generally requires providing a government-issued ID because of banking regulations. We discuss this in more detail in Chapter 7.

Supply and Demand

Like any market, the Bitcoin exchange market matches buyers who want to do one thing with sellers that are willing to do the opposite. It's a relatively large market—millions of U.S. dollars per day pass through it. It's not at the scale of the New York Stock Exchange or the dollar–euro market, which are vastly larger, but it's large enough to establish a consensus price. A person who wants to participate in this market can buy or sell at least a modest amount and will always be able to find a counterparty.

The consensus price in this market—like the price of anything in a liquid market—is set by supply and demand. By that we mean the supply of bitcoins that might potentially be sold and the demand for bitcoins by people who have dollars. Through this market mechanism, the price will be set to the level that matches supply and demand. Let's dig into this in a little more detail.

What is the supply of bitcoins? This is the number of bitcoins that you might possibly buy in one of these markets, and it is equal to the supply of bitcoins that are currently in circulation. A fixed number of bitcoins is in circulation. As of the end of 2015, it was about 15 million, and the current rules of Bitcoin state that this number will slowly go up and eventually hit a limit of 21 million.

You might also include demand deposits of bitcoins. That is, if someone has put money into their account in a Bitcoin exchange, and the exchange doesn't maintain a full reserve to meet all deposits, then there will be demand deposits at that exchange that are larger than the number of coins that the exchange is holding.

Depending on what question you're asking about the market, it might or might not be correct to include demand deposits in the supply. Basically, you should include demand deposits in a market analysis when demand-deposited money can be sold in that market. For example, if you've traded dollars for a demand deposit of bitcoins, and the exchange allows demand-deposited bitcoins to be redeemed for dollars, then they count.

It's also worth noting that when economists conventionally talk about the supply of fiat currency, they typically include in the money supply not only the currency that's in circulation—that is, paper and metal money—but also the total amount of demand deposits, for the logical reason that people can actually spend their demand-deposited money to buy things. So although it's tempting to say that the supply of bitcoins is fixed at 15 million currently or 21 million eventually, for some purposes we have to include demand deposits where those demand deposits function like money, and so the supply might not be fixed the way some Bitcoin advocates might claim. We need to look at the circumstances of the particular market we're talking about to understand what the proper definition of money supply is. But let's assume we've agreed on what supply we're using based on the market being analyzed.

Let's now look at demand. There are two main sources of demand for bitcoins: as a way of mediating fiat currency transactions and as an investment.

First we consider mediating fiat currency transactions. Imagine that Alice wants to buy something from Bob and wants to transfer a certain number of dollars to him, but they find it convenient to use Bitcoin to do this transfer. Assume here that neither Alice nor Bob is interested in holding bitcoins long term. We'll return to that possibility in a moment. So Alice would buy bitcoins for dollars and transfer them, and once they receive enough confirmations to satisfy Bob, he'll sell those bitcoins for dollars. The key point here is that the bitcoins mediating this transaction have to be taken out of circulation during the transaction. This creates a demand for bitcoins.

The second source of demand is that Bitcoin is sometimes used as an investment. That is, somebody wants to buy bitcoins and hold them in the hope that their price will go up in the future and that they'll be able to sell them at a profit. When people buy and hold, those bitcoins are taken out of circulation. When the price of Bitcoin is low, you might expect a lot of people to want to buy bitcoins as an investment, but if the price goes up very high, then the demand for bitcoins as an investment won't be as high.

A Simple Model of Market Behavior

We can do some simple economic modeling to understand how these markets behave. We won't do a full model here, although that's an interesting exercise. Let's look specifically at the transaction-mediation demand and what effect that might have on the price of bitcoins.

We start by defining some parameters. The total transaction value mediated via Bitcoin by everyone participating in the market is T. This value is measured in dollars per second. That's because we assume for simplicity that the people who want to mediate these transactions have in mind a certain dollar value of the transactions (or some other fiat currency that we'll translate into dollars). So a certain amount of dollars per second of transactions need to be mediated. The duration of time that bitcoins need to be held out of circulation to mediate a transaction is D. That's the time from when the payer buys the bitcoins to when the receiver is able to sell them back into the market, and we'll measure that in seconds. The total supply of bitcoins available for this purchase is S, which is equal to all of the hard-currency bitcoins that exist (currently about 15 million or eventually up to 21 million) minus those that are held by people as long-term investments. In other words, S is the number of bitcoins sloshing around and available for the purpose of mediating transactions. Finally, P is the price of a bitcoin, measured in dollars.

Now we can do some calculations. First we calculate how many bitcoins become available to service transactions every second. There are S bitcoins available in total, and because they're taken out of circulation for a time of D seconds, every second on average S/D of those bitcoins become newly available. They emerge from the out-of-circulation state and can be used to mediate transactions. That's the supply side.

On the demand side—the number of bitcoins per second that are needed to mediate transactions—we have T dollars worth of transactions to mediate, and to mediate 1 dollar worth of transactions, we need $1/P$ bitcoins. So T/P is the number of bitcoins per second that are needed to serve all the transactions that people want to make.

So at a particular second of time, the supply is S/D and the demand is T/P. In this market, like most markets, the price will fluctuate to bring supply into line with demand. If the supply is higher than the demand, then some bitcoins will go unsold, so people selling bitcoins will be willing to lower their asking price to sell them. And according to our formula T/P for demand, when the price drops, the demand increases, and supply and demand will reach equilibrium.

In contrast, if supply is smaller than demand, then some people want to obtain bitcoins to mediate a transaction but can't get them, because not enough bitcoins are available. Those people will then have to bid more to get their bitcoins, because there will be a lot of competition for a limited supply of bitcoins. This drives the price up, and referring to our formula again, it means that demand will come down until there is equilibrium. In equilibrium, the supply must equal the demand, so we have

$$S/D = T/P$$

which gives us a formula for the price:

$$P = TD/S$$

What does this equation tell us? We can simplify it a bit further: we can assume that D, the duration for which you need to hold a bitcoin to mediate a transaction, doesn't change. The total supply S also doesn't change, or at least it changes only slowly over time. That means the price is proportional to the demand for mediation as measured in dollars. So if the demand for mediation in dollars doubles, then the price of bitcoins should also double. We could in fact graph the price against some estimate of the demand for transaction mediation and see whether they match up. When economists do this comparison, the two do tend to match up pretty well.

Notice that the total supply S includes only the bitcoins that aren't being held as investments. So if more people are buying bitcoins as an investment, S will go down, and our formula tells us that P will go up. This makes sense—if there's more demand on the investment side, then the price that you need to pay to mediate a transaction will go up.

Now this is not a full model of the market. To have a full model, we need to take into account the activity of investors. That is, investors will demand bitcoins when they believe the price will be higher in the future, and so we need to think about investors' expectations. These expectations, of course, have something to do with the expected demand in the future. We could build a more complex model that accounts for these expectations, but we won't do that here.

The bottom line is that there is a market between bitcoins and dollars, and between bitcoins and other fiat currencies. That market has enough liquidity that you can buy or sell in modest quantities in a reliable way, although prices do fluctuate. Finally, it's possible to create an economic model to develop some idea about how supply and demand interact in this market and predict what the market might do, as long as you have a way to estimate unknowables, such as how much are people going to want to use Bitcoin to mediate transactions in the future. That kind of economic modeling is important to do and very informative, and surely there are people who are doing it in some detail today, but a detailed economic model of this market is beyond the scope of this text.

FURTHER READING

Securing bitcoins has some similarities, as well as important differences, to the way banks secure money. Chapter 10 of Ross Anderson's security textbook, titled "Banking and Bookkeeping," is a great read. The entire book is freely available online:

Anderson, Ross. *Security Engineering*. Hoboken, NJ: John Wiley & Sons, 2008.

The study analyzing closures of Bitcoin exchanges that we referenced is:
Moore, Tyler, and Nicolas Christin. "Beware the Middleman: Empirical Analysis of Bitcoin-Exchange Risk." In *Financial Cryptography and Data Security*. Heidelberg: Springer 2013.

Adi Shamir's paper on secret sharing:
Shamir, Adi. "How to Share a Secret." *Communications of the ACM* 22(11), 1979.

A paper describing Provisions, a protocol for privacy-preserving solvency proofs, is:
Dagher, Gaby, Benedikt Bünz, Joseph Bonneau, Jeremy Clark, and Dan Boneh. "Provisions: Privacy-Preserving Proofs of Solvency for Bitcoin Exchanges." In *Proceedings of the ACM Conference on Computer and Communications Security*. New York: ACM Press, 2015.

It's difficult for users to pick memorable yet hard-to-guess passwords, because modern password-cracking techniques are quite clever and effective. This paper presents one such technique:
Weir, Matt, Sudhir Aggarwal, Breno De Medeiros, and Bill Glodek. "Password Cracking Using Probabilistic Context-Free Grammars." Presented at the 2009 IEEE Symposium on Security and Privacy, Oakland, CA, 2009.

A survey of transaction fees in practice through 2014 is given in:
Möser, Malte, and Rainer Böhme. "Trends, Tips, Tolls: A Longitudinal Study of Bitcoin Transaction Fees." Presented at the Second Workshop on Bitcoin Research, Puerto Rico, 2015.

CHAPTER 5
Bitcoin Mining

This chapter is all about mining. As already discussed, Bitcoin relies on miners—they validate every transaction, build and store all the blocks, and reach consensus on which blocks to include in the block chain. We also have already seen that miners earn rewards for doing this. But many interesting questions remain unanswered. Who are the miners? How did they get into this? How do they operate? What's the business model for miners? What impact do they have on the environment? In this chapter, we answer all these questions.

5.1. THE TASK OF BITCOIN MINERS

Do you want to get into Bitcoin mining? If you do, we're not going to completely discourage you, but beware that Bitcoin mining bears many similarities to gold rushes. Historical gold rushes are full of stories of young people rushing off to find fortune, and inevitably many of them lose everything they have. A few strike it rich, but even those who do generally endure hardship along the way. We'll see in this section why Bitcoin mining shares many of the same challenges and risks as traditional gold rushes and other get-rich-quick schemes.

But first, let's look at the technical details. To be a Bitcoin miner, you have to join the Bitcoin network and connect to other nodes. Once you're connected, there are six tasks to perform:

1. *Listen for transactions.* You listen for transactions on the network and validate them by checking that signatures are correct and that the outputs being spent haven't already been spent.
2. *Maintain block chain and listen for new blocks.* You must maintain the block chain. You start by asking other nodes to give you all the historical blocks that are already part of the block chain before you joined the network. You then listen for new blocks that are being broadcast to the network. You must validate each block that you receive—by validating each transaction in the block and checking that the block contains a valid nonce. We return to the details of nonce checking later in this section.

3. *Assemble a candidate block.* Once you have an up-to-date copy of the block chain, you can begin building your own blocks. To do this, you group transactions that you have heard about into a new block that extends the latest block you know about. You must make sure that each transaction included in your block is valid.
4. *Find a nonce that makes your block valid.* This step requires the most work, and it poses all the real difficulties for miners. We discuss this step in detail shortly.
5. *Hope your block is accepted.* Even if you find a block, there's no guarantee that your block will become part of the consensus chain. There's a bit of luck here; you have to hope that other miners accept your block and start mining on top of it instead of some competitor's block.
6. *Profit.* If all other miners do accept your block, then you profit! In 2015, the block reward is 25 bitcoins, which is currently worth about $10,000. In addition, if any of the transactions in the block contained transaction fees, the miner collects those, too. So far transaction fees have been a modest source of additional income, only about 1 percent of block rewards.

We can classify the steps that a miner must take into two categories. Some tasks—validating transactions and blocks—help the Bitcoin network and are fundamental to its existence. These tasks are the reason that the Bitcoin protocol requires miners in the first place. Other tasks—the race to find blocks and profit—aren't necessary for the Bitcoin network itself but are intended to incentivize miners to perform the essential steps. Of course, both of these are necessary for Bitcoin to function as a currency, since miners need an incentive to perform the critical steps.

Finding a Valid Block

Let's return to the question of finding a nonce that makes your block valid. In Chapter 3 we saw that there are two main hash-based structures: the block chain (where each block header points to the previous block header in the chain) and a Merkle tree within each block of all transactions included in that block.

The first thing you do as a miner is to compile a set of valid transactions that you have from your pending transaction pool into a Merkle tree. Of course, you may choose how many transactions to include up to the limit on the total size of the block. You then create a block with a header that points to the previous block. The block header includes a 32-bit nonce field, and you keep trying different nonces, looking for one that causes the block's hash to be under the target—roughly speaking, to begin with the required number of zeros. As a miner, you might begin with a nonce of 0 and successively increment it by one in search of a nonce that makes the block valid (Figure 5.1).

In most cases you'll try every single possible 32-bit value for the nonce, and none of them will produce a valid hash. At this point you're going to have to make further changes. Notice in Figure 5.1 that there's an additional field in the coinbase transaction

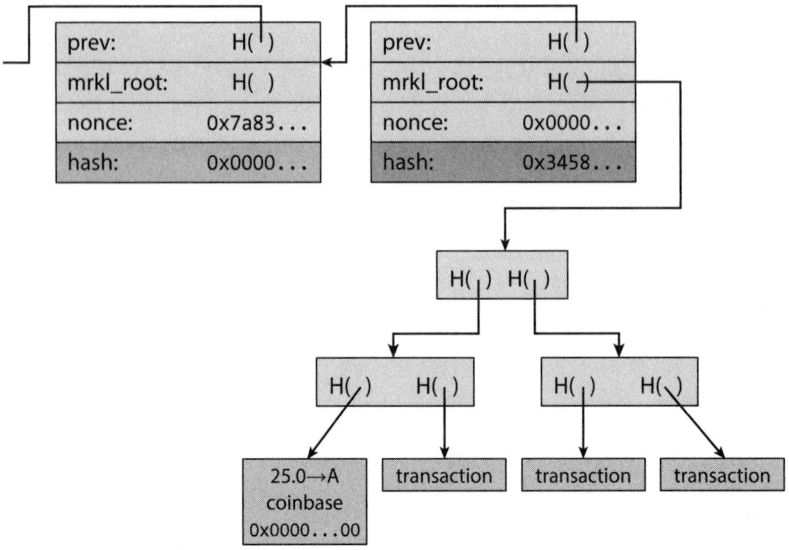

FIGURE 5.1. Finding a valid block. In this example, the miner tries a nonce of all 0s. It does not produce a valid hash output, so the miner would then proceed to try a different nonce.

that you can use a an extra nonce as well. After you've exhausted all possible nonces for the block header, you'll change the extra nonce in the coinbase transaction—say, by incrementing it by one—and then you'll start searching nonces in the block header once again.

When you change the nonce in the coinbase transaction, the entire Merkle tree of transactions has to change (Figure 5.2). Since the change of the coinbase nonce will propagate all the way up the tree, changing the extra nonce in the coinbase transaction is a much more expensive operation than changing the nonce in the block header. For this reason, miners spend most of their time changing the nonce in the block header and only change the coinbase nonce when they have exhausted all 2^{32} possible nonces in the block header without finding a valid block.

Nearly all nonces that you try aren't going to work, but if you stay at it long enough, you'll eventually find the right combination of the extra nonce in the coinbase transaction and the nonce in the block header that produce a block with a hash under the target. When you find it, you want to announce it as quickly as you can and hope that you can profit from it.

Exactly how difficult is it to find a valid block? As of the end of 2015, the mining difficulty target (in hexadecimal) is:

0000000000000000a95500000000000000000000000000000000000000000000

so the hash of any valid block has to be below this value. In other words, less than 1 in about 2^{68} nonces that you try will work, which is a really huge number. One approxima-

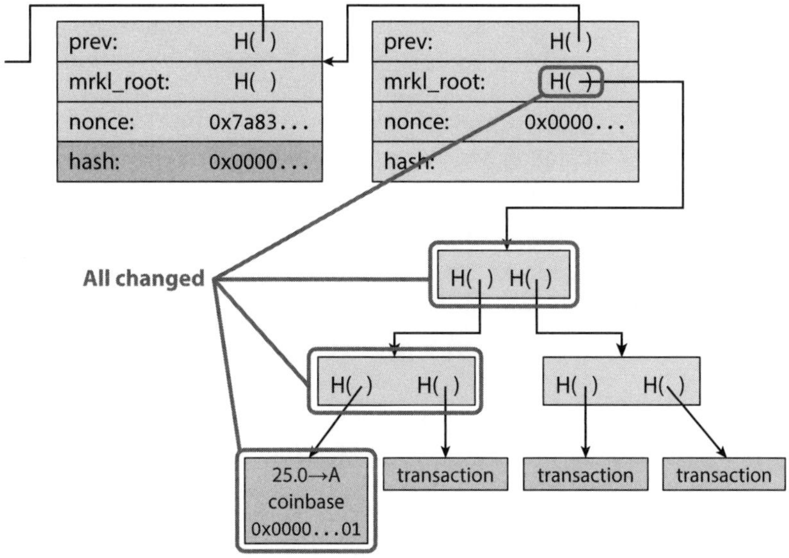

FIGURE 5.2. Changing a nonce. Changing a nonce in the coinbase transaction propagates all the way up the Merkle tree.

Is Everyone Solving the Same Puzzle?

You may be wondering: If every miner just increments the nonces as described, aren't all miners solving the same puzzle? Won't the fastest miner always win? The answer is no! First, it's unlikely that miners will be working on identical blocks, as each miner will likely include a somewhat different set of transactions and in a different order. But more importantly, even if two different miners were working on a block with identical transactions, the blocks would still differ. Recall that in the coinbase transaction, miners specify their own address as the owner of the newly minted coins. This address by itself will cause changes that propagate up to the root of the Merkle tree, ensuring that no two miners are working on exactly the same puzzle unless they share a public key. This would only happen if the two miners are part of the same mining pool (which we'll discuss shortly), in which case they'll communicate to ensure they include a distinct nonce in the coinbase transaction to avoid duplicating work.

tion is that it's greater than the human population of Earth squared. So, if every person on Earth was their own planet Earth with 7 billion people on it, the total number of people would be about 2^{65}.

Determining the Difficulty

The mining difficulty changes every 2,016 blocks, which are found about once every 2 weeks. It is adjusted based on how efficient the miners were over the period of the previous 2,016 blocks according to this formula:

$$\text{next difficulty} = (\text{previous difficulty} \cdot 2016 \cdot 10 \text{ minutes})/(\text{time to mine last 2016 blocks})$$

Note that 2,016 · 10 minutes is exactly 2 weeks, so 2,016 blocks would take 2 weeks to mine if a block were created exactly every 10 minutes. So the effect of this formula is to scale the difficulty to maintain the property that blocks should be found by the network on average about once every 10 minutes. There's nothing special about 2 weeks, but it's a good trade-off. If the period were much shorter, the difficulty might fluctuate due to random variations in the number of blocks found in each period. If the period were much longer, the network's hash power might get too far out of balance with the difficulty.

Each Bitcoin miner independently computes the difficulty and will only accept blocks that meet the difficulty that they computed. Miners who are on different branches might not compute the same difficulty value, but any two miners mining on top of the same block will agree on what the difficulty should be. This allows consensus to be reached.

You can see in Figure 5.3 that over time the mining difficulty keeps increasing. It's not necessarily a steady linear increase or an exponential increase, but it depends on activity in the market. Mining difficulty is affected by such factors as how many new miners are joining, which in turn may be affected by the current exchange rate of Bitcoin. Generally, as more miners come online and mining hardware gets more efficient, blocks are found faster and the difficulty is increased, so that it always takes about ten minutes to find a block.

In Figure 5.3 the difficulty is a step function, even though the overall network hash rate is growing smoothly. The discrete step results from the fact that the difficulty is only adjusted every 2,016 blocks.

Another way to view the network's growth rate is to consider how long it takes to find a block on average. Figure 5.4a shows how many seconds elapse between consecutive blocks in the block chain. You can see that this gradually goes down, jumps up, and then gradually goes down again. Of course what's happening is that every 2,016 blocks, the difficulty resets and the average block time goes back up to about 10 minutes. Over the next period, the difficulty stays unchanged, but more and more miners come online. Since the hash power has increased but the difficulty has not, blocks are found more quickly until the difficulty is again adjusted after 2,016 blocks, or about 2 weeks.

Even though the goal was for a block to be found every 10 minutes on average, for most of 2013 and 2014, it was closer to about 9 minutes on average and would approach 8 minutes at the end of each 2-week cycle. Quick calculations show that this requires an astonishing 25 percent growth rate every 2 weeks, or several hundredfold per year.

Unsurprisingly, this rate is not sustainable, and in 2015 the growth rate has been much slower (and occasionally negative). In Figure 5.4b, we can see that as the mining

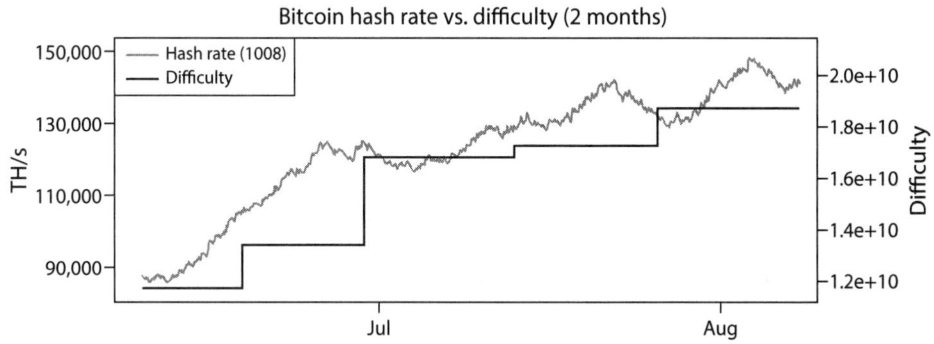

FIGURE 5.3. Mining difficulty over time (mid-2014). Note that the *y*-axis begins at 80,000 terahashes/s. The hash rate is averaged over 1,008 blocks. Source: bitcoinwisdom.com.

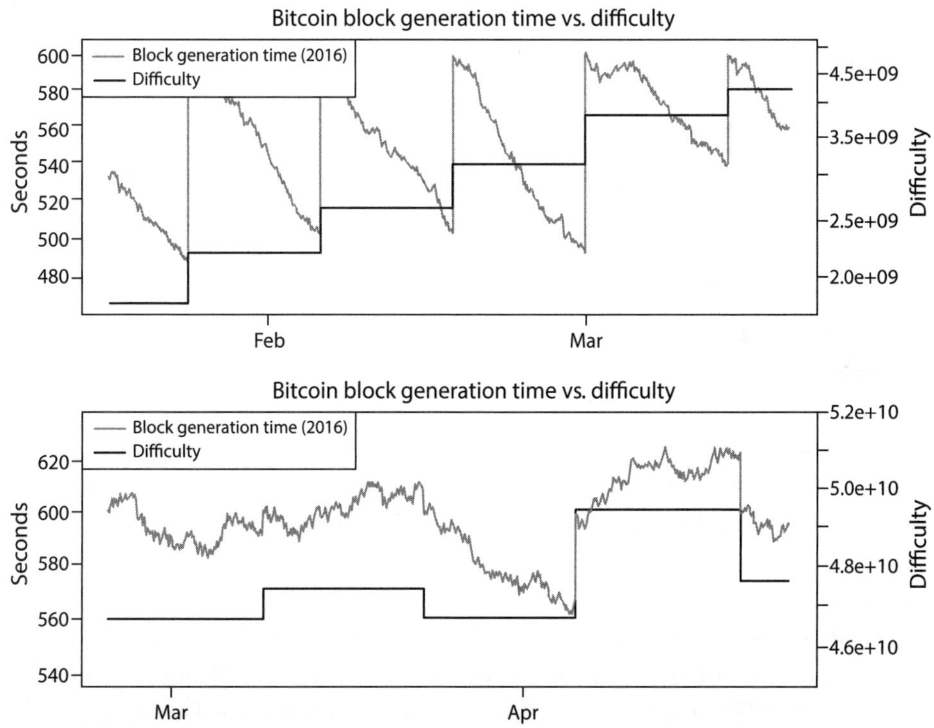

FIGURE 5.4 Time to find a block. (A) Early 2014. Note that the *y*-axis begins at 460 seconds. The block generation time is averaged over 2,016 blocks. Due to continued rapid growth in mining power during this time, the time to find a block decreased steadily within each 2-week window. (B) Early 2015. Note that the *y*-axis begins at 540 seconds. The block generation time is averaged over 2,016 blocks. As the growth of the network has slowed, the time to find each block is much closer to 10 minutes and is occasionally more than that during periods where the network's hash power actually shrinks. Source: bitcoinwisdom.com.

power is closer to a steady state, the period to find each block stays much closer to 10 minutes. It can even take longer than 10 minutes, in which case there will be a difficulty decrease. Once considered unthinkable, this has happened fairly regularly in 2015.

Although no catastrophic declines of the network's mining power have occurred so far, there's no inherent reason that cannot happen. One proposed scenario for Bitcoin's collapse is a "death spiral," in which a dropping exchange rate makes mining unprofitable for some miners, causing an exodus, in turn causing the price to drop further.

5.2. MINING HARDWARE

We've mentioned that the computation that miners have to do is difficult. In this section, we discuss why it is so computationally difficult and take a look at the hardware that miners use to perform this computation.

The core of the difficult computation miners are working on is the SHA-256 hash function. We discussed hash functions abstractly in Chapter 1. SHA-256 is a general-purpose cryptographic hash function that's part of a bigger family of functions that was standardized in 2001 (SHA stands for Secure Hash Algorithm). SHA-256 was a reasonable choice, as this was the strongest cryptographic hash function available when Bitcoin was designed. It is possible that it will become less secure over the lifetime of Bitcoin, but for now it remains secure. Its design did come from the U.S. National Security Agency, which has led to some conspiracy theories, but it's generally believed to be a very strong hash function.

A Closer Look at SHA-256

Figure 5.5 shows more detail about what actually goes on in a SHA-256 computation. We don't need to know all the details to understand how Bitcoin works, but it's good to have a general idea of the task that miners are solving.

The SHA Family

The "256" in SHA-256 comes from its 256-bit state and output. Technically, SHA-256 is one of several closely related functions in the SHA-2 family, including SHA-512 (which has a larger state and is considered more secure). There is also SHA-1, an earlier generation with 160-bit output, which is now considered insecure but is still implemented in Bitcoin script.

Although the SHA-2 family, including SHA-256, is still considered to be cryptographically secure, the next generation SHA-3 family has now been picked by an open competition held by the U.S. National Institute of Standards and Technology. SHA-3 is in the final stages of standardization today, but it wasn't available at the time Bitcoin was designed.

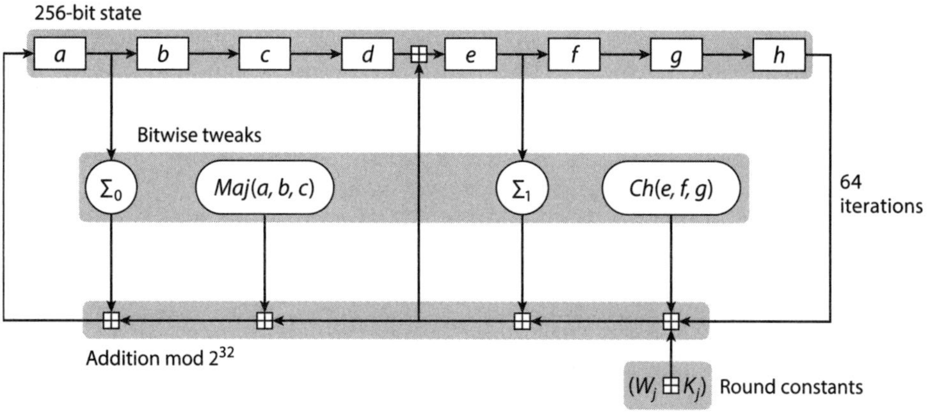

FIGURE 5.5. Structure of SHA-256. This is one round of the compression function. *Maj* is the majority function, applied bitwise. *Ch*, also applied bitwise, chooses its second or third input depending on the value of its first input. Σ_0 and Σ_1 manipulate their 32-bit word inputs via bitwise rotation (i.e., circular shift) and $\oplus$ operations.

SHA-256 maintains 256 bits of state. The state is split into eight 32-bit words, which makes it highly optimized for 32-bit hardware. In each round a number of words in the state are taken—some with small bitwise tweaks applied—and added together mod 32. The entire state is then right shifted, with the result of the addition becoming the new leftmost word of the state. The design is loosely inspired by simpler bitwise Linear Feedback Shift Registers.

Figure 5.5 shows just one round of the SHA-256 compression function. A complete computation of SHA-256 does this for 64 iterations. During each round, slightly different constants are applied, so that no two iterations are exactly the same.

The task for miners is to compute this function as quickly as possible. Remember that miners are racing against one another so the faster they can do this, the more they will earn. To do this, they need to be able to manipulate 32-bit words, perform 32-bit modular addition, and also do some bitwise logic.

As we will see shortly, Bitcoin actually requires SHA-256 to be applied twice to a block to get the hash used by the nodes. This is a quirk of Bitcoin. The reasons for the double computation are not fully specified, but at this point, it's just something that miners have to deal with.

CPU Mining

The first generation of mining was all done on general-purpose computers—that is, general-purpose central processing units (CPUs). In fact, CPU mining was as simple as running the code shown in Figure 5.6. That is, miners simply searched over nonces in a

```
TARGET = (65535 << 208) / DIFFICULTY;
coinbase_nonce = 0;
while (1) {
     header = makeBlockHeader(transactions, coinbase_nonce);
     for (header_nonce = 0; header_nonce < (1 << 32); header_nonce++){
          if (SHA256(SHA256(makeBlock(header, header_nonce))) < TARGET)
               break; //block found!
     }
     coinbase_nonce++;
}
```

FIGURE 5.6. CPU mining pseudocode.

linear fashion, computed SHA-256 in software, and checked whether the result was a valid block. Also, notice in the code that, as we mentioned, SHA-256 is applied twice.

How fast will this run on a general-purpose computer? On a high-end desktop, you might expect to compute about 20 million hashes per second. At that speed, it would take you several hundred thousand years on average at the early-2015 difficulty level (2^{67}) to find a valid block. We weren't kidding when we said mining was going to be a difficult slog!

If you're mining on a general-purpose desktop today, CPU mining is no longer profitable at the current level of difficulty. For the past few years, anyone trying to mine on a CPU probably doesn't understand how Bitcoin works and was likely pretty disappointed that they never made any money doing it.

GPU Mining

The second generation began when people started to get frustrated with how slow their CPUs were and instead used their graphics cards, or *graphics processing units* (GPUs).

Almost every modern desktop has a GPU built in to support high-performance graphics. They're designed to have high throughput and also high parallelism, both of which are useful for Bitcoin mining. Bitcoin mining can be parallelized easily, because you can try computing multiple hashes at the same time with different nonces. In 2010, the language OpenCL was released. OpenCL is a general-purpose language to do things other than graphics on a GPU. It's a high-level language, and over time people have used it to run many types of computation more quickly on graphics cards than can be done on CPUs. This paved the way for Bitcoin mining on GPUs.

Mining with GPUs had several attractive properties at the time. For one thing, they're easily available and easy for amateurs to set up. You can order graphics cards online or buy them at most big consumer electronics stores. They're the most accessible high-end hardware that's available to the general public. They also have some properties that make them specifically good for Bitcoin mining. They're designed for parallelism, so they have many arithmetic logic units that can be used for simultaneous SHA-256 computations. Some GPUs also have specific instructions to do bitwise operations that are quite useful for SHA-256.

Most GPUs can also be *overclocked*, meaning you can run them faster than they're actually designed for if you want to take on the risk that they might overheat or malfunction. This is a property gamers have demanded for years. With Bitcoin mining, it might be profitable to run the chip much faster than it was designed for, even if you induce a few errors by doing so.

For example, say you can run your GPU 50 percent faster, but doing so will cause errors in the SHA-256 computation up to 30 percent of the time. If an invalid solution is erroneously declared valid by the GPU—something that would happen rarely—you can always double check it on your CPU. However, if a valid solution is erroneously overlooked, you'd never know. But if your speed increase from overclocking can overcome the decrease in output due to errors, you'd still come out ahead. In the above example, the throughput is $1.5\times$ compared to not overclocking, whereas the success rate is $0.7\times$. The product is 1.05, which means overclocking increases your expected profits by 5 percent. People have spent considerable time optimizing exactly how much they should overclock a given chip to maximize profits.

Finally, you can drive many GPUs from one motherboard and CPU. So you can attach multiple graphics cards to the computer that runs your Bitcoin node—which gathers transactions from the network and assembles blocks—and use the GPUs to try to find the right nonces to make the SHA-256 of the block valid. Many people created some really interesting home-brewed setups like the one shown in Figure 5.7 to drive numerous GPUs from a single CPU. This was still in the early days of Bitcoin, when miners were still mostly hobbyists without much experience running servers, but they came up with some quite ingenious designs for how to pack many graphics cards into a small place and keep them cool enough to operate.

Disadvantages of GPU Mining

GPU mining has some disadvantages. GPUs have a lot of hardware built into them for doing video processing that can't be used for mining. Specifically, they have a large number of floating point units that aren't used at all in SHA-256. GPUs also don't have

> *Miners versus Gamers*
>
> According to folklore, by 2011 Bitcoin miners were purchasing enough GPUs to upset the normal market for these units. This caused friction with gamers, who found it increasingly difficult to obtain certain popular GPUs in local electronics stores. Interestingly, however, it may have increased interest in Bitcoin mining. Many of these frustrated gamers learned about the currency when investigating where all the GPUs were going, and as a result, some gamers became miners themselves!

FIGURE 5.7. Home-built rack of GPUs used for Bitcoin mining. Source: István Finta, bitcointalk.org.

the optimal thermal characteristics: when you stack them, they can overheat. They're not designed to run side by side, as configured in Figure 5.7; they're designed to be in a single box doing graphics for one computer.

GPUs can also consume a fairly large amount of power, so a lot of electricity is used relative to an ordinary computer. Another disadvantage initially was that you had to either build your own board or buy expensive boards to house multiple graphics cards.

On a really high-end GPU with aggressive tuning, you might get as high as 200 million hashes per second, an order of magnitude better than you would be doing with a CPU. But even with that improved performance, and even if you're really enterprising and ganged 100 GPUs, it would still take you hundreds of years on average to find a block at the 2015 difficulty level. As a result, GPU mining is basically dead for Bitcoin today, though it still shows up sometimes in early-stage altcoins.

Mining with Field-Programmable Gate Arrays

Around 2011, some miners started switching from GPUs to *field programmable gate arrays* (FPGAs), after the first implementation of Bitcoin mining came out in Verilog, a hardware design language used to program FPGAs. The general rationale behind FPGAs

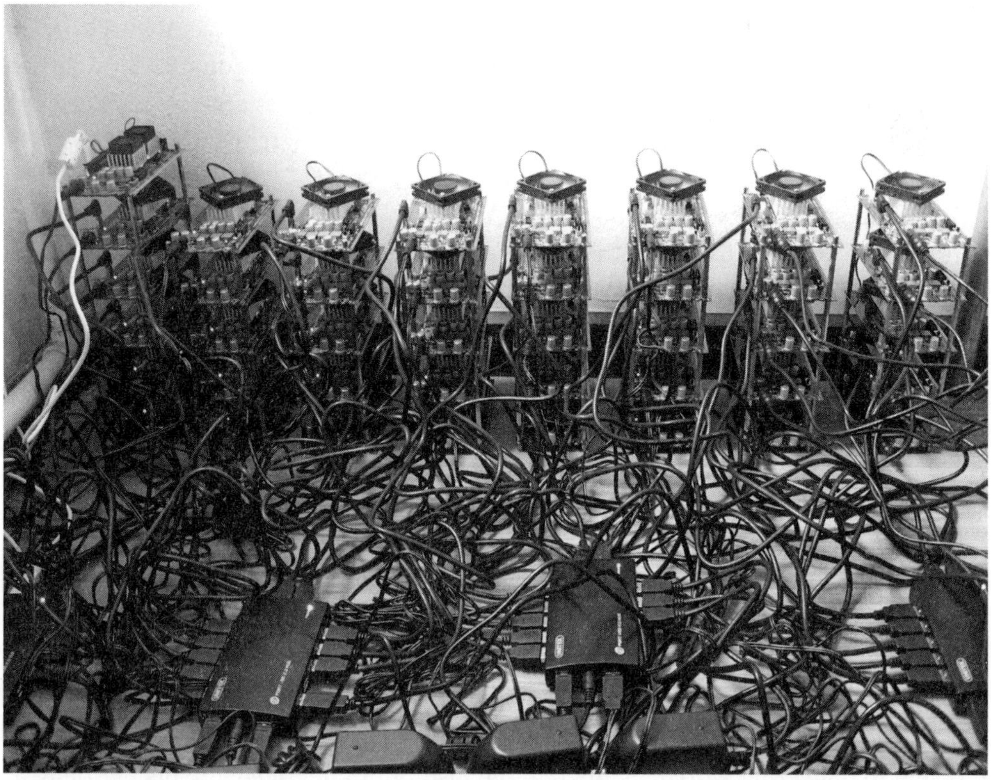

FIGURE 5.8. Home-built rack of FPGAs. Courtesy of Xiangfu Liu, www.openmobilefree.net.

is to try to approximate the performance of custom hardware while also allowing the owner of the card to customize it or reconfigure it "in the field." In contrast, custom hardware chips are designed in a factory and do the same thing forever.

FPGAs offer better performance than GPUs, particularly on "bit fiddling" operations, which are trivial to specify on an FPGA. Cooling is also easier with FPGAs, and, unlike GPUs, you can theoretically use nearly all of the transistors on the card for mining. As with GPUs, you can pack many FPGAs together and drive them from one central unit, which is exactly what people began to do (Figure 5.8). Overall, it is possible to build a big array of FPGAs more neatly than you can with graphics cards.

Using an FPGA with a careful implementation, you might get up to 1 gigahash per second, or 1 billion hashes per second. This is certainly a large performance gain over CPUs and GPUs, but even if you ganged 100 boards, each with a 1 gigahash-per-second throughput, it would still take you about a hundred years on average to find a Bitcoin block at the 2015 difficulty level.

Despite the performance gain, the days of FPGA mining were quite limited for several reasons. They were being driven harder for Bitcoin mining—by being on all the time and being overclocked—than consumer grade FPGAs were designed for.

Because of this, many people experienced errors and malfunctions in their FPGAs as they were mining. It also turned out to be difficult to optimize the 32-bit addition step, which is critical when doing SHA-256. FPGAs are also less accessible—you can't buy them at most stores, and fewer people know how to program and set up an FPGA than a GPU.

Most importantly, even though FPGAs improved performance, the cost-per-performance was only marginally improved over GPUs. This made FPGA mining a rather short-lived phenomenon. Whereas GPU mining dominated for about a year or so, the days of FPGA mining were far more limited—lasting only a few months before customized chips arrived.

Mining with Application-Specific Integrated Circuits

Mining today is dominated by Bitcoin *application-specific integrated circuits* (ASICs). These are chips that were designed, built, and optimized for the sole purpose of mining bitcoins. A few big vendors sell these to consumers with a good deal of variety: you can choose between slightly bigger and more expensive models, more compact models, as well as models with varying performance and energy-consumption specifications.

Designing ASICs requires considerable expertise, and their lead time is also quite long. Nevertheless, Bitcoin ASICs were designed and produced surprisingly quickly. In fact, analysts have said that this may be the fastest turnaround time—from specifying a problem to delivering working chips—in the history of integrated circuits. Partially as a result of this, the first few generations of Bitcoin ASICs were quite buggy, and most of them didn't quite deliver the promised performance numbers. Bitcoin ASICs have since matured, and fairly reliable ASICs are now available.

Until 2014, the lifetime of ASICs was quite short, due to the rapidly increasing network hash rate, with most boards in the early ASIC era becoming obsolete in about 6 months. During this time, the bulk of the profits were made up front. Often miners made half of the expected profits for the lifetime of the ASIC during just the first 6 weeks of using the chips. This meant shipping speed became a crucial factor in making a profit. Due to the immaturity of the industry, consumers often experienced shipping delays, with boards nearly obsolete by the time they arrived. Because the growth rate of Bitcoin's hash power has stabilized, mining equipment now has a longer lifetime, but the early era saw many frustrated customers accusing chip vendors of fraud.

For much of Bitcoin's history, the economics of mining haven't been favorable to the small miner who wants to go online, order mining equipment, and start making money. In most cases, people who placed orders for mining hardware should have lost money based on the rapid increase in mining difficulty. However, until 2013 the exchange rate of Bitcoin rose enough to prevent most miners from losing money outright. In effect, mining has been an expensive way to bet that the price of Bitcoin would rise, and many miners—even though they've made money mining bitcoins—would have been better off if they had just taken the money that they were going to spend on mining equipment, invested it in bitcoins, and eventually sold them at a profit.

You can still order Bitcoin mining equipment today and we don't want to discourage that as a way to learn about Bitcoin and cryptocurrencies. However, mining is not an advisable way to make money. Most ASICs sold commercially today are unlikely to pay for themselves in mining rewards once you factor in the price of electricity and cooling.

Professional Mining Today

Today mining has mostly moved away from individuals and toward professional mining centers. Exact details about how these centers operate are not well known, because companies protect their setups to maintain a competitive advantage. Presumably, these operations maintain profitability by buying at a bulk discount slightly newer and more efficient ASICs than are available for sale to most individuals. Figure 5.9, shows a professional mining center in the Republic of Georgia.

When determining where to set up a mining center, the three biggest considerations are climate, cost of electricity, and network speed. In particular, you want a cold climate to keep cooling costs low. Cooling is particularly challenging with Bitcoin mining, which is estimated to use an order of magnitude more electricity per square foot than traditional data centers (and hence give off an order of magnitude more heat). You obviously want cheap electricity. You also want a fast network connection to be well connected to other nodes in the Bitcoin peer-to-peer network, so that you can hear about new blocks as quickly as possible after they've been announced. Georgia and Iceland have reportedly been popular destinations for Bitcoin mining data centers.

FIGURE 5.9. BitFury mining center, a professional mining center in the Republic of Georgia. Image © Marco Krohn.

Similarities to Gold Mining

While Bitcoin "mining" may seem to be just a cute name, if we consider the evolution of mining, we can see interesting parallels between Bitcoin mining and gold mining. For starters, both saw a similar gold rush mentality with many young, amateur individuals eager to get into the business as soon as possible.

Bitcoin mining evolved from using CPUs, to GPUs, to FPGAs, and now to ASICs. Gold mining evolved from individuals with gold pans; to small groups of people with sluice boxes; to placer mining (consisting of large mining groups blasting away hillsides with water); to modern gold mining, which often uses gigantic open pit mines to extract tons of raw material from the earth (Figure 5.10). For Bitcoin and gold mining, the friendliness toward and accessibility by individuals has gone down over time, and large companies have consolidated most of the operations (and profits). Another pattern that has emerged in both endeavors is that most of the profits have been earned by those selling equipment, whether gold pans or mining ASICs, at the expense of individuals hoping to strike it rich.

The Future

Currently ASIC mining is the only realistic means to be profitable in Bitcoin, and it's not very friendly to small miners. This raises a few questions about what will happen going forward. Are small miners out of Bitcoin mining forever, or is there a way to reincorporate them? Does ASIC mining and the development of professional mining centers violate the original vision of Bitcoin, which was to have a completely decentralized system in which every individual in the network mined on their own computer?

FIGURE 5.10. Evolution of mining. A clear parallel exists between the evolution of Bitcoin mining and that of gold mining. Both were initially friendly to individuals but over time became massive operations controlled by large companies. Pit mining photo © Calistemon.

If this is indeed a violation of Satoshi Nakamoto's original vision for Bitcoin, would we be better off with a system in which the only way to mine is with CPUs? In Chapter 8, we consider these questions and look at ideas for alternative forms that might be less friendly to ASICs.

The Cycle Repeats Itself

It's worth noting that several smaller altcoins have indeed used a different puzzle than SHA-256, but have experienced a trajectory in mining that is similar to Bitcoin's. We discuss these altcoins in more detail in Chapters 8 and 10, but recall that for ASICs, there is still a long lead time between designing a chip and shipping it, so if a new altcoin uses a new puzzle (even if only a modified version of SHA-256), this will buy some time in which ASICs are not yet available. Typically, mining will proceed just as Bitcoin did: from CPUs to GPUs and/or FPGAs to ASICs (if the altcoin is very successful, e.g., LiteCoin).

Thus, one strategy for smaller miners may be to try to pioneer new altcoins that aren't yet valuable enough for large mining groups to invest in—just like small gold miners who have been driven out of proven goldfields might try prospecting unproven new areas. Of course, such pioneers would face a significant risk that the novel altcoin will never succeed.

5.3. ENERGY CONSUMPTION AND ECOLOGY

We saw how large professional mining data centers have taken over the business of Bitcoin mining, and how this parallels the movement to pit mining in gold mining. You may be aware that pit mines have been a major source of concern over the years due to the damage they cause to the environment. Bitcoin is not quite at that level yet, but it is starting to use a significant amount of energy, which has become a topic of discussion. In this section we discuss how much energy Bitcoin mining is using and what the implications are for both the currency and our planet.

Thermodynamic Limits

A physical law known as *Landauer's principle* and developed by Ralph Landauer in the 1960s states that any irreversible computation must use a minimum amount of energy. Logically, irreversible computations can be thought of as those that lose information. Specifically, the principle states that erasing any bit must consume a minimum of $kT \ln 2$ joules, where k is the Boltzmann constant (approximately 1.38×10^{-23} joules per kelvin), T is the temperature of the circuit in kelvins, and $\ln 2$ is the natural logarithm of 2, roughly 0.69. This is a tiny amount of energy per bit, but it does provide a hard lower bound on energy usage from basic physics.

We won't go through the derivation here, but the concept is that every time you flip one bit in an irreversible way, a minimum number of joules has to be used. Energy is never destroyed; it's converted from one form to another. In the case of computation, the energy is mostly transformed from electricity, which is useful, high-grade energy, into heat, which dissipates in the environment.

As a cryptographic hash function, SHA-256 is not a reversible computation. Recall from Chapter 1 that this is a basic requirement of cryptographic hash functions. So, since irreversible computation has to use some energy, and SHA-256—the basis of Bitcoin mining—is not reversible, energy consumption is an inevitable result of Bitcoin mining. That said, the limits placed by Landauer's principle are far below the amount of electricity that is being used today. We're nowhere close to the theoretical optimal consumption of computing, but even if we did reach the theoretical optimum, we would still be using energy to perform Bitcoin mining.

How does Bitcoin mining use energy? Three steps in the process require energy, some of which may not be so obvious:

1. *Embodied energy.* Bitcoin mining equipment needs to be manufactured. This requires physical mining of raw materials as well as turning these raw materials into a Bitcoin mining ASIC, both of which require energy. This is the embodied energy. As soon as you receive a Bitcoin mining ASIC in the mail, you've already consumed a lot of energy—including the shipping energy, of course—before you've even powered it on!

   Hopefully, over time the embodied energy will go down as less and less new capacity comes online. As fewer people are buying new mining ASICs, the equipment will become obsolete less quickly, and the embodied energy will be amortized over years of mining.
2. *Electricity.* When your ASIC is powered on and mining, it consumes electricity. This is the step that we know has to consume energy due to Landauer's principle. As mining rigs become more efficient, the electrical energy costs will go down. But because of Landauer's principle, we know that they will never disappear; electrical energy consumption will be a fact of life for Bitcoin miners forever.
3. *Cooling.* Bitcoin mining equipment needs to be cooled to prevent it from malfunctioning. If you're operating at a small scale in a cold climate, your cooling costs might be trivial. But even in cold climates, once enough ASICs are packed in a small space, you're going to have to pay extra to cool off your equipment from all the waste heat that it is generating. Generally, the energy used to cool off mining equipment will also be in the form of electricity.

Mining at Scale

Both embodied energy and electricity decrease (per unit of mining work completed) when operating at a large scale. It's cheaper to build chips that are designed to run in a large data center, and you can deliver the power more efficiently, because you don't need as many power supplies.

When it comes to cooling, however, the opposite is usually true: cooling costs tend to increase the larger your scale is. If you want to run a large operation and have a lot of Bitcoin mining equipment all in one place, there's less air for the heat to dissipate into in the area surrounding your equipment. Your cooling budget will therefore increase at scale (per unit of mining work completed) unless you scale your physical area along with the number of chips you have in use.

Estimating Energy Usage

How much energy is the entire Bitcoin system using? Of course, we can't compute this precisely, because it's a decentralized network with miners operating all over the place without documenting exactly what they're doing. But there are two basic approaches to estimating how much energy Bitcoin miners are using collectively. We'll do some back-of-the-envelope calculations here based on early 2015 values. These figures are very rough, both because some of the parameters are hard to estimate and because they change quickly. At best they should be treated as order-of-magnitude estimates.

TOP-DOWN APPROACH

The first approach is a top-down approach. We start with the simple fact that every time a block is found today, 25 bitcoins, worth about $6,500, are given to the miners. That's about $11 every second being created out of thin air in the Bitcoin economy and given to the miners.

Now let's ask this question: if the miners were turning all of that $11 per second into electricity, how much can they buy? Of course, miners aren't actually spending all their revenue on electricity, but this will provide an upper bound on the electricity being used. Electricity prices vary greatly, but we can use as an estimate that electricity costs about $0.10 per kilowatt-hour at an industrial rate in the United States, or equivalently, $0.03 per megajoule. If Bitcoin miners were spending all $11 per second of earnings buying electricity, they could purchase 367 megajoules per second, consuming a steady 367 megawatts.

Units of energy and power. In the International System of Units (SI), energy is measured in *joules*. A *watt* is a unit of power, where one watt is defined as one joule per second.

BOTTOM-UP APPROACH

A second way to estimate the cost is to use a bottom-up approach. In this approach, we look at the number of hashes the miners are actually computing, which we know by observing the difficulty of each block. If we then assume that all miners are using the most efficient hardware, we can derive a lower bound on the electricity consumption.

Currently, the best claimed efficiency among commercially available mining rigs is about 3 gigahashes per second per watt. That is, the most cutting-edge ASICs claim to perform 3 billion hashes per second while consuming 1 watt of power. The total network hash rate is about 350,000,000 gigahashes per second, or equivalently, 350 petahashes per second. Multiplying these two together, we see that it takes about 117 megawatts to produce that many hashes per second at that efficiency. Of course this figure excludes all of the cooling energy and all of the embodied energy that's in those chips, but we're doing an optimal calculation and deriving a lower bound, so that's okay.

Combining the top-down and bottom-up approaches, we derive a ballpark estimate of the amount of power being used for Bitcoin mining on the order of a few hundred megawatts.

How much is a megawatt? To build intuition, consider how much large power plants produce. One of the largest power plants in the world, the Three Gorges Dam in China, is a 10,000 megawatt power plant. A typical large hydroelectric power plant produces about 1,000 megawatts. The largest nuclear power plant in the world, Kashiwazaki-Kariwa in Japan, is a 7,000 megawatt plant, whereas the average nuclear power plant is about 4,000 megawatts. A major coal-fired plant produces about 2,000 megawatts.

According to our estimates then, the whole Bitcoin network is consuming perhaps 10 percent of a large power plant's output. Although this is a significant amount of power, it's still small compared to all the other things that people are using electricity for on the planet.

Is Bitcoin Mining Wasteful?

It's often said Bitcoin wastes energy, because the energy expended on SHA-256 computations does not serve any other useful purpose. However, any payment system requires energy and electricity. With traditional currency, considerable energy is consumed printing currency and running ATM machines, coin-sorting machines, cash registers, and payment processing services, as well as transporting money and gold bullion in armored cars. You could equally argue that all of this energy is wasted, in that it doesn't serve any purpose besides maintaining the currency system. So if we value Bitcoin as a useful currency system, then the energy required to support it is not really being wasted.

Still, it would be advantageous if we could replace Bitcoin mining with a less energy-intensive puzzle and still have a secure currency. We'll see in Chapter 8, however, that we don't know if that's actually possible.

Repurposing Energy

Another idea to make Bitcoin more eco-friendly is to capture the heat generated from Bitcoin mining and do something useful with it instead of just heating up the atmosphere. This model of capturing waste heat from computation is called the *data furnace* approach. The concept is that instead of buying a traditional electric heater to heat your home, or to heat water in your home, you could buy a heater that doubled as a Bitcoin mining rig, mining bitcoins and heating up your home as a by-product of that computation. It turns out that the efficiency of doing this isn't much worse than buying an electric heater, and perhaps using a data furnace would be no more complicated for home consumers than plugging their heaters into their Internet connections as well as into their electricity outlets.

There are a few drawbacks to this approach. Although it's about as efficient as using an electric heater, electric heaters are themselves much less efficient than gas heaters. Besides, what happens when everybody turns off their Bitcoin mining rig during the summer (or at least everybody in the Northern Hemisphere)? Mining hash power might go down seasonally based on how much heat people need. It might even go down on days that happen to be warmer than average! This would cause many interesting effects for Bitcoin consensus if the data furnace model actually caught on.

The question of ownership is also not clear. If you buy a Bitcoin data furnace, do you own the Bitcoin mining rewards that you get, or does the company that sold them to you? Most people don't have any interest in Bitcoin mining—and probably never will—so it might make more sense to buy it as an appliance and have the company that sold it to you keep the rewards. This might mean the heater is sold at a slight loss then, in which case some enterprising users might want to buy them and modify them to keep the mining rewards for themselves, leading to a potentially ugly digital rights management battle.

Turning Electricity into Cash

Another long-term possibility for Bitcoin is that it might provide the most efficient means of turning electricity into cash. Imagine a world in which Bitcoin mining ASICs are a readily available commodity, and the dominant cost of mining is electricity. In effect, this would mean providing free or low-cost electricity is open to new forms of abuse.

In many countries, governments subsidize electricity, particularly industrial electricity. Among other reasons, they often do so to encourage industry to locate in their country. But Bitcoin provides a good way to turn electricity into cash, which might cause governments to rethink that model if their subsidized electricity is converted en masse to bitcoins. Electricity subsidies are intended to attract businesses that will contribute to the country's economy and labor market, and subsidizing Bitcoin mining may not have the intended effect.

An even bigger problem is the billions of freely available electrical outlets around the world in people's homes, universities, hotels, airports, office buildings, and so on. People might try to plug in mining equipment so that they can profit while someone else is paying the electricity bill. In fact, they might use outdated hardware and not bother to upgrade, considering that they will not be paying the electricity bill. It is quite daunting to consider the possibility of monitoring every power outlet in the world for potential unauthorized use as a source of electricity for Bitcoin mining.

5.4. MINING POOLS

Consider the economics of being a small miner. Suppose you're an individual who spent $6,000 of your hard-earned money to buy a nice, shiny, new Bitcoin mining rig. Assume that the performance is such that you expect to find a block every 14 months (and remember that a block is worth about $10,000 as of 2015).

Amortized, the expected revenue of your miner is perhaps $400 per month once you factor in electricity and other operating costs. If you actually got a check in the mail every month for $400, it would make sense to buy the mining rig. But remember that mining is a random process. You don't know when you're going to find the next block, and until that happens you won't earn anything.

High Variance

If we look at the distribution of how many blocks you're likely to find in the first year, the variance is pretty high, and the expected number is quite low. Because you find blocks at a fixed, low rate that is independent of the time since the last block you found, your expected number of blocks is well approximated by a *Poisson distribution.* A Poisson distribution arises if you have N independent trials each with a chance λ/N of success as N approaches infinity. In Bitcoin mining, each individual nonce attempted is in fact a random trial with a small chance of success, so N is indeed large even for small miners, and the approximation is excellent.

If you expect to find about 1 block per 14 months (a Poisson distribution with $\lambda = 6/7$ blocks/year), there's a greater than 40 percent chance that you won't find any blocks in the first year. For an individual miner, this could be devastating. You spent thousands of dollars on the mining equipment, paid lots in electricity to run it, and received nothing in return. There's a roughly 36 percent chance that you'll find one block in the first year, which means maybe you're barely scraping by, provided your electricity costs aren't too high. Finally, there's a smaller chance that you'll find two or more blocks, in which case you might make out with a nice profit (Figure 5.11).

These numbers are only approximate, but the main point here is that even though the expectation is you might earn enough to make a return on your investment, the variance is sufficiently high that there's a good chance you'll make nothing at all. For a small miner, this means mining is a major gamble.

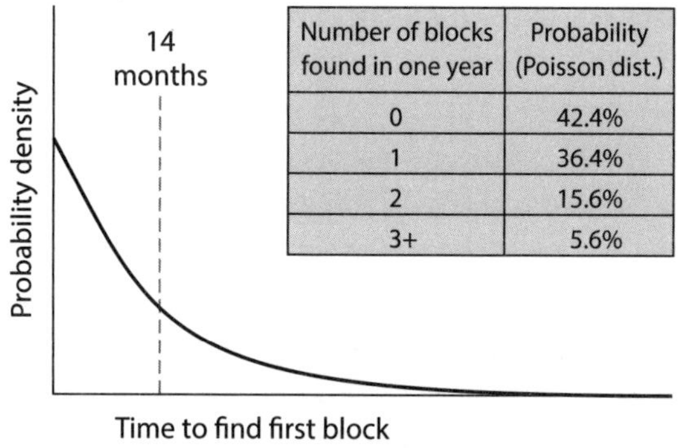

Number of blocks found in one year	Probability (Poisson dist.)
0	42.4%
1	36.4%
2	15.6%
3+	5.6%

FIGURE 5.11. Uncertainty in mining. Assuming that the global hash rate is constant and the mean time to find a block is 14 months, the variance for a small miner is quite high.

Mining Pools

Historically, when small businesspeople faced a lot of risk, they formed mutual insurance companies to lower that risk. Farmers, for example, might agree that if any individual farmer's barn burned down, the others would share their profits with that farmer. Could we have a mutual insurance model that works for small Bitcoin miners?

A *mining pool* is exactly that—mutual insurance for Bitcoin miners. A group of miners will form a pool and all attempt to mine a block with a designated coinbase recipient. That recipient is called the *pool manager*. So, no matter who actually finds the block, the pool manager will receive the rewards. The pool manager will distribute that revenue to all the participants in the pool based on how much work each participant performed. Of course, the pool manager will also probably take some kind of cut for the service of managing the pool.

Assuming everybody trusts the pool manager, this approach works well for lowering miners' variance. But how does a pool manager know how much work each member of the pool contributed? Obviously, the pool manager shouldn't simply take everyone's word for it, because people might claim that they've done more than they actually did.

Mining Shares

There's an elegant solution to this problem. Miners can prove probabilistically how much work they're doing by outputting *shares*, or near-valid blocks. Suppose the target is a number beginning with 67 zeros. A block's hash must be lower than the target for the block to be valid. In the process of searching for such a block, miners will find some blocks with hashes beginning with a lot of zeros, but not quite 67. Miners can show these nearly valid blocks to prove that they are indeed working (Figure 5.12). A share might require say 40 or 50 zeros, depending on the type of miners the pool is geared for.

The pool manager will also run a Bitcoin node on behalf of participants, collecting transactions and assembling them into a block. The manager will include her own address in the coinbase transaction and send the block to all participants in the pool. All

9D1842A2A98DEDE34E00F6B8406AED0CE11BDC906C6DB6E23BCD9DE35DC4C339
86006DC06851F801FF0322E4CB92959DB619F19A03415B0C8FE131968005B9DA
0000000004D4120FD53C6CE8F013367209E905F4AE4D7837FFCFAA22B95CEDF
60E9D45D86FA3AE285615A3972E9F85C68FEA07611830F49ED15EEE1460E83A4
00000000007EF3D0D4479C9FB96FF100601618AD56BD240EF762B1B6842D1CF5
44AEE951CD30363A0A750C81CDC4BC0D3427DACA1C878A489120EB92430866F7
D048C51CA7EA5E6B61F6B40E739F9F35E2C653A37BE7D3EA2474F5E7777C8790
00000000000000001EB96F35E74E9B0F84BC921D52EDC878A754658F23313E86
1289F7CFA4A86DEBB743D2B94AAD0A916A9282FDCA05B70E72C627FE5A592959
561BBB9E8AAC2B1DDE1E163DA1E4F05BC1A9B1E92B04DCE834A6EB827C5E2E5B
000000000082D602D87B67A42ED2BF763E92A76BE90F76A9CA71AB958EB7657A
FD639DC38BB5279885F0FC42E7FD92D37ABD7FEAFD828CEDA2731CD781DC77D7

FIGURE 5.12. Mining shares. Miners continually try to find blocks with a hash below the target. In the process, they'll find other blocks whose hashes contain fewer zeros—but are still rare enough to prove that they have been working hard. In this figure, the shaded hashes are shares, while the bold hash is from a valid block (which is also a valid share).

pool participants work on this block, and they prove that they've been working on it by sending in shares.

When a member of the pool finds a valid block, he sends it to the pool manager, who distributes the reward in proportion to the amount of work done. The miner who actually finds the block is not awarded a special bonus, so if another miner did more work, the latter miner will be paid more, even though he wasn't the one who found the valid block (Figure 5.13).

There are a few options for how exactly the pool manager calculates how much to pay each miner based on the shares they submit. We look at two of the common, simpler ones. There are many other schemes that are also used, but these illustrate the trade-offs between reward schemes.

Pay per Share

In the *pay-per-share model*, the pool manager pays a flat fee for every share above a certain difficulty for the block that the pool is working on. In this model, miners can send their shares to the pool manager right away and get paid without waiting for the pool to find a block.

In some ways, the pay-per-share model is the best for miners. They are guaranteed a certain amount of money every time they find a share. The pool managers essentially absorb all the risk, since they pay rewards even if a block is not found. Of course, as a result of the increased risk, in the pay-per-share model, the pool manager will probably charge higher fees compared with other models.

One problem with the pay-per-share model is that miners don't actually have any incentive to send valid blocks to the pool manager. That is, they can discard valid

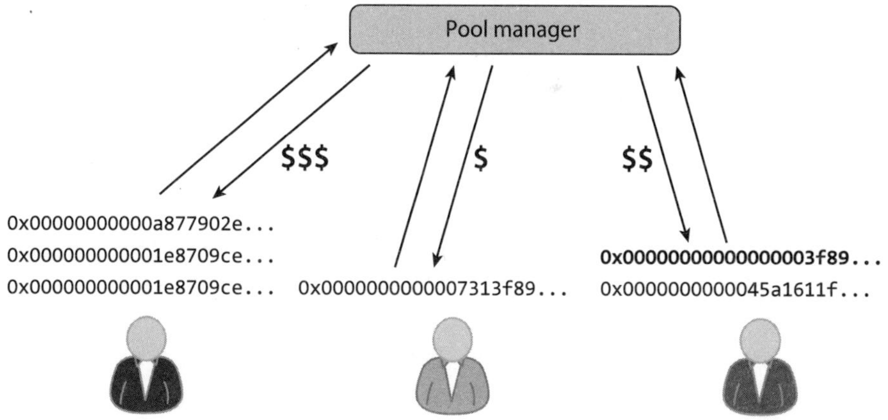

FIGURE 5.13. Mining rewards. The three participants pictured are all working on the same block. They are awarded commensurate with the amount of work done. Even though the miner on the right was the one to find the valid block, the miner on the left is paid more, since this miner did more work. There is (typically) no bonus paid to the miner who actually finds the block.

blocks but still be paid the same rewards, which will cause a big loss to the pool. A malicious pool manager might attack a competing pool in this fashion to try to drive them out of business.

Proportional

In the *proportional model*, instead of paying a flat fee per share, the amount of payment depends on whether the pool actually finds a valid block. Every time a valid block is found, the rewards from that block are distributed to the members proportional to how much work they actually did.

In the proportional model, the miners still bear some risk proportional to the risk of the pool in general. But if the pool is large enough, the variance of how often the pool finds blocks will be fairly low. Proportional payouts provide lower risk for pool managers, because they only pay out when valid blocks are found. This also gets around the problem that was mentioned for the pay-per-share model, as miners are incentivized to send in the valid blocks that they find, because that triggers revenue coming back to them.

The proportional model requires a little more work on behalf of the pool managers to verify, calculate, and distribute rewards compared to the flat pay-per-share model.

Pool Hopping

Even with just these two types of pools, we can see that miners might be incentivized to switch between the pools at different times. To see this, consider that a purely proportional pool will effectively pay out a larger amount per share if a block is found quickly, as it always pays one block reward no matter how long it has been since the last block was found.

A clever miner might try mining in a proportional pool early in the cycle (just after the previous block was found), while the rewards per share are relatively high, only to switch ("hop") to a pay-per-share pool later in the cycle, when the expected rewards from mining in the proportional pool are relatively low. As a result, proportional pools aren't really practical. More complicated schemes, such as "pay per last *N* shares submitted" are more common, but even these are subject to subtle pool-hopping behavior. How to design a mining pool reward scheme that is not vulnerable to this kind of manipulation remains an open problem.

History and Standardization

Mining pools first started around 2010 in the GPU era of Bitcoin mining. They instantly became popular for the obvious reason that they lowered the variance for the participating miners. They've become quite sophisticated now. Many protocols exist for how to run mining pools, and it has even been suggested that these mining pool protocols should be standardized as part of Bitcoin itself. Just as there's a Bitcoin protocol for running the peer-to-peer network, mining pool protocols provide a communication API (application programming interface) for the pool manager to send all members the details of the block to work on and for the miners to send back to the pool manager the shares that they're finding. The protocol getblocktemplate is officially standardized as a Bitcoin Improvement Proposal (BIP). A competing protocol, Stratum, is currently more popular in practice and is a proposed BIP. Unlike the Bitcoin protocol itself, it is only a minor inconvenience to have multiple incompatible mining pool protocols. Each pool can simply pick the protocol they prefer, and the market can decide which one is superior.

Some mining hardware even supports these protocols at the hardware level, which will ultimately somewhat limit their development flexibility. However, this makes it simple to buy a piece of mining hardware and join a pool. You just plug it into the wall—both the electricity and your network connection—choose a pool, and then the mining hardware will start immediately receiving instructions from the pool, mining and converting your electricity into money.

51 Percent Mining Pools

As of 2015, nearly all miners are mining through pools; very few miners mine solo anymore. In June 2014, GHash.IO, the largest mining pool, got so big that it actually had more than 50 percent of the entire capacity of the Bitcoin network (Figure 5.14a). Essentially GHash offered such a good deal to participating miners that the majority wanted to join.

This is something that the community had feared for a long time, and it led to a backlash against GHash. By August, GHash's market share had gone down by design, as the pool stopped accepting new participants (Figure 5.14b). Still, two mining pools controlled about half of the power in the network.

By April 2015, the situation looked very different and was less concentrated, at least superficially (Figure 5.14c). The possibility of a pool acquiring 51 percent is still a con-

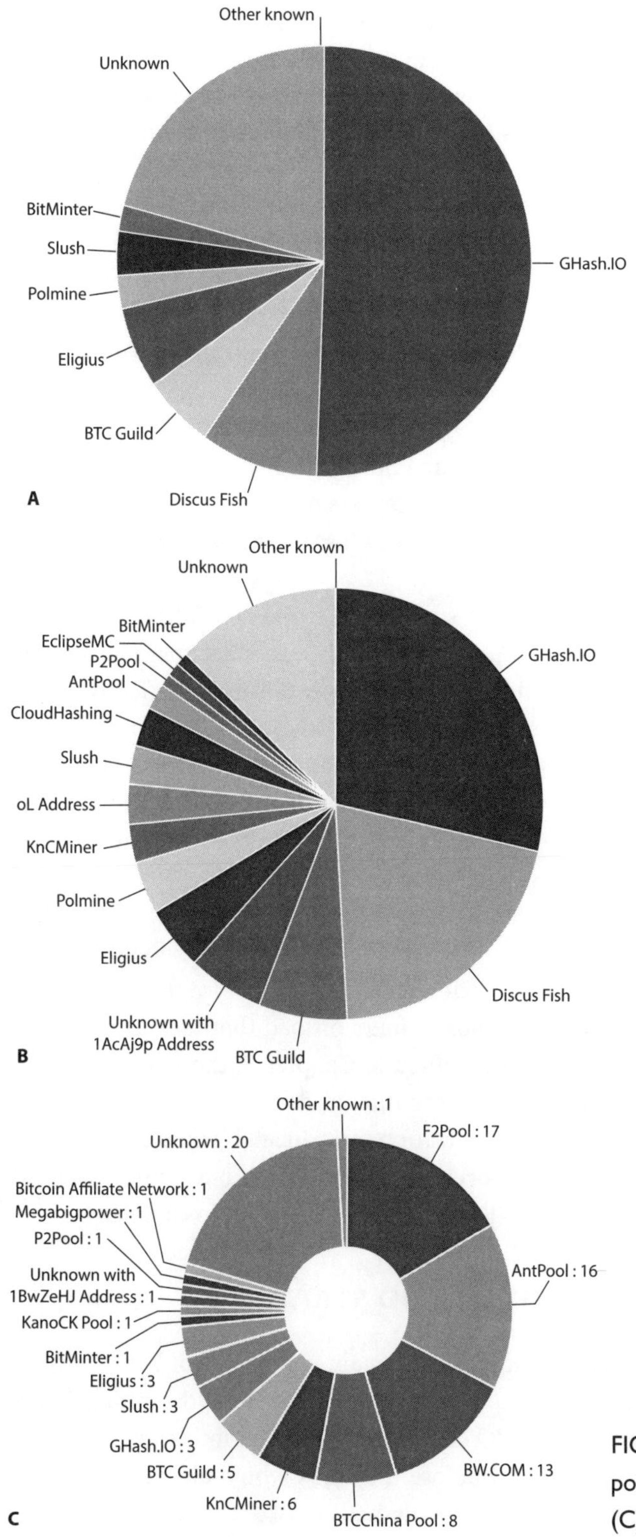

FIGURE 5.14. Hash power by mining pool. (A) June 2014. (B) August 2014. (C) April 2015. Source: blockchain.info.

cern in the community, but the negative publicity GHash received has caused pools to avoid becoming too large since then. As new miners and pools have entered the market and standardized protocols have increased the ease of switching between pools for miners, the market share of different pools has remained quite fluid. It remains to be seen how the pools will evolve in the long run.

However, it is worth noting that mining pools might be hiding actual concentration of mining power in the hands of a few large mining organizations, which can participate in multiple mining pools simultaneously to hide their true size. This practice is called *laundering hashes*. It remains unknown how concentrated physical control of mining hardware actually is, and mining pools make this quite difficult to determine.

Are Mining Pools Beneficial?

The advantages of mining pools are that they make mining much more predictable for the participants, and they make it easier for smaller miners to get involved in the game. Without mining pools, the variance would make mining infeasible for many small miners.

Another advantage of mining pools is that since there's one central pool manager who is sitting on the network and assembling blocks, it is easier to upgrade the network. Upgrading the software that the mining pool manager is running effectively updates the software that all pool members are running.

The main disadvantage of mining pools, of course, is that they are a form of centralization. It's an open question how much power the operators of a large mining pool actually have. In theory, miners are free to leave a pool if it is perceived as too powerful, but it's unclear how often miners do so in practice.

Another disadvantage of mining pools is that they reduce the number of participants actually running a fully validating Bitcoin node. Previously, all miners, no matter how small, had to run their own fully validating node. They all had to store the entire block chain and validate every transaction. Now, most miners offload that task to their pool managers. This is the main reason, as we mentioned in Chapter 3, the number of fully validated nodes may actually be going down in the Bitcoin network.

If you're concerned about the level of centralization introduced by mining pools, you might ask: Could we redesign the mining process so that we don't have any pools, and everybody has to mine for themselves? We'll consider this question in Chapter 8.

5.5. MINING INCENTIVES AND STRATEGIES

We've spent most of this chapter describing how the main challenges of being a miner are acquiring good hardware, finding cheap electricity, getting up and running as fast as you can, and hoping for some good luck. There are also some interesting strategic considerations that every miner has to make before they pick which blocks to work on.

1. *Which transactions to include.* Miners choose which transactions they include in a block. The default strategy is to include any transaction that has a transaction fee higher than some minimum.
2. *Which block to mine on.* Miners also decide which block they want to mine on top of. The default behavior for this decision is to extend the longest known valid chain.
3. *Choosing between blocks at the same height.* If two different blocks are mined and announced at around the same time, it results in a 1-block fork, with either block admissible under the longest-valid-chain policy. Miners then have to decide which block to extend. The default behavior is to build on top of the block that they heard about first.
4. *When to announce new blocks.* When they find a block, miners have to decide when to announce this to the Bitcoin network. The default behavior is to announce it immediately, but they can choose to wait some time before announcing it.

Thus miners are faced with many decisions. For each decision, there is a default strategy employed by the Bitcoin reference client, which is run by nearly all miners at the time of this writing. But it may be possible that a nondefault strategy is more profitable. Finding such scenarios and strategies is an active area of research. Let's look at several such potentially profitable deviations from default behavior (often called "attacks"). In the following discussion, we assume that a nondefault miner controls some fraction of mining power, which we denote by α.

Forking Attack

The simplest attack is a *forking attack*, and the obvious way to profit is to perform a double spend. The miner sends some money to a victim, Bob, in payment for some good or service. Bob waits and sees that the transaction paying him has indeed been included in the block chain. Perhaps he follows the common heuristic and even waits for six confirmations to be sure. Convinced that he has been paid, Bob ships the good or performs the service.

The miner now begins working on an earlier block—before the block that contains the transaction to Bob. In this forked chain, the miner inserts an alternate transaction—or a double spend—which sends the coins paid to Bob on the main chain back to one of the miner's own addresses (Figure 5.15).

For the attack to succeed, the forked chain must overtake the current longest chain. Once this occurs, the transaction paying Bob no longer exists on the consensus block chain. This will surely happen eventually if the attacking miner has a majority of the hash power—that is, if $\alpha > 0.5$. That is, even though there is a lot of random variation in when blocks are found, the chain that is growing faster on average will eventually

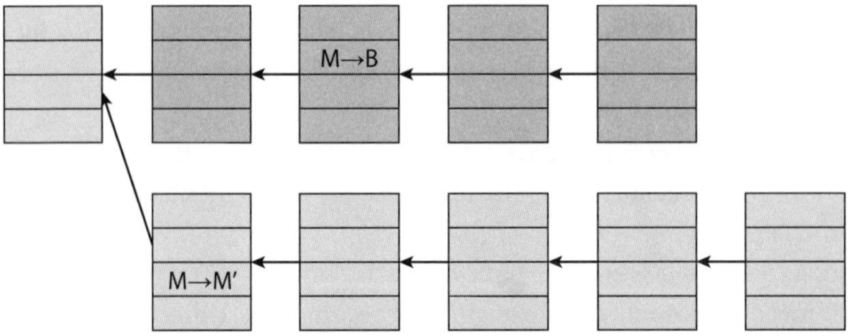

FIGURE 5.15. Forking attack. A malicious miner sends a transaction to Bob and receives some good or service in exchange for it. The miner then forks the block chain to create a longer branch containing a conflicting transaction. The payment to Bob will be invalid in this new consensus chain.

become longer. Moreover, since the miner's coins have already been spent (on the new consensus chain), the transaction paying Bob can no longer make its way onto the block chain.

Is 51 percent necessary? Launching a forking attack is certainly possible if $\alpha > 0.5$. In practice, it might be possible to perform this attack with a bit less than that because of other factors, such as network overhead. Default miners working on the main chain will generate some stale blocks for the usual reason: there is a latency for miners to hear about one another's blocks. But a centralized attacker can communicate much more quickly and produce fewer stale blocks, which might amount to a savings of 1 percent or more.

Still, at close to 50 percent, the attack may take a long time to succeed because of random chance. The attack gets much easier and more efficient the further you go over 50 percent. People often talk about a 51 percent attacker as if 51 percent were a magical threshold that suddenly enables a forking attack. In reality, it's more of a gradient.

Practical countermeasures. It's not clear whether a forking attack would actually succeed in practice. The attack is detectable, and it's possible that the community would decide to block the attack by refusing to accept the alternate chain, even though it is longer.

Attacks and the exchange rate. More importantly, it's likely that such an attack would completely crash the Bitcoin exchange rate. If a miner carried out such an attack, confidence in the system would decline, and the exchange rate would fall as participants tried to move their wealth out of the system. Thus, while an attacker with 51 percent of the hashing power might profit in the short term from double spending, they might seriously undermine their long-term earning potential to mine honestly and cash in their mining rewards.

For these reasons, perhaps a more plausible motivation for a forking attack is to specifically destroy the currency by a dramatic loss of confidence. This has been referred to as a *Goldfinger attack* after the James Bond villain who tried to irradiate all the gold in Fort Knox to make it valueless. A Goldfinger attacker's goal might be to destroy the currency, possibly to profit either by having shorted Bitcoin or by having significant holdings in some competing currency.

Forking Attack via Bribery

Buying enough hardware to control the majority of the hash power appears to be an expensive and difficult task. But there may be an easier way to launch a forking attack. Whereas it would be really expensive to directly buy enough mining capacity to have more than everybody else in the world, it might be possible to bribe the people who do control all that capacity to work on your behalf.

You could bribe miners in several ways. One way is to do this "out of band"—perhaps locate some large-scale miners and hand them an envelope of cash for working on your fork. A more clever technique is to create a new mining pool and run it at a loss, offering greater incentives than other pools offer. Even though the incentives might not be sustainable, an attacker could keep them going for long enough to successfully launch a forking attack and perhaps profit from it. A third technique is to leave big "tips" in blocks on the forking chain—big enough to cause miners to leave the longest chain and work on the forking chain in hopes that it will become the longest chain and they can collect the tips.

Whatever the mechanics of bribing are, the idea is the same: instead of actually acquiring all the mining capacity directly, the attacker just pays those who already have it to help the attacker's fork overcome the longest chain.

Perhaps miners won't want to help, because to do so would hurt the currency in which they have invested so much money and mining equipment. But even though miners as a group might want to keep the currency solvent, they don't act collectively. Individual miners might defect and accept a bribe if they thought they could make more money in the short term. This would be a classic tragedy of the commons from an economic perspective.

None of this has actually happened, and it's an open question whether a bribery attack like this could actually be viable.

Temporary Block-Withholding Attacks

Suppose you have just found a block. The default behavior is to immediately announce it to the network, but if you're carrying out a temporary *block-withholding attack*, you don't announce it right away. Instead, you try to get ahead by doing some more mining on top of this block in hopes of finding two blocks in a row before the rest of the network finds even one, keeping your blocks secret the whole time.

If you're ahead of the public block chain by two secret blocks, all of the mining effort of the rest of the network will be wasted. Other miners will mine on top of what they think is the longest chain, but as soon as they find a valid block, you can announce the two blocks that you were withholding. That would instantly be the new longest valid chain, and the block that the rest of the network worked so hard to find would immediately be orphaned (Figure 5.16). This has been called *selfish mining*. By causing the rest of the network to waste hash power trying to find a block you can immediately cause to be stale, you hope to increase your effective share of mining rewards.

The catch is that you need to get lucky to find two blocks in a row. Chances are that someone else in the network announces a valid block when you're only one block ahead. If this happens, you'll want to immediately announce your secret block yourself. This creates a one-block fork, and every miner will need to make a decision about which of those blocks to mine on. Your hope is that a large fraction of other miners will hear about your block first and decide to work on it. The viability of this attack depends heavily on your ability to win these races, so network position is critical. You could try to peer with every node, so that your block will reach most nodes first.

As it turns out, if you assume that you only have a 50 percent chance of winning these races, selfish mining is an improvement over the default strategy if your fraction of mining power is $\alpha > .25$. Even if you lose every race, selfish mining is still more profitable if $\alpha > .333$. The existence of this attack is quite surprising, and it's contrary to the original widely held belief that without a majority of the network (i.e., with $\alpha \leq .5$), there is no better mining strategy than the default. So it's not safe to assume that a miner who doesn't control 50 percent of the network doesn't have anything to gain by switching to an alternate strategy.

As of 2015, temporary block withholding is just a theoretical attack and hasn't been observed in practice. Selfish mining would be pretty easy to detect, because it would increase the rate of near-simultaneous block announcements.

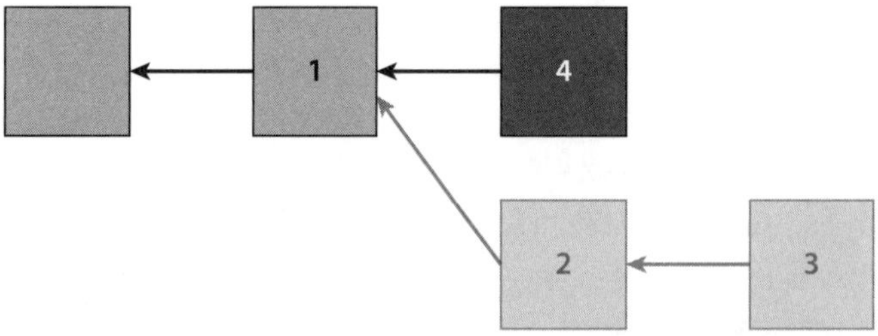

FIGURE 5.16. Selfish mining. One of several possible ways in which the attack could play out is shown. (1) Block chain before attack. (2) Attacker mines a block, withholds it, starts mining on top of it. (3) Attacker gets lucky, finds a second block before the rest of the network, continues to withhold blocks. (4) Nonattacker finds a block and broadcasts it. In response, the attacker broadcasts both his blocks, orphaning the nonattacker's block and wasting the mining power that went into finding it.

Blacklisting and Punitive Forking

Suppose you want to *blacklist* transactions from address X. In other words, you want to freeze the money held by that address, making it unspendable. Perhaps you intend to profit off of this by some sort of ransom or extortion scheme, demanding that the person you're blacklisting pay you to be taken off your blacklist. Blacklisting also might be something that you are compelled to do for legal reasons. Maybe certain addresses are designated as evil by the government. Law enforcement officials may demand that all miners operating in their jurisdiction try to blacklist those addresses.

Conventional wisdom is that there's no effective way to blacklist addresses in Bitcoin. Even if some miners refuse to include some transactions in blocks, other miners will. If you're a miner trying to blacklist, however, you could try something stronger, namely, punitive forking. You could announce that you'll refuse to work on a chain containing a transaction originating from this address. If you have a majority of the hash power, this threat should be enough to guarantee that the blacklisted transactions will never be published. Indeed, other miners would probably stop trying, as doing so would simply cause their blocks to be elided in forks.

Feather Forking

Punitive forking doesn't appear to work unless the attacker holds the majority of the network hash power. By announcing that you refuse to mine on any chain that has certain transactions, if such a chain does come into existence and is accepted by the rest of the network as the longest chain, you will have cut yourself off from the consensus chain forever (effectively introducing a hard fork), and all of your current mining will go to waste. Worse still, the blacklisted transactions will still make it into the longest chain.

In other words, a threat to blacklist certain transactions via punitive forking in the above manner is not credible as far as the other miners are concerned. But there's a much more clever way to do it, called *feather forking*. Instead of announcing that you're going to fork forever as soon as you see a transaction originating from address X, you announce that you'll attempt to fork if you see a block that has a transaction from address X, but you will give up after a while. For example, you might announce that after k blocks confirm the transaction from address X, you'll go back to the longest chain.

If you give up after one confirmation, your chance of orphaning the block with the transaction from X is α^2. The reason is that you'll have to find two consecutive blocks to get rid of the block with the transaction from address X before the rest of the network finds a block, and α^2 is the chance that you will get lucky twice.

A chance of α^2 might not seem very good. If you control 20 percent of the hash power (i.e., $\alpha = 0.20$), there's only a 4 percent chance of actually getting rid of the transaction that you don't want to see in the block chain. But it's better than it might seem, as you might motivate other miners to join you. As long as you've been public about your plans, other miners know that if they include a transaction from address *X*, they have an α^2 chance that the block that they find will end up being eliminated because of your feather-forking attack. If they don't have any strong motivation to include that transaction from address *X* and it doesn't have a high transaction fee, the α^2 chance of losing their mining reward might be a much bigger incentive than collecting the transaction fee is.

It emerges then that other miners may rationally decide to join you in enforcing the blacklist, and you can therefore enforce a blacklist even if $\alpha < .5$. The success of this attack depends entirely on how convincing you are to the other miners that you're going to fork.

Transitioning to Mining Rewards Dominated by Transaction Fees

As of 2015, transaction fees don't matter much, since block rewards provide more than 99 percent of all revenue that miners make. But every 4 years, the block reward is scheduled to be halved, and eventually it will be low enough that transaction fees will become the main source of revenue for miners. It's an open question exactly how miners will operate when transaction fees dominate their income. Will miners become more aggressive in enforcing minimum transaction fees? Will they cooperate to enforce the minimum?

Open Problems

In summary, miners are free to implement any strategy that they want, although in practice we've seen little of anything other than the default strategy. There's no complete model for miner behavior that confirms that the default strategy is optimal. In this chapter we've discussed specific examples of deviations that may be profitable for miners with sufficient hash power. Mining strategy may be an area in which practice is ahead of theory. Empirically, in a world where most miners choose the default strategy, Bitcoin seems to work well. But it is not yet clear if we can analyze Bitcoin theoretically and show that it is stable.

We also can't be sure that it will always continue to work well in practice. The facts on the ground are going to change for Bitcoin. Miners are becoming more centralized and more professional, and the network capacity is increasing. Besides, in the long run Bitcoin must contend with the transition from fixed mining rewards to transaction fees. We don't know how this will play out, and using game-theoretic models to try to predict it is a very interesting current area of research.

FURTHER READING

An excellent paper on the evolution of mining hardware is:

Taylor, Michael Bedford. "Bitcoin and the Age of Bespoke Silicon." In *Proceedings of the 2013 International Conference on Compilers, Architectures and Synthesis for Embedded Systems*. Washington, DC: IEEE Press, 2013.

A paper discussing some aspects of running a Bitcoin mining center, including cooling costs, is:

Kampl, Alex. "Analysis of Large-Scale Bitcoin Mining Operations." White paper, Allied Control, Hong Kong, 2014.

The "systematization of knowledge" paper on Bitcoin and cryptocurrencies; see especially Section III on stability:

Bonneau, Joseph, Andrew Miller, Jeremy Clark, Arvind Narayanan, Joshua A. Kroll, and Edward W. Felten. "Research Perspectives and Challenges for Bitcoin and Cryptocurrencies." Presented at the 2015 IEEE Symposium on Security and Privacy, San Jose, CA, May 2015.

A comprehensive 2011 paper analyzing different reward systems for pooled mining (some of the information is a bit out of date, but overall it's still a good resource):

Rosenfeld, Meni. "Analysis of Bitcoin Pooled Mining Reward Systems." arXiv preprint. arXiv:1112.4980 (2011).

Several papers that analyze mining strategy are:

Eyal, Ittay, and Emin Gün Sirer. "Majority Is Not Enough: Bitcoin Mining Is Vulnerable," in *Financial Cryptography and Data Security*. Berlin and Heidelberg: Springer, 2014.

Kroll, Joshua A., Ian C. Davey, and Edward W. Felten. "The Economics of Bitcoin Mining, or Bitcoin in the Presence of Adversaries." In *Proceedings of the Workshop on the Economics of Information Security 2013*. Berlin: Springer-Verlag, 2013.

Eyal, Ittay. "The Miner's Dilemma." Presented at the 2015 IEEE Symposium on Security and Privacy, San Jose, CA, May 2015.

CHAPTER 6

Bitcoin and Anonymity

Bitcoin is a secure and anonymous digital currency.
—*WikiLeaks donations page*

Bitcoin won't hide you from the NSA's prying eyes.
—*Wired UK*

One of the most controversial things about Bitcoin is its supposed anonymity. First, is Bitcoin anonymous? As you can see from the mutually contradictory quotes above, there's some confusion about this. Second, do we *want* a cryptocurrency that is truly anonymous? There are pros and cons to anonymity, which leads to more basic questions: Is having an anonymous cryptocurrency beneficial for stakeholders? Is it good for society? Is there a way to isolate the positive aspects of anonymity while doing away with the negative parts?

These questions are hard, because they depend in part on one's ethical values. We won't answer them in this chapter, though we will examine arguments for and against anonymity. Mostly we stick to studying various technologies—some already present in Bitcoin and others that have been proposed as additions to it—that aim to increase Bitcoin's anonymity. We also look at proposals for alternative cryptocurrencies whose anonymity properties differ from those of Bitcoin. These technologies raise new questions: How well do they work? How difficult would they be to adopt? What are the trade-offs to be made in adopting them?

6.1. ANONYMITY BASICS

Defining Anonymity

Before we can properly discuss whether (or to what extent) Bitcoin is anonymous, we need to define anonymity. We must understand what exactly is meant by anonymity, and the relationship between anonymity and similar terms, such as privacy.

> **Anonymity versus Pseudonymity**
>
> The distinction between anonymity and mere pseudonymity arises in a variety of other contexts. One good example is online forums. On a forum like Reddit, you pick a long-term pseudonym and interact over a period of time with that pseudonym. You could create multiple pseudonyms, or even a new one for every comment, but that would be tedious and annoying, and most people don't do it. So interacting on Reddit is usually pseudonymous but not quite anonymous. 4Chan, in contrast, is an online forum in which users generally post anonymously—with no attribution at all.

At a literal level, *anonymous* means "without a name." Two possible interpretations result when applying this definition to Bitcoin: interacting without using your real name, or interacting without using any name at all. These two interpretations lead to very different conclusions as to whether Bitcoin is anonymous. Bitcoin addresses are hashes of public keys. You don't need to use your real name to interact with the system, but you do use your public key hash as your identity. Thus, by the first interpretation, Bitcoin is anonymous. However, by the second interpretation, it is not; the address that you use is a pseudo-identity. In the language of computer science, this middle ground of using an identity that is not your real name is called *pseudonymity*.

Recall that you are free to create as many Bitcoin addresses as you like. With this in mind, you might wonder whether Bitcoin addresses really are pseudo-identities. As we'll see, this still does not make Bitcoin anonymous.

In computer science, anonymity refers to pseudonymity together with *unlinkability*. Unlinkability is a property that's defined with respect to the capabilities of a specific adversary. Intuitively, unlinkability means that if a user interacts with the system repeatedly, these different interactions should not be able to be tied to one another by the adversary in question.

Bitcoin is pseudonymous, but pseudonymity is not enough if your goal is to achieve privacy. Recall that the block chain is public, and anyone can look up all Bitcoin transactions that involved a given address. If anyone were ever able to link your Bitcoin address to your real-world identity, then all your transactions—past, present, and future—will have been linked back to your identity.

To make things worse, linking a Bitcoin address to a real-world identity is often easy. If you interact with a Bitcoin business—be it an online wallet service, exchange, or other types of merchant—they usually want your real-world identity for transactions with them. For example, an exchange might require your credit card details, or a merchant will need your shipping address.

Or you might go to a coffee shop and pay for your coffee with bitcoins. Since you're physically present in the store, the barista knows a lot about your identity, even if she doesn't ask for your real name. Your physical identity thus gets tied to one of your Bitcoin transactions, making all the other transactions that involved that address linkable to you. This is clearly not anonymous.

Side Channels

Even if a direct linkage doesn't occur, your pseudonymous profile can be *deanonymized* by exploiting *side channels*, or indirect leakages of information. For example, someone may look at a profile of pseudonymous Bitcoin transactions and note the times of day that the user is active. They can correlate this information with other publicly available information. Perhaps they'll notice that some Twitter user is active during roughly same time intervals, creating a link between the pseudonymous Bitcoin profile and a real-world identity (or at least a Twitter identity). Clearly pseudonymity does not guarantee privacy or anonymity. To achieve those, we require the stronger property of unlinkability as well.

Unlinkability

To understand unlinkability in the Bitcoin context more concretely, let's enumerate some key properties that are required for Bitcoin activity to be unlinkable:

1. It should be hard to link together different addresses of the same user.
2. It should be hard to link together different transactions made by the same user.
3. It should be hard to link the sender of a payment to its recipient.

The first two properties are intuitive, but the third one is a bit tricky. If you interpret "a payment" as a Bitcoin transaction, then the third property is clearly false. Every transaction has inputs and outputs, and these inputs and outputs inevitably appear in the block chain and are publicly linked together. However, what we mean by a "payment" is not a single Bitcoin transaction, but rather anything that has the effect of transferring bitcoins from the sender to the recipient. It might involve a roundabout series of transactions. What we want to ensure is that it's not feasible to link the sender and the ultimate recipient of the payment by looking at the block chain.

Anonymity Set

Even using our broader definition of a payment, the third property seems hard to achieve. Suppose that you pay for a product that costs a certain number of bitcoins, and you send that payment through a circuitous route of transactions. Somebody looking at the block chain will still be able to infer something from the fact that a certain number of bitcoins left one address and roughly the same number of bitcoins (minus transaction fees, perhaps) ended up at some other address. Moreover, despite the circuitous route, the initial sending and the ultimate receiving will occur in roughly the same time period, because the merchant will want to receive payment without too much of a delay.

Because of this difficulty, we usually don't try to achieve complete unlinkability among all possible transactions or addresses in the system, but rather something more limited. Given a particular adversary, the *anonymity set* of your transaction is the set of transactions that the adversary cannot distinguish from your transaction. Even if the adversary knows you made a transaction, they can only tell that it's one of the transactions in the set, but not which one it is. We try to maximize the size of the anonymity set—the set of other addresses or transactions among which we can hide.

Calculating the anonymity set is tricky. Since the anonymity set is defined with respect to a certain adversary or set of adversaries, you must first concretely define what your adversary model is. You have to reason carefully about what that adversary knows, what they don't know, and what is it that we are trying to hide from the adversary—that is, what the adversary *cannot* know for the transaction to be considered anonymous. There's no general formula for defining this set. It requires carefully analyzing each protocol and system on a case-by-case basis.

Taint Analysis

In the Bitcoin community, people often carry out intuitive analyses of anonymity services without rigorous definitions. *Taint analysis* is particularly popular: it's a way of calculating how "related" two addresses are. If bitcoins sent by an address *S* always end up at another address *R*, whether directly or after passing through some intermediate addresses, then *S* and *R* will have a high taint score. The formula accounts for transactions with multiple inputs and/or outputs and specifies how to allocate taint.

Unfortunately, taint analysis is not a good measure of Bitcoin anonymity. It implicitly assumes that the adversary is using the same mechanical calculation to link pairs of addresses. A slightly more clever adversary may use other techniques, such as looking at the timing of transactions or even exploiting idiosyncrasies of wallet software, as discussed in Section 6.2. So taint analysis might suggest that you have a high degree of anonymity in a certain situation, but in fact you might not.

Why Anonymity Is Needed

Having seen what anonymity means, let's answer some metaquestions about the concept before going further: Why do people want anonymity? What are the ethical implications of having an anonymous currency?

In block-chain-based currencies, all transactions are recorded on the ledger, which means that they are publicly and permanently traceable to the associated addresses. So the privacy of your Bitcoin transactions can potentially be far reduced compared to traditional banking. If your real-world identity is ever linked to a Bitcoin address, then you have lost privacy for all transactions—past, present, and future—associated with that address. Since the block chain is publicly available, literally anyone might be able to carry out this type of deanonymization without you even realizing that you've been identified.

With this in mind, we can identify two different motivations for having anonymous cryptocurrencies. The first is simply to achieve the level of privacy that we are already used to from traditional banking, and to mitigate the deanonymization risk that the public block chain entails. The second is to go beyond the privacy level of traditional banking and develop currencies that make it technologically infeasible for anyone to track the participants.

Ethics of Anonymity

There are many important (though often overlooked) reasons for anonymity that we take for granted with traditional currencies. Most people are uncomfortable sharing their salaries with their friends and coworkers. But if an individual's addresses in the block chain are easily identifiable, and they receive their salary in Bitcoin, it would be quite easy to infer their salary by looking for a large, regular monthly payment. Organizations also have important financial privacy concerns. For example, if a video game console manufacturer were to be observed in the block chain paying a subcontractor that manufactures virtual reality glasses, this might tip off the public (and competitors) about a new product that the console manufacturer is preparing to launch.

However, there is legitimate concern that truly anonymous cryptocurrencies can be used for money laundering or other illegal activities. The good news is that while cryptocurrency transactions themselves may be pseudonymous or anonymous, the interface between digital cash and fiat currencies is not. In fact, these flows are highly regulated, as discussed in Chapter 7. So cryptocurrencies are no panacea for money laundering or other financial crimes.

Nevertheless one may ask: Can the technology be designed in such a way that only the good uses of anonymity are allowed and the bad uses are somehow prohibited? This is in fact a recurring plea to computer security and privacy researchers. Unfortunately, it never turns out to be possible. The reason is that use cases that we classify as good or bad from a moral viewpoint turn out to be technologically identical. In Bitcoin, it's not clear how we could task miners with making moral decisions about which transactions to include.

Our view is that the potential good that's enabled by having anonymous cryptocurrencies warrants their existence, and that we should separate the technical anonymity properties of the system from the legal principles we apply when using the currency. This solution is not completely satisfactory, but it's perhaps the best way to achieve a favorable trade-off.

Anonymization versus Decentralization

A recurring theme throughout this chapter is that the design criteria of anonymization and decentralization are often in conflict with one another. If you recall Chaum's ecash, discussed in the Foreword, it achieved perfect anonymity in a sense, but through an interactive blind-signature protocol with a central authority, a bank. As you can imagine, such protocols are difficult to decentralize. Also, decentralization requires that we have a mechanism to trace transactions and prevent double spending. This public traceability of transactions is a threat to anonymity.

Tor

The moral dilemma of how to deal with a technology that has both good and bad uses is by no means unique to Bitcoin. Another system whose anonymity is controversial is Tor, an anonymous communication network.

On one hand, Tor is used by ordinary people who want to protect themselves from being tracked online. It's used by journalists, activists, and dissidents to speak freely online without fear of retribution by oppressive regimes. It's also used by law enforcement agents who want to monitor suspects online without revealing their IP addresses (after all, ranges or blocks of IP addresses assigned to different organizations, including law enforcement agencies, tend to be well known). Clearly, Tor has many applications that we might morally approve of. On the other hand, it also has clearly bad uses: operators of botnets use it to issue commands to the infected machines under their control, and it's used to distribute images of child sexual abuse.

Distinguishing between these uses at a technical level is essentially impossible. The Tor developers and the Tor community have grappled extensively with this conundrum. Society at large has grappled with it to some degree as well. We seem to have concluded that overall, it's better for the world that the technology exists. In fact, one of the main funding sources of the Tor project is the U.S. State Department. They're interested in Tor because it enables free speech online for dissidents in oppressive regimes. Meanwhile, law enforcement agencies seem to have grudgingly accepted Tor's existence and have developed ways to work around it. The FBI has regularly managed to bust websites on the "dark net" that distribute child sexual abuse images, even though these sites hide behind Tor. Often this is because the operators tripped up. Technology is only a tool, and perpetrators of crimes live in the real world, where they may leave physical evidence or commit human errors when interacting with the technology.

In Section 6.5, we discuss Zerocoin and Zerocash, anonymous decentralized cryptocurrencies that have some similarities to Chaum's ecash, but they have to tackle thorny cryptographic challenges because of these two limitations.

6.2. HOW TO DEANONYMIZE BITCOIN

As mentioned before, Bitcoin is only pseudonymous, so all of your transactions or addresses could potentially be linked together. Let's take a closer look at how that might actually happen.

Figure 6.1 shows a snippet of the Wikileaks donation page (including the quote at the beginning of the chapter). Notice the refresh button next to the donation address. As you might expect, clicking the button will replace the donation address with an entirely new, freshly generated address. Similarly, if you refresh the page or close it and visit it later, it will have another address, never previously seen. That's because Wikileaks wants to make sure that each donation they receive goes to a new public key

Bitcoin is a secure and anonymous digital currency. Bitcoins cannot be easily tracked back to you, and are safer and faster alternative to other donation methods. You can send BTC to the following address:

13DFamCvSxG8EG16VyXzdpfqxyooifswYx

FIGURE 6.1. Snippet from Wikileaks donation page. Notice the refresh icon next to the Bitcoin address. Wikileaks follows the Bitcoin best practice of generating a new receiving address for every donation.

that they create just for that purpose. Wikileaks is taking maximal advantage of the ability to create new pseudonyms. This is in fact best practice for anonymity used by Bitcoin wallets.

You might think that these different addresses must be unlinkable. Wikileaks receives each donation separately, and presumably it can also spend each donation separately. But these activities can potentially be linked, as we now discuss.

Linking

Suppose Alice wants to buy a teapot that costs 8 BTC (more likely 0.08 BTC, at 2015 exchange rates). Suppose, further, that her bitcoins are in three separate unspent outputs at different addresses whose amounts are 3, 5, and 6 BTC, respectively. Alice

Stealth Addresses

Suppose Bob wants to advertise his donation address on a billboard, in addition to on his website. Now there is no way to show a different address to each user, and it would seem inevitable that the donations the site receives at this address will be easily linkable to Bob's site.

A neat solution to this problem is the use of *stealth addresses*. It allows the recipient Bob to post a static "permanent" address from which any sender Alice can derive new addresses, for which only Bob will know the private key.

How is this done? Recall that ECDSA public keys are of the form g^x, where x is the private key, and the address is $H(g^x)$. To enable stealth addresses, Bob will have to advertise the public key itself, rather than the much shorter hash value. Then Alice can pick a random value r, compute $(g^x)^r = g^{xr}$, and send money to this public key. If Alice is able to separately send the value r to Bob, he can compute the correct private key xr to spend the money sent to g^{xr}.

This method isn't ideal, as Alice has to send r to Bob, and Bitcoin transactions are supposed to work even when Bob is offline. To fix this, there are more complicated protocols that allow Alice to effectively embed r in the Bitcoin transaction itself. Then Bob can later scan the block chain, detect transactions intended for him, and recover the private key. This approach is used in Dark Wallet, a wallet designed to increase privacy, and a similar concept is used in the altcoin CryptoNote.

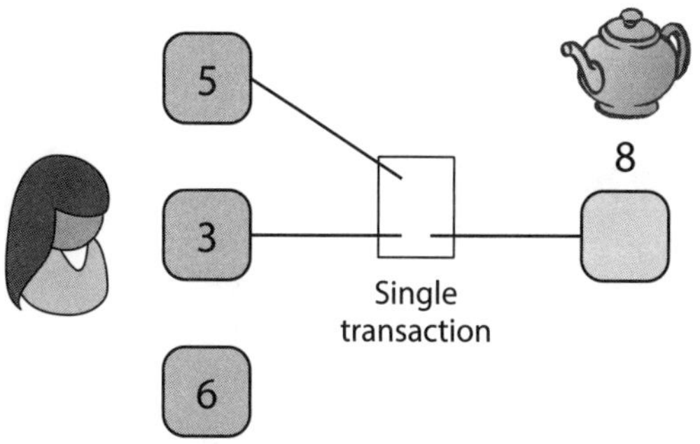

FIGURE 6.2. Multi-input transaction. To pay for the teapot, Alice has to create a single transaction having inputs that are at two different addresses. In doing so, Alice reveals that these two addresses are controlled by a single entity.

doesn't actually have an address with 8 BTC sitting in it, so she must combine two of her outputs as inputs to a single transaction that she pays to the store (Figure 6.2).

But this transaction reveals something. It is recorded permanently in the block chain, and anyone who sees it can infer that the two inputs to the transaction are most likely under the control of the same user. In other words, *shared spending is evidence of joint control* of the different input addresses. There could be exceptions, of course. Perhaps Alice and Bob are roommates and agree to jointly purchase the teapot by each supplying one transaction input. But by and large, joint inputs imply joint control.

But it doesn't stop there. The adversary can repeat this process and transitively link an entire cluster of transactions as belonging to a single entity. If another address is linked to either one of Alice's addresses in this manner, then the adversary knows that all three addresses belong to the same entity, and he can use this observation to cluster addresses. In general, if an output at a new address is spent together with one from any of the addresses in the cluster, then this new address can also be added to the cluster.

In Section 6.4 we discuss an anonymity technique called "CoinJoin," which works by violating this assumption. But for now, if you assume that people are using regular Bitcoin wallet software without any special anonymity techniques, then this method of linking addresses by clustering tends to be pretty robust. We haven't yet seen how to link these clusters to real-world identities, but we'll get to that shortly.

Change Address Randomization

An early version of the Bitcoin-Qt library (which is now called Bitcoin Core) had a bug that always put the change address as the first output in a transaction with two outputs. Thus it was trivial to identify the change address in many transactions. This bug was fixed in 2012, but it highlights an important point: wallet software has an important role to play in protecting anonymity. If you're developing wallet software, there are many pitfalls you should be aware of; in particular, you should always choose the position of the change address at random to avoid giving too much away to an adversary!

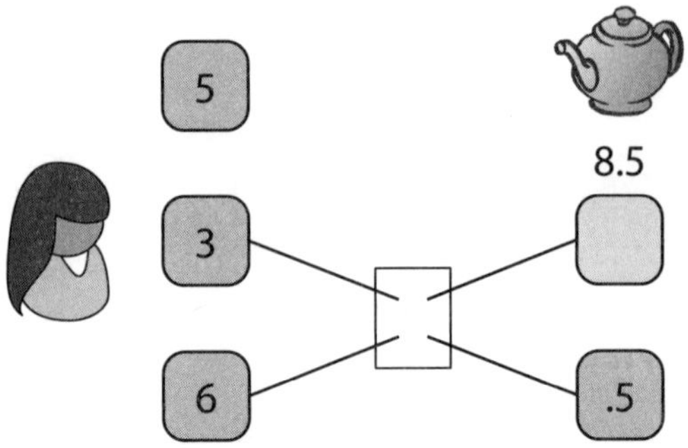

FIGURE 6.3. Change address. To pay for the teapot, Alice has to create a transaction with one output that goes to the merchant and another output that sends change back to herself.

Going back to our example, suppose the price of the teapot has gone up from 8 BTC to 8.5 BTC. Alice can no longer find a set of unspent outputs that she can combine to produce the exact change needed for the teapot. Instead, she exploits the fact that transactions can have multiple outputs, as shown in Figure 6.3. One of the outputs is the store's payment address and the other is a "change" address owned by Alice.

Now consider this transaction from the viewpoint of an adversary. They can deduce that the two input addresses belong to the same user. They might further suspect that one of the output addresses also belongs to that same user, but they have no way to determine which one that is. Just because the 0.5 output is smaller doesn't mean that it's the change address. Alice might have 10,000 BTC sitting in a transaction, and she might spend 8.5 BTC on the teapot and send the remaining 9,991.5 BTC back to herself. In that scenario, the bigger output is in fact the change address.

A somewhat better guess is that if the teapot had cost only 0.5 BTC, then Alice wouldn't have had to create a transaction with two different inputs, since either the 3 BTC or the 6 BTC input would have been sufficient by itself. But the effectiveness of this type of heuristic depends entirely on the implementation details of commonly used wallet software. There's nothing preventing wallets (or users) from combining transactions even when not strictly necessary.

Idioms of Use

Implementation details of this sort are called *idioms of use*. In 2013, a group of researchers led by Sarah Meiklejohn found an idiom of use that was true for most wallet software and led to a powerful heuristic for identifying change addresses. Specifically, they found that wallets typically generate a fresh address when a change address is required. Because of this idiom of use, change addresses are generally addresses that have never before appeared in the block chain. In contrast, nonchange outputs are often not new addresses and may have appeared previously in the block chain. An adversary can use this knowledge to distinguish change addresses and link them with the input addresses.

Exploiting idioms of use can be error prone. The fact that change addresses are fresh addresses just happens to be a feature of wallet software. It was true in 2013 when the researchers tested it. Maybe it's still true, but maybe it's not. Users may choose to override this default behavior. Most importantly, a user who is aware of this technique can easily evade it. Even in 2013, the researchers found that it produced many false positives, in which the technique clustered together addresses that didn't actually belong to the same entity. They reported that the method needed significant manual oversight and intervention to prune these false positives.

Attaching Real-World Identities to Clusters

Figure 6.4 shows how Meiklejohn et al. clustered Bitcoin addresses using basic idioms of use as heuristics. But the graph is not labeled—identities are not yet attached to the clusters.

We might be able to make some educated guesses based on what we know about the Bitcoin economy. Back in 2013, Mt. Gox was the largest Bitcoin exchange, so we might guess that the largest filled circle represents addresses controlled by them. We might also notice that the small cluster on the left has a tiny volume (represented by its small filled circle) in bitcoins, despite having the largest number of transactions. This fits the pattern

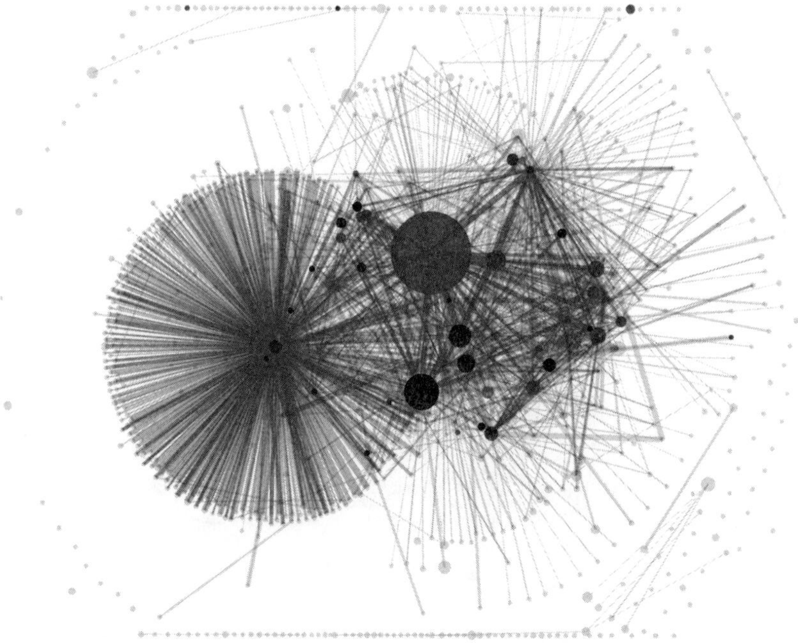

FIGURE 6.4. Clustering of addresses. In the 2013 paper "A Fistful of Bitcoins: Characterizing Payments among Men with No Names," Meiklejohn et al. combined the shared-spending heuristic and the fresh-change-address heuristic to cluster Bitcoin addresses. The sizes of these circles represent the quantity of money flowing into those clusters, and each edge represents a transaction.

of the gambling service Satoshi Dice, which is a popular game in which you submit small wagers in bitcoins. Overall, this isn't a great way to identify clusters. It requires knowledge and guesswork and will only work for the most prominent services.

Tagging by Transacting

What about just visiting the website for each exchange or merchant and looking up the address they advertise for receiving bitcoins? That doesn't quite work, however, because most services will advertise a new address for every transaction, and the address shown to you is not yet in the block chain. There's no point in waiting, either, because that address will never be shown to anyone else.

The only way to reliably infer addresses is to actually transact with that service provider—depositing bitcoins, purchasing an item, and so on. When you send bitcoins to or receive bitcoins from the service provider, you will then know one of their addresses, which will soon end up in the block chain (and in one of the clusters). You can then tag that entire cluster with the service provider's identity.

This is is exactly what the "Fistful of Bitcoins" researchers (and others since) have done. They bought a variety of things, joined mining pools, used Bitcoin exchanges, wallet services, and gambling sites, and interacted in a variety of other ways with service providers, conducting 344 transactions in all.

In Figure 6.5, we again show the clusters of Figure 6.4, but this time with the labels attached. Our guesses about Mt. Gox and Satoshi Dice were correct, but the researchers

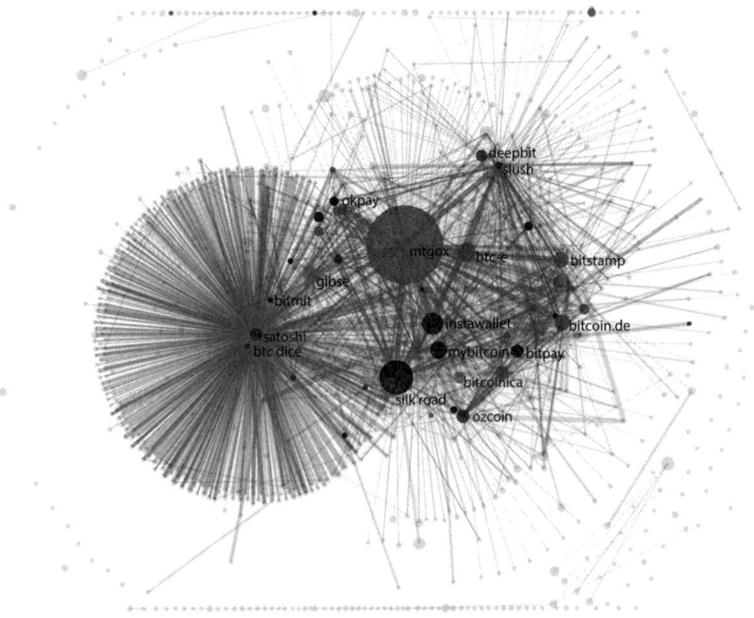

FIGURE 6.5. Labeled clusters. By transacting with various Bitcoin service providers, Meiklejohn et al. were able to attach real-world identities to their clusters.

were able to identify numerous other service providers that would have been hard to identify without transacting with them.

Identifying Individuals

Can we do the same thing for individuals? That is, can we connect little clusters corresponding to individuals to their real-life identities?

Directly transacting. Anyone who transacts with an individual—an online or offline merchant, an exchange, or a friend who splits a dinner bill using Bitcoin—knows at least one address belonging to that individual.

Via service providers. In the course of using Bitcoin over a few months or years, most users eventually interact with an exchange or other centralized service provider. These service providers typically ask users for their identities—often they're legally required to, as we discuss in Chapter 7. If law enforcement wants to identify a user, they can turn to these service providers.

Carelessness. People often post their Bitcoin addresses in public forums. A common reason is to request donations. When someone does this, it creates a link between their identity and one of their addresses. If they don't use the anonymity services that we discuss in the following sections, they risk having all their transactions deanonymized.

Attacks on privacy become more effective with time. History shows that deanonymization algorithms usually improve over time when the data is publicly available, as more researchers study the problem and identify new attack techniques. Besides, more auxiliary information becomes available that attackers can use to attach identities to clusters. This is something to worry about if you care about privacy.

The deanonymization techniques examined so far are all based on analyzing the graphs of transactions in the block chain. They are collectively known as *transaction graph analysis.*

Network-Layer Deanonymization

A completely different way in which users can be deanonymized does not rely on the transaction graph. Recall that to post a transaction to the block chain, one typically broadcasts it to Bitcoin's peer-to-peer network, where messages are sent that don't necessarily get permanently recorded in the block chain.

In networking terminology, the block chain is called the *application layer* and the peer-to-peer network is the *network layer.* Network-layer deanonymization was first pointed out by Dan Kaminsky at the 2011 Black Hat conference. He noticed that when a node creates a transaction, it connects to many nodes at once and broadcasts the transaction. If sufficiently many nodes on the network collude with one another (or are run by the same adversary), they could figure out the first node to broadcast any transaction. Presumably, that would be a node that's run by the user who created the transaction. The adversary could then link the transaction to the node's IP address. An IP address is close to a real-world identity; there are many ways to try to unmask the

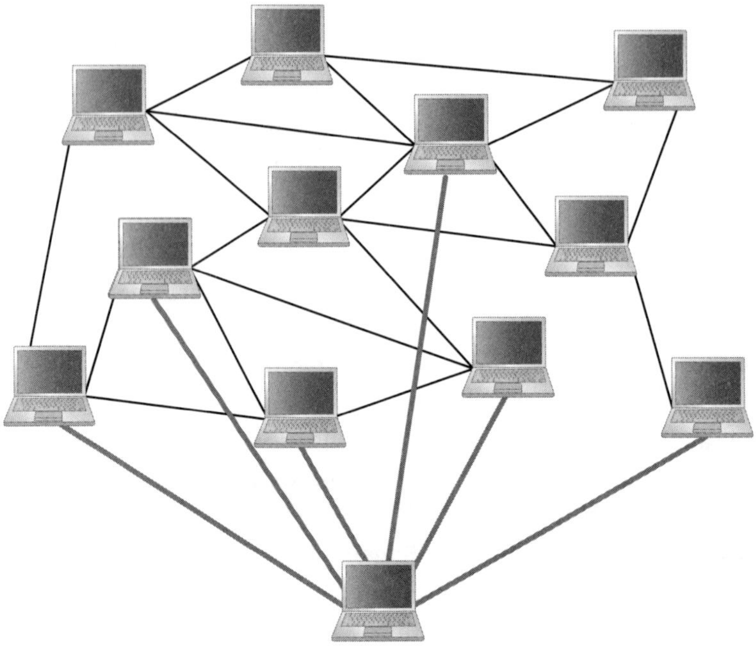

FIGURE 6.6. Network-level deanonymization. As Dan Kaminsky pointed out in his 2011 Black Hat talk, "the first node to inform you of a transaction is probably the source of it." This heuristic is amplified when multiple nodes cooperate and identify the same source.

person behind an IP address. Thus, network-layer deanonymization is a serious problem for privacy (Figure 6.6).

Luckily, this problem of communications anonymity has already been the subject of considerable research. As discussed in Section 6.1, the widely deployed system called Tor can be used for communicating anonymously.

There are a couple of caveats to using Tor as a network-layer anonymity solution for Bitcoin. First, subtle interactions may occur between the Tor protocol and any protocol that's overlaid on it, resulting in new ways to breach anonymity. Indeed, researchers have found potential security problems with using Bitcoin-over-Tor, so this must be done with extreme caution. Second, other anonymous communication technologies might be better suited to use in Bitcoin. Tor is intended for "low-latency" activities, such as web browsing, where you don't want to sit around waiting for too long. It makes some compromises to achieve anonymity with low latency. Bitcoin, by comparison, is a high-latency system, because it takes a while for transactions to be confirmed in the block chain. In theory, at least, you might want to use an alternative anonymity technique such as a *mix net* (see Section 6.3), but as of this writing, Tor has the advantage of being an actual system that has a large user base and whose security has been intensely studied.

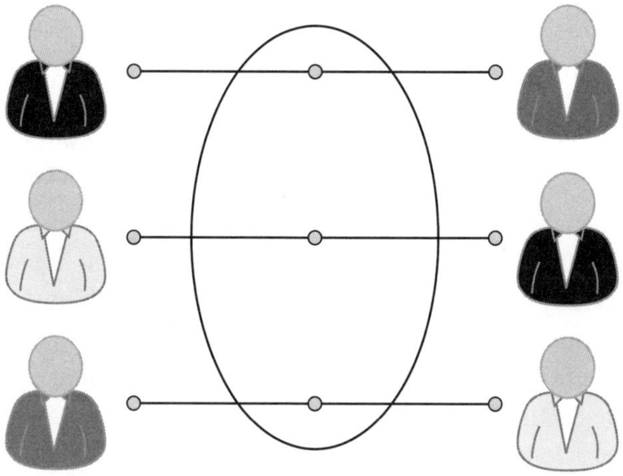

FIGURE 6.7. Mixing. Users send coins to an intermediary and get back coins that were deposited by other users. This makes it harder to trace a user's coins on the block chain.

So far, we've seen that different addresses might be linked together by transaction graph analysis and that they might also be linkable to a real-world identity. We've also seen that a transaction or address could get linked to an IP address based on the peer-to-peer network. The latter problem is relatively easy to solve, even if it can't be considered completely solved yet. The former problem is much trickier, and the rest of this chapter deals with ways to solve it.

6.3. MIXING

Several mechanisms can make transaction graph analysis less effective. One such technique is *mixing*. The intuition behind it is simple: if you want anonymity, use an intermediary. This principle is not specific to Bitcoin and is useful in many situations where anonymity is a goal. Mixing is illustrated in Figure 6.7.

Online Wallets as Mixes

If you recall our discussion of online wallets (Section 4.4), they may seem to be suitable as intermediaries. Online wallets are services where you can store your bitcoins online and withdraw them at some later date. Typically the coins that you withdraw won't be the same as the coins you deposited. Do online wallets provide effective mixing, then?

Online wallets do provide a measure of unlinkability that can foil attempts at transaction graph analysis—in one case, prominent researchers had to retract a claim that had received a lot of publicity, because the link they thought they'd found was a spurious one caused by an online wallet.

However, using online wallets for mixing has several signficant limitations. First, most online wallets don't actually promise to mix users' funds; instead, they do it because it simplifies the engineering. You have no guarantee that they won't change their behavior. Second, even if they do mix funds, they will almost certainly maintain records internally that will allow them to link your deposit to your withdrawal. This is a prudent choice for wallet services for reasons of both security and legal compliance. So if your threat model includes the possibility of the service provider itself tracking you, or getting hacked, or being compelled to hand over its records, you're back to square one. Third, in addition to keeping logs internally, reputable and regulated services will also require and record your identity (we discuss regulation in more detail in Chapter 7). You won't be able to simply create an account with a username and password. So in one sense, you are worse off than if you did not use the wallet service.

The anonymity provided by online wallets is similar to that provided by the traditional banking system. There are centralized intermediaries that know a lot about our transactions, but from the point of view of a stranger with no privileged information, we have a reasonable degree of privacy. But as we discussed, the public nature of the block chain means that if something goes wrong (say, a wallet or exchange service gets hacked and records are exposed), the privacy risk is worse than with the traditional system. Besides, most people who turn to Bitcoin for anonymity tend to do so because they are unhappy with anonymity properties of the traditional system and want a better (or a different kind of) anonymity guarantee. These are the motivations behind dedicated mixing services.

Dedicated Mixing Services

In contrast to online wallets, dedicated mixes promise not to keep records; nor do they require your identity. You don't even need a username or other pseudonym to interact

> **Terminology: Mix versus Laundry**
>
> In this book, the term *mix* refers to a dedicated mixing service. An equivalent term that some people prefer is *mixer*.
>
> You might also encounter the term *laundry*. We don't like this term, because it needlessly attaches a moral judgement to something that's a purely technical concept. As we've seen, there are good reasons you might want to protect your privacy in Bitcoin and use mixes for everyday privacy. Of course, we must also acknowledge the bad uses, but using the term "laundry" promotes the negative connotation, as it implies that your coins are "dirty" and you need to clean them.
>
> There is also the term *tumbler*, which refers to tumbling drums. Such drums are used in clothes dryers as well as in "tumbling boxes" that clean and polish gemstones. It isn't clear whether it is the mixing action of tumbling drums or their cleaning effect that inspired the use of the word in the Bitcoin context. Regardless, we'll stick to the term "mix."

with the mix. You send your bitcoins to an address provided by the mix, and you tell the mix a destination address to send bitcoins to. Hopefully, the mix will soon send you (other) bitcoins to the address you specified. It's essentially a swap.

Although it's good that dedicated mixes promise not to keep records, you still have to trust them to keep that promise. And you have to trust that they'll send you back your coins at all. Since mixes aren't a place where you store your bitcoins, unlike wallets, you'll want your coins back relatively quickly, which means that the pool of other coins that your deposit will be mixed with is relatively small—those that were deposited at roughly the same time.

Guidelines for Mixing

A group of researchers, including four of the five authors of this textbook, studied mixes and proposed a set of guidelines for improving the way that mixes operate, both in terms of increasing anonymity and in terms of the security of entrusting your coins to the mix. Here we discuss each of these guidelines.

USE A SERIES OF MIXES

The first principle is to use a series of mixes, one after the other, instead of just a single mix (Figure 6.8). This is a well-known and well-established principle—for example, Tor uses a series of three routers for anonymous communication. This reduces your reliance on the trustworthiness of any single mix. As long as any one of the mixes in the series keeps its promise and deletes its records, you have reason to expect that no one will be able to link your first input to the ultimate output that you receive.

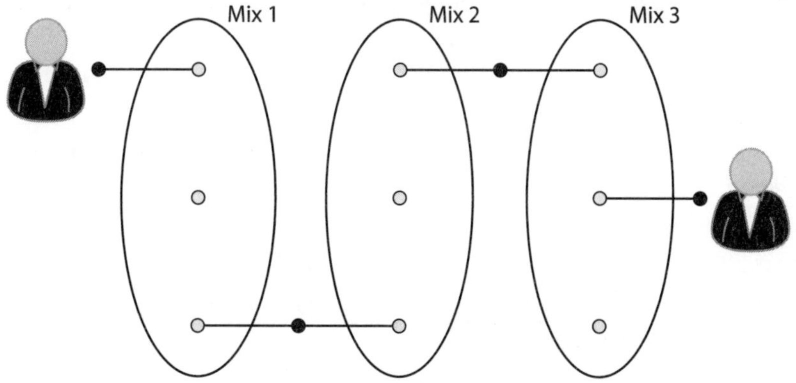

FIGURE 6.8. Series of mixes. We begin with a user who has a coin that we assume the adversary has managed to link to the user. The user sends the coin through various mixes, each time providing a freshly generated output address to the mix. Provided that at least one of these mixes destroys its records of the input-to-output address mapping, and there are no side-channel leaks of information, an adversary won't be able to link the user's original coin to his final one.

USE UNIFORM TRANSACTIONS

If mix transactions by different users involved different quantities of bitcoins, then mixing wouldn't be very effective. Since the value going into the mix and coming out of it would have to be preserved, the user's coins could be linked as they flow through the mix, or at least the size of the anonymity set could be greatly diminished.

Instead, we want mix transactions to be uniform in value, so that linkability is minimized. All mixes should agree on a standard *chunk size*, a fixed value that incoming mix transactions must have. This would increase the anonymity set, as all transactions going through *any* mix would look the same and would not be distinguishable based on their value. Moreover, having a uniform size across all mixes would make it easy to use a series of mixes without having to split or merge transactions.

In practice, it might be difficult to agree on a single chunk size that works for all users. If the chunk size is too large, users wanting to mix a small amount of money won't be able to. But if it is too small, users wanting to mix a large amount of money will need to divide it into a huge number of chunks, which might be inefficient and costly. Multiple standard chunk sizes would improve performance but also split the anonymity sets by chunk size. Perhaps a series of two or three increasing chunk sizes would provide a reasonable trade-off between efficiency and privacy.

CLIENT SIDE SHOULD BE AUTOMATED

In addition to trying to link coins based on transaction values, a clever adversary might attempt various other ways to deanonymize, for example, by observing the timing of transactions. These attacks can be avoided, but the precautions necessary are too complex and cumbersome for human users. Instead, the client-side functionality for interacting with mixes should be automated and built into privacy-friendly wallet software.

FEES SHOULD BE ALL OR NOTHING

Mixes are businesses and expect to be paid for their services. One way for a mix to charge fees is to take a cut of each transaction that users send in. But this is problematic for anonymity, because mix transactions can no longer be in standard chunk sizes. (If users try to split and merge their slightly smaller chunks back to the original chunk size, it introduces serious and hard-to-analyze anonymity risks because of the new linkages between coins that are introduced.)

Don't confuse mixing fees with transaction fees, which are collected by miners. Mixing fees are separate from and in addition to such fees.

To avoid this problem, mixing fees should be all or nothing and be applied probabilistically. In other words, the mix should swallow the whole chunk with a small probability or return it in its entirety. For example, if the mix wants to charge a 0.1 percent mixing fee, then one out of every 1,000 times the mix should swallow the entire chunk, whereas 999 times out of 1,000, the mix should process and return the entire chunk without taking any mixing fee.

This feat is tricky to accomplish. The mix must make a probabilistic decision and convince the user that it didn't cheat: that it didn't bias its random number generator so that it has (say) a 1 percent probability of retaining a chunk as a fee, instead of 0.1 percent. Cryptography provides a way to do this; see the 2014 "Mixcoin" paper by Bonneau et al. in the Further Reading section for details. The paper also discusses various ways in which mixes can improve their trustworthiness.

Mixing in Practice

As of 2015, there is no functional mix ecosystem. Many mix services are available, but they have low volumes and therefore small anonymity sets. Worse, many mixes have been reported to steal bitcoins. Perhaps the difficulty of bootstrapping such an ecosystem is one reason it has never been established. Given the dodgy reputation of mixes, not many people want to use them, resulting in low transaction volumes and hence poor anonymity. There's an old saying that anonymity loves company—that is, the more people using an anonymity service, the better anonymity it can provide. Furthermore, in the absence of much money to be made from providing the advertised services, mix operators might be tempted to steal funds instead, perpetuating the cycle of untrustworthy mixes.

Today's mixes don't follow any of the principles we have laid out. Each mix operates independently and typically provides a web interface, with which the user interacts manually to specify the receiving address and any other necessary parameters. The user chooses the amount to be mixed. The mix will take a cut of every transaction as a mixing fee and send the rest to the destination address.

We think it's necessary for mixes (and wallet software) to move to the model presented here to achieve strong anonymity, resist clever attacks, provide a usable interface, and attract high volumes. But it remains to be seen whether a robust mix ecosystem will ever evolve.

6.4. DECENTRALIZED MIXING

Decentralized mixing eliminates mixing services and replaces them with a peer-to-peer protocol by which a group of users can mix their coins. As you can imagine, this approach is philosophically better aligned with Bitcoin than the centralized mixing services discussed in Section 6.3.

Decentralization also has more practical advantages. First, it doesn't have the bootstrapping problem: users don't have to wait for reputable centralized mixes to come into existence. Second, theft is impossible in decentralized mixing; the protocol ensures that when you put in bitcoins to be mixed, you'll get back bitcoins of equal value. Because of this, even though some central coordination turns out to be helpful in decentralized mixing, it's easier for someone to set up such a service, because they don't have to convince users of their trustworthiness. Finally, in some ways decentralized mixing can provide better anonymity.

CoinJoin

The main proposal for decentralized mixing is CoinJoin. In this protocol, different users jointly create a single Bitcoin transaction that combines all their inputs. The key technical principle that enables CoinJoin to work is this: when a transaction has multiple inputs coming from different addresses, the signatures corresponding to each input are separate from and independent of one another. So these different addresses could be controlled by different people. You don't need one party to collect all the private keys (Figure 6.9).

This allows a group of users to mix their coins with a single transaction. Each user supplies an input and output address, and together the users form a transaction with these addresses. The order of the input and output addresses is randomized, so an adversary who isn't part of this group of users will be unable to determine the mapping between inputs and outputs. Participants check that their output address is included in the transaction and that it receives the same amount of bitcoins that they input (minus any transaction fees). Once they have confirmed this, they sign the transaction.

Somebody looking at this transaction on the block chain—even if they know that it is a CoinJoin transaction—will be unable to determine the mapping between the inputs and outputs. From an outsider's perspective, the coins have been mixed, which is the essence of CoinJoin.

What we've described so far is just one round of mixing. But the principles discussed

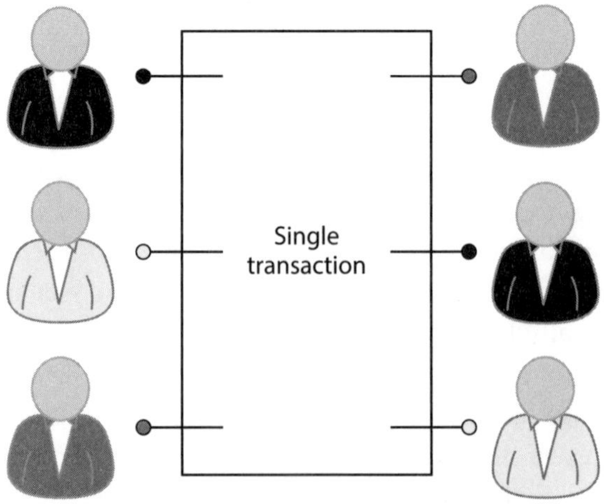

FIGURE 6.9. A Coinjoin transaction.

in Section 6.3 still apply. Users should repeat this process with (presumably) different groups of users. They should also make sure that the chunk sizes are standardized, so that side channels are not introduced.

Let's now delve into the details of CoinJoin, which can be broken into five steps:

1. Find peers who want to mix.
2. Exchange input/output addresses.
3. Construct the transaction.
4. Send the transaction around to each participant. Each peer signs after verifying their output is present.
5. Broadcast the transaction.

To begin the process, a group of peers who all want to mix need to find one another. This step can be facilitated by servers acting as "watering holes," allowing users to connect and group together. Unlike centralized mixes, these servers are not in a position to steal users' funds or compromise anonymity.

Once a peer group has formed, the peers must exchange their input and output addresses with one another. It's important for participants to exchange these addresses in such a way that even the other members of the peer group do not know the mapping between input and output addresses. Otherwise, even if peers execute a CoinJoin transaction with a supposedly random set of peers, an adversary might be able to weasel her way into the group and note the mapping of inputs to outputs. To swap addresses in an unlinkable way requires an anonymous communication protocol. The Tor network could be used, which we discussed earlier, or a special-purpose anonymous routing protocol called a "decryption mix-net."

Once the inputs and outputs have been communicated, one of these users—it doesn't matter who—will then construct the transaction corresponding to these inputs and outputs. The unsigned transaction will then be passed around; each peer will verify that its input and output addresses are included correctly and then sign.

If all peers follow the protocol, this system works well. Any peer can assemble the transaction, and any peer can broadcast the transaction to the network. Two of them could even broadcast it independently; it will be published only once to the block chain, of course. But if one or more of the peers wants to be disruptive, it's easy for them to launch a denial-of-service attack, preventing the protocol from completing.

In particular, a peer could participate in the first phase of the protocol, providing its input and output addresses, but then refuse to sign in the second phase. Alternately, after signing the transaction, a disruptive peer can try to take the input that he provided to the peers and spend it in some other transaction instead. If the alternate transaction wins the race on the network, it will be confirmed first, and the CoinJoin transaction will be rejected as a double spend.

Several proposals have been made to prevent denial of service in CoinJoin. One is to impose a cost to participate in the protocol, either via a proof of work (analogous to mining), or by a proof of burn, a technique to provably destroy a small quantity of bitcoins that you own, which we studied in Chapter 3. Alternatively, there are cryptographic ways to identify noncompliant participants and kick them out of the group. For details, see the Further Reading section at the end of this chapter.

High-Level Flows

We mentioned side channels in Section 6.1. We now take a closer look at how tricky side channels can be. Suppose Alice receives a specific amount of bitcoins, say 43.12312 BTC, at a particular address on a weekly basis, perhaps as her salary. Suppose further that she has a habit of automatically and immediately transferring 5 percent of that amount to her retirement account, which is another Bitcoin address. We call this transfer pattern a *high-level flow*. No mixing strategy can effectively hide the fact that there's a relationship between the two addresses in this scenario. Think about the patterns that will be visible on the block chain: the specific amounts and timing are extraordinarily unlikely to occur by chance.

One technique that can help regain unlinkability in the presence of high-level flows is called *merge avoidance*, proposed by Bitcoin developer Mike Hearn. Generally, to make a payment, a user creates a single transaction that combines as many coins as necessary to pay the entire amount to a single address. What if the user could avoid the need to merge and consequently link all of her inputs? The merge avoidance protocol enables this by allowing the receiver of a payment to provide multiple output addresses—as many as necessary. The sender and receiver agree on a set of denominations to break up the payment into and carry it out using multiple transactions, as shown in Figure 6.10.

Assuming the store eventually combines these two payments with many other inputs from other payments it has received, it will no longer be obvious that these two addresses were associated with each other. The store should avoid recombining these two coins as soon as it receives them, or else it would be clear that they came from the same

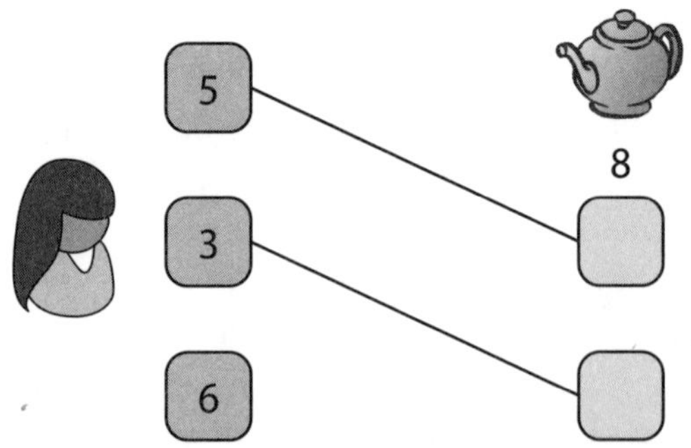

FIGURE 6.10. Merge avoidance. Alice wishes to buy a teapot for 8 BTC. The store gives her two addresses, and she pays 5 BTC to one and 3 BTC to the other, matching her available coins. This method avoids revealing that these two addresses both belong to the same entity.

entity. Also, Alice might want to avoid sending the two payments at the same time, which might similarly reveal this information.

Generally, merge avoidance can help mitigate the problem of high-level flows: an adversary might not be able to discern a flow if it is broken up into many smaller flows that aren't linked to one another. In the example of Alice funding her retirement account, she would need to use merge avoidance both when receiving her salary as well as when transferring a portion of it to her retirement fund. Merge avoidance also defeats address clustering techniques that rely on coins being spent jointly in a single transaction.

6.5. ZEROCOIN AND ZEROCASH

No cryptocurrency anonymity solutions have caused as much excitement as *Zerocoin* and its successor *Zerocash*. That's both because of the ingenious cryptography that they employ and because of the powerful anonymity that they promise. Whereas all of the anonymity-enhancing technologies discussed so far add anonymity on top of the core protocol, Zerocoin and Zerocash incorporate anonymity at the protocol level. We present a high-level view of the protocol here and necessarily simplify some details, but you can find references to the original papers in the Further Reading section at the end of the chapter.

Compatibility. As we'll see, the strong anonymity guarantees of Zerocoin and Zerocash come at a cost: unlike centralized mixing and CoinJoin, these protocols are not compatible with Bitcoin as it stands today. It is technically possible to deploy Zerocoin with a soft fork to Bitcoin, but the practical difficulties are serious enough to make this infeasible. With Zerocash, a fork is not even possible, and an altcoin is the only option.

Cryptographic guarantees. Zerocoin and Zerocash incorporate protocol-level mixing, and the anonymity properties come with cryptographic guarantees. These guarantees are qualitatively better than those of the other mixing technologies that we have discussed. You don't need to trust anybody—mixes, peers, or intermediaries of any kind, or even miners and the consensus protocol—to ensure your privacy. The promise of anonymity relies only on the adversary's computational limits, as with most cryptographic guarantees.

Zerocoin

To explain Zerocoin, we first introduce the concept of Basecoin. Basecoin is a Bitcoin-like altcoin, and Zerocoin is an extension of this altcoin. The key feature that provides anonymity is that you can convert basecoins into zerocoins and back again, and when you do that, it breaks the link between the original basecoin and the new basecoin. In this system, Basecoin is the currency that you transact in, and Zerocoin just provides a mechanism to trade your basecoins in for new ones that are unlinkable to the old ones.

You can view each zerocoin you own as a token that you can use to prove that you owned a basecoin and made it unspendable. The proof does not reveal which basecoin you owned, merely that you did own a basecoin. You can later redeem this proof for a new basecoin by presenting the proof to the miners. An analogy is entering a casino and exchanging your cash for poker chips. These serve as proof that you deposited some cash, which you can later exchange for different cash of the same value on exiting the casino. Of course, unlike poker chips, you can't actually do anything with a zerocoin except hold on to it and later redeem it for a basecoin.

To make this work in a cryptocurrency, these proofs are implemented cryptographically. We need to make sure that each proof can be used only once to redeem a basecoin. Otherwise, it would be possible to acquire basecoins for free by turning a basecoin into a zerocoin and then redeeming it more than once.

Zero-Knowledge Proofs

The key cryptographic tool used is a *zero-knowledge proof*, which is a way for somebody to prove a (mathematical) statement without revealing any other information that leads to that statement being true. For example, suppose you've done a lot of work to solve a hash puzzle, and you want to convince someone of this. In other words, you want to prove the statement

$$\text{I know } x \text{ such that } H(x \parallel \text{other known inputs}) < \langle\text{target}\rangle$$

You could, of course, do this by revealing x. But a zero-knowledge proof allows you to do this in such a way that the other person is no wiser about the value of x after seeing the proof than they were before.

You can also prove such statements as "I know x such that $H(x)$ belongs to the following set: $\{\ldots\}$." The proof would reveal nothing about x, nor about which element of the set equals $H(x)$. Zerocoin crucially relies on zero-knowledge proofs, and in fact the statements proved in Zerocoin are very similar to the latter example. In this book, we treat zero-knowledge proofs as black boxes. We present the properties achieved by zero-knowledge proofs and show where they are necessary in the protocol, but we do not delve into the technical details of how these proofs are implemented. Zero-knowledge proofs are a cornerstone of modern cryptography and form the basis of many protocols. We refer the motivated reader to the Further Reading section for more detailed treatments.

Minting Zerocoins

Zerocoins come into existence by minting, and anybody can mint a zerocoin. They come in standard denominations. For simplicity, assume that there is only one denomination worth 1.0 zerocoins, and that each zerocoin is worth 1 basecoin. While anyone can mint a zerocoin, just minting one doesn't automatically give it any value—you can't

FIGURE 6.11. Committing to a serial number. The real-world analog of a cryptographic commitment is sealing a value inside an envelope.

get free money. It acquires value only when you put it onto the block chain, and doing that will require giving up 1 basecoin.

To mint a zerocoin, you use a cryptographic commitment. Recall from Chapter 1 that a commitment scheme is the cryptographic analog of sealing a value in an envelope and putting it on a table in everyone's view (Figure 6.11).

Minting a zerocoin is done in three steps:

1. Generate serial number *S* and a random secret *r*.
2. Compute *Commit(S, r)*, the commitment to the serial number.
3. Publish the commitment on the block chain, as shown in Figure 6.12. This burns a basecoin, making it unspendable, and creates a zerocoin. Keep *S* and *r* secret for now.

To spend a zerocoin and redeem a new basecoin, you need to prove that you previously minted a zerocoin. You could do this by opening your previous commitment, that is, revealing *S* and *r*. But this makes the link between your old basecoin and your new one apparent. How can you break the link? This is where the zero-knowledge proof comes in. At any point, there will be many commitments on the block chain—let's call them $c_1, c_2, \ldots, c_n$.

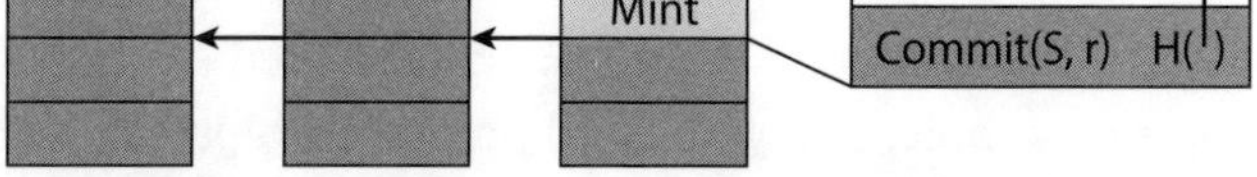

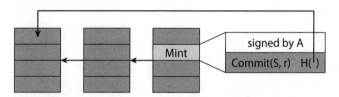

FIGURE 6.12. Putting a zerocoin on the block chain. To put a zerocoin on the blockchain requires a special mint transaction whose output "address" is the cryptographic commitment of the zerocoin's serial number. The input of the mint transaction is a basecoin, which has now been spent creating the zerocoin. The transaction does *not* reveal the serial number.

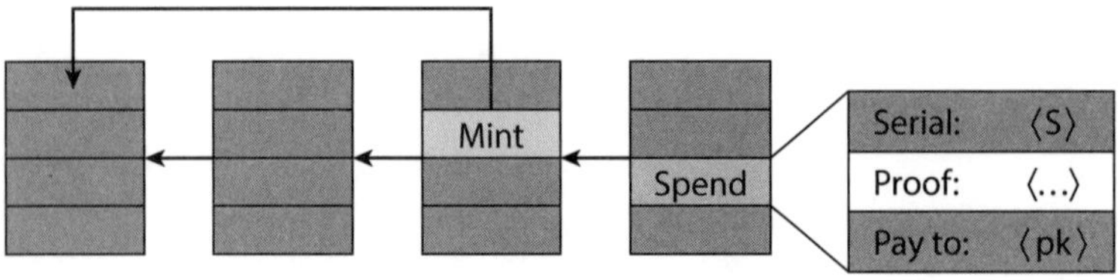

FIGURE 6.13. Spending a zerocoin. The spend transaction reveals the serial number S committed by the earlier mint transaction, along with a zero-knowledge proof that S corresponds to *some* earlier mint transaction. Unlike a mint transaction (or a normal Bitcoin/Basecoin transaction), the spend transaction has no inputs, and hence no signature. Instead the zero-knowledge proof serves to establish its validity.

Here are the steps that go into spending a zerocoin with serial number S to redeem a new basecoin (Figure 6.13):

- Create a special "spend" transaction that contains S, along with a zero-knowledge proof of the statement:

  "I know r such that $Commit(S, r)$ is in the set $\{c_1, c_2, \ldots, c_n\}$"

- Miners will verify your zero-knowledge proof, which establishes your *ability* to open one of the zerocoin commitments on the block chain without actually opening it.
- Miners will also check that the serial number S has never been used in any previous spend transaction (since that would be a double spend).
- The output of your spend transaction will now act as a new basecoin. For the output address, you should use an address that you own.

Once you spend a zerocoin, the serial number becomes public, and you will never be able to redeem this serial number again. And since there is only one serial number for each zerocoin, it means that each zerocoin can only be spent once, exactly as we required for security.

Anonymity. Observe that r is kept secret throughout; neither the mint nor the spend transaction reveals it. That means nobody knows which serial number corresponds to which zerocoin. This is the key concept behind Zerocoin's anonymity. There is no link on the block chain between the mint transaction that committed a serial number S and the spend transaction that later revealed S to redeem a basecoin. This magical sounding property is possible through cryptography, but it is not achievable in a physical, envelope-based system. It's as if there were a bunch of sealed envelopes containing different serial numbers on a table, and you could prove that a particular serial number is one of them without having to reveal which envelope and without having to open any of them.

Efficiency. Recall the statement that's proved in a spend transaction:

"I know r such that $Commit(S, r)$ is in the set $\{c_1, c_2, \ldots, c_n\}$"

This sounds like it would be horribly inefficient to implement, because the size of the zero-knowledge proofs would grow linearly as n increases, which is the number of zerocoins that have ever been minted. Remarkably, Zerocoin manages to make the size of these proofs only logarithmic in n. Note that even though the *statement* to be proved has a linear length, it doesn't need to be included along with the proof. The statement is implicit; it can be inferred by the miners, since they know the set of all zerocoins on the block chain. The proof itself can be much shorter. Nevertheless, compared to Bitcoin, Zerocoin still adds quite a sizable overhead, with proofs being about 50 kilobytes in size.

Trusted Setup

One of the cryptographic tools used in building Zerocoin (RSA accumulators) requires a one-time *trusted setup*. Specifically, a trusted party needs to choose two large primes p and q and publish $N = p \cdot q$, which is a parameter that everybody will use for the lifetime of the system. Think of N as a public key, except that it is for all of Zerocoin as opposed to one particular entity. As long as the trusted party destroys any record of p and q, the system is believed to be secure. In particular, this belief rests on the widely held assumption that it's infeasible to factor a number that is a product of two large primes. But if *anyone* knows the secret factors p and q (called the "trapdoor"), then they'd be able to create new zerocoins for themselves without being detected. So these secret inputs must be used once when generating the public parameters and then securely destroyed.

There's an interesting sociological problem here. It's not clear how an entity could choose N and convince everybody that they have securely destroyed the factors p and q that were used during the setup. Various proposals for how to achieve this have been made, including "threshold cryptography" techniques, which allow a set of delegates to jointly compute N in such a way that as long as any one of them deletes their secret inputs, the system will remain secure.

It's also possible to use a slightly different cryptographic construction to avoid the need for a trusted setup. Specifically, it has been shown that simply generating a very large random value for N is secure with high probability, because the number probably cannot be completely factored. Unfortunately, this carries a huge efficiency hit and is thus not considered practical.

Zerocash

Zerocash is a different anonymous cryptocurrency that builds on the concept of Zerocoin but takes the cryptography to the next level. It uses a cryptographic technique called "zero-knowledge succinct noninteractive arguments of knowledge" (zk-SNARKs), which are a way of making zero-knowledge proofs much more compact and efficient to verify. The upshot is that the efficiency of the system overall is improved to the point that it becomes possible to run the whole network without needing a basecoin. All transactions can be done in a zero-knowledge manner. As discussed, Zerocoin supports regular transactions for when you don't need unlinkability, augmented with computationally expensive transactions that are used only for mixing. The mix transactions are of fixed denominations, and splitting and merging of values can happen only in Basecoin. In Zerocash, that distinction is gone. The transaction amounts are now inside the commitments and are no longer visible on the block chain. The cryptographic proofs ensure that the splitting and merging are done correctly and that users can't create zerocash out of thin air.

The only thing that the ledger records publicly is the existence of these transactions, along with proofs that allow the miners to verify all the properties needed for the correct functioning of the system. Neither addresses nor values are revealed on the block chain at any point. The only users who need to know the amount of a transaction are the sender and the receiver of that particular transaction. The miners don't need to know transaction amounts. Of course, if there is a transaction fee, the miners need to know that fee, but that doesn't really compromise your anonymity.

The ability to run as an entirely untraceable system of transactions puts Zerocash in a category of its own as far as anonymity and privacy are concerned. Zerocash is immune to the side-channel attacks against mixing, because the public ledger no longer contains transaction amounts.

Setting Up Zerocash

In terms of its technical properties, Zerocash might sound too good to be true. There is indeed a catch. Just like Zerocoin, Zerocash requires public parameters to set up the zero-knowledge proof system. But unlike Zerocoin, which requires just one number N (which is only a few hundred bytes), Zerocash requires an enormous set of public parameters—more than a gigabyte long. Once again, to generate these public parameters, Zerocash requires random and secret inputs, and if *anyone* knows these secret inputs, it compromises the security of the system by enabling undetectable double spends.

We won't delve any deeper into the challenge of setting up a zk-SNARK system here. It remains an active area of research, but as of 2015, no one knows exactly how to set up the system in practice in a sufficiently trustworthy way. To date, zk-SNARKs have not been used in practice.

Putting It All Together

Let's now compare the solutions that we have discussed, both in terms of the anonymity properties that they provide and in terms of how deployable they are in practice (Table 6.1).

We start with Bitcoin itself, which is already deployed and is considered the default system here. But it's only pseudonymous, and powerful transaction graph analyses can be deployed against it. We looked at ways to cluster large groups of addresses, and how to sometimes attach real-world identities to those clusters.

TABLE 6.1. COMPARISON OF THE ANONYMITY TECHNOLOGIES PRESENTED IN THIS CHAPTER

System	Type	Anonymity attacks	Deployability
Bitcoin	Pseudonymous	Transaction graph analysis	Default
Manual mixing	Mix	Transaction graph analysis, bad mixes/peers	Usable today
Chain of mixes or CoinJoins	Mix	Side channels, bad mixes/peers	Bitcoin-compatible
Zerocoin	Cryptographic mix	Side channels (possibly)	Altcoin, trusted setup
Zerocash	Untraceable	None known	Altcoin, trusted setup

The next level of anonymity is to use a single mix in a manual way, or to do a CoinJoin by finding peers manually. This obscures the link between input and output but leaves too many potential clues in the transaction graph. Besides, mixes and peers could be malicious, hacked, or coerced into revealing their records. Although far from perfect in terms of anonymity, mixing services exist, so this option is usable today.

The third level we considered is a chain of mixes or CoinJoins. The anonymity improvement results from reduced reliance on any single mix or group of peers. Features like standardized chunk sizes and client-side automation can minimize information leaks, but some side channels are still present. There's also the danger of an adversary who controls or colludes with multiple mixes or peers. Wallets and services that implement a chain of mixes could be deployed and adopted today, but to our knowledge, a secure mix-chain solution isn't yet readily available.

Zerocoin bakes cryptography directly into the protocol and brings a mathematical guarantee of anonymity. We think some side channels are still possible, but it's certainly superior to the other mixing-based solutions. However, Zerocoin would have to be launched as an altcoin.

Finally, we looked at Zerocash. Due to its improved efficiency, Zerocash can be run as a fully untraceable—and not just anonymous—cryptocurrency. However, like Zerocoin, Zerocash is not Bitcoin compatible. Worse, it requires a complex setup process that the community is still figuring out how best to accomplish.

We've covered a lot of technology in this chapter. Now let's take a step back. Bitcoin's pseudonymity (and potential for anonymity) is powerful, and gains power when combined with other technologies, particularly anonymous communication. As we'll see in Chapter 7, this is the potent combination behind the Silk Road and other anonymous online marketplaces.

Despite its power, anonymity is fragile. One mistake can create an unwanted, irreversible link. But anonymity is worth protecting, since it has many good uses in addition to the obvious bad ones. Although these moral distinctions are important, they are not expressible at a technical level. Anonymity technologies seem to be deeply and inherently morally ambiguous, and as a society we must learn to live with this fact.

Bitcoin anonymity is an active area of technical innovation as well as ethical debate.

We still do not know which anonymity system for Bitcoin, if any, is going to become prominent or mainstream. That's a great opportunity for you—whether a developer, a policymaker, or a user—to get involved and make a contribution. Hopefully what you've learned in this chapter has given you the right background to do that.

FURTHER READING

Even more so than the topics discussed in previous chapters, anonymity technologies are constantly developing and are an active area of cryptocurrency research. The best way to keep up with the latest in this field is to begin with the papers listed here and to look for papers that cite them.

The "Fistful of Bitcoins" paper on transaction graph analysis is:

Meiklejohn, Sarah, Marjori Pomarole, Grant Jordan, Kirill Levchenko, Damon McCoy, Geoffrey M. Voelker, and Stefan Savage. "A Fistful of Bitcoins: Characterizing Payments among Men with No Names." In *Proceedings of the 2013 Conference on Internet Measurement*, New York: ACM, 2013.

A study of mixing technologies and the source of the principles for effective mixing that we discussed can be found in:

Bonneau, Joseph, Arvind Narayanan, Andrew Miller, Jeremy Clark, Joshua A. Kroll, and Edward W. Felten. "Mixcoin: Anonymity for Bitcoin with Accountable Mixes." In *Financial Cryptography and Data Security*. Berlin: Springer, 2014.

A study of mixing services in practice, showing that many are not reputable, is:

Möser, Malte, Rainer Böhme, and Dominic Breuker. "An Inquiry into Money Laundering Tools in the Bitcoin Ecosystem." In *2013 eCrime Researchers Summit*. Washington, DC: IEEE, 2013.

CoinJoin was presented on the Bitcoin forums by Bitcoin Core developer Greg Maxwell:

Maxwell, Gregory. "CoinJoin: Bitcoin Privacy for the Real World." Bitcoin Forum, 2013. Available at https://bitcointalk.org/index.php?topic=279249.0.

Zerocoin was developed by cryptographers from Johns Hopkins University. Zerocoin and Zerocash have the most complex cryptography of any scheme we've discussed in this book:

Miers, Ian, Christina Garman, Matthew Green, and Aviel D. Rubin. "Zerocoin: Anonymous Distributed E-Cash from Bitcoin." In *Proceedings of the 2013 IEEE Symposium on Security and Privacy*. Washington, DC: IEEE, 2013.

The Zerocoin authors teamed up with other researchers who had developed the SNARK technique. This collaboration resulted in Zerocash:

Ben Sasson, Eli, Alessandro Chiesa, Christina Garman, Matthew Green, Ian Miers, Eran Tromer, and Madars Virza. "Zerocash: Decentralized Anonymous Payments from Bitcoin." In *Proceedings of the 2013 IEEE Symposium on Security and Privacy*. Washington, DC: IEEE, 2013.

An alternative design to Zerocoin is CryptoNote, which uses different cryptography and offers different anonymity properties. We didn't discuss it in this chapter for lack of space, but it is an interesting design approach:

van Saberhagen, Nicolas. "CryptoNote v. 2.0." Available at https://cryptonote.org/whitepaper.pdf.

This classic book on cryptography includes a chapter on zero-knowledge proofs:

Goldreich, Oded. *Foundations of Cryptography*, Volume 1. Cambridge: Cambridge University Press, 2007.

This paper describes the technical design of the anonymous communication network Tor:

Dingledine, Roger, Nick Mathewson, and Paul Syverson. "Tor: The Second-Generation Onion Router." Washington, DC: Naval Research Lab, 2004.

The "systematization of knowledge" paper on Bitcoin and cryptocurrencies is the following. See especially Section VII on anonymity and privacy:

Bonneau, Joseph, Andrew Miller, Jeremy Clark, Arvind Narayanan, Joshua A. Kroll, and Edward W. Felten. "Research Perspectives and Challenges for Bitcoin and Cryptocurrencies." Presented at the 2015 IEEE Security and Privacy Conference, San Jose, CA, 2015.

CHAPTER 7

Community, Politics, and Regulation

In this chapter, we look at all the ways that the world of Bitcoin and cryptocurrency technology touches the world of people. We discuss the Bitcoin community's internal politics as well as the ways that Bitcoin interacts with traditional politics, namely, law enforcement and regulation issues.

7.1. CONSENSUS IN BITCOIN

First, consider consensus in Bitcoin, that is, the way that the operation of Bitcoin relies on the formation of consensus among individuals. Three kinds of consensus have to operate for Bitcoin to be successful.

Consensus about rules. By rules we mean things like what makes a transaction or a block valid, the core protocols and data formats involved in making Bitcoin work. You need to have a consensus about these things so that all the different participants in the system can talk to one another and agree on what's happening.

Consensus about history. That is, participants must agree on what is and isn't in the block chain and therefore reach a consensus about which transactions have occurred. Once this is established, what follows is a consensus about which coins—which unspent outputs—exist and who owns them. This consensus results from the processes—considered in Chapters 1 and 2—from which the block chain is built and by which nodes come to agree about the contents of the block chain. This is the most familiar and most technically intricate kind of consensus in Bitcoin.

Consensus about the value of coins. The third form of consensus is the general agreement that bitcoins are valuable and in particular the consensus that if someone gives you a bitcoin today, then tomorrow you will be able to redeem or trade it for something of value. Any currency, whether a fiat currency like the dollar or cryptocurrency like Bitcoin, relies on the consensus that it has value. That is, you need people to generally accept that it's exchangeable for something else of value, now and in the future.

In a fiat currency, the third type of consensus is the *only* kind of consensus. The rules don't emerge by consensus—what is and isn't a dollar bill is declared by fiat. History is

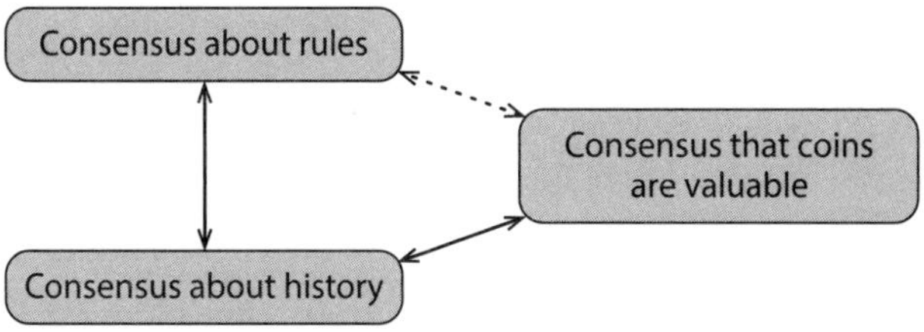

FIGURE 7.1. Relationships among the three forms of consensus in Bitcoin.

not salient, but state is (i.e., who owns what). State is either determined by physical possession, as with cash, or relegated to professional record keepers (i.e., banks). In cryptocurrencies, however, rules and history are also subject to consensus.

In Bitcoin, this third form of consensus, unlike the others, is a bit circular. In other words, my belief that the bitcoins I'm receiving today are of value depends on my expectation that tomorrow other people will believe the same thing. So consensus on value relies on believing that consensus on value will continue. This is sometimes called the "Tinkerbell effect" by analogy to the story of Peter Pan, where it's said that Tinkerbell exists because you believe in her.

Whether circular or not, the consensus on value seems to exist and is important in the operation of Bitcoin. What's important about all three forms of consensus is that they're intertwined with one another, as Figure 7.1 shows.

First of all, consensus on rules and on history are linked. Without knowing which blocks are valid, you can't reach consensus on the block chain. And without consensus on which blocks are in the block chain, you can't know whether a transaction is valid or whether it is an attempt to spend an already-spent output.

Consensus on history and on the value of coins are also tied together. The consensus on history means that we agree on who owns which coins, which is a prerequisite for believing that the coins have value—without a consensus that I own a particular coin, I can't have any expectation that people will accept that coin from me as payment in the future. It's true in reverse as well—as we saw in Chapter 2, consensus about value is what incentivizes miners to maintain the security of the block chain, which establishes a consensus on history.

The genius in Bitcoin's original design was in recognizing that it would be difficult to establish any one of these types of consensus by itself. Consensus about the rules in a worldwide decentralized environment with no notion of identity is unlikely.

Similarly, reaching a consensus about history is a difficult distributed data structure problem that is not likely to be solvable on its own. And a consensus that some kind of cryptocurrency has value is also hard to achieve. What the design of Bitcoin and the continued operation of Bitcoin show is that even if you can't build any one of these forms of consensus by itself, you can somehow combine the three and get them to operate in an interdependent way. So when we talk about how the Bitcoin community operates, we have to bear in mind that Bitcoin relies on agreement by the participants, and that consensus is a fragile construct that consists of interlinked technical and social components.

7.2. BITCOIN CORE SOFTWARE

Bitcoin Core is a piece of open-source software that is a focal point for discussion and debate about Bitcoin's rules. The software is licensed under the MIT license, which is a very permissive open-source license. It allows the software to be used for almost any purpose as long as the source is attributed and the MIT license is not stripped out. Bitcoin Core is the most widely used Bitcoin software, and even those who don't use it tend to defer to its definitions of the Bitcoin rules. That is, people building alternative Bitcoin software typically mimic the rule-defining parts of the Bitcoin Core software—those parts that check validity of transactions and blocks.

Bitcoin Core is the de facto rulebook of Bitcoin. If you want to know what's valid in Bitcoin, you should consult the Bitcoin Core software—or explanations of it.

Bitcoin Improvement Proposals

Anyone can contribute technical improvements via "pull requests" to Bitcoin Core, a familiar process in the world of open-source software. More substantial changes, especially protocol modifications, use a process called "Bitcoin Improvement Proposals" (BIPs). These are formal proposals for changes to Bitcoin. Typically a BIP includes a technical specification for a proposed change as well as a rationale for it. So if you have an idea for how to improve Bitcoin by making some technical change, you're encouraged to write up one of these documents and to publish it as part of the BIP series, and that will then kick off a discussion in the community about what to do. While the formal process is open to anyone, there's a learning curve for participation, just as for any open-source project.

BIPs are published in a numbered series. Each one has a champion, that is, an author who evangelizes in favor of it, coordinates discussion, and tries to build a consensus in the community in favor of going forward with or implementing his or her particular proposal.

The above applies to proposals to change the technology. Other BIPs are purely informational and exist to disseminate knowledge about Bitcoin or to standardize some part of the protocol previously only specified in source code. Yet other BIPs are process oriented and discuss how things should be decided in the Bitcoin community.

In summary, Bitcoin has a rulebook as well as a process for proposing, specifying, and discussing rule changes, namely, BIPs.

Bitcoin Core Developers

To understand the role of the Bitcoin Core software requires understanding the role of Bitcoin Core developers. The original code was written by Satoshi Nakamoto, whom we discuss in Section 7.4. Nakamoto is no longer active; instead a group of developers maintain Bitcoin Core. Hundreds of developers contributed code to the project, but only a handful have direct "commit" access to the Core repository. The Core developers lead the effort to continue development of the software and are in charge of what code gets pushed into new versions of Bitcoin Core.

How powerful are these people? In one sense they're very powerful, because you could argue that any of the rule changes to the code that they make will get shipped in Bitcoin Core and will be followed by default. These are the people who can write in the de facto rulebook of Bitcoin. In another sense, they're not powerful at all. Because it's open-source software, anyone can copy and modify it (i.e., fork the software at any time), and so if the lead developers start behaving in a way that the community doesn't like, the community can go in a different direction.

In a sense, the lead developers are leading the parade. They're out in front, marching, and the parade will generally follow them when they turn a corner. But if they try to lead the march down a disastrous route, then the parade members might decide to go in a different direction. The lead developers can urge the community on, but they don't have formal power to force people to follow them if they take the system in a technical direction that the community doesn't like.

Let's consider what you as a user of the system can do if you don't like how the rules are trending or the way it's being run, and compare it to a centralized currency like a fiat currency. In a centralized currency if you don't like what's going on, you have a right to exit, that is, you can stop using it. You'd have to try to sell any currency you hold, and you might have to move to someplace with a different fiat currency. With a centralized currency, opting out is really your only alternative to participating.

With Bitcoin, you certainly have the right to exit, but because it operates as an open-source system, you additionally have the right to fork the rules. That means you, and some of your friends and colleagues, can decide that you would rather operate under a different rule set, and you can fork the rules and go in a different direction from the lead developers. The right to fork is more empowering for users than the right to exit, and therefore the community has more power in an open-source system like Bitcoin than it would in a purely centralized system. So although the lead developers might look like a centralized entity controlling things, in fact they don't have the power that a purely centralized manager or software owner would have.

Forks in the Rules

One way to fork the software and the rules is to start a new block chain with a new genesis block. This is a popular option for creating altcoins, which we discuss in Chap-

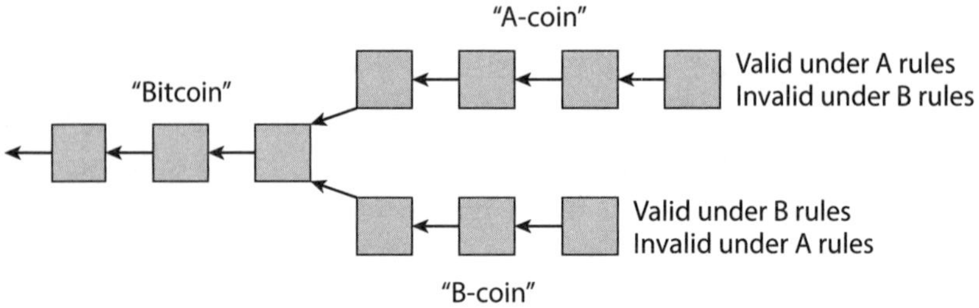

FIGURE 7.2. A fork in the currency. If a fork in the rules leads to a hard fork in the block chain, the currency itself forks, and two new currencies result.

ter 10. But for now let's consider a different type of fork in the rules, one in which those who fork decide to fork the block chain as well.

If you recall the distinction between a hard fork and a soft fork from Chapter 3, we're talking about a hard fork here. At the point when there's a disagreement about the rules, a fork will occur in the block chain, resulting in two branches. One branch is valid under rule set A but invalid under rule set B, and vice versa. Once the miners operating under the two rule sets separate, they can't come back together, because each branch will contain transactions or blocks that are invalid according to the other rule set (Figure 7.2).

We can think of the currency that had existed up until the fork as being Bitcoin—the big happy Bitcoin that everyone agreed on. After the fork, it's as if two new currencies emerge, A-coin corresponding to rule set A and B-coin corresponding to rule set B. At the moment of the fork, everyone who owned one bitcoin receives one A-coin and one B-coin. From that point on, A-coin and B-coin operate as separate currencies, and they might operate independently. The two groups might continue to evolve their rules in different ways.

We should emphasize that not just the software, or the rules, or the software implementing the rules forked—the currency itself forked. This is an interesting event that can happen in a cryptocurrency but couldn't happen in a traditional currency, where the option of forking is not available to users. To our knowledge, neither Bitcoin nor any altcoin has ever forked in this way, but it's a fascinating possibility.

How might people respond to such a fork? It depends on why the fork happened. The first case is where the fork was not intended as a disagreement about the rules, but instead as a way of starting an altcoin. Someone might start an altcoin by forking Bitcoin's block chain if they want to start with a rule set similar to Bitcoin's. This doesn't really pose a problem for the community—the altcoin goes its separate way, the branches coexist peacefully, and some people will prefer to use bitcoins while others will prefer the altcoin. But as we said earlier, as far as we know, no one has ever started an altcoin by forking Bitcoin's or another existing altcoin's block chain. They've always started with a new genesis block.

The interesting case is if the fork reflects a fight between two groups about what the future of Bitcoin should be—in other words, a rebellion in the Bitcoin community, where a subgroup decides to break off, because they think they have a better idea about how the system should be run. In that case, the two branches are rivals and will fight for market share. A-coin and B-coin will each try to persuade more merchants to accept it and more people to buy it. Each will want to be perceived as the "real Bitcoin." There may be a public-relations fight, where each claims legitimacy and portrays the other as a weird splinter group.

The probable outcome is that one branch will eventually win and the other will fade away. These sorts of competitions tend to tip in one direction. Once one of the two is viewed as more legitimate and obtains a bigger market share, the network effect will prevail, and the other becomes a niche currency that will eventually fade away. The rule set and the governance structure of the winner will become the de facto rule set and governance structure of Bitcoin.

7.3. STAKEHOLDERS: WHO'S IN CHARGE?

Who are the stakeholders in Bitcoin, and who's really in charge? We've seen how Bitcoin relies on consensus and how its rulebook is written in practice. We've analyzed the possibility of a fork or a fight about what the rules should be. Now let's take up the question of who has the power to determine who might win such a fight.

In other words, if there's a discussion and negotiation in the community about rule setting, and that negotiation fails, we want to know what will determine the outcome. Generally speaking, in any negotiation, the party that has the best alternative to a negotiated agreement has the advantage in a negotiation. So figuring out who might win a fight will indicate who has the upper hand in community discussions and negotiations about the future of Bitcoin.

We can make claims on behalf of many different stakeholders:

1. Core developers have the power—they write the rulebook, and almost everybody uses their code.
2. Miners have the power—they write history and decide which transactions are valid. If miners decide to follow a certain set of rules, arguably everyone else has to follow it. The fork with more mining power behind it will build a stronger, more secure block chain and so has some ability to push the rules in a particular direction. Just how much power they have depends on whether it's a hard fork or a soft fork, but either way they have some power.
3. Investors have the power—they buy and hold bitcoins, so it's the investors who decide whether Bitcoin has any value. You could argue that although the developers control consensus about the rules and the miners control consensus about history, it is the investors who control the consensus that Bitcoin has value. In the case of a hard fork, if investors mostly decide to put their money in either A-coin or B-coin, that branch will be perceived as legitimate.

4. Merchants and their customers have the power—they generate the primary demand for Bitcoin. Although investors provide some of the demand that supports the price of the currency, the primary demand driving the price of the currency, as we saw in Chapter 4, arises from a desire to mediate transactions using Bitcoin as a payment technology. Investors, according to this argument, are just guessing where the primary demand will be in the future.
5. Payment services have the power—they're the ones that handle transactions. A lot of merchants don't care which currency they follow and simply want to use a payment service that will give them dollars at the end of the day, allow their customers to pay using a cryptocurrency, and handle all the risk. So maybe payment services drive primary demand and merchants, customers, and investors will follow them.

As you may have guessed, there's some merit to all these arguments, and all of those entities have some power. To succeed, a coin needs all these forms of consensus—a stable rulebook written by developers, mining power, investment, participation by merchants and customers, and the payment services that support them. So all these parties have some power in controlling the outcome of a fight over the future of Bitcoin, and there's no one that we can point to as being the definite winner. It's a big, ugly, messy consensus-building exercise.

Another player relevant to the governance of Bitcoin is the Bitcoin Foundation. It was founded in 2012 as a nonprofit. It plays two main roles. The first is funding some of the Core developers out of the foundation's assets, so that they can work full time on developing the software. The second is talking to government, especially the U.S. government, as the "voice of Bitcoin."

Some members of the Bitcoin community believe that Bitcoin should operate outside of and apart from traditional national governments. They believe Bitcoin should operate across borders and shouldn't explain or justify itself to governments or negotiate with them. Others take a different view. They view regulation as inevitable, desirable, or both. They would like the interests of the Bitcoin community to be represented in government and for the community's arguments to be heard. The Foundation arose partly to fill this need, and it's fair to say that its dealings with government have done a lot to smooth the road for an understanding and acceptance of Bitcoin.

The Foundation has experienced quite a bit of controversy. Some board members

Governance of Open Protocols

We've described a system where numerous stakeholders with imperfectly aligned interests collaborate on open protocols and software and try to reach technical and social consensus. This might remind you of the architecture of the Internet itself. There are indeed many similarities between the development process of Bitcoin Core and that of the Internet. For example, the BIP process is reminiscent of the RFC, or Request for Comments, which is a type of standards-setting document for the Internet.

have gotten into criminal or financial trouble, and there have been questions about the extent to which some of them represent the community. The Foundation struggled with members of the board who became liabilities and had to be replaced on short notice. It's been accused of lacking transparency and of being effectively bankrupt. As of 2015, it's at best unclear whether the Bitcoin Foundation will have much of a role in Bitcoin's future.

A different nonprofit group, Coin Center, launched in September 2014 and based in Washington, DC, has taken on one of the roles the Bitcoin Foundation played, namely, advocacy and talking to government. Coin Center acts as a think tank. It has operated without much controversy as of early 2015. Neither the Bitcoin Foundation nor Coin Center is in charge of Bitcoin any more than the other stakeholders are. The success and perceived legitimacy of any such representative entity will be driven by how much support—and funding—it can obtain from the community over time, like everything else in this kind of open-source ecosystem.

To summarize, no one entity or group is definitively in control of Bitcoin's evolution. In another sense, everybody is in charge, because the consensus on how the system will operate—the three interlocking forms of consensus on rules, on history, and on value—governs Bitcoin. Any rule set, group, or governance structure that can maintain that consensus over time will, in a very real sense, be in charge of Bitcoin.

7.4. ROOTS OF BITCOIN

Let's look at the roots of Bitcoin—how it got started, what its precursors were, and what we know about its mysterious founder.

Cypherpunk and Digital Cash

One precursor of Bitcoin that's worth discussing is *cypherpunk*, a movement that brought together two viewpoints. First was libertarianism and in particular the idea that society would be better off with either no or minimal government. Second, the movement coupled that libertarian (or perhaps even anarchist) notion with the idea of strong cryptography and in particular public-key cryptography, which started in the late 1970s. The cypherpunk movement consisted of people who believed that with strong online privacy and strong cryptography, they could redesign the architecture of the way people interact. In this world, cypherpunks believed, people could protect themselves and their interests more effectively and with much less activity by (or, as they would say, interference from) government.

One of the challenges in the cypherpunk movement was how to deal with money in a future cypherpunk world where people would interact online via strong technical and cryptographic measures. This inspired much research, led especially by the early digital cash work of David Chaum and others, that aimed to create new forms of digital value that functioned like money (specifically, cash), in the sense of being anonymous and easily exchangeable. The story of how these technical ideas were developed and why early digital cash *didn't* sweep the world is an interesting one (see the Foreword). In any event, early work in that area came together with cypherpunk beliefs—in particular, the desire to have a strong currency that would be decentralized, online, and relatively private—to sow the seeds from which Bitcoin would be born. It's also the basis for the philosophy that many of Bitcoin's supporters follow.

Satoshi Nakamoto

Bitcoin began in 2008 with the release of a white paper titled "Bitcoin: A Peer to Peer Electronic Cash System" that was authored by Satoshi Nakamoto. This paper, which was made freely available online, is the initial description of what Bitcoin is, how it works, and the philosophy behind its design. It's still a good resource to get a quick idea of how Bitcoin's technical design and philosophy were specified. Open-source software implementing that specification was released soon after by the same Satoshi Nakamoto, and that's where everything started. To this day, Satoshi is one of the central mysteries of Bitcoin.

In an important sense, it doesn't matter that we don't know Satoshi's identity, because of the notable feature of Bitcoin that it is decentralized and has no single entity in charge. Satoshi's not in charge, and in fact has not been active since handing over control of the Bitcoin source code to other developers in mid-2010. To some extent it doesn't really matter what Satoshi thinks anymore. Any special influence that Satoshi has is only because of respect that Satoshi has in the Bitcoin community.

Growth

Bitcoin has grown considerably since the system became operational in January 2009. The growth is obvious in the plot of transaction volume over time (Figure 7.3) and in that of the number of transactions over time (Figure 7.4), although the all-time peak price, as of 2015, was back in late 2013. Sometimes the growth has been gradual, but

Who Is Satoshi Nakamoto?

"Satoshi Nakamoto" is almost certainly a pseudonym. Satoshi claimed to be a 37-year-old man living in Japan (as of 2009). However, there is no evidence that Satoshi spoke or understood Japanese, but we do know that Satoshi writes fairly fluently in English, although sometimes using American spelling and sometimes British spelling. Numerous attempts have been made to examine Satoshi's text, code, post times, machine identifiers, and so on to try to answer some basic questions: What is Satoshi's native language? Where is Satoshi from? There have even been attempts to use *stylometry* (the algorithmic analysis of text for writer-specific patterns) to uncover Satoshi's identity. The real identity of Satoshi is still unknown, despite occasional confident pronouncements by individuals and, at least once, a news organization. See the Foreword for a longer discussion of what we know about Satoshi.

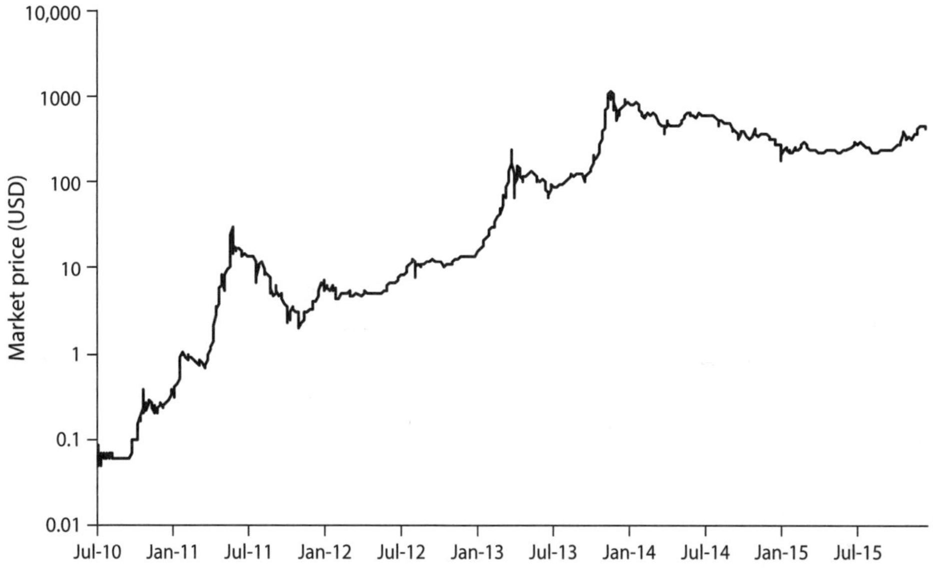

FIGURE 7.3. Market price of Bitcoin (7-day average). Note the logarithmic scale. Source: bitcoincharts .com.

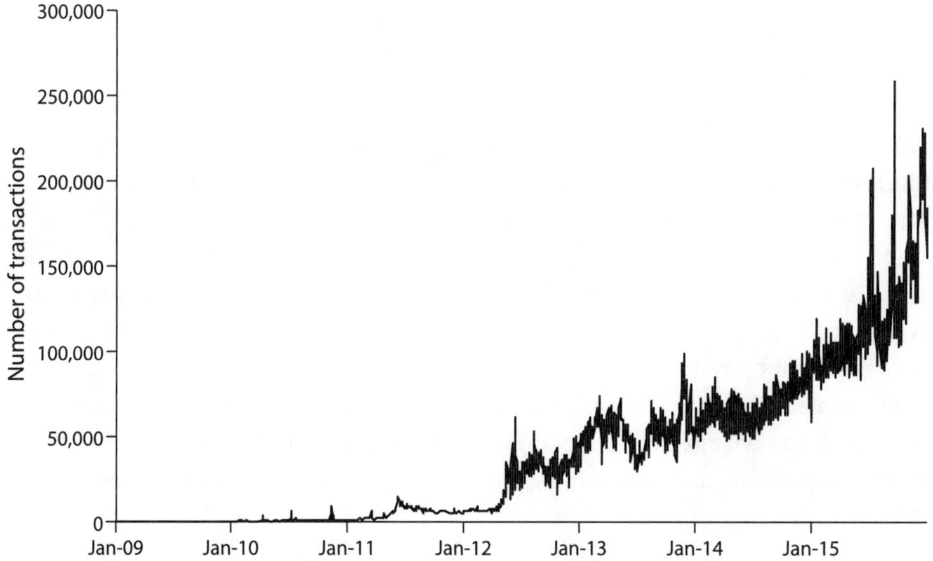

FIGURE 7.4. Daily transaction volume (7-day average). Source: bitcoincharts.com.

there have been jumps or spurts, often corresponding to newsworthy events. Generally speaking, the growth has accelerated over time.

7.5. GOVERNMENTS NOTICE BITCOIN

The rest of this chapter is about governments—government interaction with Bitcoin and attempts to regulate the currency. Let's start with the moment when governments noticed Bitcoin, that is, when Bitcoin became a big enough phenomenon that government started to worry about the impact it might have and how to react to it. In this section and the next one, we discuss why governments might worry about Bitcoin specifically. Then in Section 7.7 we turn to areas where Bitcoin businesses may be regulated for similar reasons as other types of businesses. Finally, in Section 7.8, we look at a case study of a proposed regulation that combines elements of regular consumer financial protection with Bitcoin-specific aspects.

Capital Controls

One reason governments would notice a digital currency like Bitcoin is that untraceable digital cash, if it exists, defeats capital controls. Capital controls are rules or laws that a country has in place that are designed to limit the flow of capital (money and other assets) into or out of the country. By putting controls on banks, investments, and so on, the country can try to regulate these flows.

Bitcoin is an easy way, under some circumstances, to defeat capital controls. Someone can simply buy bitcoins with capital inside the country, transmit those bitcoins outside the country electronically, and then trade them for capital or wealth. That would let them export capital or wealth—or, conversely, import it—without governmental control. Because wealth in this electronic form can move so easily across borders and can't really be controlled, a government that wants to enforce capital controls in a world with Bitcoin has to try to disconnect the Bitcoin world from the local fiat currency banking system. That would make it infeasible for someone to turn large amounts of local currency into bitcoins, or the reverse. We have indeed seen countries trying to protect their capital controls do exactly that, with China being a notable example. China has engaged in increasingly strong measures to try to disconnect bitcoins from the Chinese fiat currency banking system by preventing businesses from exchanging bitcoins for yuan.

Crime

Another reason governments might worry about untraceable digital cash is that it makes certain kinds of crimes easier to commit—in particular, crimes like kidnapping and extortion that involve the payment of a ransom. Those crimes become easier when payments can be made from a distance and anonymously.

Law enforcement against kidnappers, for example, often has relied on exploiting the hand-off of money from the victim or the victim's family to the criminals. When that can be done at a distance in an anonymous way, it becomes much harder for law enforcement to follow the money. Another example is the CryptoLocker malware, which encrypts victims' files and demands ransoms in Bitcoin (or other types of electronic money) to decrypt them. So the crime and the payment are both carried out at a distance. Similarly, tax evasion is facilitated when people can move money around readily and engage in transactions that are not easily tied to a particular individual or identity. Finally, the sale of illegal items becomes potentially easier when the funds can be transferred at a distance without being processed by regulated institutions.

Silk Road

A good example of these possibilities is Silk Road, a self-styled "anonymous marketplace," which has also been called "the eBay for illegal drugs." Figure 7.5 shows a screenshot of Silk Road's website when it was operating. Illegal drugs were the primary items for sale, with a smattering of other categories that you can see on the left in the figure.

Silk Road allowed sellers to advertise goods for sale and buyers to buy them. The goods were delivered typically through the mail or through shipment services, and payment was made in bitcoins. The website operated as a Tor hidden service, a concept discussed in Chapter 6. As you can see in the screenshot, its address was http://silkroadvb5piz3r.onion. This way the server's location was hidden from law enforcement.

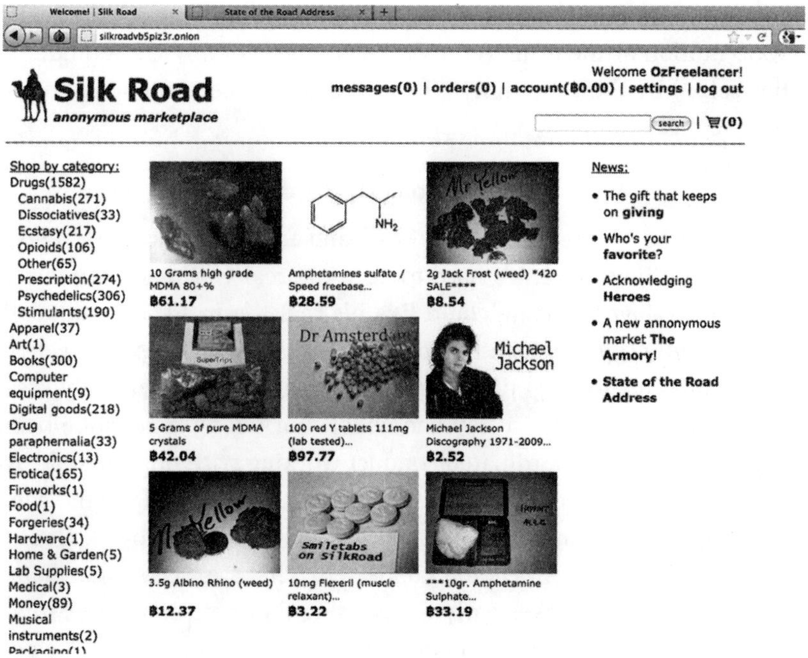

FIGURE 7.5. Screenshot of the Silk Road website (April 2012).

Because of the use of bitcoins for payment, it was also difficult for law enforcement to follow the money and identify market participants.

Silk Road held the bitcoins in escrow while the goods were shipped. This innovative escrow system helped protect the buyers and sellers against cheating by other parties. The bitcoins would be released once the buyer certified that the goods had arrived. There was also an eBay-like reputation system that allowed buyers and sellers to get reputations for following through on their deals, and by using that reputation system, Silk Road was able to give the market participants an incentive to play by the rules. So Silk Road was innovative among criminal markets in finding ways of enforcing the rules of the criminal market at a distance, which is something that criminal markets in the past have had difficulty doing.

Silk Road was run by a person who called himself Dread Pirate Roberts—obviously a pseudonym, which you might recognize as a reference to the hero of the novel/film *The Princess Bride*. The website operated from February 2011 until October 2013. Silk Road was shut down after the arrest of its operator Ross Ulbricht, who was later identified as Dread Pirate Roberts. Ulbricht had tried to cover his tracks by operating pseudonymous accounts and by using Tor, anonymous remailers, and so on. The U.S. government was nevertheless able to connect the dots and tie him to Silk Road activity—to the servers and the bitcoins he controlled as the operator of Silk Road. He was convicted of various crimes relating to operating the website. He was also charged with attempted murder for hire, although fortunately he was sufficiently incompetent at it that nobody actually got killed.

In the course of taking down Silk Road, the FBI seized about 174,000 BTC, worth more than $30 million at the time. As with the proceeds of any crime under U.S. law, they could be seized by the government. Later the government auctioned off a portion of the seized bitcoins.

Lessons from Silk Road

Several lessons can be learned from Silk Road and from the encounter between law enforcement and Ulbricht. First, it's hard to keep the real world and the virtual world separate. Ulbricht believed that he could live his real life in society and at the same time have a secret identity in which he operated a sizable business and technology infrastructure. It's difficult to keep these worlds apart and not accidentally create some linkage between them. It's hard to stay anonymous for a long time while being active and engaging in a course of coordinated conduct working with other people over time. If a connection ever links those two identities—say, you slip up and use the name of one while wearing the mask of another—that link can never be destroyed. Over time the different anonymous identities become connected. That's exactly what happened to Ulbricht—he made a few mistakes early on by using the same computers to access his personal accounts and Dread Pirate Robert's accounts. These mistakes were enough for investigators eventually to discover his offline identity.

Another lesson is that law enforcement can follow the money. Even before Ulbricht's arrest, the FBI knew that certain Bitcoin addresses were controlled by the operator of Silk Road, and they were watching those addresses. The result is that Ulbricht, while wealthy according to the block chain, was not actually able to benefit from that wealth, because any attempt to transfer those assets into dollars would have resulted in a traceable event and probably would have resulted in rapid arrest. So although Ulbricht was the owner of something like 174,000 BTC, in the real world, he was not living like a king. He lived in a one-bedroom apartment in San Francisco while apparently unable to access the wealth that he had accumulated.

In short, if you intend to operate an underground criminal enterprise—and obviously, we wouldn't recommend this career path—then it's a lot harder to do than you might think. Technologies like Bitcoin and Tor are not bulletproof, and law enforcement agencies still have significant tools at their disposal. Although there's been some panic in the world of law enforcement over the rise of Bitcoin, these agencies can still follow the money up to a point, and they still have substantial ability to investigate crimes and make life difficult for people who want to engage in coordinated criminal action.

At the same time, by taking down Silk Road, law enforcement has not shut down Bitcoin-based hidden markets for illegal drugs. In fact, after the demise of Silk Road, there has been a mushrooming of such markets. Some of the more prominent ones are Sheep Marketplace, Silk Road 2, Black Market Reloaded, Evolution, and Agora. Most of these are now defunct, either due to law enforcement actions or theft, often by insiders. However, research has found that the total volume of sales has only gone up, with law enforcement actions against individual sites not significantly slowing the growth of this underground market. To address the security risk of the site operator disappearing with buyers' escrowed funds, the newer marketplaces use multisignature escrow (discussed in Chapter 3) rather than Silk Road's model of depositing the funds with the market operator.

7.6. ANTI-MONEY LAUNDERING

In this section we'll look at money laundering and the anti-money-laundering (AML) rules that governments have imposed, especially in the United States, that affect some Bitcoin-related businesses.

The goal of AML policy is to prevent large flows of money from crossing borders or moving between the underground and legitimate economies without being detected. In Section 7.5 we looked at capital controls that exist to prevent money from crossing borders. In some cases, countries don't object to money crossing borders, but they want to know who's transferring what to whom and where that money came from.

AML policy is intended to make certain kinds of crime more difficult, especially organized crime. Organized crime groups often receive large sums of money in one place and want to move it elsewhere, but they don't want to explain where that money came from—hence the desire to move money across borders. Or they might find themselves making a lot of money in an underground economy and wanting to transfer it to the legitimate economy, so that they can spend it on luxury goods or other items. AML, then, has the goals of making it harder to move money around this way and making it easier to catch people trying to do it.

Know Your Customer

One of the essential countermeasures against money laundering is "Know Your Customer" (KYC) laws. The details can be a bit complicated and will depend on your locale, but the basic idea is this: KYC rules require certain kinds of businesses that handle money to do three things:

1. *Identify and authenticate clients.* Obtain some kind of proof that clients really are who they claim they are and that those claimed identities correspond to a real-world identity. So a person can't just walk in and claim to be John Smith from 123 Main Street in AnyTown, USA—they have to provide reliable identification documents.
2. *Evaluate risk of client.* Determine the risk of a certain client engaging in underground activities. This will be based on how the client behaves—how long-standing their business relationship is with the company, how well known they are in the community, and various other factors. KYC rules generally require covered companies to monitor clients whose activities seem riskier.
3. *Watch for anomalous behavior.* Watch for behavior that seems to be indicative of money laundering or criminal activity. KYC often requires a company to terminate business with clients who look dodgy, or who are unable to authenticate themselves or their activities sufficiently to meet the requirements of the law.

Mandatory Reporting

Mandatory reporting requirements in the United States can significantly impact Bitcoin businesses. Companies in a broad range of sectors have to report currency transactions that are more than $10,000. They must file what's called a "currency transaction report," stating what the transaction is and who the other party to it is. They are also required to authenticate who that party is. Once reported, the information is entered into government databases and then might be analyzed to look for patterns of behavior indicative of money laundering.

Companies are also required to watch for clients who might be "structuring" transactions to avoid reporting, like engaging in a series of $9,999 transactions to get around the $10,000 reporting rule. Companies that see evidence of structuring must report it by filing a Suspicious Activity Report. Again, the information goes into a government database and might lead to investigation of the client.

These requirements differ significantly by country. We're not by any means trying to give you legal advice. This discussion is meant to give you an idea about what kind of requirements are imposed by AML rules. That said, take note that governments—of the United States and other countries—tend to take AML rules very seriously and impose harsh criminal penalties for violations. These aren't rules that you can just ignore and deal with if a government lodges a complaint against you later.

Bitcoin businesses have been shut down—sometimes temporarily, sometimes permanently. Businesspeople have been arrested, and people have gone to jail for not following these rules. This is an area where government will enforce the law vigorously, regardless of whether fiat currency or Bitcoin is used. Government agencies have enforced these laws against Bitcoin-based businesses ever since they noticed that Bitcoin was large enough to pose a risk of money laundering. If you're interested in starting any kind of business that will handle large volumes of currency, you need to consult with a lawyer who understands these rules.

7.7. REGULATION

Now let's directly address the "R" word—regulation. Regulation often gets a bad name, especially among the kind of people who tend to like Bitcoin. As the argument goes, regulation is "some bureaucrat who doesn't know my business or what I'm trying to do, coming in and messing things up. It's a burden. It's stupid and pointless." This argument is common and easy to sympathize with, and although it's often at least partially correct, we won't dwell on it here.

Instead, in this section we look in some detail at reasons regulations might sometimes be justified, because that argument is not as well understood. To be clear, the fact that we're spending most of this section talking about why regulation might be good shouldn't be read as an endorsement of widespread regulation. But we want to bring a bit more balance to the discussion in a community where regulation is often considered to be inherently bad.

The ultimate argument in favor of regulation is this: when markets fail and produce outcomes that are bad—and are agreed to be bad by pretty much everyone in the market—then regulation can step in and try to address the failure. So the argument for regulation, when there is an argument, starts with the idea that markets don't always result in optimal outcomes.

Let's make this concept a bit more precise, using terms from economics. At issue is a market failure, and by that we don't simply mean that something bad is happening, or somebody feels they are getting ripped off or treated unfairly. We mean that there is an alternate allocation of goods to the market participants that would result in *everybody* being better off, or at least not worse off. Such an alternate allocation is called a *Pareto improvement.*

Lemons Market

Let's discuss one way in which the market can fail, a classic example called the *lemons market*. The name originated in the context of selling cars, but the idea is not limited to that market. Suppose that all cars are either of low quality or high quality (with nothing in between). A high-quality car costs a bit more to manufacture than a low-quality car, but it's much better for the consumer who buys it.

If the market is operating well (if it's *efficient*, as economists call it), it will deliver mostly high-quality cars to consumers. That's because even though the high-quality car is somewhat costlier, most consumers prefer it and are willing to pay more for it. So under certain assumptions, a market will provide this happy outcome.

But suppose customers can't tell low-quality cars from high-quality ones. A low-quality car (a "lemon") sitting on the lot may look pretty good, but you can't really tell whether it's going to break down tomorrow or run for a long time. The dealer probably knows if it's a lemon, but you as the customer can't tell.

Think about the incentives that drive people in this kind of lemons market. As a consumer, you're not willing to pay extra for a high-quality car, because you just can't tell the difference before purchasing the car. Even if the used-car dealer says that a car is perfect and costs only an extra $100, you don't have a good reason to trust the dealer.

As a consequence, producers can't make any extra money by selling a high-quality car. In fact, they lose money by selling a high-quality car, because it costs more to produce, and they don't get any price premium. So the market gets stuck at an equilibrium where only low-quality cars are produced, and consumers are relatively unhappy with them.

This outcome is worse for everybody than a properly functioning market would be. It's worse for buyers, because they have to make do with low-quality cars. In a more efficient market, they could have bought a car that was much better for a slightly higher price. It's also worse for producers—since the cars that are on the market are all lemons, consumers don't buy as many cars as they might otherwise, so there's less money to be made selling cars than there would be in a healthy market.

This phenomenon is known as a market failure. Lemons markets are not inherently about cars. Any goods (or "widgets") for sale that suffer from *asymmetric information* (in which either sellers or buyers have much better information about the quality of the good than the other party does) may result in a market failure. The economics literature provides many more examples beyond car markets.

Fixing a Lemons Market

Some market-based approaches try to fix a lemons market. One approach relies on seller reputation. The idea is that if a seller consistently tells the truth to consumers about which widgets are high versus low quality, then the seller might acquire a reputation for telling the truth. Once they have that reputation, they may be able to sell high-quality widgets for a higher price, because consumers will believe them, and therefore the market can operate more efficiently.

This approach only works sometimes, depending on the precise assumptions you make about the market. Of course, it will never work as well as a market where consumers can actually tell the difference in quality. For one thing, it takes a while for a producer to build up a good reputation. That means they have to sell high-quality widgets at low prices for a while until consumers learn that they're telling the truth. That makes it harder for an honest seller to get into the market.

The other potential problem is that a seller, even if they've been honest up to now, no longer has the incentive to be honest if they want to get out of the market (say, if their sales are shrinking). In that case, their incentive is to massively cheat people all at once and then exit the market. So reputation doesn't work well at either the beginning or end of a seller's presence in the market.

A reputation-based approach also tends not to work in businesses where consumers don't do repeat business with the same entity, or where the product category is very new, and therefore not enough time has elapsed for sellers to build up a reputation. A high-tech market like Bitcoin exchanges suffers just those problems.

The other market-based approach to fixing a lemons market is warranties. The idea is that a seller could provide a warranty to a buyer that says if the widget turns out to be low quality, the seller will provide an exchange or a refund. That can work well up to a point, but this fix also has a problem: a warranty is just another kind of product that can also come in high- or low-quality versions! A low-quality warranty is one that the seller doesn't honor when you come back with the broken product. They renege on their promise, or they make you jump through all kinds of hoops to redeem the warranty.

Regulatory Fixes

So if a lemons market has developed, and if these market-based approaches don't work for the particular market, then regulation might be able to help. Specifically, there are three ways in which regulation might be able to address the problem.

First, regulation could require disclosure. It could require, say, that all widgets be labeled as high or low quality, combined with penalties on the firms for lying. That gives consumers the information that they were missing. A second approach to regulation is to have quality standards so that no widget can be sold unless it meets some standard of quality testing, with that standard set so that only high-quality widgets can pass the test. That would result in a market that again has only one kind of widget, but at least it's high quality, assuming that the regulation works as intended. The third approach is to require all sellers to issue warranties and then enforce the operation of those warranties, so that sellers are held to the promises that they make.

Any of these forms of regulation could obviously fail—it might not work as intended, might be poorly written or misapplied, or might be burdensome on sellers. But there's at least the possibility that regulation of this type could help address market failure due to a lemons market. People who argue for regulation of Bitcoin exchanges, for example, sometimes point to them as an example of a lemons market.

Collusion and Antitrust Law

Another example of markets not operating optimally is price fixing. Price fixing is when different sellers collude with one another and agree to raise prices or to not lower them. A related situation is where companies that would otherwise compete with one another agree not to compete. For example, if there were two bakeries in town, they might agree that one of them will only sell muffins and the other will only sell bagels, and that way there's less competition between them than there would be if they both sold muffins and bagels. As a result of the reduced competition, presumably prices go up, and the merchants are able to foil the operation of the market.

After all, the reason that the market protects consumers well in its normal operation is through the vehicle of competition. Sellers have to compete to offer the best goods at the best price to consumers, and if they don't compete in that way then they won't get business. An agreement to fix prices or otherwise collude circumvents that competition. When people take steps that prevent competition, that's another kind of market failure.

These kinds of agreements—to raise prices or to not compete—are illegal in most jurisdictions. This is part of antitrust law or competition law. The goal of this body of law is to prevent deliberate actions that limit or harm competition. More generally, it limits actions other than simply offering good products at good prices, such as attempts to reduce competition through mergers. Antitrust law is complicated, and we've given you only a sketch of it, but it's another instance of how the market can fail and how the law can and will step in to rectify it.

7.8. NEW YORK'S BITLICENSE

So far we've discussed regulation in general: different forms of regulation, and why regulation might be justified in some cases and might make good economic sense. Now let's turn to an effort by one state to introduce specific regulation of Bitcoin, namely, New York State's BitLicense. The details are not crucial for our purposes, because our goal isn't so much to help you understand a specific piece of regulation. Rather, we want to help you understand the kinds of things regulators are doing and give you a sense of how they think about the problem.

The BitLicense proposal was issued in July 2014 and revised in response to comments from the Bitcoin community, industry, the public, and other stakeholders. It came into effect in August 2015. It was issued by the New York Department of Financial Services (NYDFS), the state agency that regulates the financial industry. Of course, the state of New York has the world's largest financial center, and so this part of the state government is used to dealing with relatively large institutions.

Who's Covered

BitLicense is a set of codes, rules, and regulations dealing with virtual currencies. Fundamentally, it requires you to obtain a so-called BitLicense from NYDFS if you wanted to do any of the things listed below:

> Virtual Currency Business Activity means the conduct of any one of the following types of activities involving New York or a New York Resident:
>
> 1. receiving Virtual Currency for Transmission or Transmitting Virtual Currency, except where the transaction is undertaken for non-financial purposes and does not involve the transfer of more than a nominal amount of Virtual Currency;
> 2. storing, holding, or maintaining custody or control of Virtual Currency on behalf of others;
> 3. buying and selling Virtual Currency as a customer business;
> 4. performing Exchange Services as a customer business; or
> 5. controlling, administering, or issuing a Virtual Currency.
>
> The development and dissemination of software in and of itself does not constitute Virtual Currency Business Activity.
>
> (Excerpt from the text of the NYDFS BitLicense regulation)

The text refers to "activities involving New York or a New York resident," reflecting the regulatory authority of NYDFS. Yet the impacts of regulations like these extend well beyond the borders of the state, for two reasons. First, for states with significant populations, such as New York or California, faced with the choice between complying with state laws and not doing business with consumers in those states, most companies will choose to comply. Second, some states are generally perceived as leaders in regulating certain economic sectors—finance in the case of New York, technology in the case of California. That means that other U.S. states often follow the direction that the leaders set.

Notice the exception for nonfinancial uses in the first category—this was added in the second revision, and it is a good change. It's a carve-out for just the kind of Bitcoin-as-a-platform applications discussed starting in Chapter 9. The second category might cover things like wallet services. As for the third category, it appears that you can buy and sell bitcoins for yourself, but doing it as a customer business requires a BitLicense. The fourth category is self-explanatory. The final one might apply more to altcoins, many of which are somewhat centralized, than to Bitcoin. We look at altcoins in Chapter 10.

The software-development exception at the end of the text is again an important one.

The language wasn't in the original version, which provoked an outcry from the community. NYDFS superintendent Benjamin Lawsky clarified soon after that the intent was not to regulate developers, miners, or individuals using Bitcoin. The final version contains the two explicit exceptions listed above.

Requirements

Covered entities have to apply for a license. Detailed language in the proposal explains how to apply for a license, which you can read (see the Further Reading section at the end of this chapter), but roughly speaking, you have to provide information on the ownership of your enterprise, on your finances and insurance, and on your business plan—generally enough to allow the NYDFS to know who you are, how well backed you are, where your money comes from, and what you're planning to do. And you have to pay an application fee.

If you get a license, you would then have to provide updated information to NYDFS about ownership, finances, insurance, and so on. You'd have to provide periodic financial statements, so they could keep track of how you're doing financially. You'd be required to maintain a financial reserve, the amount of which will be set by NYDFS based on various factors about your business.

The proposal includes rules about how you would keep custody of consumer assets. It may include AML rules that might or might not go beyond what's already required by existing laws. There are rules about having a security plan and penetration testing and so on. There are rules about disaster recovery—you have to have a disaster-recovery plan that meets various criteria. And there are rules about record keeping—you have to keep records and make them available to the NYDFS under certain circumstances. You must have written policies about compliance, and you must designate a compliance officer—someone in your organization who's in charge of compliance and has the necessary authority. There's a requirement that you disclose risk to consumers, so that consumers understand the risks of doing business with you.

As you can see, the requirements are substantial, and they're analogous to the sort of requirements for a mutual fund or a publicly traded stock. This makes BitLicense a major step in the history of Bitcoin. Perhaps other jurisdictions will also start to regulate Bitcoin transactions, and Bitcoin businesses will begin to converge on the traditional model of regulated financial institutions.

This would in some ways be contrary to the cypherpunk or cypher-libertarian ideas about what Bitcoin should be. But it is perhaps inevitable that as soon as Bitcoin became really valuable, Bitcoin businesses became big businesses, and government became interested, regulation would ensue. Bitcoin businesses touch real people and the fiat currency economy. If Bitcoin is big enough to matter, then it is big enough to be regulated. It represents a retreat from what the original advocates of Bitcoin had in mind, but in another way it represents the Bitcoin ecosystem growing up and integrating into the regular economy. Regardless of your stance on it, regulation is starting to happen, and if you're interested in starting a Bitcoin business, you need to pay attention to this trend.

Will this effort to regulate Bitcoin be a success? There are different ways to look at it, but here's one way to evaluate the effectiveness of regulations like BitLicense with respect to the public policy goal of improving the quality of Bitcoin businesses: if companies start advertising to customers outside New York that they can be trusted because they have a BitLicense, and if that argument is convincing to consumers when they're picking a company to do business with, then regulation will be working in the way that its advocates wanted it to. Whether that will happen and how it will affect the future of Bitcoin is something that we'll have to wait and see.

FURTHER READING

Two papers that contain many interesting details of how Silk Road and its successors have operated are:

Christin, Nicolas. "Traveling the Silk Road: A Measurement Analysis of a Large Anonymous Online Marketplace." In *Proceedings of the 22nd International Conference on the World Wide Web*. New York: ACM, 2013.

Soska, Kyle, and Nicolas Christin. "Measuring the Longitudinal Evolution of the Online Anonymous Marketplace Ecosystem." In *Proceedings of the 24th USENIX Security Symposium*. Berkeley, CA: USENIX, 2015.

This is a guide to the regulatory issues that Bitcoin raises:

Brito, Jerry, and Andrea Castillo. *Bitcoin: A Primer for Policymakers*. Fairfax, VA: Mercatus Center at George Mason University, 2013.

A nontechnical book that looks at the Bitcoin community and some of its prominent characters is:

Popper, Nathaniel. *Digital Gold: Bitcoin and the Inside Story of the Misfits and Millionaires Trying to Reinvent Money*. New York: Harper, 2015.

A popular exposition of early work on digital cash, combined with a vision for a world with digital privacy, is:

Chaum, David. "Security without Identification: Transaction Systems to Make Big Brother Obsolete." *Communications of the ACM*, 28(70), 1985.

A survey of the economics of information security, which discusses several reasons for market failure, is:

Anderson, Ross, and Tyler Moore. "The Economics of Information Security." *Science* 314 (5799), 2006.

A discussion of Bitcoin-specific economic issues and regulatory options can be found in:

Böhme, Rainer, Nicolas Christin, Benjamin Edelman, and Tyler Moore. "Bitcoin: Economics, Technology, and Governance." *Journal of Economic Perspectives* 29(2), 2015.

The text of the BitLicense proposal can be found in:

New York State Department of Financial Services. "Regulations of the Superintendent of Financial Services. Part 200: Virtual Currencies." 2015. Available at http://www.dfs.ny.gov/legal/regulations/adoptions/dfsp200t.pdf.

CHAPTER 8

Alternative Mining Puzzles

Mining puzzles are at the core of Bitcoin, because their difficulty limits the ability of any one party to control the consensus process. Because Bitcoin miners earn rewards for the puzzles that they solve, we expect that they'll spend considerable effort trying to find any available shortcuts to solve these puzzles faster or more efficiently, in the hope of increasing their profits. In contrast, to minimize their costs, miners might be incentivized to skip any work that would benefit the network but doesn't directly contribute to solving puzzles any faster. So the design of the puzzle plays an important role in steering and guiding participation in the network.

In this chapter, we discuss a variety of possible alternative puzzle designs, assuming that Bitcoin's puzzle could be modified or even redesigned from scratch. A classic design challenge has been to make a puzzle that is ASIC resistant, leveling the playing field between users with ordinary computing equipment and users with optimized custom hardware (see Section 5.2). What else could we design the puzzle to achieve? What other kinds of behaviors would we like to encourage or discourage? We discuss a few examples with various interesting properties, from decreasing energy consumption to having some socially useful side effects to discouraging the formation of mining pools. Some of these designs are already used by altcoins, while others are research ideas that might be used in the future.

8.1. ESSENTIAL PUZZLE REQUIREMENTS

We start by looking at some essential security requirements for mining puzzles. It does no good to introduce fancy new features if the puzzle doesn't continue to satisfy the basic requirements needed to keep Bitcoin secure.

There are many possible requirements, some of which were discussed in Chapters 2 and 5. Mining puzzles need to be quick to verify, because every node on the network validates every puzzle solution—even nodes that aren't involved in mining directly, including SPV clients. Adjustable difficulty is also necessary, so that the difficulty of the puzzle can be changed over time as new users enter the network with increasing amounts of hash power contributed. This enables the puzzle to be difficult enough that attacks on the block chain are costly, but puzzle solutions are still found at a fairly steady rate (about once every 10 minutes in Bitcoin).

What exactly is Bitcoin's mining puzzle? So far we've just called it "Bitcoin's puzzle." More precisely, it is a *partial hash-preimage puzzle*, since the goal is to find preimages for a partially specified hash output—namely, an output below a certain target value. Some other rare property could also work, such as finding a block whose hash has at least k bits set to zero, but comparing the output to a target is probably the simplest.

It's easy to see how Bitcoin's SHA-256 hash-based mining puzzle already satisfies these two requirements. It can be made arbitrarily more difficult by tweaking a single parameter (the *target*). Checking solutions is trivial, requiring just a single SHA-256 computation and a comparison, no matter how difficult the puzzle was to solve.

Another central requirement is more subtle: the chance of winning a puzzle solution in any unit of time should be roughly proportional to the hash power used. This means that really large miners with powerful hardware should only have proportional advantage in being the next miner to find a puzzle solution. Even small miners should have some proportional chance of being successful and receiving compensation.

To illustrate this point, consider a bad puzzle that doesn't satisfy this requirement. Suppose a mining puzzle takes exactly n steps to find a solution. For example, instead of finding a block whose SHA-256 hash is below a certain target, we could require computing n consecutive SHA-256 hashes. This wouldn't be efficient to check, but never mind that for now. The bigger problem here is that since it takes exactly n steps to find a solution, then the fastest miner in the network will always be the one who wins the next reward. It would soon become clear which miner was solving every puzzle, and other miners would have no incentive to participate at all.

Again, a good puzzle gives every miner the chance of winning the next puzzle solution in proportion to the amount of hash power they contribute. Imagine throwing a dart at a board randomly, with different sized targets corresponding to the mining power held by different miners. This requirement means that the odds of solving the puzzle must be independent of how much work you have already spent trying to solve it (because big miners will have always spent more work). This is why a good mining puzzle is called *progress free*.

From a mathematical perspective, this means that a good mining puzzle must be a *memoryless process*—anything else would inevitably reward miners for past progress in some way. Therefore, any feasible puzzle will inherently involve some sort of trial-and-error process. The time to find a solution will therefore inevitably form an exponential distribution, as we saw in Chapter 2.

Adjustable difficulty, fast verification, and progress freeness are three crucial properties of Bitcoin mining puzzles. SHA-256-based partial preimage finding certainly satisfies all three. Some people argue that other properties satisfied by Bitcoin's mining puzzle are also essential, but we'll discuss other potential requirements as they come up while we explore other potential functions.

8.2. ASIC-RESISTANT PUZZLES

We start with the challenge of designing an *ASIC-resistant* puzzle, which has been by far the most widely discussed and sought after type of alternative mining puzzle. As discussed in Chapter 5, Bitcoin mining was initially done primarily with ordinary computers, eventually extended to GPUs and customized FPGA devices, and now is almost exclusively done by powerful optimized ASIC chips. These ASICs are so much more efficient than general-purpose computing equipment that mining with an ordinary computer (or even some early generation ASICs) is no longer worth the price of electricity, even if the hardware is free.

This transition has meant that most individuals participating in the Bitcoin ecosystem (e.g., customers or merchants transacting using Bitcoin) no longer have any role in the mining process. Some members of the Bitcoin community think that a small group of professional miners controlling the mining process is a dangerous development. In Satoshi Nakamoto's original paper on Bitcoin, the phrase "one-CPU-one-vote" was used, which has sometimes been taken to mean Bitcoin should be a democratic system owned by all of its users.

Others think that the rise of ASICs is inevitable and is not detrimental to Bitcoin, and that the desire for ASIC resistance is simply nostalgia for the "the good old days." Without taking a side on whether ASIC resistance is desirable, we can dive into the technical challenges and some of the proposed approaches for achieving this goal.

What Does ASIC Resistance Mean?

Generally speaking, we want to disincentivize the use of custom-built hardware for mining. Interpreting this strictly would mean designing a puzzle for which existing general-purpose computers are already the cheapest and most efficient devices. But this would be impossible. After all, general-purpose computers already have special-purpose optimizations. Not all products have the same optimizations, and they change with time. For example, in the past decade Intel and AMD have both added support for special instructions (often called "adding hardware support") to compute the Advanced Encryption Standard block cipher more efficiently. So some computers will always be less efficient than others at mining. Besides, it's hard to imagine designing a mining puzzle that would rely on features like the speakers and screen that most individuals' personal computers have. So special-purpose machines stripped of these features would still probably be cheaper and more efficient.

So in reality our goal is a more modest one: coming up with a puzzle that reduces the gap between the most cost-effective customized hardware and what most general-purpose computers can do. ASICs will inevitably be somewhat more efficient, but if we could limit this advantage to an order of magnitude or less, it might still be economical for individual users to mine with the computers they already have.

Memory-Hard Puzzles

The most widely used puzzles designed to be ASIC resistant are called *memory-hard* puzzles—puzzles that require a large amount of memory to compute, instead of, or in addition to, a lot of CPU time. A similar but different concept is *memory-bound* puzzles, in which the time to access memory dominates the total computation time. A puzzle can be just memory hard without being memory bound, or memory bound without being memory hard, or both. It's a subtle but important distinction arising from the fact that even if CPU speed is the bottleneck for computation *time*, the *cost* of solving a large number of such puzzles in parallel might still be dominated by the cost of memory, or vice versa. Typically, for a computational puzzle we want something that is memory hard *and* memory bound, ensuring that a large amount of memory is required, and this is the limiting factor.

Why might memory-hard and memory-bound puzzles help ASIC resistance? The logical operations required to compute modern hash functions are only a small part of what goes on in a CPU, meaning that for Bitcoin's puzzle, ASICs get a lot of mileage by not implementing any of the unnecessary functionality. A related factor is that the variation in memory performance (and cost per unit of performance) is much lower than the variation in computing speeds across different types of processors. So if we could design a puzzle that was memory hard, requiring relatively simple computation but lots of memory, then the cost of solving a puzzle would improve at the slower rate of memory-cost improvements.

SHA-256 is decidedly not memory hard, as we've seen, requiring only a tiny 256-bit state, which easily fits into CPU registers. But it isn't too difficult to design a memory-hard proof-of-work puzzle.

Scrypt

The most popular memory-hard puzzle is called *scrypt*. This puzzle is already widely used in Litecoin, the second-most popular cryptocurrency, and a variety of other Bitcoin alternatives.

Scrypt is a memory-hard hash function, originally designed for hashing passwords in a way that is difficult to brute force, so the mining puzzle is the same as Bitcoin's partial hash-preimage puzzle except with scrypt replacing SHA-256.

That scrypt existed prior to Bitcoin and has been used for password hashing gives some confidence in its security. Password hashing has a similar goal of ASIC resistance, because for security we want an attacker with customized hardware to not be able to compute password hashes much faster than the legitimate user or server, who presumably have only general-purpose computers.

```
1 def scrypt(N, seed):
2     V = [0] * N // initialize memory buffer of length N

     // Fill up memory buffer with pseudorandom data
3    V[0] = seed
4    for i = 1 to N:
5       V[i] = SHA-256(V[i-1])

     // Access memory buffer in a pseudorandom order
6    X = SHA-256(V[N-1])
7    for i = 1 to N:
8       j = X % N // Choose a random index based on X
9       X = SHA-256(X ^ V[j]) // Update X based on this index

10    return X
```

FIGURE 8.1. Scrypt pseudocode.

Scrypt basically works in two steps. The first step involves filling a large buffer of random access memory (RAM) with random data. The second step involves reading from (and updating) this memory in a pseudorandom order, requiring that the entire buffer is stored in RAM.

Figure 8.1 shows scrypt pseudocode. It demonstrates the core principles, but we've omitted a few details: in reality scrypt works on slightly larger blocks of data, and the algorithm for filling up the buffer is somewhat more complex.

To see why scrypt is memory hard, imagine trying to compute the same value without using the buffer V (see Figure 8.1). This would certainly be possible—however, in line 9, we would need to recompute the value $V[j]$ on the fly, which would require computing j iterations of SHA-256. Because the value of j during each iteration of the loop will be pseudorandomly chosen between 0 and $N - 1$, this will require about $N/2$ SHA-256 computations. This means computing the entire function will now take $N \cdot N/2 = N^2/2$ SHA-256 computations, instead of just $2N$ if a buffer is used! Thus, the use of memory converts scrypt from an $O(N)$ function to an $O(N^2)$ one. It should be simple to choose N large enough such that the $O(N^2)$ is slow enough to make using memory the faster option.

Time-Memory Trade-Offs

While it would be much slower to compute scrypt without the help of a large memory buffer, it is still possible to use less memory at the cost of slightly more computation. Suppose that we use a buffer of size $N/2$ (instead of size N). Now, we could store only the values $V[j]$ if j is even, discarding the values for which j is odd. In the second loop, about half of the time an odd value of j will be chosen, but this is now fairly easy to compute on the fly—we simply compute SHA-256($V[j - 1]$), since $V[j - 1]$ will be in our buffer. Since this happens about half the time, it adds $N/2$ extra SHA-256 computations.

Thus, halving our memory requirement increases the number of SHA-256 computations by only a quarter (from $2N$ to $5N/2$). In general, we could store only every kth row of the buffer V, using N/k memory and computing $(k + 3)N/2$ iterations of SHA-256. In the limit, if we set $k = N$, we're back up to our earlier calculation, where the running time becomes $O(N^2)$. These numbers don't apply precisely for scrypt itself, but the asymptotic estimates do.

There are alternate designs that mitigate the ability to trade off memory with time. For example, if the buffer is continually updated in the second loop, it makes the time-memory trade-off less effective, as the updates will have to be stored.

Verification Cost

Another limitation of scrypt is that it takes as much memory to verify as it does to compute. To make the memory hardness meaningful, N will need to be fairly large. This means that a single computation of scrypt is orders of magnitude more expensive than a single iteration of SHA-256, which is all that is needed to check Bitcoin's simpler mining puzzle.

This expense has some negative consequences, as every client in the network must repeat this computation to check that a claimed new block is valid. This could slow down propagation and acceptance of new blocks and increase the risk of forks. It also means every client (even lightweight SPV clients) must have enough memory to compute the function efficiently. As a result, the amount of memory N that can be used for scrypt in a cryptocurrency is somewhat limited by practical concerns.

Until recently, it wasn't known whether it was possible to design a mining puzzle that was memory hard to compute but fast (and memory easy) to verify. This property is not useful for password hashing, which had been the primary use case for memory-hard functions before their use in cryptocurrencies.

In 2014, a new puzzle, *Cuckoo Cycle*, was proposed by John Tromp. Cuckoo Cycle is based on the difficulty of finding cycles in a graph generated from a cuckoo hash table, a data structure that itself was only proposed in 2001. There isn't any known way to compute it without building up a large hash table, but it can be checked simply by checking that a (relatively small) cycle has been found.

This puzzle might make memory-hard or memory-bound proof of work much more practical for use in Bitcoin consensus. Unfortunately, there is no mathematical proof that this function can't be computed efficiently without using memory. Often, new cryptographic algorithms appear secure, but the community is not convinced until they have been around for many years without an attack being found. For this reason, and due to its recent discovery, Cuckoo Cycle has not been used by any cryptocurrency as of 2015.

Scrypt in Practice

Scrypt has been used in many cryptocurrencies, including several popular ones, such as Litecoin. The results have been somewhat mixed. Scrypt ASICs are already available for the parameters chosen by Litecoin (and copied by many other altcoins). Surprisingly, the performance improvement of these ASICs compared to general-purpose computers has been equal to or larger than that for SHA-256! Thus, scrypt was decidedly not ASIC resistant in the end, as least as used by Litecoin. The developers of Litecoin initially claimed ASIC resistance was a key advantage over Bitcoin, but have since admitted this is no longer the case.

The lack of ASIC resistance may be a result of the relatively low value of N (the memory usage parameter) used by Litecoin, requiring only 128 kilobytes to compute (or less if a time-memory trade-off is used, which was commonly done on GPUs to get the entire buffer to fit in a faster cache). This low N value has made it relatively easy to design lightweight mining ASICs without a complicated memory access bus needed to access gigabytes of RAM, as general-purpose computers have. Litecoin developers didn't choose a value that was much higher (which would make ASICs more difficult to design), because they considered the verification cost impractical.

Other Approaches to ASIC Resistance

Recall that our original goal was simply to make it hard to build ASICs with dramatic performance speedups. Memory hardness is only one approach to this goal.

The other approaches, unfortunately, are not very scientific and have not been as rigorously designed or attacked as memory-hard functions. The best known is X11, which is simply a combination of 11 different hash functions introduced by an altcoin called "Darkcoin" (later renamed DASH) and since used by several others. The goal of X11 is to make it considerably more complicated to design an efficient ASIC, as all 11 functions must be implemented in hardware. But this is nothing more than an inconvenience for hardware designers. If an ASIC were built for X11, it would surely make CPU and GPU mining obsolete.

Another approach that has been proposed, but not actually implemented, is to have a mining puzzle that's a moving target. That is, the mining puzzle itself would change, just as the difficulty periodically changes in Bitcoin. Ideally, the puzzle would change

> **Where Did X11's Hash Functions Come From?**
>
> From 2007 to 2012, the U.S. National Institute of Standards ran a competition to choose a new hash function family to be the SHA-3 standard. This produced a large number of hash functions that were submitted as candidates, complete with design documents and source code. While many of these candidates were shown not to be cryptographically secure during the competition, 24 survived without any known cryptographic attacks. X11 chose 11 of these, including Keccak, the ultimate competition winner.

in such a way that optimized mining hardware for the previous puzzle would no longer be useful for the new one. It's unclear exactly how to actually change the puzzle once every so often to obtain the security requirements. If the decision were to be made by the developers of an altcoin, it might be an unacceptable source of centralization. For example, the developers might choose a new puzzle for which they have already developed hardware (or just an optimized FPGA implementation), giving them an early advantage.

Perhaps the sequence of puzzles could be generated automatically, but this seems difficult as well. One idea might be to take a large set of hash functions (e.g., the 24 SHA-3 candidates that were not broken) and use each for 6 months to 1 year, too short a time for hardware to be developed. Of course, if the schedule were known in advance, then the hardware could simply be designed to ship just in time for the introduction of each function being used.

The ASIC Honeymoon

The lack of ASICs for X11 so far, even though they are clearly possible to build, demonstrates a potentially useful pattern. Because no altcoins using X11 have a particularly high market share, there simply hasn't been a large enough market for anybody to build ASICs for X11 yet. In general, designing ASICs has high up-front costs (in both time and money) and relatively low marginal costs per unit of hardware produced. Thus, for new and unproven cryptocurrencies, it is not worth making an investment to build hardware if the currency might fail before the new hardware is available for mining. Even when a clear market exists, there is a time delay before hardware units will be ready. It took more than a year for the first Bitcoin ASICs to be shipped from when they were first designed, and this was considered to be lightning fast for the hardware industry.

Thus, any new altcoin with a new mining puzzle is likely to experience an *ASIC honeymoon*, during which time GPU and FGPA mining (and potentially even CPU mining) will be profitable. It may not be possible to stem the tide of ASICs forever, but there is perhaps some value in making it appealing for individuals to participate in mining (and earn some units of the new currency) while it is bootstrapping.

Arguments against ASIC Resistance

We've seen that it may be impossible to achieve ASIC resistance in the long run. But there are also arguments that it is risky to move away from the relatively proven SHA-256 mining puzzle toward a new puzzle that might be weaker cryptographically. Furthermore, SHA-256-mining ASICs are already being designed at close to the modern limits on hardware efficiency, meaning the exponential growth period is probably over, and SHA-256 mining will therefore offer the most stability to the network.

Finally, it can be argued that even in the short run, ASIC resistance is a bad feature to have. Recall from Chapter 3 that even for a 51 percent miner, many types of attack aren't rational for her to attempt, because it could crash the exchange rate and decimate the value of the miner's investment in hardware, since the bitcoins she earns from mining will be worth much less.

With a highly ASIC-resistant puzzle, this security argument might fall apart. For example, an attacker might be able to rent a huge amount of generic computing power temporarily (from a service, such as Amazon's EC2), use it to attack, and then suffer no monetary consequences as she no longer needs to rent the capacity after the attack. In contrast, with an ASIC-friendly puzzle, such an attacker would inherently need to control a large number of ASICs, which are useful only for mining the cryptocurrency. Such an attacker would be maximally invested in the future success of the currency. Following this argument to its logical conclusion, to maximize security, perhaps mining puzzles should not only enable efficient mining ASICs to be be built, but be designed such that those ASICs are completely useless outside of the cryptocurrency!

8.3. PROOF OF USEFUL WORK

In Chapter 5, we discussed how the energy consumed (some would say wasted) by Bitcoin mining, referred to as *negative externalities* by economists, is a potential concern. We estimated that Bitcoin mining consumes several hundred megawatts of power. The obvious question is whether there is some puzzle for which the work done to solve it provides some other benefit to society. This would amount to a form of recycling and could help increase political support for cryptocurrencies. Of course, this puzzle would still need to satisfy several basic requirements to make it suitable for use in a consensus protocol.

Previous Distributed Computing Projects

The idea of using idle computers (or "spare cycles") for good is much older than Bitcoin. Table 8.1 lists a few of the most popular volunteer computing projects. All these projects have a property that might make them suitable for use as a computational puzzle: they involve some sort of a "needle in a haystack" problem that has a large space of potential solutions, and small portions of the search space can be checked relatively quickly and in parallel. For example, in SETI@home, volunteers are given small portions of observed radio signals to scan for potential patterns, while in distributed .net, volunteers are given a small range of potential secret keys to test.

Volunteer computing projects have succeeded by assigning small portions of the solution space to individuals for checking. In fact, this paradigm is so common that a specific library called "BOINC" (Berkeley Open Infrastructure for Network Computing) was developed to make it easy to parcel out small pieces of work for individuals to finish.

In these applications, volunteers were motivated mainly by interest in the underlying problem, though these projects also often use leaderboards for volunteers to show off how much computation they have contributed. This has led to some attempts to game

TABLE 8.1. POPULAR VOLUNTEER COMPUTING PROJECTS

Project	Founded	Goal	Impact
Great Internet Mersenne Prime Search	1996	Finding large Mersenne primes	Found the new "largest prime number" twelve straight times, including $2^{57885161} - 1$
distributed.net	1997	Cryptographic brute-force demos	First successful public brute force of a 64-bit cryptographic key
SETI@home	1999	Identifying signs of extraterrestrial life	Largest project to date with more than 5 million participants
Folding@home	2000	Atomic-level simulations of protein folding	Greatest computing capacity of any volunteer computing project; more than 118 scientific papers

the leaderboards by reporting work that wasn't actually finished, requiring some projects to resort to sending a small amount of redundant work to detect cheating. For use in a cryptocurrency, of course, the motivation is primarily monetary, and we can expect participants to attempt to cheat as much as technically possible.

Challenges in Adapting Useful Puzzles to Proof of Work

Given the success of these projects, we might attempt to simply use these problems directly. For example, in the case of SETI@home, where volunteers are given segments of radio observations that they test for statistical anomalies, we might decide that statistical anomalies that are rarer than some threshold are considered "winning" solutions to the puzzle and allow any miner who finds one to create a block.

There are a few problems with this idea. First, note that potential solutions are not all equally likely to be a winning solution. Participants might realize that certain segments are more likely to produce anomalies than others. With a centralized project, participants are assigned work so all segments can be analyzed eventually (perhaps with more promising segments given priority). For mining, however, any miner can attempt any segment, meaning miners might flock to try the most likely segments first. This could mean the puzzle is not entirely progress free, if faster miners know they can test the most promising segments first. Compare this to Bitcoin's puzzle, in which any nonce is equally likely as any other to produce a valid block, so all miners are incentivized to choose random nonces to try. The problem here demonstrates a key property of Bitcoin's puzzle that we previously took for granted: an *equiprobable solution space.*

Next, consider the problem that SETI@home has a fixed amount of data to analyze based on observations taken by radio telescopes. It's possible that as mining power increased, there would be no more raw data to analyze. Compare this again to Bitcoin, in which an effectively infinite number of SHA-256 puzzles can be created. This reveals another important requirement: an *inexhaustible puzzle space* is needed.

Finally, consider that SETI@home uses a trusted, centralized set of administrators to curate the new radio data and determine what participants should be looking for.

Again, since we are using our puzzle to build a consensus algorithm we can't assume a centralized party to manage the puzzle. Thus, we need a puzzle that can be *algorithmically generated.*

Which Volunteer Computing Projects Might Be Suitable as Puzzles?

Returning to Table 8.1, we can see that SETI@home and Folding@home clearly won't work for a decentralized consensus protocol. Both probably lack all three properties we've now added to our list. The cryptographic brute-force problems taken on by distributed.net could work, although they are typically chosen in response to specific decryption challenges that have been set by companies looking to evaluate the security of certain algorithms. These can't be algorithmically generated. We can algorithmically generate decryption challenges to be broken by brute forcing, but in a sense this is exactly what SHA-256 partial preimage finding already does, and it serves no beneficial function.

This leaves the Great Internet Mersenne Prime Search, which turns out to be close to workable. The challenges can be algorithmically generated (find a prime larger than the previous one), and the puzzle space is inexhaustible. In fact, it's infinite, since it has been proven that there are an infinite number of prime numbers (and an infinite number of Mersenne Primes in particular).

The only real drawback is that large Mersenne Primes take a long time to find and are very rare. In fact, the Great Internet Mersenne Prime Search has found only 14 Mersenne primes in over 18 years! It clearly wouldn't work to add less than one block per year to a block chain. This specific problem appears to lack the adjustable difficulty property that we stated was essential in Section 8.1. It turns out, however, that a similar problem involving finding prime numbers appears workable as a computational puzzle.

Primecoin

As of 2015, the only proof-of-useful-work system deployed in practice is Primecoin. The challenge in Primecoin is to find a *Cunningham chain* of prime numbers. A Cunningham chain is a sequence of k prime numbers $p_1, p_2, \ldots, p_k$ such that $p_i = 2p_{i-1} + 1$ for each number in the chain. That is, you take a prime number, double it and add one to get another prime number, and continue until you get a composite number. The sequence 2, 5, 11, 23, 47 is a Cunningham chain of length 5. The potential sixth number in the chain, 95, is not prime ($95 = 5 \cdot 19$). The longest known Cunningham chain is of length 19 (starting at 79,910,197,721,667,870,187,016,101). It is conjectured and widely believed, but not proven, that there exist Cunningham chains of length k for any k.

Now, to turn this into a computational puzzle, we need three parameters m, n, and k, which we will explain momentarily. For a given challenge x (the hash of the previous block), we take the first m bits of x and consider any chain of length k or greater in which the first prime in the chain is an n-bit prime and has the same m leading bits as x to be a valid solution. Note that we can adjust n and k to make the puzzle harder. Increasing k (the required chain length) makes the problem exponentially harder, while increasing n (the size of the starting prime) makes it polynomially harder. This provides fine-tuning of the difficulty. The value of m just needs to be large enough that trying to precompute solutions before seeing the value of the previous block is infeasible.

All the other properties we have discussed appear to be provided: solutions are relatively quick to verify, the problem is progress free, the problem space is infinite (assuming some well-studied mathematical conjectures about the distribution of prime numbers are true), and puzzles can be algorithmically generated. Indeed, this puzzle has been in use for Primecoin for almost 2 years and has produced the largest-known primes in Cunningham chains for many values of k. Primecoin has since expanded to include additional, similar types of prime chains in its proof of work, including "second kind" Cunningham chains in which $p_i = 2p_{i-1} - 1$.

This example provides strong evidence that it is possible to make proof of useful work practical in some limited circumstances. Of course, it's debatable the extent to which finding large Cunningham chains is useful. They may have some applied purpose in the future, and they certainly stand as a small contribution to our collective mathematical knowledge. Currently, however, they have no known practical applications.

Permacoin and Proof of Storage

A different approach to proof of useful work is *proof of storage* (also sometimes called *proof of retrievability*). Rather than requiring a solely computational puzzle, what if we could design a puzzle that required storing a large amount of data to compute? If this data were useful, then miners' investment in mining hardware would effectively be contributing to a widely distributed and replicated archival storage system.

Consider *Permacoin*, the first proposal for proof of storage for use in consensus. We begin with a large file F. For now, assume everybody agrees on the value of F and the file will not change. For example, F might be chosen by a trusted dealer when a cryptocurrency is launched, much as any new currency needs to agree on a genesis block to get going. This file would ideally be of public value. For example, experimental data collected from the Large Hadron Collider already consists of several hundred petabytes. Providing a free backup to this data would be quite useful.

Of course, since F is a huge file, most participants would not be able to store the entire file. But we already know how to use cryptographic hash functions to ensure everybody agrees on F without knowing the entire contents of the file. The simplest approach would be for everybody to agree on $H(F)$, but a better approach is to represent F using a large Merkle tree and have all participants agree on the value of the root. Now, everybody can agree on the value of F, and it is efficient to prove that any portion of F is correct.

In Permacoin, each miner M stores a random subset $F_M \subseteq F$. To achieve this, when the

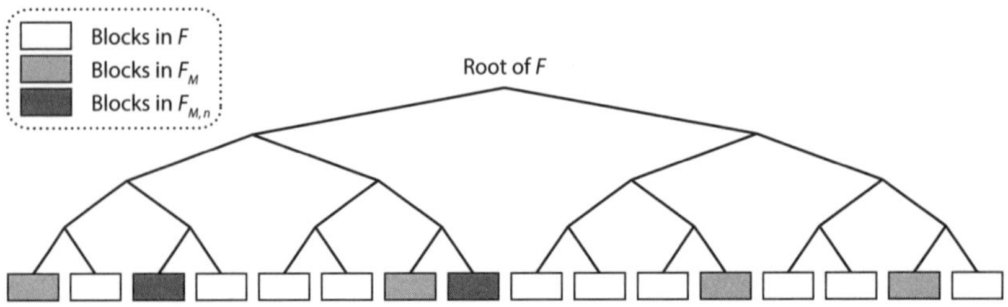

FIGURE 8.2. Choosing random blocks in a file in Permacoin. In this example, $k_1 = 6$ and $k_2 = 2$. In a real implementation, these parameters would be much larger.

miner generates a public key K_M, which he will use to receive funds, he hashes his public key to generate a pseudorandom set of blocks F_M, which he must store to be able to mine. This subset will be of some fixed number of blocks k_1. We have to assume here that miners have some way to fetch those blocks when they start mining—perhaps downloading them from a canonical source (Figure 8.2).

Once the miner has stored F_M locally, the puzzle is fairly similar to conventional SHA-256 mining. Given a previous block hash x, the miner chooses a random nonce value n and hashes this to generate a pseudorandom subset $F_{M,n} \subseteq F_M$, consisting of $k_2 < k_1$ blocks. Note that this subset depends both on the nonce the miner has chosen and his public key. Finally, the miner computes a SHA-256 hash of n and the blocks in F_k. If the value of this hash is below a target difficulty, he has found a valid solution.

Verifying a solution requires the following steps:

- Verify that $F_{M,n}$ was correctly generated from the miner's public key K_M and nonce n.
- Verify that each block of $F_{M,n}$ is correct by verifying its path in the Merkle tree to the globally-agreed-on root of F.
- Verify that $H(F_{M,n} \| n)$ is less than the target difficulty.

It should be easy to see why solving the puzzle requires the miner to store all of $F_{M,n}$ locally. For each nonce, the miner needs to test the hash of a random subset of blocks of $F_{M,n}$, which would be prohibitively slow to fetch over the network from remote storage.

Unlike the case with scrypt, there are no reasonable time-memory trade-offs, provided that k_2 is big enough. If a miner stored only half of F_M locally, and $k_2 = 20$, they'd have to try a million nonces before they found one that didn't require any blocks to be fetched over the network. So decreasing their storage burden by a constant factor increases their computational burden exponentially. Of course, setting k_2 to be too large would not be very efficient, since k_2 Merkle tree paths must be transmitted and verified in any valid solution.

There is also a trade-off in setting k_1. The smaller k_1 is, the less storage is needed to function as a miner, and hence mining is more democratic. However, this also means larger miners have no incentive to store more than k_1 blocks of F, even if they have the ability to store more.

As usual, this example is a slight simplification of the full Permacoin proposal, but it is enough to understand the key design components. The biggest practical challenge, of course, is finding a suitably large file that is important, public, and in need of additional replication. There are also significant complexities if the file F changes over time, as well as with adjusting the mining difficulty over time.

Long-Term Challenges and Economics

To summarize this section, proof of useful work is a natural goal, but it is quite challenging to achieve it, given the other requirements of a good computational puzzle for a consensus protocol. Although at least two examples are known that are technically feasible, Primecoin and Permacoin, both carry some technical drawbacks (primarily longer verification time of purported solutions). Furthermore, both provide fairly minor public benefits compared to the scale of effort we've seen levied in Bitcoin mining, with millions of dollars' worth of capital and megawatts of electricity consumed.

There is an interesting economic argument that the benefit of any proof of useful work should be a pure *public good.* In economics, a public good is one that is nonexcludable, meaning nobody can be prevented from using it, and nonrivalrous, meaning the good's use by others does not affect its value. The classic example is a lighthouse.

Some of the examples we discussed here, such as protein folding, might not be a pure public good, because some firms (e.g., large pharmaceutical corporations) may benefit more from increased knowledge about protein folding than others. Essentially, mining would be cheaper for these parties, since they are gaining more benefit from the public benefits than others would gain.

8.4. NONOUTSOURCEABLE PUZZLES

Let's turn to another potential design goal for alternative mining puzzles: preventing the formation of mining pools. As discussed in Chapter 5 and elsewhere, most Bitcoin miners mine as part of a pool rather than independently. This has resulted in a few large pools that together represent most of the mining power. Since each pool is operated by a central pool administrator, some stakeholders feel this is a dangerous trend away from Bitcoin's core design principle of decentralization and can compromise its security.

A mining pool with a majority share is an obvious problem, but any large, centrally managed pool might implement a nondefault mining strategy and attack the network. Such pools are also a juicy target for hackers to try to compromise, resulting in hacker control of a large amount of mining power. The pool operators might collude to censor transactions or enforce high transaction fees. At the very least, having most miners in pools also means that most miners aren't running a fully validating node.

Interestingly, these concerns have an analogy in the realm of voting. It's illegal in the United States and many other nations for individuals to sell their votes. Arguably, participating in a pool controlled by someone else is akin to selling your vote in the Bitcoin consensus protocol.

Technical Requirements for Pools

Recall that mining pools appear to be an emergent phenomenon. There's no evidence that Satoshi was thinking of mining pools at the time of Bitcoin's original design. It wasn't apparent for a few years that efficient pools could be established among many individuals who don't know or trust one another.

As we saw in Chapter 5, mining pools typically work by designating a pool operator with a well-known public key. Each of the participating miners mines as usual but sends in shares to the pool operator. These shares are "near misses," or partial solutions, which would be valid solutions at a lower difficulty level. This shows the pool operator how much work the miner is performing. When one of the pool participants finds a valid block, the pool operator then distributes the rewards among the pool participants based on the number of shares they have submitted. As discussed in Chapter 5, there are many formulas for dividing up the revenue, but all mining pools follow this basic structure.

The existence of pools thus relies on at least two technical properties of Bitcoin. The first is that it's easy for miners to prove (probabilistically) how much work they are doing by submitting shares. By choosing a low enough threshold for shares, miners can easily prove how much work they are performing with arbitrary precision, regardless of the actual difficulty of finding a valid block. This facet of mining puzzles appears difficult to change, given that we need a puzzle that can be created with arbitrary difficulty.

Second, pool members can easily prove to the pool operator that they're following the rules and working to find valid blocks, which would reward the pool as a whole. The shares that miners submit constitute such a proof, because the pool's public key is committed to in the coinbase transaction included in the block's Merkle tree of transactions. Once a miner finds a block or even a share, they can't change which public key is the recipient of the newly minted coins.

Block-Discarding Attacks

This scheme for implementing mining pools has one weakness: Nothing guarantees that participating miners actually submit valid blocks to the pool manager in the event that they find them. Suppose that a pool member is upset with a large mining pool. She can participate in the pool by mining and submitting shares as usual, but if she actually finds a valid block that would reward the pool, she can simply discard it and not tell the pool operator about it.

This attack reduces the pool's overall mining power, as none of the attacker's work

Block-Discarding Attacks between Pools

People assumed for years that it can't be profitable for a participant to discard valid blocks found on behalf of the pool. It turns out this strategy can be profitable if one mining pool uses it to attack another. This was proposed apocryphally many times and was first thoroughly analyzed in a paper by Ittay Eyal in 2015.

Consider a simple case: suppose two mining pools, A and B, each have 50 percent of the total mining capacity. Now suppose B uses half of its mining power (25 percent of the total capacity) to mine as a member in pool A, but discards all blocks found. We can show, in a simplified model, that B will now earn 5/9 of the total rewards, greater than the 50 percent it would earn by mining normally. In this simple case, dedicating half of its mining power to attacking can be shown to be the optimal strategy for pool B.

The situation grows more complicated with multiple pools. Block discarding has not been observed in practice on a large scale as of 2015. But it remains possible that in the long run, attacks like this one will bring the viability of large mining pools into question.

is contributing to finding valid blocks. However, the attacker will still be rewarded, as she appears to be submitting valid shares and is simply not finding any valid blocks. If the mining pool is designed to be revenue-neutral (that is, all mining rewards are redistributed back to participants), then this attack can cause the pool to run at a loss.

This attack is sometimes called a *vigilante* or *sabotage* attack and is considered to be a form of vandalism, because the attack appears to be costly for both the attacker and the pool. The attacker loses money, because every block discarded would have led to some proportion of the block rewards being returned to the attacker. Of course, the attacker still gets rewards for other puzzle solutions that are found.

It appears that a rational attacker wouldn't employ this strategy, since she would lose money without gaining anything tangible. It turns out (quite surprisingly) that there are cases where this strategy can be profitable. We want to design an entirely new mining puzzle formulation that ensures this strategy is always profitable.

Rewarding Sabotage

Our design goal is to make it so that miners are incentivized to mine in a pool but not submit valid blocks to the pool manager. Currently, only the pool manager can collect the mining rewards, because the manager requires all participants to include a specific public key in the coinbase transaction of blocks they are mining. Proper inclusion can be easily checked in submitted partial solutions. The pool manager is the only party that knows the private key and hence can determine where the newly minted coins go.

But what if we required that all participants also knew the private key (and hence could redirect the funds after mining a block?). To do this, we need a puzzle in which each solution attempt requires knowledge of the private key in the coinbase transaction. We can change the puzzle from "find a block whose hash is below a certain target" to "find a block for which the hash of *a signature* on the block is below a certain target." This signature must be computed using the same public key used in the coinbase transaction.

Such a puzzle leaves would-be pool operators with two untenable choices. They might distribute the private key to all pool participants, in which case any of the latter can steal all of the funds. Alternately, they can perform the signatures on behalf of pool participants. Computing a signature is orders of magnitude more expensive than computing a hash, however, so in this case the pool manager would be doing the majority of the heavy lifting. It would be better for the pool manager to simply be a solo miner.

Pros and Cons of Nonoutsourceable Mining

Since this puzzle can't effectively be outsourced to an untrusted participant, it is much more challenging, if not outright impossible, to form a mining pool with untrusted participants. It effectively prevents all pools, even efforts to make a decentralized pool without a pool manager, such as P2Pool.

There's an argument that deploying such a puzzle might perversely lead to more centralization, not less, because it would discourage small miners from participating due to the high variance they would face. This would leave only large mining operations. Currently, while pools may nominally control a large amount of mining power, it isn't clear that they can use this power to launch an attack without having many of their members defect. It remains an open question which risk is worse—that of large mining pools or of limiting mining to operators large enough to live with a high variance.

The holy grail would be to design a consensus protocol that is intrinsically low variance by rewarding miners a small amount for lower-difficulty puzzles. Then miners don't need to form pools, and yet small miners may still participate. Simply decreasing the average time between blocks won't work—it would need to be decreased by a factor of 1,000 or more for the resulting variance to be equivalent to that of today's large mining pools. But then the delay between blocks would be less than a second, and the number of stale blocks would be chaotically high. It remains an open question whether there is an alternate version of the consensus protocol that would enable easier mining puzzles without requiring near-instantaneous broadcast of all solutions.

8.5. PROOF OF STAKE AND VIRTUAL MINING

To wrap up this chapter, let's look at the idea of replacing computational puzzles with *virtual mining*. This term refers to a disparate set of approaches, but they all have in common that they require only a small expenditure of computational resources by participating miners.

Closing the Loop on Mining

As a thought experiment, suppose Bitcoin or another cryptocurrency becomes the dominant form of payment globally. Miners would start with some initial holding of crypto-

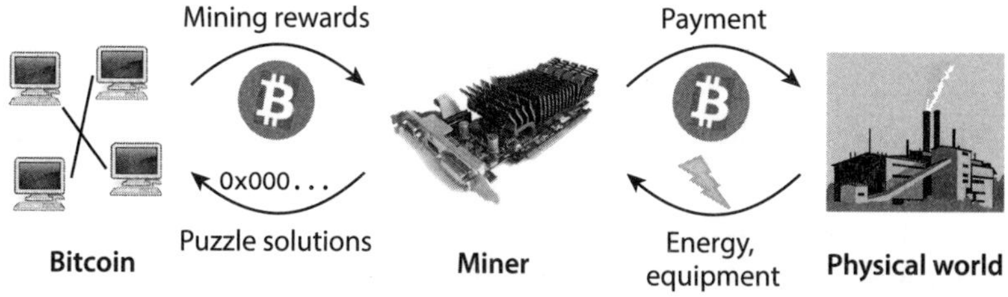

FIGURE 8.3. Cycle of Bitcoin mining. ASUS NVIDIA GeForce 210 silent graphics card with HDMI courtesy of Joydeep. Factory image courtesy of Dtbohrer.

currency, use it to purchase mining equipment and electricity, consume these resources, and in the process, acquire new cryptocurrency in the form of mining rewards (Figure 8.3). This process continually burns energy and raw materials.

Once mining hardware becomes a commodity and electricity is a commodity (as it generally already is), no miner would have a significant advantage over any other miner in terms of how efficiently they could convert their initial cryptocurrency holdings into mining rewards. Barring minor variations in efficiency, whoever invests the most into mining will receive the most rewards.

The basic question motivating virtual mining is: what would happen if we removed the step of spending money on power and equipment? After all, this process is primarily used to prove who has invested the most in mining. Why not simply allocate mining "power" directly to all currency holders in proportion to how much currency they actually hold?

Recall that the original goal of Bitcoin mining was to enable a form of voting on the state of the block chain, with miners with more computing power gaining more votes. We could instead design the voting system so that votes are determined by how much currency one currently holds.

Advantages of Virtual Mining

The primary advantage of this approach is obvious: it removes the wasteful right half of the mining cycle from Figure 8.3, leaving us with a closed system, as shown in Figure 8.4.

In addition to simplicity, this approach would dramatically reduce Bitcoin's environmental footprint. It wouldn't reduce energy consumption to zero, because miners will

FIGURE 8.4. Virtual mining cycle.

always have to expend some computational resources to communicate with the network and validate. Some virtual mining schemes also require a small amount of computational mining as well. But in either case, nearly all mining work performed in Bitcoin can potentially be eliminated.

Virtual mining may also reduce the trend toward centralization. Because no mining hardware is involved, there is no concern about an ASIC advantage; any miner is able to mine as efficiently as all others. Any virtual mining puzzle achieves all of the goals of ASIC-resistant puzzles.

Perhaps most importantly, virtual mining might solve the problem we discussed in the context of ASIC-resistant puzzles, namely, that miners may not be invested in the long-term health of the currency. Anybody who holds any bitcoins is effectively a stakeholder in the currency, and a powerful virtual miner (such as one who holds 51 percent or more of all currency) is a very large stakeholder. This miner has an incentive to do things that would benefit the system as a whole, because such actions increase the value of the coins that he holds. This argument is even stronger than the argument that a miner sitting on a large stock of mining equipment whose value depends on the future of the currency will not behave maliciously.

This virtual mining argument is where the term *proof of stake* comes from. Even more than eliminating mining and saving energy, perhaps the most fundamental motivation for virtual mining is to ensure that mining is done by stakeholders in the currency who have the strongest incentives to be good stewards of the system.

Implementing Virtual Mining: Peercoin

Many variations of virtual mining exist, of which we describe a few of the most common ideas. These ideas have not yet been studied in a scientific and rigorous way, nor have they undergone the level of practical testing that proof of work has, due to Bitcoin's popularity.

To start with, consider the approach taken by Peercoin, which was launched in 2012 as the first altcoin using proof of stake. Peercoin is a hybrid proof-of-work/proof-of-stake algorithm in which stake is denominated by "coin-age." The coin-age of a specific unspent transaction output is the product of the amount held by that output and the number of blocks that output has remained unspent. To mine a block in Peercoin, miners must solve a SHA-256-based computational puzzle just like in Bitcoin. However, the difficulty of this puzzle is adjusted down based on how much coin-age the miners are willing to consume. To do this, the block includes a special "coinstake" transaction, in which some transactions are spent simply to reset their coin-age to zero. The sum of the coin-ages consumed in the coinstake transaction determines how difficult the proof-of-work puzzle is to make a given block valid.

It is possible for miners to mine with very little stake and a large amount of computational power, but the difficulty formula is chosen to make it dramatically easier to find a block if some coin-age is consumed. The effect of the computational puzzle is mainly to ensure that the process is randomized if two miners attempt to consume a similar quantity of coin-age.

Many virtual mining altcoins have adopted slightly different designs, including Nxt, BitShares, BlackCoin, and Reddcoin. In each of these currencies, some amount of stake is used to make a computational puzzle vastly easier, purportedly to the point that the computational puzzle is no longer the main challenge in mining.

Alternate Forms of Stake

Two alternatives to this hybrid model are worth discussing:

- *Proof of stake.* The purest form of proof of stake is simply to make mining easier for those who can show they control a large amount of currency. This approach is similar to Peercoin's proof of coin-age, only with age not taken into account. The downside of this approach is that unlike coin-age, which resets after successful mining, the richest participants are always given the easiest mining puzzle.
- *Proof of deposit.* In this formulation, when coins are used by a miner to mint a block, they become frozen for a set number of blocks. This can be thought of as a mirror of coin-age: instead of rewarding a miner for holding coins that remain unspent for a long time in the past, this system rewards miners who are willing to keep coins unspent for a long time into the future. In both approaches, miners' stake effectively comes from the opportunity cost of not being able to use the coins to perform other actions.

The Nothing-at-Stake Problem

Virtual mining is an active area of ongoing research, and there are significant open problems. Although a few other cryptocurrencies have launched and survived using virtual mining, they have faced the same pressure as Bitcoin to withstand motivated attackers.

The generic vulnerability of virtual mining schemes is what's often called the *nothing-at-stake* problem or *stake-grinding attacks.* Suppose an attacker with a proportion $\alpha < 0.5$ of the stake is attempting to create a fork of k blocks. As discussed in Chapter 2, this attack will fail with a high probability (specifically, the probability of success decreases exponentially with k). In traditional mining, a failed attack has a significant opportunity cost, because that miner could have been earning mining rewards during the mining process instead of wasting mining resources on the failed attack.

With virtual mining, this opportunity cost doesn't exist. A miner can use his stake to mine in the current longest chain while simultaneously attempting to create a fork. If his fork succeeds, it will have consumed a large amount of his stake. If it fails, the record of it failing will not be reflected on the eventual longest chain. Thus, rational miners might constantly attempt to fork the chain.

Forking Attacks and Checkpointing

When you download Bitcoin Core, it comes hardcoded with a few checkpoints, or hashes of past blocks. This is primarily intended to make the initial download of the block chain smoother. Without checkpoints, other nodes could flood you with fake—yet valid—blocks and branches. It is easy for an attacker today to generate blocks with valid puzzle solutions at a low block height, that is, close to the genesis block, since the difficulty at the beginning was relatively miniscule. You'd eventually figure out that those blocks are not on the longest valid branch (more precisely, the valid branch with the highest total difficulty), but you'd have to waste resources doing so.

Some altcoins, especially virtual mining schemes, have adopted a strong form of checkpointing as a defense against forking attacks. Nodes receive regular checkpoint updates from designated checkpoint nodes, signed by a designated private key. Nodes will discard branches that conflict with checkpoints. This allows the checkpoint operator, typically the altcoin creator, to pick a winner in case of a fork and even "roll back" blocks. This design is interesting, but it is no longer a decentralized consensus protocol.

For Ethereum (an altcoin launched in mid-2015 that is discussed in Chapter 10), a proposal called "Slasher" allows punishment of miners who attempt to fork the chain. In Slasher, using stake to mine requires signing the current block with the private key corresponding to the transactions making up the miner's stake. If a miner ever uses the same stake to sign two inconsistent chains (neither of which is a prefix of the other), Slasher allows other miners to enter these two signatures later on in the block chain as proof of misbehavior and collect a portion of this stake as a bounty. Although this proposed mechanism appears to provide an effective solution, the details of the protocol are quite complicated, and it has yet to be deployed successfully.

Finally, as we've seen for traditional mining schemes, miners may simply not have a strong incentive to attack because this would damage the system and undermine their stake, even if the attack is successful.

Other Drawbacks of Virtual Mining

Two other drawbacks are worth mentioning. The first is that some forms of virtual mining, even in the absence of stake grinding, might make some types of attacks easier, because it is possible to "save up" for a burst of mining power. For example, a large amount of coin-stake can be pooled to enable a dramatic surge of mining to, perhaps, introduce a fork. This is possible even if a system like Slasher is used to discourage mining on two chains at once. To discourage this type of attack, Peercoin limits the age parameter to 90 days when computing coin-age.

A second issue is that if a miner in a virtual mining system obtains 51 percent of the available stake, she can maintain it forever by only mining on top of her own blocks, essentially taking control of the block chain. Even if a new stake emerges from mining rewards and transaction fees, the 51 percent miner will obtain this new stake, and her share of the total stake will slowly approach 100 percent. In traditional mining, even if a 51 percent miner exists, it is always possible that some new miner will emerge with more mining equipment and energy and will reduce the majority miner. It is much more difficult to avoid this problem in virtual mining.

Can Virtual Mining Actually Work?

Virtual mining remains somewhat controversial in the mainstream Bitcoin community. There is an argument that security fundamentally requires burning real resources, requiring real computational hardware and expending real electrical power to find puzzle solutions. If this argument is believed, then the apparent waste generated by the proof-of-work system can be interpreted as the cost of the security that the system provides. But this argument hasn't been proven, just as the security of virtual mining hasn't been proven.

In summary, it may be desirable to change numerous aspects of Bitcoin's mining puzzle, and this has been an area of furious research and innovation. So far, however, none of the alternatives seems to have both demonstrated theoretical soundness and found practical adoption. For example, even though scrypt has been a popular choice in altcoins, it hasn't actually achieved ASIC resistance, and its usefulness is unclear. It is entirely possible that alternative mining puzzles will find more success in the future. After all, Bitcoin itself came after decades of failed attempts to create a cryptocurrency, and it managed to hit the sweet spot between principled design and practical trade-offs.

FURTHER READING

The paper that defines memory-hard functions and proposes scrypt is:

Percival, Colin. "Stronger Key Derivation via Sequential Memory-Hard Functions," 2009. Available at https://www.bsdcan.org/2009/schedule/attachments/87_scrypt.pdf.

Earlier papers on memory-bound functions include:

Abadi, Martin, Mike Burrows, Mark Manasse, and Ted Wobber. "Moderately Hard, Memory-Bound Functions." *ACM Transactions on Internet Technology* 5(2), 2005.

Dwork, Cynthia, Andrew Goldberg, and Moni Naor. "On Memory-Bound Functions for Fighting Spam." In *Advances in Cryptology—Crypto 2003*. Berlin: Springer, 2003.

The Cuckoo Cycle proposal can be found in:

Tromp, John. "Cuckoo Cycle: A Memory-Hard Proof-of-Work System." IACR Cryptology ePrint Archive, 2014. Available at https://eprint.iacr.org/2014/059.pdf.

The Permacoin proposal is in:

Miller, Andrew, Ari Juels, Elaine Shi, Bryan Parno, and Justin Katz. "Permacoin: Repurposing Bitcoin Work for Data Preservation." In *Proceedings of the 2014 IEEE Symposium on Security and Privacy*, 2014. Available at http://research.microsoft.com/pubs/217984/permacoin.pdf.

This paper discusses different hash function designs and the SHA-3 contest:

Preneel, Bart. "The First 30 Years of Cryptographic Hash Functions and the NIST SHA-3 Competition." In *Topics in Cryptology—CT-RSA, 2010*. Berlin: Springer, 2010.

The proposal for nonoutsourceable puzzles is:

Miller, Andrew, Elaine Shi, Ahmed Kosba, and Jonathan Katz. "Nonoutsourceable Scratch-Off Puzzles to Discourage Bitcoin Mining Coalitions." In *Proceedings of the 22nd ACM Conference on Computer and Communications Security*, forthcoming.

CHAPTER 9
Bitcoin as a Platform

In earlier chapters, we developed the technical underpinnings of Bitcoin and saw how it can be used as a currency. Now we'll look at applications other than currency that we can build using Bitcoin as a central component. Some of these rely on Bitcoin as it is today, without any modifications, and many others would require only small modifications.

We've chosen these applications for a combination of practical usefulness and intellectual interest. This list is not in any way exhaustive, but seeing how these applications work (or could work, since many are only ideas or proposals) will give you insight into the many ways in which Bitcoin's functionality can be repurposed.

9.1. BITCOIN AS AN APPEND-ONLY LOG

It's helpful to think about Bitcoin as an *append-only log*—a data structure to which we can write new data, and one where data is tamper proof and available forever once it has been written. We also have a secure notion of ordering: we can tell if one piece of data was written to the log before or after another piece. This ordering arises from the block hash pointers, not the block timestamps—a block's timestamp can in fact be a lower (earlier) value than its predecessor. That's because miners can lie about timestamps, miners' clocks may not be synchronized, and there is latency on the network. That said, if a block timestamp appears to be off by more than a few hours, then other miners will reject it, so we can rely on the timestamps being approximately correct. As we'll see, these properties turn out to be quite useful.

Secure Timestamping

The append-only log can be used to build a secure timestamping system from Bitcoin. We want to be able to prove that we know some value x at some specific time T. We might not want to actually reveal x at time T. Instead, we only want to reveal x when we actually make the proof, which may be much later than T (and of course if we knew it at T, we still know it after T). However, once we have made the proof, we want the evidence to be permanent.

Recall from Chapter 1 that we can use hash functions to commit to data. Instead of publishing the data x that we want to prove that we know, we can publish just the hash $H(x)$ to the block chain. The properties of the hash function guarantee that we can't later find some different value y with the same value, that is, $y \neq x$ such that $H(x) = H(y)$. We also rely on the convenient property that the hash of x doesn't reveal any information about x, as long as x is chosen from a distribution with high min-entropy, that is, it is sufficiently unpredictable. If x doesn't have this property, then we can pick a random number r with high min-entropy and use $H(r \| x)$ as the commitment, as discussed in Chapter 1.

The main idea is that we can publish just the hash $H(r \| x)$ at time T, and then at some point later on we can reveal r and x. Anybody can look at the append-only log and be convinced that we must have known x at the time we published $H(r \| x)$, because there is no other feasible way to have generated that data.

Applications of Timestamping

What could we do with this kind of secure timestamping? One possible use is to prove prior knowledge of some idea. Suppose we wanted to prove that some invention we filed a patent on was actually in our heads much earlier. We could do this by publishing the hash of a design document or schematic when we first thought of the invention—without revealing to anybody what the idea is. Later on, when the patent is filed or the idea publicized, we can publish the original documents and information, so that anybody can confirm that we must have known the idea earlier, when we published the commitment to it.

We can also prove that someone else has received a message we sent them. Suppose Alice hires Bob to perform a programming job; their contract requires Bob to submit his work to Alice by a specific time. Both parties want to make sure that if there is a dispute later about whether Bob submitted the work or whether the code performed to specification, they have proof of what was submitted and when. To ensure this, they can mutually agree to publish a hash of Bob's submitted work signed by both parties. If either party later lies about what was submitted or when, the other party can prove them wrong (say, in a court of arbitration) by revealing the input to the hash.

Many other interesting systems and protocols can be built using only the secure-timestamping feature of Bitcoin. There's even an entire public-key signature scheme (called the "Guy Fawkes signature scheme") that just uses hash functions and an append-only log. It doesn't require any of the cryptography usually used for public-key signatures.

Attacks on Proofs of "Clairvoyance"

One thing that we can't do with secure timestamping alone—although it would be nice if we could—is to prove clairvoyance (the ability to predict future events). This might seem possible. The idea would be to publish a commitment to a description of an event that's about to occur (such as the outcome of a sporting event or of an election) and

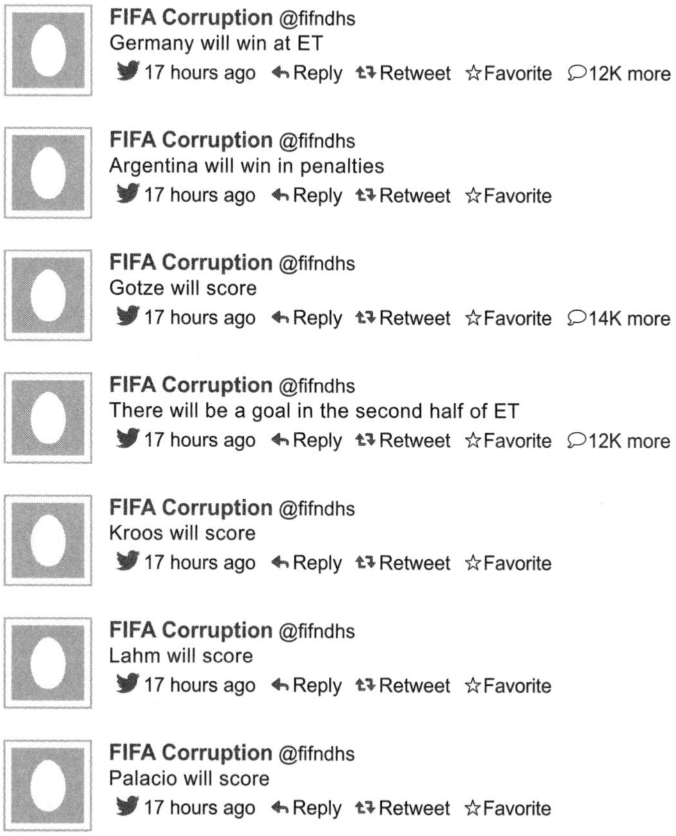

FIGURE 9.1. Attempted proof of clairvoyance. A Twitter account that attempted to "prove" that the 2014 FIFA Men's World Cup Final was rigged by "predicting" the outcome of the match. The first, third, and fourth tweets ended up being true; the rest were deleted after the match.

then later reveal that information to prove we predicted the event ahead of time. But does this work?

In late 2014, during the final match of the World Cup, someone used this method to "prove" that the Fédération Internationale de Football Association (FIFA), the organization running the World Cup, was corrupt. After the match was over, a Twitter account received significant attention for having tweeted about several events that occurred during the game, timestamped before the match even began. For example, it correctly tweeted that Germany would win in extra time and that Mario Götze would score. Seemingly this proves that either the owner of this Twitter account could predict the future or that the match was rigged. But in fact the account had tweeted every possible outcome before the match started. For every player involved in the match, there was a tweet predicting that he would score, a tweet for every conceivable final score of the game, and so on (Figure 9.1). Before the match ended, all the false predictions were deleted, leaving the Twitter account with only true "predictions."

The same basic attack can be performed against any secure timestamping system. You simply commit to a variety of possible outcomes and then only reveal the commitments that turn out to be true. This means that if you actually do have the ability to predict the future and want to prove it, you must prove that you are timestamping one specific prediction rather than multiple predictions. If you are publishing hash-based commitments, this is difficult to do, especially in Bitcoin, since the secure timestamping system does not tie commitments to any individual's public identity. If you don't reveal them, it is easy to publish a large number of commitments, and the ones you never reveal cannot easily be traced back to you.

Secure Timestamping the Old-Fashioned Way

Here's a simple low-tech way to do secure timestamping: publish the hash of your data in a newspaper, or some other media widely seen by the public, by purchasing an advertisement. Archives of old newspaper issues are maintained at libraries and online. This method provides a high degree of assurance that you knew that data on the day the newspaper was published. Later, when you want to reveal the data you committed, you can even take out a second advertisement to publish the data in the same newspaper.

Secure Timestamping in Bitcoin

If we want to use Bitcoin instead of newspapers for timestamping, where should we place the hash commitment? Somewhere in a transaction? Or directly in a block?

The simplest solution (and the one people came up with first) is instead of sending money to the hash of a public key, just send it to the hash of your data. This "burns" those coins, that is, makes them unspendable and hence lost forever, since you don't know the private key corresponding to that address. To keep your cost down, you'd want to send a very small amount, such as 1 satoshi (the minimum possible transaction value in Bitcoin).

Although this approach is simple, the need to burn coins is a disadvantage (although the amount burned is probably negligible compared to the transaction fees incurred). A bigger problem is that Bitcoin miners have no way to know that the transaction output is unspendable, so they must track it forever. The community frowns on the method for this reason.

A more sophisticated approach, called *CommitCoin*, allows you to encode your data into the *private* key. Recall that in Chapter 1, we said: "With ECDSA, a good source of randomness is essential, because a bad source will likely leak your key. It makes intuitive sense that if you use bad randomness when generating a key, then the key that you generate will likely not be secure. But it's a quirk of ECDSA that, even if you use bad randomness only when making a signature and you use your perfectly good key, the bad signature will also leak your private key."

CommitCoin exploits this property. We generate a new private key that encodes the

```
OP_RETURN <H(data)>
```

FIGURE 9.2. Timestamping using OP_RETURN. A provably "unspendable" transaction output script that embeds a data commitment.

commitment, and we derive its corresponding public key. Then we send a tiny transaction (e.g., 2,000 satoshi) to that address, and subsequently send it back in two chunks of 1,000 satoshi each. Crucially, when sending it back, we use the same randomness both times for signing the transaction. This allows anyone looking at the block chain to compute the private key, which contains the commitment, using the two signatures.

Compared to encoding your commitment in the public key, this CommitCoin transaction avoids the need to burn coins and for miners to track an unspendable output forever. However, it is quite complex.

Unspendable Outputs

As of 2015, the preferred way to do Bitcoin timestamping is with an OP_RETURN transaction, which results in a provably unspendable output (Figure 9.2). The OP_RETURN instruction returns immediately with an error, so that this script can never be run successfully, and the data you include is ignored. As shown in Chapter 3, this can be used both as a proof of burn and to encode arbitrary data. As of 2015, OP_RETURN allows 80 bytes of data to be pushed, which is more than enough for a hash function output (32 bytes for SHA-256).

This method avoids bloat in the unspent transaction output set, since miners will prune OP_RETURN outputs. The cost of such a commitment is essentially the cost of one transaction fee. The cost can be reduced even further by using a single commitment for multiple values. As of 2015, there are already several website services that help with this. They collect commitments from different users and combine them into a large Merkle tree, publishing one unspendable output containing the Merkle tree root. This tree acts like a commitment for all the data that users wanted to timestamp that day.

Illicit Content

One downside of being able to write arbitrary data into the block chain is that people might abuse the feature. In most countries, it is illegal to possess or distribute some kinds of content, notably child pornography, and penalties can be severe. Copyright laws also restrict the distribution of some content.

Several individuals have tried doing things like this to "grief" (i.e., to harass or annoy) the Bitcoin community. For example, there have been reports of links to pornography published in the Bitcoin block chain. The goal of these griefers is to make it dangerous to download the block chain onto your hard drive and to run a full node, since to do so might mean storing and transmitting material whose possession or dissemination is illegal.

There's no good way to prevent people from writing arbitrary data into the Bitcoin block chain. One possible countermeasure is to only accept Pay-to-Script-Hash transactions. This would make it a bit more expensive to write in arbitrary data, but it still wouldn't prevent it.

Fortunately, the law is not an algorithm. It is tempting to try to "hack" the law by technical means to produce unexpected or unintended outcomes, but this is not easy. Laws are intended to be interpreted by humans and incorporate factors such as intent. For example, U.S. Code 2252, the section of U.S. federal law that pertains to possession, distribution, and receipt of child pornography, uses the wording "*knowingly* possesses, or *knowingly* accesses with intent to view" when describing prohibited activities (emphasis ours).

It is also worth noting that because of the size limitations discussed above, data such as images (except, perhaps, tiny ones) cannot be directly written into the Bitcoin block chain. They will either have to be hosted externally, with only links written into the block chain, or be encoded in a cumbersome way across multiple transactions. Finally, most Bitcoin clients do not ship with the ability to decode and view data written into transactions, let alone data that's encoded across multiple transactions.

Overlay Currencies

On the positive side, since any data can be written into Bitcoin, we can also build an entirely new currency system on top of Bitcoin without needing to develop a new consensus mechanism. We can simply use Bitcoin as it exists today as an append-only log, and write all of the data that we need for our new currency directly into the Bitcoin block chain. We call this currency an *overlay currency*. Bitcoin serves as the underlying substrate, and the data of the overlay currency is written into the Bitcoin block chain using unspendable transaction outputs.

Of course, Bitcoin miners will not actually validate what you're writing into the block chain, since they don't know (and don't care!) whether the data you write is valid under the rules of your new currency. Anyone who's willing to pay the Bitcoin transaction fees can write anything in there. Instead, you must develop more complicated logic for validating transactions in the new currency, and this logic must reside in each end-user client that participates in sending or receiving this currency.

For example, in an overlay currency, miners are no longer able to reject double spends. Instead, every user of the overlay currency has to look at the history of what's been written in the block chain. If an overlay transaction attempts to spend an overlay coin that has already been spent, then that second transaction should simply be ignored. For this reason, there's no such thing as a lightweight SPV client for overlay currencies.

Counterparty is a prominent overlay currency. All Counterparty transactions are written into the Bitcoin block chain. During 2014, between 0.5 percent and 1 percent of all Bitcoin transactions carried Counterparty data. This currency also supports a much larger and richer feature set than Bitcoin. The idea is that since Counterparty doesn't have to develop a new consensus algorithm, and since Bitcoin miners don't need to know about the Counterparty rules, the developers can instead focus on developing interesting features, such as smart contracts and user-defined currencies. The Counterparty API can be much larger than the Bitcoin API, since Bitcoin miners don't need to understand it or approve of it.

The potential to develop a new currency without having to create a new consensus system is appealing. You don't even need to encourage new miners to join your system, and you can add new features without needing to change Bitcoin. However, such systems are still reliant on Bitcoin—for example, they are subject to the same fee requirements as other Bitcoin transactions. This approach can also be inefficient: nodes on the overlay currency may need to process a lot of data, because Bitcoin nodes don't filter these transactions for the user.

9.2. BITCOINS AS "SMART PROPERTY"

Now we discuss using bitcoins to represent something other than a unit of currency in the Bitcoin system.

Recall from Chapter 6 that you can trace ownership of value in the Bitcoin system over time simply by following the transaction graph. Keep in mind the caveat: there's no such thing as a "bitcoin" per se—just unspent transaction outputs, which we refer to as coins. Every bitcoin has a history that anybody can view in the block chain. A coin's history traces all the way back to one or more coinbase transactions in which coins were originally minted. As discussed earlier, this is bad for anonymity, since you can often track ownership of coins this way.

Smart Property

Could this traceability property be useful? We've already seen why it can be bad for privacy because of the potential for deanonymizing users. In this section, we consider how this property can also give meaning to the history of a bitcoin.

> **Fungibility**
>
> The fact that bitcoins have histories means that bitcoins aren't *fungible*. In economics, a fungible good is one where all individual units are equivalent and can be substituted for one another. For example, gold is fungible, since 1 ounce of (pure) gold can be substituted for any other ounce of gold. But this isn't always true of Bitcoin, because every bitcoin is unique and has a different history.
>
> In many contexts, this history may not matter, but if the history is meaningful to someone you want to trade with, it may mean that your 1.0 BTC is not the same as their 1.0 BTC. Maybe they wouldn't be willing to exchange theirs with yours, because they prefer the history of their coin to that of yours. For example, just as coin collectors value old coins, someday bitcoin collectors might place special value on coins originating in the genesis block or some other early block in Bitcoin's history.

FIGURE 9.3. Adding useful metadata to ordinary banknotes.

Let's think about the significance of giving meaning to the history of ordinary offline physical currency. Suppose we wanted to add metadata to offline currency. In fact, some people already do this. For example, they write various messages on banknotes, often as a joke or a political protest. This generally doesn't affect the value of the banknote and is just a novelty.

But what if we could have *authenticated* metadata attached to our currency—metadata that cannot easily be duplicated? One way to achieve this is to include a cryptographic signature in the metadata and tie this metadata to the serial number of the banknote.

What could this be used for? Say a baseball team wants to use dollar bills as tickets. This way they no longer have to go through the hassle of printing their own tickets and making sure that no one can print counterfeit tickets. The New York Yankees could simply assert that the dollar bill with a specific serial number now represents a ticket to a specific game and a specific seat. These dollar bills would be distributed in the same ways that paper tickets are normally distributed, such as by being mailed to fans when they buy tickets online. Whoever is holding that note has the right to enter the stadium, sit in the assigned seat, and watch the game, with no other questions asked. The banknote itself is the ticket!

To add authenticity, the Yankees could use digital signatures. They'd sign a message that includes the specific game date, the seat number, and the serial number of the bill—and stamp the message and the signature right on the bill. A two-dimensional barcode would be a convenient form for that data. Alternatively, the stadium could maintain a database that lists the serial numbers and corresponding seat numbers for each game. They could check the database for this information when a ticketholder enters the gate, which removes the need to stamp the banknotes.

What does this buy us? Now currency can represent many things. Besides the example of a sports ticket, there are many other applications. We inherit the anticounterfeiting property that banknotes already have. Governments work hard to ensure that it's difficult to duplicate a banknote! Also, the underlying currency value of the banknote is maintained. After the fan redeems the ticket, the banknote is perfectly usable as regular currency. It may be a problem if everybody wants to physically stamp metadata on currency, but this problem goes away if we use the database approach.

Of course, the useful meaning of this new metadata is only as good as our trust in the issuer who signed it. Someone must know that there's a specific key used to sign valid Yankees' tickets—or download the Yankees' database—to recognize its value as a ticket. To anyone else, it would just look like a dollar bill. But that's actually a desirable property, since once the ticket has fulfilled its purpose, it can go back into circulation as an ordinary dollar bill.

Colored Coins

Can we do the same thing digitally on top of Bitcoin? We'd like to keep Bitcoin's nice features, such as the ability to transact online, fast transaction settlement, and nonreliance on a bank.

The main idea is to stamp some Bitcoins with a "color," and track that color stamp even as the coin changes hands, just as we are able to stamp metadata onto a physical currency. A bitcoin stamped with a color still functions as a valid bitcoin, but additionally carries this metadata.

To achieve this, in one transaction, called the "issuing" transaction, we insert some extra metadata that declares some of the outputs to have a specific color. An example is illustrated in Figure 9.4. In one transaction, we issue five "light-gray" bitcoins in one transaction output, while the other output continues to be normal uncolored bitcoins. Someone else, perhaps with a different signing key, issues "dark-gray" bitcoins in a different transaction. We call these "colors" for intuitiveness, but in practice the colors are just bit strings. The only property that matters is that coins of the same color and same value are equivalent.

Now we have bitcoins with different colors associated with them. We can still do all the normal things we do with bitcoin transactions. We could have another bitcoin transaction that takes several inputs: some dark-gray coins, some light-gray coins, some uncolored coins, and shuffles them around. It can have some outputs that maintain the colors. Some metadata may need to be included in the transaction to determine which color goes with which transaction output. We can split a transaction output of four green coins into two smaller green coins. Later on we could combine multiple green coins into one big green coin.

OpenAssets

As of 2015, the most popular proposal for implementing this overlay in Bitcoin is called OpenAssets. Assets are issued using a special Pay-to-Script-Hash address. If you want to issue colored coins, you first choose a Pay-to-Script-Hash address to use. Any coin that transfers through that address and comes in without a color will leave with the color designated by that address. For this to be meaningful, you'd have to publicize that ad-

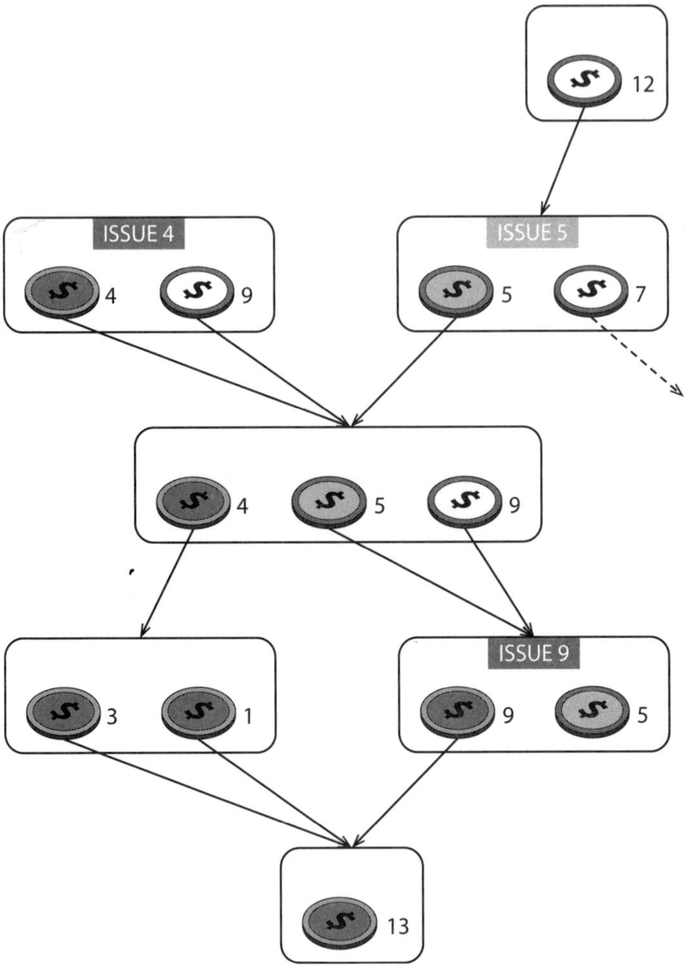

FIGURE 9.4. Colored coins. The transaction graph shown illustrates issuance and propagation of "color."

dress somewhere. There are various exchanges that track which addresses confer which colors onto coins. Since coins can sequentially pass through more than one color-issuing address, they can have more than one color.

Every time you make a transaction that involves colored coins, you have to insert a special marker output. This is a provably unspendable output, similar to what was used for timestamping data commitments. The metadata embedded in the marker output encodes details about how the incoming color value should be divided among the different outputs.

As noted earlier, this practice is compatible with Bitcoin. Since it doesn't require changing Bitcoin, the community of miners tends not to discourage or interfere with these schemes. It allows anybody to declare any color they want without having to ask a central authority for the right to issue colored coins. If there are others who understand and abide by the meaning you ascribe to the color you issue, your colored coins may attain additional value beyond their nominal bitcoin value. For example, if the Yankees issue colored coins, these coins will be able to function as tickets to a game, provided the stadium operators understand their meaning and let you in based on colored-coin tickets.

One disadvantage of this scheme is that we have to put the unspendable marker output into every transaction. This adds a bit of overhead, since we must forfeit some money every time we want to trade a colored coin. A second disadvantage is that miners don't check the validity of colored coins, only the underlying bitcoins. To verify that a colored coin you receive is valid, you have to check the entire transaction history that the coin was involved in, or trust a third party to do the checking for you. In particular, you can't use a thin SPV client like you can for regular Bitcoin. That makes it harder to use colored coins on computationally limited devices like mobile phones.

Uses of Colored Coins and Smart Property

Stock in a company. A frequently cited motivation for smart property is stock in a company. A company wishing to issue colored coins as stock would publicize its issuing address, and bitcoins that are colored with this address function as shares. One satoshi might represent one share in the company. Shareholders can then trade the stock on the block chain without needing a centralized intermediary like a stock exchange. Of course, shareholders will have to trust that the company will honor the shares. For example, the company may promise to disburse dividends proportionally to each stock or to give shareholders voting power in the company's decisions. With traditional shares, these promises are enforced legally. As of 2015, colored coins or other block chain–based assets don't have legal recognition in any jurisdiction.

Physical property. Another potential use is that colored coins might represent a claim to some real-world property. For example, a colored coin could be associated with a house or a car. Maybe you have a sophisticated car that actually tracks a specific colored coin on the block chain and automatically starts and drives for anybody who owns that colored coin. Then you could sell your car, or at least transfer control of it, simply by making a single transaction in the block chain. We'll see in Chapter 11 how this ability can potentially be implemented technologically as well as the social and legal obstacles to making it happen. But the dream of colored coins and smart property is that any real-world property could be represented in the world of Bitcoin and transferred or traded as easily as bitcoins themselves.

Domain names. As a final example, consider using colored coins to perform some of the functions of the existing Domain Name System: tracking the ownership and transfer of Internet domain names as well as the mapping of domain names to IP addresses. The domain name market has a variety of interesting properties: there are a potentially infinite number of names, these names have widely different values based on their memorability and other factors, and the same name might have very different utility to different people. It is possible to use colored coins to handle domain name registration and the functions we listed. However, supporting this application has also been the focus of a prominent altcoin called "Namecoin," which we consider in detail in Chapter 10. Each approach has benefits: colored coins give you the security of Bitcoin's block chain, whereas the altcoin makes it easier to implement the complex logic needed for domain name ownership, transfer, and IP address mapping.

9.3. SECURE MULTIPARTY LOTTERIES IN BITCOIN

Let's consider hosting a "coin flip" game in Bitcoin. Again, we start by describing the offline version of what we're trying to build.

Alice and Bob want to bet $5. They both agree to the bet ahead of time and the method for determining the winner. Bob will flip a coin in the air, and while it's rotating, Alice calls out "heads" or "tails." When the coin lands, they both immediately know who won the bet, and they both have assurance that the outcome was random and that neither of them was able to influence the outcome.

The sequence of steps in this ceremony as well as the physics of coin flipping play a crucial role in convincing both parties that the game is fair. One shortcoming of this scheme is that both parties have to be present at the same place at the same time. Also, both parties still have to trust that whoever loses will pay up. In the online world, we'd like to be able to have a lottery that is just as fair but also solves the problem of making sure the loser pays.

At first this might seem like a rather peculiar and limited application to be studying in detail. Amusingly, Bitcoin-based betting services such as Satoshi Dice—which rely on a trusted party, unlike the system we'd like to design—have proven very popular, at times representing a large fraction of all Bitcoin transactions on the network.

The real reason we want to study cryptographic coin flipping, however, is that if we can design a secure protocol for it, we can use those techniques to build many other interesting and useful protocols. Cryptographers study *secure multiparty computation*, where two or more mutually untrusting parties each have some data and want to compute a result that depends on all of their data, but without revealing the data to one another. Think of a sealed-bid auction, but without a trusted auctioneer. Often, these computations need to be randomized, say, to break ties. Finally, we might want the result of the computation to determine a monetary outcome in an irrevocable way. Maybe we want to ensure that the winning bidder in the auction pays the seller; perhaps we even want to ensure that the seller's (smart) property being auctioned is automatically transferred to the winning bidder. Alternatively, maybe we want to penalize parties if they deviate from the protocol.

In other words, a secure multiparty lottery is a simple setting in which to study an extraordinarily powerful paradigm: mutually untrusting participants with sensitive inputs jointly executing a program that has the power to manipulate not only bits, but also money.

Coin Flipping Online

The first challenge is replacing the coin flip mechanism with some online equivalent. Suppose we now have three parties, Alice, Bob, and Carol, who all want to select a number, 1, 2, or 3, with equal probability. Here's one attempt at such a protocol. Each of them picks a large random number—Alice chooses x, Bob y, and Carol z. They tell one another their numbers, and they compute the output as $(x + y + z) \% 3$.

If all of them chose their random numbers independently, this method would indeed work. But remember that we're doing this over the Internet, and there's no way to insist that they all send their numbers "simultaneously." Alice might wait until she hears Bob's and Carol's numbers before broadcasting hers. If she does this, you can see how it's trivial for her to make the final output whatever she wants. We can't design the protocol to convince every party that none of the other parties cheated.

To solve this problem, we can once again use hash commitments. First, each participant picks a large random number and publishes a hash of this number. Once this is done, each of them reveals the number they picked. The others then check that the revealed numbers hash to the values published in the first step, and they compute the final outcome from the three random numbers, as shown here:

Round 1:
Each party picks a large random string—Alice picks x, Bob picks y, and Carol picks z.
The parties publish $H(x)$, $H(y)$, $H(z)$, respectively.
Each party checks that $H(x)$, $H(y)$, $H(z)$ are all distinct values (otherwise aborts the protocol).
Round 2:
The three parties reveal their values, x, y, and z.
Each party checks that the revealed values agree with the hashes published in round 1.
The outcome is $(x + y + z) \% 3$.

The reason this protocol works is twofold. First, since the hash inputs x, y, and z are large random numbers, no party can predict the others' inputs after the first round. Second, if (say) Alice chooses her input randomly as specified by the protocol, she can be sure that the final output will be random, regardless of whether Bob and Carol choose their inputs randomly.

Fairness

What happens if somebody fails to reveal their commitment? In round 2 of the protocol, suppose Carol waits until Alice and Bob have revealed their secrets. Carol, before re-

```
scriptPubKey:
        OP_IF
              <AlicePubKey> OP_CHECKSIGVERIFY <BobPubKey> OP_CHECKSIG
        OP_ELSE
              <AlicePubKey> OP_CHECKSIGVERIFY OP_HASH <H(x)> OP_EQUAL
        OP_ENDIF

scriptSig for Case 1:
        <BobSignature> <AliceSignature> 0
scriptSig for Case 2:
        x <AliceSignature> 1
```

FIGURE 9.5. The transaction output scriptPubKey and scriptSigs used in a timed hash commitment.

vealing hers, realizes that she's going to lose if she does. So she might refuse to publish her random number—she can claim to have forgotten it or pretend to go offline. Alice and Bob would likely be suspicious, but they would have no good recourse.

What we'd like is a scheme where whoever makes a commitment is forced to reveal it within some time limit. This is an instance of a cryptographic property called *fairness*. Bitcoin provides us with an excellent mechanism for this.

Let's say that Alice wants to make a *timed commitment*, and Bob is the only other person who is concerned with it. First, Alice puts up a bond, in the form of a Bitcoin transaction output script that specifies that it can be spent in one of two ways. One way is with a signed transaction from both Alice and Bob. The other way to spend it is with a signature from just Alice, but only if she also reveals her random number. If Alice's random string is x, then the scriptPubKey actually contains the value $H(x)$.

Next, Alice and Bob both sign a transaction that pays the bond to Bob (which is one of the two ways it can be spent). Why would Alice agree to this? The transaction carries an `nLockTime` value that guarantees Bob can't claim the bond before some time t. Since Alice plans to reveal her committed value before then and recover the bond, it is safe for her to sign this transaction (Figure 9.5).

Now if Alice leaves without revealing her value, Bob can claim the bond at time t. This doesn't force Alice to reveal her commitment but she will lose the entire bond that she put up. So the guarantee that she'll reveal her secret value depends on the amount of money she's willing to put in the bond.

How can we use this timed hash commitment to implement our secure lottery? We'll have almost the same structure as before, except instead of using the simple hash commitments, we use these timed commitments. Whoever does not reveal their random value before the deadline will forfeit a security deposit that's used to compensate the other two players. Revealing the random value is now simply a matter of recovering the bond by providing the correct secret input x.

This lottery scheme can be implemented on top of Bitcoin. But it's a bit complicated, and the timed hash commitments require multiple nonstandard transactions. When there are n parties in the lottery, n^2 commitments are needed, since each party must put up a bond for every other party. The players have to escrow more money in total than they are even betting. But it is reasonable for a small number of participants, and there are variants with better efficiency. Most importantly, it serves as an existence proof that seemingly impossible protocols—such as flipping a virtual coin on the Internet and penalizing a party for aborting the protocol—are possible in the Bitcoin world.

9.4. BITCOIN AS A PUBLIC RANDOMNESS SOURCE

In Section 9.3, we showed how a group of people can jointly choose a fair random value. In this section, we discuss using Bitcoin to generate random values that are fair to anyone in the public. Why would we want this ability? Let's discuss a few examples of applications that already rely on public sources of random values.

NBA Draft Lottery

One example that occurs every spring in the United States is the NBA draft lottery. All 30 teams in the NBA get together and randomly choose—with some weighting based on how each team performed in the previous season—the order in which teams get to select the top amateur players in the country who are ready to turn professional. This was first done in 1985. The lottery was conducted on live television and involved picking envelopes after they were shuffled in a transparent spinning drum. This lottery generated a bit of controversy then, because the New York Knicks won in the first year and were able to draft the highly sought after center Patrick Ewing (an eventual member of the Basketball Hall of Fame). Since the lottery was filmed in New York City, some fans of other teams alleged that the process was rigged in favor of the Knicks.

Conspiracy theories abound for how the NBA might have rigged this process, such as the famous "bent corner" theory, suggesting that the Knicks' envelope had its corner bent so the commissioner could distinguish it from the others by touch. Another theory suggests the Knicks' envelope was kept in a freezer, and the commissioner simply grabbed the one cold envelope. These theories show why it is hard to hold a drawing like this and prove that it was fair—there are many plausible avenues for cheating. Just think of what professional sleight-of-hand magicians can appear to do! Even today, this lottery occurs every year, and each time it leads to a variety of conspiracy theories and rumors that the lottery isn't a fair random drawing.

U.S. Military Draft Lottery

A more serious example comes from 1969, when a conscription lottery was held in the United States to determine which young men would be required to join the armed services. Most of them were sent to fight in the Vietnam war. A procedure similar to the NBA lottery was used, carried out by several representatives from the U.S. Congress and broadcast on live television (Figure 9.6). They dumped small capsules labeled with each day of the year into a large plastic drum, and then took turns reaching in to pull the

FIGURE 9.6. Image from the 1969 (Vietnam War) military draft lottery.

numbers out. Men eligible to be drafted were given a priority number based on the day of the year their birthday fell on. The priority number determined the order in which they would be drafted.

The 1969 draft was the first time this lottery procedure was used on a national scale. The goal was to make the process more fair (by taking it out of the hands of thousands of local draft boards) and to demonstrate to the public that it was a random process. Unfortunately, the lottery was botched. Within a week, statisticians looking at the data noticed an anomalous pattern (illustrated in Figure 9.7). Days late in the year received low draft numbers. Though the deviation is subtle, it is statistically significant and highly unlikely to have happened by chance. When they reviewed the tapes, it turned

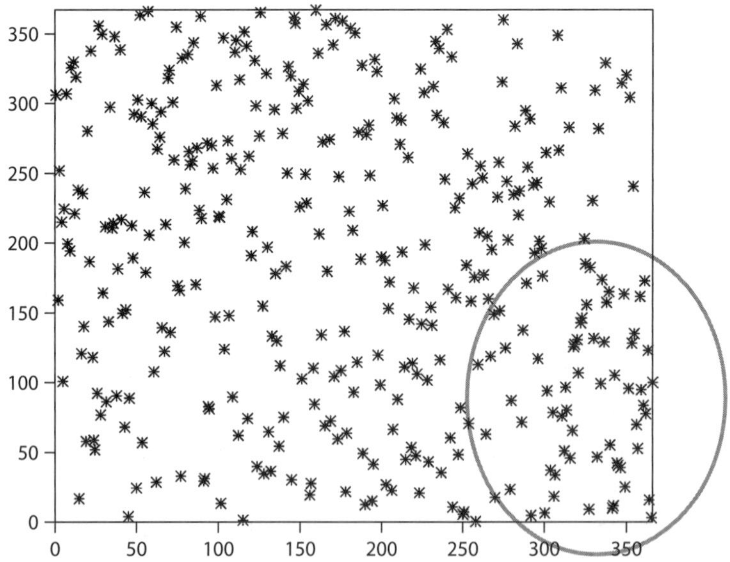

FIGURE 9.7. Statistical bias of the 1969 draft lottery. Day of the year (x-axis) versus lottery number (y-axis). Courtesy of Stannered.

out that the drum was rotated exactly an even number of times, such that the capsules that started out on top tended to still be on the top. There wasn't sufficient mixing to make it a statistically random draw.

What both of those examples show is that it's hard to generate public randomness and convince the public that the result is truly random. There's a risk that the process might not be free of influence. There's also a risk that even if the process is random, the public won't believe it.

Cryptographic Beacons

Public displays of randomness using a wheel, flipping coins, rolling dice, and so on have been so popular throughout history because they're cheap and easy to understand. But they are not so suitable for large-scale scenarios, because they're difficult to audit. Even if the video of the procedure appears legitimate, people may reasonably be suspicious that the lottery conductor has performed some sleight of hand to rig the process.

Could we do better cryptographically? Let's use the term *cryptographic beacon* to refer to a service that provides a public source of randomness. The idea is that the beacon will continuously publish new random data at a regular rate that nobody can predict in advance. Hopefully everybody agrees that there's no way for anyone to predict what the beacon will output next, so everybody can rely on it as a fair random value.

If a perfect cryptographic beacon existed, then it could be used for any public lottery. Even if you just wanted to play bingo at your local social club, you wouldn't need to use a large drum of numbers. If everybody trusted the beacon, you would save a lot of effort compared to using physical displays of randomness.

Cryptographers have proposed many other applications of public randomness, including voting systems, zero-knowledge proofs, and cut-and-choose protocols. Many of these can be done much more simply and efficiently using a perfect cryptographic beacon. Unfortunately, we haven't found a perfect way to implement such a beacon yet.

National Institute of Standards and Technology Beacon

The National Institute of Standards and Technology (NIST) has, since 2011, run its own beacon service. They claim to generate their random numbers through a complicated laboratory setup involving two entangled photons. The idea is to provide strong guarantees that the numbers are random, because they are generated from a quantum mechanical phenomenon. If you accept the Heisenberg uncertainty principle and other widely accepted laws of physics, then this beacon should be truly random and unpredictable. The service is set up so that it produces new random data every 60 seconds along with a digital signature over the data. The NIST beacon provides a convenient interface for programmatic applications: the numbers can simply be read out from a web feed.

This quantum mechanical procedure is in some sense the limit for physical displays of randomness. But it does nothing to alleviate the essential problem of trust—you have to trust that NIST is in fact carrying out the procedure as they claim. You have to trust that somewhere in a building in Maryland, NIST has an actual laboratory that produces these numbers and that they aren't simply staging the procedure. You also have to believe that they aren't reserving the ability to deliberately overwrite some of the random values before they publish them.

Other Potential Ways to Build a Beacon: Natural Phenomena

What about an alternate approach, where we use some natural phenomenon that everybody can observe? Perhaps we could use details about the weather, such as what temperature it's going to be tomorrow at a specific place, or how strong the wind will be, or whether it will rain. Of course, we have some ability to predict the weather ahead of time, but not precisely, so perhaps we can use the least significant bits of the measured values as a random number generator. The limitation here is that all participants need to be at the same place to get the same measurements.

To avoid this problem, we could turn to sunspots, which are bursts of activity on the surface of the Sun (Figure 9.8). Another example is cosmic background radiation, which is noise that you can listen to with a radio antenna from any point on the planet; everybody should be able to read the same value. These are phenomena that happen at such a large scale that it's easy to convince yourself that nobody will succeed in rigging the process. It's far-fetched to imagine that somebody would fly a spacecraft toward the surface of the Sun to somehow tamper with it just to rig some lottery back on Earth. So these approaches have several good properties: public observability, security against manipulation, and (in most cases) an acceptable level of unpredictability.

One problem with these approaches is that they're fairly slow. For example, if your random signal is the daily high temperature, then you only get one reading per day.

FIGURE 9.8. NASA image of sunspots. Courtesy: NASA.

The surface of the Sun doesn't change too often. In many cryptographic applications, random bits are used as input to a *pseudorandom generator*. For the pseudorandom generator to be secure, the input needs to be 80 bits (or more) in length. It might take a while for 80 bits of randomness to accumulate with sources based on weather and astronomy.

Besides, it requires expertise to measure sunspots, so you'd effectively need to rely on some trusted observer to publish the measurements. However, there could be many trusted observers, and we can hope that they'd "keep each other honest." Applications that consume beacons, or users of such applications, could choose which of the observers to rely on. They can also easily switch observers at any time. This property is called "trust agility" and is arguably superior to having a single entity, such as NIST, produce the beacon.

There's a deeper problem, one that at first sight might seem trivial. How do we turn a real-world observation—a temperature, a photograph of sunspots—into a string of bits in such a way that every observer will end up with the same bit string? We could try quantizing the measurement: for example, we could express the temperature in Fahrenheit and use the first decimal digit as the beacon output. But unless every observer's thermometer is unrealistically precise, there will be times when some observers will read the temperature as (say) 62.7 and others will read it as 62.8. It seems that no matter which natural phenomenon we pick and what protocol we use, there will always be "corner cases," where different observers will end up with different bit strings. For a cryptographic beacon, even a small probability of inconsistent measurements may be unacceptable, because it will cause the random bits output by a pseudorandom generator to be completely different.

Financial Data

A similar idea is to use feeds of financial data, such as stock market prices. Again, these are publicly observable values. Unlike natural phenomena, they are reported as digital values, so the problem of inconsistent observations goes away. There's strong reason to believe that predicting low-level fluctuations in stock prices is difficult: if you could predict within a penny what the final price of a specific stock will be on the New York Stock Exchange tomorrow, you could make a lot of profit as a day trader. Someone could try to influence the price by buying or selling the stock to drive it to a specific value, but that has a real cost that you can't avoid.

However, this approach also has the problem of relying on a trusted party, namely, the stock exchange. Even though the stock exchange has a strong incentive to establish its integrity, they still might be suspected of trying to manipulate the price of a stock by a penny (e.g., by inserting their own order into the order book) if it would let them rig a valuable lottery.

All the approaches considered so far seem to require having a trusted party who has influence over some crucial part of the process.

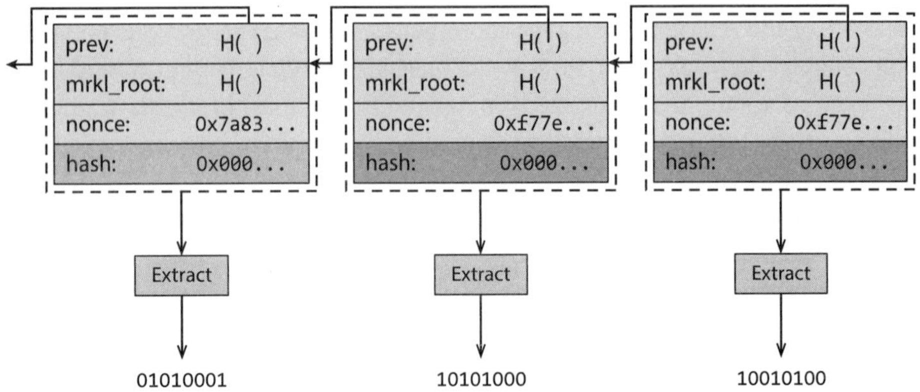

FIGURE 9.9. Bitcoin as a beacon. We can extract public randomness by applying a function called a "randomness extractor" to the headers of blocks in the block chain.

Using Bitcoin as a Beacon

A major theme throughout this book has been that Bitcoin is a promising technology for removing centralized trust from protocols in ways we didn't previously think were possible. Can we use Bitcoin as a random beacon? We'd like to extract random data from the Bitcoin block chain while keeping the decentralized properties that make Bitcoin itself so attractive.

Recall that miners must compute lots of random hash values while they're attempting to find a winning block. Perhaps this means that no one can predict or influence what the next block hash will be without actually doing the work of mining. Of course the first several bits of any block hash will be zero, but it turns out that under suitable assumptions, the only way to predict the remaining bits would be to influence them by finding a winning block and selectively discarding it (Figure 9.9).

That makes it simple to turn the block chain into a randomness beacon. For every block in the chain, we apply a "randomness extractor" to the value of the block header. A randomness extractor, roughly speaking, is like a hash function that is designed to squeeze all the random entropy of the input into the one uniformly random string. Every time a block is published, we have new beacon output.

Evaluating the Security of a Bitcoin Beacon

Suppose you're participating in a lottery whose outcome is determined by the output of the Bitcoin beacon for some prespecified future block at height h in the block chain. There are N players in this lottery, and each of them is betting B bitcoins. If you're also a miner, you might get lucky and find a hash puzzle solution for block h. Then you have the choice of whether or not to publish the block. If you don't like the lottery outcome that would result from your publishing the block you found, you can simply discard it and let the lottery be determined by whoever else publishes block B. However, you'd forfeit the revenue that you could earn from that block.

Let's calculate how big the bet B needs to be for you to find the selective discarding strategy worthwhile. You successfully find a block at block height h and realize that if you publish it, you will definitely lose the lottery, whereas if you discard the block, you still have a $1/N$ chance of winning $B \cdot N$ bitcoins. That means it will be rational to discard the block if your expected payout of $(1/N) \cdot B \cdot N$ bitcoins (i.e., B bitcoins) is greater than the reward for mining a block (25 BTC in 2015, ignoring transaction fees). So the attack is profitable if $B > 25$. In 2015, 25 BTC was worth more than $5,000. So if the bet per player is less than $5,000, the lottery will be secure against this attack, assuming that the players are rational.

One of the advantages of this scheme is that it's a fully decentralized beacon, with no central point of trust. Compared to some other beacon proposals, it is fairly fast. It can create an output roughly every 10 minutes. It's also useful to be able to estimate the cost to an attacker to manipulate the beacon outputs using our simple model above.

A downside of using Bitcoin as a beacon is that its timing is somewhat imprecise. Suppose we want to read the value of the beacon tomorrow at noon. We don't know exactly which block will be the latest block at that time. Although on average a block will be published within 10 minutes before or after noon, there is some variance. We also have to plan to tolerate a bit more delay if we want to reduce the likelihood of the block we look at being lost in a short fork. As is usual in Bitcoin, we'd want to wait for roughly six blocks to arrive before we believe that the beacon value has truly settled.

Another disadvantage is that the cost of manipulating the beacon value may be too low for some applications we care about. If we were actually running the NBA draft, where there are tens of millions of dollars at stake, it may suddenly look worthwhile for one of the teams to start bribing Bitcoin miners to manipulate this process. It remains an open question whether we can extend this construction to make it secure when millions of dollars are at stake.

Finally, our security evaluation ignores some real-life factors. For example, a miner who is part of a mining pool doesn't lose much by discarding a block, since they're rewarded on the basis of shares rather than blocks. For now, Bitcoin beacons are an interesting but unproven idea.

Scripting Support for Beacons

What if we extended Bitcoin's scripting language with a special opcode to read beacon values? Currently there's no way to have any randomness in Bitcoin scripts. That's by design, because miners have to verify scripts, and they all want to agree on whether a script is valid or not. But if we use the beacon value, it's a public source of verifiable randomness. We could use the beacon to add randomness into transaction scripts that every miner could agree on.

Suppose we had an opcode that would make a random decision based on the beacon output of the previous block. We could replace the entire complicated lottery protocol with just one script that reads the beacon value and assigns the output to one of n keys. It wouldn't require a multiround protocol, security deposits, or timed hash commitments.

One drawback of this idea is that it would now be possible for miners to manipulate the lottery simply by delaying the lottery transaction until a later block, if they find that including the transaction in the block they're mining would cause them to lose the lottery. It no longer requires forfeiting block rewards. The beacon opcode could be modified to avoid this attack. Instead of referring to the previous block, you specify to use the beacon value at a particular block height.

9.5. PREDICTION MARKETS AND REAL-WORLD DATA FEEDS

Finally, we look at how to implement a *prediction market* in a decentralized way using cryptocurrencies and the related topic of bringing real-world data into Bitcoin. A prediction market allows people to come together to make bets on future events, such as a sports game or an election. Participants in a prediction market buy, sell, and trade "shares" in specific outcomes of such events.

Let's walk through an example to clarify the concepts underpinning prediction markets. The 2014 World Cup was held in Brazil. Suppose there were a market where you could buy and sell shares associated with each team, and each share for the team that wins will ultimately be worth $1, and all the other shares are worth 0. Going into the tournament, every team would start out with some nonzero price, based on what the market believes their chances of winning are. Examples are shown in Table 9.1 for six different teams.

In the pretournament phase, Germany shares are trading for about 12 cents, which means that the market roughly believes Germany has a 12 percent chance of winning. As the tournament progresses, these prices will fluctuate, reflecting how the market participants adjust their beliefs of how likely each team is to win.

In our example, England was initially trading at 5 cents but went to 0 after the group stage. That's because England was knocked out in the group stage. There's no longer any way for them to win, and the price reflects that; their shares are now worthless. In contrast, the U.S. team that was initially thought to have little chance of surviving the group stage turned out to do very well. If you had thought to buy U.S. shares in the beginning when they were cheap (1 cent), you could sell them immediately after the group stage for 6 cents. You'd get back six times the money you bet. You wouldn't have to wait until after the end of the tournament to make a profit. Even though the U.S. team didn't end up winning the tournament, you'd be able to profit from the fact that you anticipated a change in beliefs about their chances of winning after their strong performance in the group stage.

In the semifinals, only four teams are left. The United States and England have been knocked out, so their share prices have already gone to 0. Now every remaining team

TABLE 9.1. PRICES IN DOLLARS IN A HYPOTHETICAL PREDICTION MARKET FOR A SELECTION OF TEAMS DURING THE 2014 WORLD CUP

Team	Germany	Argentina	Brazil	United States	England	Netherlands
Pre-tournament	0.12	0.09	0.22	0.01	0.05	0.03
After group stage	0.18	0.15	0.31	0.06	0.00	0.05
Before semifinals	0.26	0.21	0.45	0.00	0.00	0.08
Before finals	0.64	0.36	0.00	0.00	0.00	0.00
Final	1	0	0	0	0	0

Notes: The price of a share betting on the U.S. team to win the cup rose from 1 cent to 6 cents after the United States performed well at the group stage. A share in Brazil rose progressively to 45 cents as Brazil advanced into the semifinals and then lost its entire value after Brazil lost its semifinal match. After the tournament, only shares in Germany (which won the tournament) had any value.

has a relatively high price, and their share prices should add up to 1.0. Brazil in particular was favored to win, and thus had the highest price. In fact, Brazil lost in the semifinals, and their share price went to zero. In the span of a couple of hours, the market's beliefs changed dramatically. You would have been able to profit in a very short time frame if you were confident going in to the match that Brazil was overrated; you could take a "short position" on Brazil or bet on the other teams (or do both).

Going into the finals only two teams are left, and their shares again add up to 1.0. At the end of the tournament, of course, the only shares that finally have any value are those of the German team, since they ended up winning.

Obviously, one way to have made a profit would have been to buy shares in Germany at the beginning for 12 cents and hold them all the way to the end. This is basically how traditional sports betting works—you place a bet before the tournament starts and collect the payout after it ends. However, in a prediction market, there are many other ways to play and to profit. You can invest in any team at any time, and you can profit

The Power of Prediction Markets

Economists tend to be enthusiastic about prediction markets. Information that's relevant to forecasting future events is often widely dispersed, and prediction markets are an excellent mechanism to aggregate that information by giving participants a way to profit from their knowledge. Under suitable economic models, the market price of shares can be interpreted as the probability of the outcome, although there are concerns that real prediction markets suffer from biases. Empirically, prediction markets have held up well against other forecasting methods, such as polling and expert panels.

However, prediction markets face many regulatory uncertainties and hurdles. Intrade was the most popular prediction market on the Internet before it ran into regulatory compliance issues in the United States and shut down in 2013. Many economists were disappointed by its closure, because they thought we lost a valuable social tool that revealed useful information about the future.

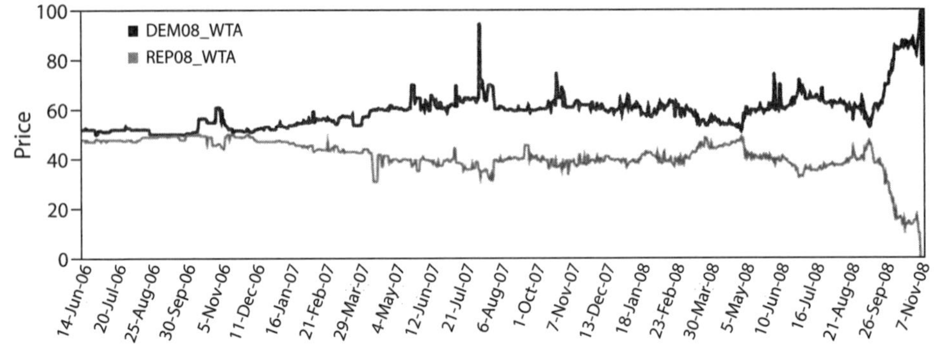

FIGURE 9.10. Prediction market shares. The price of prediction market shares for the 2008 U.S. presidential election. Source: Iowa Electronic Markets.

solely on the ability to predict that people's beliefs will change, regardless of the final outcome.

Here's another example, this time from a real prediction market. Before the 2008 U.S. presidential election, the Iowa Electronic Markets allowed people to buy shares for whether Barack Obama or John McCain would win. In Figure 9.10, the price of Barack Obama shares is shown in black and that for McCain in gray. You can see that as the months of the campaigning unfolded, people's beliefs about who would win fluctuated. But by the day before the election, Obama was given a 90 percent chance of winning. The market was well aware that the outcome was essentially settled before votes were cast.

Decentralized Prediction Markets

What would it take to build a *decentralized* prediction market? Several tasks will need to be decentralized. We need a way of accepting money and disbursing payouts, and of enforcing that the correct amounts are paid out according to the outcome. We especially need decentralized arbitration. Arbitration is the process of asserting which outcomes actually happened. Most of the time, in the case of a national election or a sports match, it's pretty obvious who won and who lost. But there are also many gray areas. Finally, the order book—which is a way for people to find counterparties to trade shares with—must be decentralized. We'll go through each of these challenges in order.

Let's design a hypothetical altcoin called "Futurecoin" that has explicit support for prediction markets. We need a few new transaction types that perform functions specific to prediction markets. The functions might look something like Figure 9.11.

`CreateMarket` allows any user to create a prediction market for any event by specifying an arbitrator (in terms of a public key), who is authorized to declare the outcome of that event, and the number of possible outcomes. The `event_id` is an arbitrary string that ties together the different transactions that refer to the same market. Futurecoin

`CreateMarket(event_id, arbitrator_key, num_outcomes)`
create a new prediction market, specifying the arbitrator and parameters

`BuyPortfolio(event_id)`
purchase one share in every outcome for 1 futurecoin

`TradeShares(...)`
transfer shares in exchange for futurecoins

`SellPortfolio(event_id)`
redeem one share in every outcome for 1 futurecoin

`CloseMarket(event_id, outcome_id)`
close the market for the specified event by converting all shares of the specified outcome into 1 newly minted futurecoin and destroying all shares of all other outcomes in the event (`outcome_id` is an integer between 1 and `num_outcomes` for the event)

FIGURE 9.11. New transaction types in Futurecoin. Futurecoin is a hypothetical altcoin that implements a decentralized prediction market.

doesn't care about what real-world event `event_id` refers to, nor what the outcomes are, and there is no way to specify these in the system. Users will have to obtain this information from the market creator (who will typically be the same as the arbitrator). We'll discuss different options for arbitration shortly.

Payment and Settlement

`BuyPortfolio` lets you purchase a portfolio of shares of some event. For the price of one futurecoin, you can buy one share in *every* possible outcome of the event. Suppose we're betting on the 2014 World Cup. There are 32 teams that could win. For one coin, you could buy 32 shares, one for each team—this is clearly "worth" exactly one coin since exactly one of the teams will ultimately win. Any user can unilaterally create a `BuyPortfolio` without needing a counterparty. The transaction essentially destroys one futurecoin provided as input by the user and creates one new share in every outcome. There is also a transaction type to sell a portfolio, which lets you sell (or burn) a share in every outcome to get one futurecoin back. For one futurecoin, you can buy a share in every outcome, and then you can turn a share in every outcome back into a futurecoin.

You can also trade shares for futurecoins, or one kind of share for another kind of share, as long as you can find someone to trade with. This case is much more interesting. You could spend a futurecoin to buy a share in every outcome, and then sell off the shares in outcomes you don't think are likely to occur. For the teams you don't want to bet on, you could sell those shares to someone else who does want to bet on that team. Once you do this, you no longer have a balanced portfolio on every team, and you can no longer automatically redeem your portfolio for one futurecoin. Instead you have to wait until the bet ends to redeem your shares—and if the team(s) you bet on didn't win, you might not be able to redeem them for anything at all. However, you could also profit directly by trading. You could buy a balanced portfolio, wait for prices to change, and then sell all shares directly for futurecoins, which you could then trade for Bitcoin or any other currency of your choice.

Prediction Market Arbitration

How can we do arbitration in a decentralized way? How can we make assertions about who actually won, so people can redeem their winning shares at the end? The simplest system is to have a trusted arbitrator, which is what `CreateMarket` does (see Figure 9.11). Any user can launch a market where they are the arbitrator (or designate someone else as the arbitrator). They can create a transaction and announce that they are opening a market on the World Cup outcomes. They will decide who won in the end, and if you trust them, then you should be willing to accept their signature on a `CloseMarket` transaction as evidence of the outcome.

As in many other markets, we imagine that over time, some entities will build reputations as reliable arbitrators. Then they would have some incentive to arbitrate correctly to maintain their valuable reputations. But there's always the risk that they could steal a lot of money—more than their reputation is worth—by rigging a bet. This would be dangerous in a prediction market. For example, in the World Cup market, the arbitrator could assert that Argentina won, even though they actually lost. If the arbitrator had bet heavily on Argentina themselves, then they might be able to profit enough from it to justify ruining their reputation.

Could we have a more decentralized arbitration system? One option is to designate multiple arbitrators, with the outcome being decided based on the majority. Some options are based on voting—either by all users who hold shares in the market or by miners of the cryptocurrency. Proposals along these lines often suggest penalizing participants for voting against the majority. But there are many potential problems with these approaches, and we don't know how well they would work in practice.

A further wrinkle is that sometimes reality is complicated. In addition to the problem of arbitrators lying, there might be a legitimate dispute over the outcome of the event. Our favorite example is from the 2014 Super Bowl. There's a tradition at the Super Bowl of the winning team dumping a bucket of Gatorade on their head coach. People like to bet on the color of the Gatorade that the winning team uses for this celebration, and this betting has happened for two or three decades. In 2014, bets were placed on yellow, orange, and all the other colors of Gatorade. But that year, an unprecedented outcome made it hard to settle the bet. When the Seahawks won, they dumped orange Gatorade on their head coach, Pete Carroll. Then a little later, a few other players decided to do it again and dump another bucket of Gatorade on him. The first bucket contained orange Gatorade, and the second bucket contained yellow Gatorade.

If you were running a prediction market where people had bet on the color of the Gatorade, how would you handle this scenario? It's not clear if orange, yellow, or both should win. What happened in practice with several sports betting services is that they decided it was better to lose some money to maintain their reputations. As a show of good faith to their customers, they paid out winnings to anyone who bet on either orange or yellow.

Of course, in a decentralized prediction market this isn't so easy, because you can't just create money out of thin air to pay both sets of parties. Instead, the arbitrator could split the winnings equally among both orange and yellow. Instead of closing at a value of 1.0, both shares would close at a value of 0.5. You could define the contract carefully to avoid this confusion, but you can't be sure you've anticipated every possibility. The lesson here is that arbitration is partly a social problem, and no technical solution is going to be perfect.

Data Feeds

The idea of arbitration leads to a more general concept: extending cryptocurrencies with a mechanism to assert facts about the real world. We call such a mechanism a *data feed.* A fact might be about typical prediction-market events, like who won an election, or the price of a stock or commodity on a certain day, or any other real-world data of importance. If we had such facts available in Bitcoin, the scripting language would be able to use them as inputs. For example, a script might be able to load the current price of copper onto the stack and make decisions based on the value.

If trusted data feeds existed, we could place—and automatically settle—bets on sports matches or the future price of commodities. A prediction market is only one application that data feeds would enable. You could hedge risks in your investment portfolio by making bets against the price of stocks you own. And you could derive a variety of financial instruments like forwards and futures that are ordinarily traded in financial markets. Wouldn't it be great if we could do all this in Bitcoin?

We can separate the technical question of how to represent real-world facts in Bitcoin (or an altcoin) from the sociotechnical question of how to improve our confidence in the correctness of the feed. We've already looked at the former question when discussing options for arbitration.

A clever way to encode data feeds into ordinary Bitcoin is called "Reality Keys." In this system, the arbitrator creates a pair of signing keys for every outcome of every event of interest—one key pair for "Yes," and one key pair for "No." The artitrator publishes the public keys when the event is first registered, and later publishes exactly one of the two *private* keys when the outcome is settled. If Alice were betting against Bob that the outcome would occur, they could send their wagers to a Bitcoin output that can either be claimed by Alice using a signature from Alice and from the "Yes" key, or claimed by Bob using a signature from Bob and from the "No" key. This procedure falls well short of the ideal goal of being able to use data feed values as script inputs in arbitrary ways, but it allows simple applications like the wager described above. Note that the arbitrator doesn't need to know about or get involved in the specific wager between Alice and Bob.

Order Books

The final piece of a prediction market is a decentralized order book. Once again this concept is pretty general, and realizing it would allow many other applications. What's an order book? In real prediction markets, or most financial markets, there is no single market price. Instead there are *bids* and *asks*, which are listed in the *order book*. A bid is the highest price that anyone is willing to buy a share for, and the ask is the lowest price that anyone is willing to sell the share for. Typically the ask is greater than the bid (otherwise there would be two participants who would be matched up, a trade would occur, and at least one of the orders would no longer remain in the order book). A participant who wants to buy a share right away can do so at the ask price, and a participant who wants to sell right away can do so at the bid price. These are called "market orders," since they execute at market price, as opposed to the "limit orders" that are recorded in the order book that execute at the specified limit price (or better).

Traditionally this has been done in a centralized way with a single order-book service (typically an exchange) that collects all the orders. The problem, as is typical of centralized services, is that a dishonest exchange might profit at the expense of the participants. If the exchange receives a market buy order, they might themselves buy from the best ask before placing the order they received, then turn around and sell the shares they just bought at a higher price, pocketing the difference. This practice is called "frontrunning." It shows up in a variety of financial settings and is considered a crime. Centralized order books require legal enforcement to discourage frontrunning and ensure confidence in the integrity of the system.

In a decentralized order book, we can't rely on strong legal enforcement. But there's a clever solution, which is to simply forget about frontrunning. Instead of declaring it a crime and defending against it, we'll call it a feature. The idea is that anybody can submit limit orders to miners by broadcasting transactions, and miners can match any two orders as long as the bid is greater than or equal to the ask. The miner simply gets to keep the difference as a form of transaction fee. Now miners have no incentive to frontrun, because frontrunning an order will never be more profitable than simply fulfilling it and capturing the surplus.

This is an elegant way to build a decentralized order book. The main downside is the miner fees that traders must pay. To avoid paying that fee, people might submit much more conservative orders and may not be willing to reveal up front the best price at which they are willing to trade. This might make the market less efficient. We don't yet know how this kind of order book, with miners matching orders, will function in practice, but it seems to be a promising idea.

In conclusion, Bitcoin as it is today can act as a platform for a variety of applications. But for some applications, Bitcoin only takes us so far. It doesn't have all the features we need for a secure decentralized prediction market or a decentralized order book.

But what if we could start from scratch and forget about soft forks, hard forks, and other challenges when bolting new features on to Bitcoin? We've learned a lot since 2008, when Bitcoin first came out. Why not design a new cryptocurrency from scratch and make everything better?

In the next chapter, we look at altcoins, which are attempts to do just that. We discuss all the promising ideas and the challenges to be faced when starting a new cryptocurrency.

FURTHER READING

Project pages and specifications of two of the overlay protocols we looked at can be found in:

The Counterparty Protocol Specification. Available at https://github.com/CounterpartyXCP/Documentation/blob/master/Developers/protocol_specification.md.

The OpenAssets Protocol. Available at https://github.com/OpenAssets/open-assets-protocol.

The secure multiparty lottery protocol we described is from the following paper, which is not for the faint of heart:

Andrychowicz, Marcin, Stefan Dziembowski, Daniel Malinowski, and Lukasz Mazurek. "Secure Multiparty Computations on Bitcoin." Presented at the 2014 IEEE Symposium on Security and Privacy, San Jose, CA, 2014. Available at https://eprint.iacr.org/2013/784.pdf.

The following are papers by economists on the power of prediction markets:

Wolfers, Justin, and Eric Zitzewitz. "Prediction Markets." Paper w10504. Cambridge, MA: National Bureau of Economic Research, 2004.

Arrow, Kenneth J., Robert Forsythe, Michael Gorham, Robert Hahn, Robin Hanson, et al. "The Promise of Prediction Markets." *Science* 320, 2008.

The prediction market design we described is from this paper, coauthored by several of the present authors:

Clark, Jeremy, Joseph Bonneau, Edward W. Felten, Joshua A. Kroll, Andrew Miller, and Arvind Narayanan. "On Decentralizing Prediction Markets and Order Books." Presented at the Workshop on the Economics of Information Security, State College, PA, 2014. Available at http://www.jbonneau.com/doc/CBEKMN14-WEIS-decentralizing_prediction_markets.pdf.

CHAPTER 10

Altcoins and the Cryptocurrency Ecosystem

Bitcoin is just one component (albeit an important one) of a broader ecosystem of alternative, but often quite similar, currencies called *altcoins*. In this chapter, we look at altcoins and the ecosystem of cryptocurrencies.

10.1. ALTCOINS: HISTORY AND MOTIVATION

Bitcoin was launched in January 2009. It wasn't for another 2 years, until the middle of 2011, that the first Bitcoin-like derived system, Namecoin, was launched. The rate of altcoin launches exploded in 2013, and hundreds have since followed (Figure 10.1). How many are there in all? An exact number is impossible to calculate, because it's not clear which altcoins are worth counting. For example, if someone announces an altcoin and perhaps releases some source code, but no one has started mining or using it yet, does that count? Other altcoins have been launched and seen some initial use, but then died quickly after their launch.

It's also not quite clear what is an altcoin, as opposed to simply another cryptographic currency. After all, there were various cryptocurrency proposals and systems that predated Bitcoin, and they are usually not called "altcoins." Many altcoins borrow concepts from Bitcoin, often directly forking its code base or otherwise adopting some of its code. Some make only minor modifications to Bitcoin, such as changing the value of some parameters of the system, and continue to incorporate changes made by Bitcoin's developers. To date, all altcoins that we know of begin with a new genesis block and their own alternate view of transaction history, rather than forking Bitcoin's block chain after a certain point in history. For our purposes, we don't need a precise definition of an altcoin. Instead we'll loosely refer to any cryptocurrency launched since Bitcoin as an altcoin.

Here we mention in passing non-altcoin systems like Ripple and Stellar: these are distributed consensus protocols in the tradition considered in Chapter 2. These systems achieve consensus in a model where nodes have identifiers and need to be aware of one another. Bitcoin, of course, radically departs from this model. In both Ripple and Stellar, the consensus protocol supports a payment/settlement network, and each system

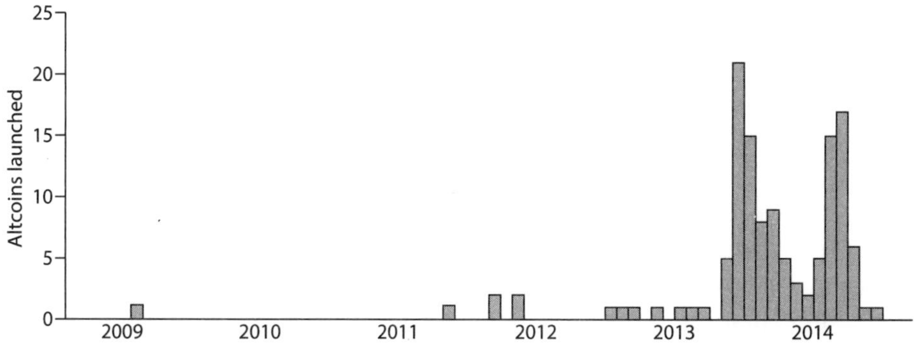

FIGURE 10.1. Altcoins launched per month (measured by genesis block creation).

has a native currency. Despite these similarities with altcoins, we don't consider them to be in the scope of this book.

Reasons for Launching Altcoins

Every altcoin needs some kind of story to tell. If an altcoin can't claim some characteristic that distinguishes it from all the others, there is no reason for it to exist. In the simplest case, an altcoin simply changes some of the built-in parameters to Bitcoin. These parameters include, for example, the average time between blocks, the block size limit, the schedule of rewards being created, and the inflation rate of the altcoin.

There can also be more complex technical differences, which makes the altcoin more interesting. For example, additions to the scripting language can express different kinds of transactions or security properties. Mining could work differently, and the consensus algorithm could be significantly different from Bitcoin's.

Sometimes altcoins are launched with a theme or a sense of a community that the altcoin is intended to support or be associated with, often giving members of this community a special role or abilities in the altcoin. We look at examples of all of these possibilities later in this section.

How to Launch an Altcoin

Consider what's involved in the process of launching an altcoin and what happens after launch. As we mentioned, creating an altcoin involves creating a new reference client, typically by forking the existing code base of some existing, more well-established altcoin, or of Bitcoin itself. The easy part is to add in technical features or modified parameters you think will work out well. In fact, there was once a website called "Coingen" that would automate this process for a small fee. It allowed you to specify various parameters like the average block time and the proof-of-work algorithm you wanted, in addition to a name for your altcoin, a three-letter currency code, and a logo. Then at the click of a button you'd download a fork of Bitcoin with the parameters you chose, and you (and others) could immediately start running it.

The hard part is bootstrapping adoption of your altcoin. You can fork the source code and you can announce it publicly, but at this point, nobody is using your altcoin. So it has no market value (since nobody wants the coins) and no security (since there aren't miners yet). Chapter 7 described the various stakeholders in Bitcoin: developers, miners, investors, merchants, customers, and payment services. Eventually you'll have to attract all these types of participants to your altcoin economy to get it off the ground.

These groups are important and interrelated. The challenge of assembling them is analogous to that involved in launching any other platform and getting it adopted. If you wanted to launch a new smartphone operating system, say, you'd need to attract users, device manufacturers, app developers, and various other stakeholders, and each of these groups needs the others.

Attracting miners has special importance for cryptocurrencies, because without adequate hash power behind an altcoin, security may fail badly if double spending and forks are possible. In fact, your altcoin might be run over entirely; we look at "altcoin infanticide" in Section 10.4. There is no simple recipe for bootstrapping adoption, but in general, miners will come once they believe the mining rewards they could earn would be worth the effort. To encourage them, many altcoins give early miners greater rewards. Bitcoin, of course, pioneered this approach, but some altcoins have taken a more aggressive approach to rewarding early miners.

Convincing a community of people that the altcoin is valuable is the most difficult trick. As discussed in Chapter 7, even for Bitcoin, it's not clear exactly how this process was bootstrapped, as it relies on the Tinkerbell effect. Fostering this belief ties back to why altcoins need a good narrative: to get off the ground, its community must believe that the new altcoin is going to become valuable (and believe that others will believe it is valuable, and so on). Other important elements usually follow miners and early adopters. These include having your altcoin listed on exchanges and developing various types of supporting infrastructure, ranging from an advocacy foundation to tools for exploring the block chain.

Pump-and-Dump Scams

When the creators of an altcoin have succeeded in bootstrapping a community and a real exchange market, they have often found themselves very wealthy. That's because they almost certainly own a large quantity of coins—for example by being early miners before the hash rate increases, or even "pre-mining," which we discuss below. Once the altcoin's exchange rate rises, the founders will be in a position to sell off their coins if they choose to.

The possibility of getting rich has attracted entrepreneurial individuals and venture capital to altcoins, and, unsurprisingly, it has also attracted scammers. Indeed, the line between the two is sometimes a bit blurry. A scammer might use a variety of methods to exaggerate an altcoin's potential and drum up interest. They may hype up its supposed technical merits, fake the appearance of grassroots support, purchase the altcoin on the market at inflated prices, and so on.

In fact, this scam can be pulled off even by someone who is not the founder of an altcoin. They would first need to buy up shares of some obscure altcoin, then convince the public of this coin's supposed undiscovered potential (i.e., pump the altcoin). If they succeed in inflating the price this way, they can unload their shares and reap a profit (i.e., dump their coins). At this point, investors will probably become wise to the fraud and the price will plummet, with many people left holding worthless coins. This kind of pump-and-dump fraud has long been perpetrated in mainstream finance, using obscure, low-priced stocks, and it was common in the early days of altcoins, when enthusiasm was high and investors struggled to differentiate truly innovative altcoins from "me-too" systems with slick marketing but no real innovation. As a result, users and investors are wary of altcoins today.

Initial Allocation

In Bitcoin, currency is allocated to users solely through mining. But for various reasons, altcoin developers have sought other ways of initial currency allocation in addition to mining.

Developers may pre-mine the currency, that is, reserve some portion of the money supply for themselves or some other designated entity (e.g., a nonprofit foundation with a charter to develop the currency). The idea is that the possibility of a windfall gives developers more of an incentive to spend time creating and bootstrapping a new cryptocurrency. Sometimes they go further and have a pre-sale, where they sell these pre-mined units to other speculators for bitcoins or fiat currency. This is somewhat analogous to investing in a startup: the speculators can strike it rich if the altcoin makes it big.

Another motivation for seeking additional methods of initial allocation is to ensure the development of a diverse community of early adopters who own the currency and have a stake in its success, given that mining today is rather centralized and might lead to concentrated ownership of assets. A clever way to enable diverse ownership is to allocate altcoin units to existing Bitcoin owners.

How can we technically design the system so that anyone who owns bitcoins can claim their share of the altcoin, with this claim being automatically adjudicated? One option is a proof of burn, which we discussed in Chapter 3: users can claim units of a new altcoin in proportion to a quantity of bitcoins they provably destroy. The owner will commit to some data in the proof of burn, such as a special string identifying the specific altcoin, to show that they are burning bitcoins solely to earn new units of this specific altcoin (Figure 10.2).

Allocating altcoins via a proof of burn is also called a *one-way peg* or *price ceiling*. Associating one altcoin unit to (say) one bitcoin doesn't actually make it worth one

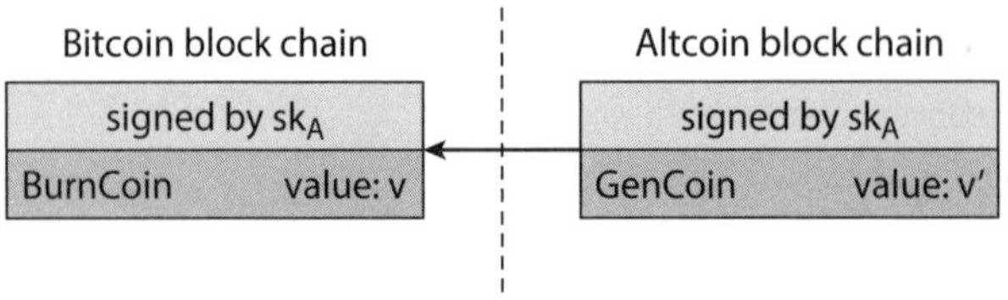

FIGURE 10.2. Allocating altcoins via proof of burn. The altcoin supports a GenCoin transaction that takes a *Bitcoin* transaction as input. GenCoin is signed by the same private key that signed the proof of burn (using the same signature scheme). This ensures that the same user who burned bitcoins also created the GenCoin. If the peg ratio is 1:1, then v' must be no greater than v.

bitcoin. It ensures instead that the altcoin will be worth *at most* one bitcoin, since one bitcoin can always be cashed in for an altcoin, but not vice versa.

There's a less heavy-handed alternative: require proving ownership of bitcoins, but not burning them, to claim altcoins. Specifically, the altcoin would designate a Bitcoin block height (perhaps coinciding with the launch date of the altcoin), during which anyone who owned an unspent Bitcoin transaction output as of that block would be able to claim a proportional amount of altcoins (Figure 10.3). In this system, no fixed relationship exists between the price of a bitcoin and that of an altcoin, because bitcoins aren't being converted to altcoins via proof of burn.

Of course, to make these conversions happen, altcoin miners need to stay on top of the Bitcoin block chain as well. The altcoin must specify what counts as a confirmed Bitcoin transaction. One option is to require some fixed number (e.g., six) of confirmations. Another option is to specify the most recent Bitcoin block in each altcoin block. This way, Bitcoin transactions become immediately available to spend in the altcoin. This is analogous to the fact that within Bitcoin itself, transaction outputs can be spent in the next block or even in the same block. Merge mining, which we discuss in Section 10.4, is one way to tie altcoin blocks to Bitcoin blocks.

Finally, donating already-allocated coins is another way of increasing the diversity of the currency owners. One method is tipping: various services allow sending tips to

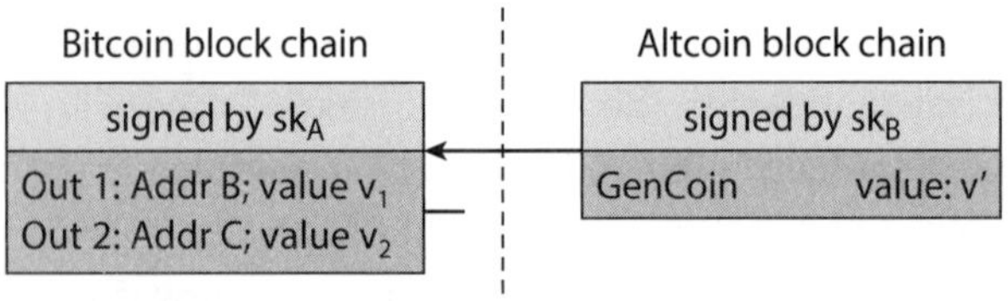

FIGURE 10.3. Allocating altcoins by proving ownership of bitcoins. The input to GenCoin is one or more unspent Bitcoin transaction outputs at the designated block height. It is to be signed by the private keys that control those unspent outputs, as in any normal Bitcoin transaction. Here the Bitcoin transaction shown has two unspent transaction outputs, to addresses B and C, at the designated block height. The owner of address B has claimed their altcoins, but the owner of address C has not yet done so. If the peg ratio is 1:1, then v' must be no greater than v_1.

an email address or a social media account, which is partly a way to incentivize the recipient to learn about and have a stake in the currency. The tipping service keeps the coins in escrow, and recipients get a message telling them that they have coins they can collect. The recipients can claim the coins by authenticating themselves to the service via their email address or social media account. They'll also need to install wallet software or enable another way to receive coins. Another donation method is a faucet: these are services that give out a small quantity of coins to anyone who visits a site and perhaps enters an email address.

10.2. A FEW ALTCOINS IN DETAIL

Here we focus on a few of the oldest altcoins and study their features in more detail.

Namecoin

We've seen how Bitcoin's block chain is a secure, global database. Once data has been written to it, this data is tamper-proof, and its inclusion can be proved forever. Could we modify Bitcoin's design to support other applications of secure global databases, such as a naming system?

We need a few ground rules to make this database more useful for noncurrency applications. First, we agree to view data entries as name/value pairs, with names being globally unique. This allows everyone to look up the value mapped to a name, just like a hash table or a database with a primary-key field. To enforce the global uniqueness of names, if a name/value pair has the same name as a previous database entry, then we view it as an update to the value rather than a new entry.

Second, we agree that only the user who initially created the entry for a particular name is allowed to make updates to that name. We can easily enforce this by associating each name with a Bitcoin address and requiring the update transactions to be signed by the private key for that address.

We could do all this on top of Bitcoin, just as we could build any overlay currency using Bitcoin as an append-only log (see Chapter 9). But it's simpler to do it in an altcoin, because we can take this "gentleman's agreement" and write it into the rules of the altcoin. These rules would then be inviolable and enforced by the miners, rather than requiring each user (i.e., full node) to check the rules and independently decide what to do if they are violated. Done properly, this implementation would even allow SPV-style proofs: a lightweight client would be able to submit a query (i.e., a name) to a server running a full node, and the server would return a value for that name, along with a proof that the returned value is in fact the latest update for that name in the database.

That's Namecoin in a nutshell. It's a global name/value store, where each user can register one or more names (for a nominal fee) and then issue updates to the values of any of their names. Users can also transfer control of their names to others. In fact, you can make a transaction that transfers your domain to someone, and at the same time transfers units of the Namecoin currency from them to you. Since this is a single atomic transaction, it's a secure way to sell your domain to someone you've never met and don't trust. As of 2015, Namecoin doesn't support secure lightweight clients, but an extension that supports them has been proposed.

Namecoin's goal is to provide a decentralized version of the Domain Name System (DNS), the names in the database being domain names and the values being IP addresses. You can't use this by default with an unmodified browser, but you can download a browser plugin for, say, Firefox or Chrome that would allow you to type in an address like example.bit—any domain name that ends in ".bit"—and it will look up the location in the Namecoin registry instead of the traditional DNS.

Namecoin is technically interesting, and it's also historically interesting—it was in fact the first altcoin to be launched, in April 2011, a little more than 2 years after Bitcoin was launched. It features merge mining (see Section 10.4).

Namecoin isn't used very much as of 2015. Nearly all registered domains are taken by "squatters," hoping (but failing so far) to sell their names for a profit. Namecoin supporters tend to argue that the existing DNS puts too much control over a critical component of the Internet into the hands of a single entity. This view is popular in the Bitcoin community, as you can imagine, but it doesn't look like mainstream users are clamoring for an alternative to DNS, robbing Namecoin of the killer app it needs to enjoy significant adoption.

Litecoin

Litecoin was also launched in 2011, sometime after Namecoin. As of 2015, Litecoin is the number one altcoin in terms of overall popularity and user base. It is also the most widely forked codebase. In fact, it has been forked more times than Bitcoin itself.

The main technical distinction between Litecoin and Bitcoin is that Litecoin features a memory-hard mining puzzle (based on scrypt), which we discussed in Chapter 8. When Litecoin was launched, Bitcoin mining was in the GPU era, and so the goal of Litecoin's use of a memory-hard mining puzzle was GPU resistance. When it was launched, you could still mine on Litecoin with a CPU, long after this had become futile for Bitcoin. But since then, Litecoin hasn't succeeded in resisting the transition to GPU mining and then to ASICs. Each of those mining transitions took a bit longer in Litecoin than in Bitcoin, but it's not clear whether this is because Litecoin's puzzle was actually harder to implement in hardware or simply because Litecoin's lower exchange rate provided less incentive to do so.

In any case, the performance improvements of ASICs compared to CPU mining are roughly similar for Litecoin as they are for Bitcoin. In this sense, Litecoin failed in its original goal of creating a more decentralized system by maintaining a community of CPU miners. But, importantly, this narrative still worked for bootstrapping Litecoin—it attracted many adopters who ended up staying even after the original premise failed. Litecoin has since explicitly changed its narrative, stating that its initial allocation was more fair than Bitcoin's, because it resisted ASICs for longer.

Litecoin also makes a few minor parameter changes: for example, blocks in Litecoin arrive four times faster than in Bitcoin, every 2.5 minutes. Litecoin otherwise borrows as much from Bitcoin as possible. In fact, its development has followed Bitcoin, so that as patches and improvements have been made to Bitcoin, Litecoin has also adopted them.

Dogecoin

Dogecoin has perhaps been the most colorful of all altcoins to date. It was released in late 2013, and what distinguishes it is not primarily technical (it is a close fork of Litecoin) but rather a set of community values: tipping, generosity, and not taking cryptocurrency so seriously. Indeed, it is named after Doge, an amusing Internet meme featuring a grammatically challenged Shiba Inu dog (Figure 10.4). The community has had several interesting and successful marketing campaigns, such as sponsoring a NASCAR driver and putting Dogecoin logos all over his car. They also raised more than $30,000 to support the Jamaica National Bobsled Team, so that the team could travel and compete in the 2014 Winter Olympics. Amusingly, this closely mirrors the plot to the 1990s movie *Cool Runnings*.

The combination of the community's generosity, PR activities, and the inherent meme value of Doge meant that Dogecoin became popular in 2014. It appears that many of the early adopters were unfamiliar with cryptocurrencies prior to Dogecoin, providing a new community to bootstrap the currency's value without having to offer a compelling story in terms of advantage over other currencies. Dogecoin showed that bootstrapping can be successful with a nontechnical narrative. But like many Internet

FIGURE 10.4. One of several Dogecoin logos. The selling point is humor more than technical innovation. Logo of Dogecoin, Copyright © 2013–2014 Dogecoin Developers.

phenomena, the popularity has not lasted, and Dogecoin's exchange rate has since tanked.

10.3. RELATIONSHIP BETWEEN BITCOIN AND ALTCOINS

We can use various metrics to get a sense of the relative size or impact of different altcoins.

Comparing Altcoins

MARKET CAPITALIZATION

Traditionally, market capitalization ("market cap") is a simple method of estimating the value of a public corporation by multiplying the price of a share by the total number of shares outstanding. In the context of altcoins, this market cap is often similarly used to estimate the total value of the altcoin by multiplying the price of an individual unit of the altcoin (measured, perhaps, at the most popular third-party exchanges) by the total number of units of currency of the altcoin thought to be in circulation. By this metric, Bitcoin is by far the largest—as of 2015, it accounts for more than 90 percent of the overall market cap of all of cryptocurrencies combined. The relative ranking of the other altcoins tends to vary quite a lot, but the point is that most altcoins are comparatively tiny in terms of monetary value.

It's important not to read too much into the market cap. First, it isn't necessarily how much it would cost for someone to buy up all the coins in circulation. That number might be higher or lower, because large orders will move the price of the currency. Second, even though the calculation considers only the coins currently in circulation, we should expect that market participants factor into the exchange rate the fact that new coins will come into circulation in the future, which further complicates the interpretation of the number. Finally, we cannot even accurately estimate the true number of coins currently in circulation, because the owners of some coins may have lost their private keys, and we have no way to know what percentage of coins have been lost.

MINING POWER

If two altcoins use the same mining puzzle, we can directly compare them by how much mining power all the altcoin's miners have. This is often just called the "hash rate" due to the prominence of hash-based puzzles. For example, Zetacoin is an altcoin that uses SHA-256 mining puzzles, just as Bitcoin does, and it has a network hash rate of about 5 terahashes/second (5×10^{12} hashes/second) as of December 2015. This number is about a hundred-thousandth of Bitcoin's mining power. It's trickier to compare the mining power between coins that use different mining puzzles, because the puzzles may take different amounts of time to compute. Besides, mining hardware specialized for one of the coins won't necessarily be usable for mining (including attacking) the other coin.

Even for an altcoin using a completely unique mining puzzle, we can still learn something from the relative change in mining power over time. Growth in mining power indicates either that more participants have joined or that they have upgraded to more powerful mining equipment. Loss of mining power usually means some miners have abandoned the altcoin and is typically an ominous sign.

OTHER INDICATORS

There are several other indicators we can look at. Changes in an altcoin's exchange rate over time gives us clues about its health and tends to correlate with changes in its hash rate over long time periods. Exchange volume on various third-party exchanges is a measure of activity and interest in the altcoin. In contrast, the volume of transactions that have been made on the altcoin's block chain doesn't tell us much, since it could simply be users shuffling their own coins around in their wallet, perhaps even automatically. Finally, we can also look at how many merchants and payment processors support the altcoin—only the most prominent currencies tend to be supported by payment processors.

Economic View of Bitcoin-Altcoin Interactions

The relationship between Bitcoin and altcoins is complicated. In one sense, cryptocurrencies compete with one another, because they all offer a way to make online payments. If there are two standards, protocols, or formats in competition that are roughly equivalent in terms of what they offer, then one of them will usually come to dominate, because of what economists call "network effects."

For example, Blu-ray and HD DVD were in fierce competition in the mid-to-late 2000s to be the successor to the DVD format. Gradually, Blu-ray started to become more popular, in large part because the popular PlayStation 3 console functioned as a Blu-ray player. This made Blu-ray a more attractive format for movie studios, and this popularity fed on itself: as more movies were released for Blu-ray, more consumers bought standalone Blu-ray players, leading to more movie releases and so on. Similarly, if your friends all have Blu-ray players, you'd want to buy one yourself rather than an HD DVD player, because you'd be able to easily swap movies with them. Within about 2 years, HD DVD was a historical footnote.

This line of reasoning suggests that one cryptocurrency—presumably Bitcoin, which is far and away the most popular one today—will dominate, even if some successor systems could be arguably technically superior. But that would be an oversimplification. Competition among cryptocurrencies is not as hostile as the competition between disc formats for at least two reasons.

First, it's relatively easy for users to convert one cryptocurrency into another, and for vendors to accept more than one cryptocurrency, which means that multiple cryptocur-

> **Who Wins the Race?**
>
> Long before HD DVD, there have been countless examples of technological standards that rapidly lost out to a competitor and slid into obscurity, from Betamax analog video tapes to Russian gauge railroad tracks. If you've never heard of these outmoded standards, network effects are the reason. Sometimes, as in the case of Thomas Edison's direct-current power grid versus Nikola Tesla's alternating-current power grid, the winner (AC) was determined by overwhelming technical superiority. In many other cases though, such as Betamax tapes losing to VHS tapes, the loser may have actually been technically superior, with network effects being strong enough to overcome a slight technological disadvantage.

rencies can more easily coexist and thrive. In economics terms, cryptocurrencies exhibit relatively low *switching costs*. Compare this situation to that for DVD players, where most people really don't want two bulky machines in their homes and can't convert their existing library of discs if they change to a machine that plays the other format. Switching costs are certainly not zero for cryptocurrencies. For example, users might buy hardware wallets that can't be upgraded. But by and large, it's easy to switch cryptocurrencies or to use more than one at the same time.

Second, as mentioned earlier, many altcoins have unique features that provide them with a distinct reason for existing. These altcoins shouldn't be seen as mere substitutes for Bitcoin; they may be orthogonal, or perhaps even complementary. Viewed this way, complementary altcoins actually increase the usefulness of Bitcoin rather than compete with it. If Namecoin succeeds, for example, Bitcoin users have one more useful thing they can do with their bitcoins.

But this picture of happy cooperation is also an oversimplification. Some altcoins, like Litecoin, simply try to achieve the same functionality as Bitcoin but in a different, perhaps more efficient, manner. Even when new functionality is being offered, often those use cases can in fact be achieved in Bitcoin itself, albeit in a less elegant way (we have more to say about this in Chapter 11). Supporters of the do-it-on-top-of-Bitcoin model argue that having numerous altcoins divides the hash power available and makes each currency less secure.

In contrast, supporters of altcoins argue that these alternate currencies allow market forces to determine which features are worth having, which systems are technically superior, and so on. They further argue that having numerous altcoins limits the damage of a potential catastrophic failure of any one system. They point out that Bitcoin developers are highly risk averse, and that adding new features to Bitcoin via a soft or a hard fork is slow and difficult. In contrast, it is easy to try out a new idea using an altcoin; altcoins can be seen as a research-and-development test bed for potential Bitcoin features.

The practical upshot is that there is some tension between supporters of Bitcoin and those of altcoins, but also a sense of collaboration.

10.4. ALTCOIN INFANTICIDE AND MERGE MINING

In this section and the next one, we set aside issues of culture, politics, and economics. Instead we focus on the technical interactions between Bitcoin and altcoins.

Altcoin Infanticide

As of 2015, Bitcoin's hash power dwarfs that of any other altcoin. Indeed, Bitcoin has powerful miners and mining pools that control more mining power than that deployed for entire altcoins. Such a miner or entity could easily carry out an attack against a small altcoin (if it uses the same SHA-256 mining puzzle as Bitcoin), causing forks and general havoc, which are often sufficient to kill the altcoin. We call this phenomenon *altcoin infanticide.*

Why would anyone do this, given that they must use their valuable mining power to do so and won't gain a significant monetary reward? Take the case of the 2012 attack on a small altcoin called CoiledCoin: the operator of the Bitcoin mining pool Eligius decided that CoiledCoin was a scam and an affront to the cryptocurrency ecosystem. So Eligius pointed its mining resources at CoiledCoin, mining blocks that reversed days' worth of CoiledCoin transaction history as well as mining a long chain with empty blocks, effectively causing a denial-of-service attack, which prevented CoiledCoin users from making any transactions. After a fairly short siege, users abandoned CoiledCoin, and it no longer exists. In this example and in other altcoin infanticide attacks, the attacker is motivated by something other than direct profit.

Merge Mining

By default—say, if an altcoin forks the Bitcoin source code but makes no other changes—mining on the altcoin is exclusive. That is, you can try to solve the mining puzzle solution to find a valid block for the altcoin or for Bitcoin, but you can't try to solve both puzzles at once. Of course, you can divide your mining resources to dedicate some to mining on the altcoin and some to mining on Bitcoin. You can even divide among multiple different altcoins and adjust your allocations over time, but there's no way to get your mining power to do double duty.

With exclusive mining, network effects can make it difficult for an altcoin to bootstrap. If you wanted to launch an altcoin and convince today's Bitcoin miners to participate in your network, they would have to stop mining Bitcoin (with at least some of their resources), which would mean an immediate loss of Bitcoin mining rewards. This means your altcoin is likely to remain small in terms of hashing power and more vulnerable to infanticide-style attacks by Bitcoin miners.

Can we design an altcoin so that it's possible to mine blocks both on the altcoin and on Bitcoin at the same time? To do that, we need to create blocks that include transactions from both Bitcoin and the altcoin, making them valid in both block chains. It's easy to design the altcoin so that it allows Bitcoin transactions in its blocks, because we can write the rules of the altcoin however we want. The reverse is harder. Where can we put altcoin transactions in Bitcoin blocks? Chapters 3 and 9 discussed how to put arbitrary data into Bitcoin blocks, but the bandwidth of these methods is very limited.

There's a trick, though: even if we can't put the contents of the altcoin's transactions into Bitcoin blocks, we can put a summary of the altcoin transactions into Bitcoin blocks in the form of a hash pointer to the altcoin block. Finding a way to put a single hash pointer into each Bitcoin block is easy. Specifically, recall that each Bitcoin block has a special transaction—the coinbase transaction—that the miner uses to create new coins as a block reward. The scriptSig field of this transaction has no significance and can therefore be used to store arbitrary data (there's no need to sign the Coinbase transaction, since it's not spending any previous transaction outputs). So in a merge-mined altcoin, the mining task is to compute *Bitcoin* blocks whose Coinbase scriptSig contains a hash pointer to an altcoin block.

This block can now do double duty: to Bitcoin clients, it looks just like any other Bitcoin block, with a hash in the coinbase transaction that can be ignored. Altcoin clients know how to interpret the block by ignoring the Bitcoin transactions and looking at the altcoin transactions committed to by the hash in the coinbase transaction. Although this doesn't require any changes to Bitcoin, it does require the altcoin to specifically understand Bitcoin and accept merge-mined blocks.

If our altcoin is merge mined, we hope that many Bitcoin miners will mine it, because doing so doesn't require any additional hash power. It requires a modicum of additional computational resources for processing blocks and transactions, and miners need to know and care enough about our altcoin to bother to mine it. Suppose that 25 percent of Bitcoin miners by hash power are mining our altcoin. Then on average, 25 percent of Bitcoin blocks contain pointers to altcoin blocks. It seems, then, that in our altcoin a new block would be mined on average every 40 minutes. Worse, while the altcoin is still being bootstrapped and the fraction of Bitcoin miners mining it is tiny, the time between blocks will be hours or days, which is unacceptable.

Can we ensure that blocks of a merge-mined altcoin are created at a steady rate, as high or low as we want, irrespective of the fraction of Bitcoin miners mining it? The answer is yes. The trick is that even though the mining task for the altcoin is the same as that for Bitcoin, the mining *target* need not be. The altcoin network computes the target and difficulty for its blocks independently of the Bitcoin network. Just as Bitcoin adjusts its mining target so that blocks are found every 10 minutes on average, the altcoin would adjust its own target, so that blocks in the altcoin are found every 10 minutes (or any other fixed interval).

The altcoin's target then will typically be much less than Bitcoin's target, and some (or even most) altcoin blocks will not be pointed to by valid Bitcoin blocks. But that's okay! You should think of the Bitcoin and the altcoin block chains as two parallel chains, with occasional pointers from a Bitcoin block to an altcoin block. This is illus-

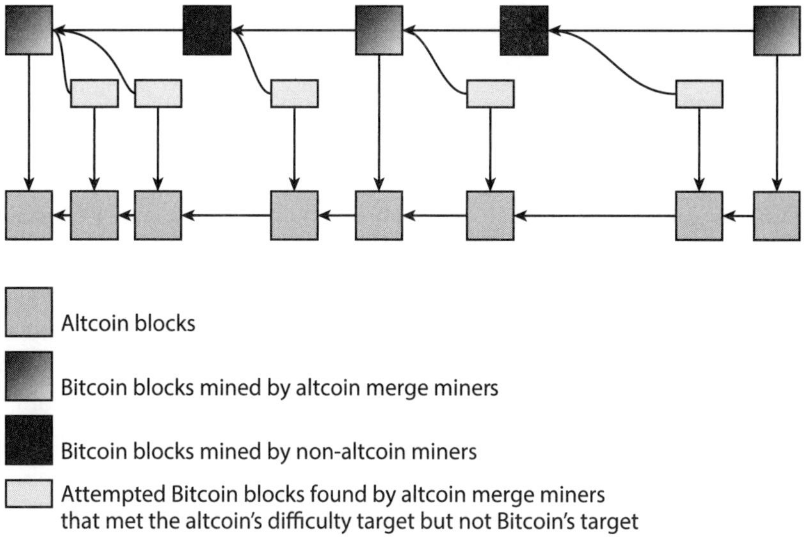

FIGURE 10.5. Merge mining. Bitcoin and altcoin block chains are shown, as well as the interactions between them.

trated in Figure 10.5. In this example, 60 percent of Bitcoin miners mine the altcoin, and the altcoin's time-between-blocks is 5 minutes. This means that the altcoin's difficulty is 60 percent × 5/10 = 30 percent that of Bitcoin. Note that 40 percent of Bitcoin blocks do not contain hash pointers to altcoin blocks in this example.

Conversely, every valid altcoin block results from an attempt at mining a Bitcoin block, but only 30 percent of them actually meet Bitcoin's difficulty target. For the other 70 percent of altcoin blocks, the altcoin network needs to be able to verify the mining puzzle solution. The simple way to do this is to broadcast the Bitcoin near-block in addition to the altcoin block. But a cleverer way is to broadcast just the header of the Bitcoin near-block and the Merkle proof of inclusion of the Coinbase transaction in the Bitcoin block.

It's also possible (although rarely seen) for the altcoin to actually have a more difficult puzzle than Bitcoin has. This is unusual, because most altcoins want to have blocks found more often than once per 10 minutes, but if for some reason you wanted a slower rate, it would be easy to achieve. In this case, you would see some Bitcoin blocks that the miner hoped would also become altcoin blocks, but they would be rejected on the altcoin network, because they failed to meet the harder difficulty target.

Finally, note that any number of altcoins can be simultaneously merge mined with Bitcoin, and every miner is free to pick an arbitrary subset of altcoins to merge mine. In this case, the Coinbase scriptSig would itself be a Merkle tree of hash pointers to various altcoin blocks. Note the levels of complexity: verifying the inclusion of an altcoin transaction requires verifying, among other things: (1) a Merkle proof of inclusion of the altcoin transaction in the altcoin block, (2) a Merkle proof of inclusion of the altcoin block hash in the Coinbase scriptSig, and (3) a Merkle proof of inclusion of the Coinbase scriptSig in the Bitcoin block or near-block!

Merge Mining and Security

Merge mining is a mixed blessing. It makes bootstrapping easier, as we've discussed, and the resulting boost to your altcoin's total hash power increases its resilience to attack. An adversary who is looking to buy computing power to destroy your altcoin will need to make an enormous up-front investment.

However, one could argue that this is a false sense of security, because such an adversary would presumably recoup the cost of his investment by mining Bitcoin, and the marginal cost to attack your altcoin is trivial. This is easier to appreciate if we think about an adversary who is already a large Bitcoin miner. Indeed, CoiledCoin, the altcoin that suffered infanticide (described earlier in this section), was merge mined. The Eligius mining pool and its participants did not need to stop Bitcoin mining to attack CoiledCoin. In fact, the pool participants were not even aware that their computing resources were being used in the attack!

By contemplating a rational miner deciding whether or not to merge mine, we can discover more problems with the security of merge mining. Recall that, roughly speaking, mining makes sense if the expected reward equals or exceeds the expected costs. For Bitcoin mining, the cost is primarily that of hash computation. But for someone who's already a Bitcoin miner deciding whether to merge mine an altcoin, there is no additional cost from hashing. Instead, the additional costs arise from two factors: (1) the computation, bandwidth, and storage needed to validate the altcoin transactions and (2) the need to keep software up to date and perhaps make informed decisions if the altcoin is undergoing hard or soft forks.

This reasoning yields two insights. First, merge mining has strong economies of scale, because all miners incur roughly the same costs regardless of their hash power. This is in stark contrast to Bitcoin, where cost is proportional to hash power, to a first approximation. So for a low-value altcoin, a small solo miner will find it unprofitable to merge mine it, because the cost exceeds the meager reward they will make due to their low hash power. Keep in mind that as of 2015, the potential revenue from mining altcoins remains a small fraction of Bitcoin mining revenue. This argument predicts that com-

> **Trends in Altcoin Mining Puzzles**
>
> As of 2015, few altcoins launch with the same SHA-256 mining puzzle as Bitcoin, with or without merge mining, which suggests that it is perhaps considered a security risk. Scrypt is a much more popular choice, which makes Bitcoin ASICs useless for mining or attacking such altcoins. Of course, scrypt ASICs being manufactured for Litecoin mining could be used to attack them.

pared to Bitcoin, merge-mined altcoins will have a greater centralization or concentration of mining power.

A related prediction is that most miners will choose to outsource their transaction validations. The smaller the altcoin, the greater the incentive to outsource will be. The natural way to do this is to join a Bitcoin mining pool. That's because pools typically take those computations out of miners' hands. The pool operator assembles a Bitcoin block that incorporates blocks from (zero or more) altcoins, after validating the transactions in the Bitcoin block as well as any altcoin blocks. The miner merely tries to solve for the nonce. These predictions are borne out in practice. For example, GHash.IO, at one time the largest Bitcoin mining pool, allows merge mining of Namecoin, IXCoin, and DevCoin. So those currencies became the most popular merge-mined altcoins.

The second insight from the economic reasoning is perhaps even more worrying for security than the concentration of mining power. When miners' primary cost is proof of work, by design there is no way for miners to game the system. There is no shortcut to mining, given the security of hash functions, and additionally other miners easily can and will verify the proof of work. Both assumptions fail when the cost is that of transaction validation. A miner could assume that transactions they heard about are valid and hope to get away with not checking them. Besides, for other miners to validate a block and its transactions is just as much work as it was for the miner who found it. For these reasons, we should expect that at least for small merge miners, there's an incentive to skimp on validation. The existence of improperly validating miners makes attacks easier, because a malicious miner can create a block that will cause the rest of the miners to disagree on what the longest valid branch is.

To summarize, merge mining solves one security problem but creates many others, in part because the economics of merge mining differ in important ways from the economics of exclusive mining. Overall, it's far from clear that merge mining is a good idea for a new altcoin concerned about mining attacks.

10.5. ATOMIC CROSS-CHAIN SWAPS

In Bitcoin, it's straightforward to create a single transaction that swaps currency or assets controlled by different people or entities. This is the intuition behind CoinJoin, which we studied in Chapter 6. It is also useful for trading smart property, which we looked at briefly in Chapter 9 and return to in Chapter 11. The same idea enables selling domain names in Namecoin, as mentioned earlier in this chapter.

But in all these cases, the swap transactions are confined to a single block chain, even if they involve different types of assets in that block chain. In general, a transaction on one altcoin is entirely independent of and has no way of referring to a transaction that happens on some other altcoin's transaction history. But is this a fundamental limitation, or is there some way to swap one type of coin for another? That is, if Alice wants

1. Alice generates a refundable deposit of *a* altcoins as follows:
   - 1.1 Alice generates a random string *x* and computes the hash $h = H(x)$
   - 1.2 Alice generates **DepositA** as shown below, but doesn't publish it yet
   - 1.3 Alice generates **RefundA**, and gets Bob's signature on it
   - 1.4 Once Bob signs **RefundA**, she publishes **DepositA** (but doesn't publish **RefundA**)
2. Bob generates a refundable deposit of *b* bitcoins as follows:
   - 2.1 Bob generates **DepositB** as shown below, but doesn't publish it yet
   - 2.2 Bob generates **RefundB**, and gets Alice's signature on it
   - 2.2 Once Alice signs **RefundB**, he publishes **DepositB** (but doesn't publish **RefundB**)
3. Case 1: Alice goes through with the swap
   - 3.1 Alice claims the bitcoins by time T_1, revealing *x* to Bob (and everyone) in the process
   - 3.2 Bob claims the altcoins by time T_2

   Case 2: Alice changes her mind, does not claim the altcoins, does not reveal *x* to Bob
   - 3.1 Bob claims his altcoin refund at time T_1
   - 3.2 Alice claims her Bitcoin refund at time T_2

DepositA [Altcoin block chain]

Input:	Alice's coins of value *a*
ScriptPubKey:	Redeemable by providing either (*sigA* and *sigB*) or *sigB* and *x* s.t. *H*(*x*) = <h>

RefundA [Altcoin block chain]

Input:	DepositA
Output:	AddrA
Timelock:	T_2
ScriptSig:	*sigA, sigB*

DepositB [Bitcoin block chain]

Input:	Bob's coins of value *b*
ScriptPubKey:	Redeemable by providing either (*sigA* and *sigB*) or *sigA* and *x* s.t. *H*(*x*) = <h>

RefundB [Bitcoin block chain]

Input:	DepositB
Output:	AddrB
Timelock:	T_1
ScriptSig:	*sigA, sigB*

FIGURE 10.6. Atomic cross-chain swap protocol.

to sell a quantity *a* of altcoins to Bob in exchange for a quantity *b* of his bitcoins, can they do so in an atomic fashion, without having to trust each other or relying on an intermediary such as an exchange service? At first sight this seems impossible, because there is no way to force transactions on two different block chains to happen simultaneously. If one of them—say, Alice—carries out her transfer before the other does, what prevents Bob from reneging on his side of the bargain?

The solution is clever and involves cryptographic commitments and time-locked deposits, both of which are techniques we've seen before (see Chapters 1 and 3, respectively). Figure 10.6 describes the protocol. For the moment, assume that blocks in the two block chains are generated in lockstep: one block is generated every time unit. Let *T* represent the time at the start of the protocol.

In step 1, Alice deposits altcoins of value a that can be redeemed in one of two ways ("deposit" simply means sending those coins to a ScriptPubKey that specifies two possible conditions for spending it). First, if Alice and Bob mutually agree, they can redeem it. Indeed, Alice publishes the deposit only after making sure to get a refund transaction signed by Bob—this allows her to redeem her deposit if 2 time units elapse and it hasn't already been claimed.

The other way to claim Alice's deposit, at any time, is by providing Bob's signature as well as the value x that opens the hash commitment h. Note that we write $<h>$ in *DepositA* to indicate that Alice literally writes the value of h into the ScriptPubKey. Since x is known only to Alice, at the end of stage 1 neither party is able to claim the deposit this way. The idea is that Bob will learn the value x, enabling him to claim the altcoins, if and only if Alice claims his bitcoins, as we'll see.

Step 2 is roughly the reverse of step 1: Bob deposits bitcoins of value b so that they can be redeemed in one of two ways. The key difference is that he doesn't pick a new secret; instead, he uses the same hash value h (he would just copy the value from the *DepositA* transaction to the *DepositB* transaction). This is the key to tying together transactions on the two block chains.

At this point the ball is in Alice's court. She could change her mind about the swap—if at time T_1 Alice hasn't done anything to reveal x to Bob, he will simply claim his deposit and quit the protocol. Alice's other option is to claim Bob's bitcoins before time T_1. But she can only do this by creating and broadcasting a scriptSig containing the value x; Bob can listen to this broadcast and use the value same x to claim Alice's altcoins, completing the swap.

Note that if Alice tries to claim Bob's bitcoins a tad too late (after time T_1 but before time T_2), Bob might be able to claim *both* deposits. Similarly, if Alice claims Bob's bitcoins on time but Bob waits too long, Alice might be able to go home with both deposits. But this is not a problem: we are happy as long as there is no way for a player deviating from the protocol to cheat the other player.

Finally, blocks in Bitcoin or any altcoin don't arrive in fixed time steps, which introduces some messiness, particularly as the two chains may not be synchronized. Let's say both block chains have an average time of 10 minutes between blocks. Then we'd want to pick a "time unit" of, say, 1 hour. In other words, we'd want to have T_1 be at least `current_altcoin_block + 12` and T_2 be at least `current_bitcoin_block + 6`, possibly with a greater safety margin.

Unfortunately, there's a small but nonzero chance that the next 12 altcoin blocks will be found before the next 6 Bitcoin blocks. In this case, Alice might be able to claim both deposits. This probability can be made arbitrarily small by increasing the time unit, but at the expense of transaction speed.

This is a neat protocol, but as of 2015, no one uses it. Instead, cryptocurrencies are traded on traditional, centralized exchanges. There are many reasons to use a centralized exchange. The first is the complexity, inconvenience, and slowness of the protocol.

Second, although the protocol prevents theft, it cannot prevent a denial of service. Someone might advertise offers at amazing exchange rates, only to quit after step 1 or step 2, wasting everyone else's time. To mitigate this and to aggregate and match people's offers, you probably need a centralized exchange anyway—albeit one that can't steal your coins and hence doesn't need to be trusted—further diminishing the usefulness of the protocol.

10.6. SIDECHAINS: BITCOIN-BACKED ALTCOINS

In Section 10.1, we discussed two ways to allocate units of a new altcoin to existing owners of bitcoins: (1) requiring provably burning bitcoins to acquire altcoins or (2) simply allocating altcoins to existing holders of bitcoins based on bitcoin addresses that own unspent transaction outputs. As we saw, neither of these allows bilaterally pegging the price of the altcoin to that of Bitcoin. Without such pegging, the price of an altcoin is likely to be volatile during its bootstrapping phase. The motivation for sidechains is the view that this price volatility is problematic: it is a distraction and makes it difficult for altcoins to compete on their technical merits.

Here's what we need in terms of technical features to be able to actually peg the altcoin's price to Bitcoin's at a fixed exchange rate. First, you should be able to put a bitcoin that you own into some sort of escrow and mint one altcoin (or a fixed quantity of altcoins). You should be able to spend this altcoin normally on the altcoin block chain. Finally, you should be able to burn an altcoin that you own and redeem a previously escrowed bitcoin. This is similar to Zerocoin (see Section 6.5), where we escrow basecoins to create zerocoins, but the difference is that here we need to do it across two different block chains.

The bad news is that, as far as we know, there is no way to achieve this without modifying Bitcoin, because Bitcoin transactions can't depend on events happening in another block chain. Bitcoin script simply isn't powerful enough to verify an entire separate block chain. The good news is that it can be enabled with a relatively practical soft-fork modification to Bitcoin, and that's the idea behind sidechains. The sidechains vision is that of numerous flourishing altcoins that rapidly innovate and experiment, using Bitcoin as a sort of reserve currency. As of 2015 it is only a proposal, but one that is being actively worked on and has serious traction in the Bitcoin community. The proposal is still in flux, and we take the liberty of simplifying some details for pedagogical purposes.

The obvious but impractical way to extend Bitcoin to allow converting coins from a sidechain back to bitcoins is this: encode all of the sidechain's rules into Bitcoin, including validating all of the sidechain's transactions and checking the sidechain's proof of work. The reason this approach is impractical is that the resulting extensions to Bitcoin's script would be too complex, and the verification effort needed for Bitcoin nodes would be prohibitive. Besides, the complexity and effort would grow with the number of pegged sidechains.

The SPV Trick

The trick to avoiding this complexity is to use *SPV proofs*. Recall from Chapter 3 that Simplified Payment Verification is used by lightweight clients, such as mobile apps for Bitcoin. SPV nodes don't validate transactions they're not interested in; they merely verify block headers. Instead of worrying about the longest *valid* branch, SPV clients merely look for evidence that the transaction they care about is in the longest branch, valid or not, and that it has received some number of confirmations. They assume that the miners who created these blocks wouldn't have made the effort to mine them without validating the transactions in those blocks.

Perhaps, then, we could extend Bitcoin's script with an instruction to verify a proof that a particular transaction (e.g., one that destroyed a coin) happened in the sidechain. The Bitcoin nodes doing this verification would still be fully validating as far as Bitcoin's block chain is concerned, but they would do relatively lightweight SPV verification of events in the sidechain.

Contesting a Transfer

This approach is better but still not ideal. To do even simplified verification, Bitcoin nodes would still have to connect to the sidechain's peer-to-peer network (for each pegged sidechain!) and track all sidechain block headers, so that the nodes can determine the longest sidechain branch. Instead, when a transaction tries to convert a coin in a sidechain back into a bitcoin, we want the sidechain to contain all the information that Bitcoin nodes need to verify its legitimacy (i.e., to verify that a particular sidechain transaction happened). This is the notion of an "SPV proof."

Here we present one way in which it could work, with the caveat that this component of sidechains is still an area of research. To reference a sidechain transaction in Bitcoin, the user must provide (1) proof of inclusion of the sidechain transaction in a sidechain block and (2) sidechain block headers showing that this block has received a certain number of confirmations that cumulatively represent a certain amount of proof of work. Bitcoin nodes will verify these claims but will make no attempt to verify that the chain of block headers presented is the longest. Instead, they will wait for a defined period, say a day or two, to allow other users to present evidence that the block headers presented in step 2 are *not* on the longest branch. If such evidence is presented within the defined period, the provisional acceptance of the sidechain transaction in Bitcoin will be invalidated.

The rationale is that if an SPV proof has been presented that shouldn't be accepted because the transaction is not on the longest branch, there must be *some* sidechain user who will be harmed by the acceptance of this proof. This user will have the incentive to present evidence to invalidate the proof. If there is no user who will be harmed (perhaps there was a fork or reorganization of the sidechain, but the transaction in question was also present in the other branch) then there is no harm in accepting the proof.

More generally, the system doesn't try to be bulletproof against problems in sidechains, and it won't prevent you from shooting yourself in the foot. If you transfer your bitcoin into a sidechain that has broken crypto, for example, someone else might be able to steal your coin on the sidechain and convert it back into a bitcoin. Or all mining on the sidechain might collapse due to bugs, with the locked bitcoins lost forever. But what the proposal does ensure is that problems on sidechains can't damage Bitcoin. In particular, the same coin can't be redeemed twice from a sidechain regardless of how buggy the sidechain may may be—that is, sidechains won't allow you to mint bitcoins.

Compact SPV Proofs via Proof-of-Work Samples

There is one final difficulty. Some of the sidechains might have a high block rate, perhaps one block every few seconds. In this case, even verifying SPV proofs might be too onerous for Bitcoin nodes. It turns out that we can use a clever statistical technique to decrease the amount of computation needed to verify N block confirmations from $O(N)$ to a number that grows much slower than linearly.

The intuition is this: when we're verifying that a block is buried deep in the block chain, we're verifying that each block that builds on it meets the target difficulty (i.e., it satisfies $hash < target$). Now the hash values of these blocks will be uniformly distributed in the interval $(0, target)$, which means that statistically about 25 percent of those blocks will in fact satisfy $hash < target/4$. In fact, the amount of work needed to find $N/4$ blocks that each satisfy $hash < target/4$ is the same as the amount of work needed to compute N blocks each satisfying $hash < target$. There is of course nothing special about the number 4; we could replace it by any factor.

This logic means that if we had some way of knowing which blocks in the chain satisfied $hash < target/4$ and verified only those blocks (or block headers), we'd be done, having put in only one-fourth of the verification work! How would we know which blocks satisfy $hash < target/4$? The blocks themselves could tell us, as shown in Figure 10.7. Each block would contain a pointer both to its predecessor as well as to the most recent block that satisfied $hash < target/4$.

How far can we push this approach? Can we pick arbitrarily large multiples? Not really. The logic here is similar to pooled mining, but in reverse. In pooled mining, the pool operator verifies shares, which are blocks with a lowered difficulty (that is, a higher target value). Miners find many more shares than blocks, so the operator must do extra work to verify them. The benefit of doing so is the ability to estimate the miner's hash power much more accurately—the variance of the estimate is lower.

Here we see the opposite trade-off. As we do less and less work to estimate the total amount of work that has gone into building the chain, our estimate will have a greater and greater variance. Here's an example. Suppose $N = 4$, so that without the above

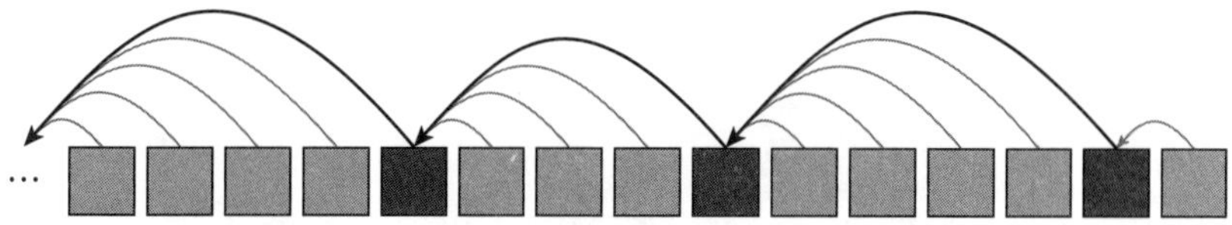

FIGURE 10.7. Proof-of-work skiplist. Blocks contain pointers both to the previous block and to the nearest block that satisfies *hash* < *target* /4. The concept could be applied recursively, with a third level of pointers to blocks satisfying *hash* < *target*/16, and so on.

skiplist solution, we'd check that there are 4 blocks that satisfy *hash* < *target*. The expected amount of work that an adversary must do to fool us is 4 times the average amount of work needed to find a block.

Suppose the adversary only does half this amount of work. If we do the math, it turns out that this adversary has a 14 percent chance of finding 4 blocks that satisfy *hash* < *target*. But with a skiplist solution with a factor of 4, the adversary's task would be to find a single block that satisfies *hash* < *target*/4. In this scenario, the lazy adversary who only does half the expected amount of work will be able to fool us with a probability of 40 percent instead of 14 percent.

10.7. ETHEREUM AND SMART CONTRACTS

We have seen several ways to use Bitcoin's scripting language to support interesting applications, such as an escrowed payment transaction. We've also seen how Bitcoin script is somewhat limited, with a small instruction set that isn't Turing complete (see Section 3.2). As a result, some new altcoins propose adding application-specific functionality. Namecoin was the first example, but many others have proposed cryptocurrencies much like Bitcoin but supporting gambling, stock issuance, prediction markets, and so on.

What if, instead of needing to launch a new system to support every application, we built a cryptocurrency that could support any application we might dream up in the future? This is what Turing completeness is all about: a Turing-complete programming language lets you specify any functionality that is possible to program into a Turing machine, an abstract model of a computer that is believed to be capable of computing any function that can be computed at all. As a consequence, every Turing-complete programming language—including familiar ones, such as Java, Python, and Lisp—is identical in the set of computations that it allows to be expressed. In a certain theoretical sense, Turing completeness is the best we can hope for in a programming language in terms of expressive power, ignoring practical matters, such as simplicity and performance.

To some extent, the situation today harkens back to the early days of computers themselves in the 1940s: increasingly complicated machines were being built for vari-

FIGURE 10.8. Rebuilt Bombe machine located at the Bletchley Park museum, UK. The Bombe was a special-purpose computer designed by Alan Turing to crack German Enigma ciphers. Will Ethereum do to application-specific altcoins what the general-purpose computer did to Bombe-like contraptions? Photo by Tom Yates.

ous specific applications during World War II (such as brute-forcing keys used by mechanical cipher machines or determining firing trajectories for naval artillery), motivating researchers to build the first reprogrammable general-purpose computers that could be used for any conceivable applications (Figure 10.8).

Ethereum is an ambitious altcoin that aims to provide a Turing-complete programming language for writing scripts or "contracts." While there are other proposals to do this, Ethereum is the most notable: it introduced several novel technical ideas; held a successful crowd-funding campaign, raising $20 million over several months; and adopted aggressive choices for parameters, such as block time. In this section, we provide a brief overview of Ethereum—though the system is complex enough that we could easily devote an entire second book to it!

Smart Contract Programming Model

The term *smart contract* was first used to describe the use of computer systems (or other automated means) to enforce contracts. As an example, you could think of a vending machine as a mechanical smart contract that enforces an agreement between you and the machine's owner involving the purchase of a candy bar.

In Ethereum, a contract is a program that lives on the block chain. Anybody can create an Ethereum contract, for a small fee, by uploading its program code in a special transaction. This contract is written in bytecode and executed by a special Ethereum-specific virtual machine, usually just called "EVM." Once uploaded, the contract will live on the block chain. It has its own balance of funds, other users can make procedure calls through whatever API the program exposes, and the contract can send and receive money.

A Simple Example: Namecoin in Ethereum

We claimed that Ethereum can be used to implement any application-specific altcoin's functionality. As a simple example, we can show how to implement Namecoin-style functionality in a simple Ethereum contract.

One example implementation is shown in Figure 10.9. It is coded in Solidity, Ethereum's high-level programming language for defining contracts. This contract implements a crude name/value store or name registry, in which names are assigned values once and for all. The contract defines a data variable, `registryTable`, which is a mapping from 32-byte strings to public keys. Initially, it maps every string to the null address 0x0000000000 . . . 000. This contract also defines a single entry point, called `claimName`. This entry point accepts a single argument, `name`. First, the contract makes sure that the caller has sent a value of at least 10 wei, wei being the smallest currency unit in Ethereum. If insufficient funds have been sent, the contract terminates with an error (the `throw` statement does this), and no action is taken. If sufficient funds are sent and the name is not yet taken, then it is permanently assigned the value of whichever address invoked this function.

That's all this contract can do in eight lines of code. But we could add all the other features of Namecoin with a little more work. For example, we could store more data with each mapping than just the address of the entity that claimed it. We could require name owners to re-register periodically by storing a "last updated" time and allowing other users to claim names that haven't been updated in a long time.

We might also want to add a second function to allow the money to be withdrawn. As currently programmed, the money will just accumulate in the contract forever, es-

```
contract NameRegistry {
      mapping(bytes32 => address) public registryTable;
      function claimName(bytes32 name) {
            if (msg.value < 10) {
                  throw;
            }
            if (registryTable[name] == 0) {
                  registryTable[name] = msg.sender;
            }
      }
}
```

FIGURE 10.9. Simple Ethereum smart contract implementing a name registry.

sentially being removed from circulation. Of course, in the function allowing money to be withdrawn, we'd better make sure to check that the caller is the owner of the contract. Anybody can call any function on an Ethereum contract, but the calls are signed, so we can securely identify who the caller is.

Gas, Incentives, and Security

Unlike Bitcoin, Ethereum supports loops, although we didn't need them in our first example. That should immediately raise alarm bells. If there are loops, there can be infinite loops. In general, Ethereum contracts might run forever for a variety of reasons. A famous result in computer science (the undecidability of the Halting Problem) states that there's no algorithm that can look at a program's source code and always correctly determine whether it will run forever or not. So how can we prevent contracts from running forever?

More generally, we need some way to limit contracts that take a long time to run, even if that time is finite. Ethereum uses a mechanism called *gas* to achieve this. Essentially, executing each virtual-machine instruction costs a small amount of money (gas). Different operations cost different amounts. Basic operations like addition or comparison cost 1 gas, whereas computing a SHA-3 hash (available as a built-in instruction) costs 20 gas, and writing a 256-bit word to persistent storage costs 100 gas. Every transaction also costs 21,000 gas right off the bat. You can think of Ethereum like flying on an ultra-discount airline: you pay to get on board and you pay extra for everything you do from there. The complete list of instructions available in Ethereum and the gas cost of each is fixed; changing these would require a hard fork, just like changing the semantics of Bitcoin's scripting language would.

Gas is paid for using Ethereum's built-in currency, called "ether." It's just called "gas" when being used to pay for contract execution. Every transaction can specify the "gas price," that is, how much ether it will pay per unit of gas consumed. The gas price offered is like the transaction fee in Bitcoin: miners are free to publish transactions with any gas price, and each miner can independently decide their fee structure. This should result in a market price for gas reflecting supply and demand. As of early 2016, however, the network remains experimental and has coalesced around a default of 50 gigawei per unit of gas (50 gigawei is 5×10^{-8} ether, or about 3×10^{-10} BTC, given the ether-BTC exchange rate at the end of 2015).

Every call must specify up front how much gas it is willing to spend (the "gas limit"). If this value is hit (running out of gas), execution halts, all changes to the program's state are undone, and the miner pockets the gas anyway. So it's very important not to run out of gas.

The gas requirement means that very expensive computations are not suitable for Ethereum. The system is not designed to be a cloud-computing service, where you go to pay others to do a difficult computation that you're unable to do yourself. Services like Amazon's Elastic Compute Cloud or Microsoft's Azure provide millions of times more bang for your buck. In contrast, Ethereum is suitable for implementing security protocol logic. Essentially, it provides a service that two (or more) anonymous parties can count on to behave as specified.

The security of Ethereum's block chain is not nearly as well established as Bitcoin's. Theoretically, the system is much more complex and therefore harder to reason about mathematically. Practically, Ethereum hasn't been around for very long and hasn't been subject to the same kind of scrutiny as Bitcoin has. In particular, there are concerns that the cost of transaction processing throws Bitcoin-style incentive arguments out of whack, similar to our discussion about merge mining. When transaction processing is a nontrivial fraction of a miner's total cost, the system favors larger miners, since this cost is independent of hash power. More importantly, the gas payment goes only to the miner who initially includes the transaction in a block. But all miners building on that block must also validate the transaction, and they don't get paid for doing so. Thus they have an incentive to skip validation. As we saw earlier, this can be dangerous for the health of the block chain.

A Second Example: Chess in Ethereum

We still haven't said much about what you can do with Ethereum that's new, so let's look at a second example. Suppose Alice wants to challenge Bob to a game of chess with money on the line. The only problem is that Alice and Bob live in different countries and neither trusts each other to pay if they lose. This is a problem Ethereum can solve!

Alice will write an Ethereum program that implements the rules of chess and upload it to Ethereum. She'll send the contract a quantity of ether equal to the amount she wants to bet. Bob can see this contract, and if he decides to accept the challenge, he can start the game by sending his own betting stake to the contract. Before doing this, Bob should make sure the contract is correctly written in that it implements chess and will ultimately send all of its value to the winning player.

Once both players have sent their stakes in, the contract should check that the stakes are equal, assuming they're making an even wager. At this point the game is afoot, and there should be no way for either player to extract the money from the contract without actually winning the game, or for anyone else to extract the money under any circumstance.

Alice and Bob will take turns sending a transaction to the contract, which indicates the next move they'd like to play. The contract, of course, must ensure that each move is sent in only by the player whose turn it is to move, and not by the other player or by someone else entirely. Remember that every transaction (which causes the contract to execute a function) is signed by the caller, so the contract can verify the identity of the source. The contract will also have to check all the rules of chess. If a player tries to move a pawn three spaces, that transaction will have to be rejected.

Eventually, the game will end. After each move, the contract must check whether either player is mated, or if the game is a draw by stalemate or one of the other drawing conditions in chess. Players should also be able to send in a move indicating their resignation. When the game ends, the contract can terminate itself and send all of the money to the winning player or split the money in case of a draw.

Conceptually, this is a simple application of Ethereum, but there are subtleties. What if a player in a losing position simply walks away? The contract will need a mechanism that awards the money to the opponent if a player hasn't submitted a valid move in a specified period of time.

Which player gets to move first? "Playing white" confers a slight advantage in chess, so both players want this advantage. This points to a difficulty faced by many Ethereum contracts: there is no built-in source of randomness. This is a hard problem, as the random number generator needs to be verifiable by all miners (so they can check that the contract was executed correctly) but shouldn't be predictable for either player (or else they might refuse to join if they know they will have to play second).

This is the problem of randomness beacons. As discussed in Section 9.4, the contract might hash the value of the next block in the block chain after both players have joined. For our specific application, the problem is a bit easier, since only Alice and Bob need to be convinced that the coin flip is random, not the whole world. So they might use the approach from Section 9.3: they both submit the hash of a random value, then both reveal the inputs and derive the random bit from the inputs. Both approaches have been seen in practice.

Other Applications

Playing chess might be fun, but the real excitement about Ethereum concerns financial applications. Many of the applications we've discussed in the text so far, including prediction markets, smart property, escrowed payments, micropayment channels, and mixing services, can be implemented in Ethereum. Subtleties plague all these applications, but they are all possible and in most cases are much simpler to implement than the types of bolt-on protocols we've seen with Bitcoin. There are also a host of other applications, like auctions and order books, that we haven't talked about but whose implementation in Ethereum is generating enthusiam among users.

State and account balances in Ethereum. In Chapter 3, we discussed two ways to design a ledger: account based and transaction based. In a transaction-based ledger like Bitcoin, the block chain stores only transactions (plus a small amount of metadata in the block headers). To make it easier to validate transactions, Bitcoin treats coins as immutable, and transaction outputs must be spent in their entirety, with change addresses used if necessary. Effectively, transactions operate on a global state, which is a list of unspent transaction outputs, but this state is never made explicit in the Bitcoin protocol and is simply something miners create on their own to speed up verification.

In contrast, Ethereum uses an account-based model. Since Ethereum already stores a data structure mapping contract addresses to state, it is natural to also store the account balance of every regular address (also called an "owned address") in the system. So instead of representing payments using an acyclic transaction graph, where each transaction spends some inputs and creates some outputs, Ethereum just stores a balance for each address like a traditional bank might store the balance of each account number.

Data structures in Ethereum. In Chapter 3, we said that an account-based ledger would necessitate fancy data structures for record keeping. Ethereum has just such data structures. Specifically, every block contains a digest of the current state (balance and transaction count) of every address as well as the state (balance and storage) of every contract. Each contract's storage tree maps arbitrary 256-bit addresses to 256-bit words, making for a whopping $2^{256} \times 256 = 2^{264}$ bytes of storage! Of course, you could never fill up all of this storage, but that's the theoretical space. The digest makes it easy to prove that a given address has a given balance or storage state. For example, Alice can prove to Bob what her balance is without Bob having to scan the entire block chain to verify the proof.

The simple binary Merkle tree used in Bitcoin would work for this purpose, as it allows efficient proofs of inclusion (provided miners ensure that no tree will include two different states for the same address). But we also want fast lookups and the ability to efficiently update an address's value. To do this Ethereum uses a slightly more complicated tree structure called a *Patricia tree,* also known as a prefix tree, trie, or radix tree. Each Ethereum block includes the root of a Merkle Patricia tree (i.e., a Patricia tree with hash pointers) committing to the state of every address, including contract addresses. Each contract's state, in turn, includes a tree committing to the entire state of its storage.

Another tricky issue with an account-based ledger is preventing replay attacks. In Bitcoin, since every transaction consumes its input unspent transaction outputs, the same signed transaction can never be valid twice. With Ethereum's design, we need to make sure that if Alice signs a transaction saying "pay 1 ether to Bob," Bob can't broadcast the transaction over and over again until Alice's account is drained. To avoid this, every account in Ethereum has a transaction counter tracking how many transactions it has sent. The statement Alice really signs is "I authorize my *n*th transaction to be a payment of 1 ether to Bob." This transaction can't be replayed, because after it is processed, Alice's transaction counter will increment and is part of the global state.

To summarize, Ethereum uses more powerful data structures than Bitcoin does as part of its ledger. Although we haven't looked at the details, it allows efficient proofs of a variety of types of statements about accounts, contracts, and transactions.

Ethereum Project

Ethereum was initially described in late 2013 and launched its first release, dubbed "Frontier," in 2015. Ethereum used a pre-sale, making units of the ether currency publicly available for a fixed price in Bitcoin, with all of the proceeds going to the Ethereum Foundation.

This is a slower pace of development compared to many altcoins, but it reflects the greater complexity of Ethereum. In addition to EVM, a new programming model, and new data structures, Ethereum made significant changes to Bitcoin's consensus protocol as well. The block time is targeted at 12 seconds instead of 10 minutes. To lessen the impact of stale blocks, which comprise a larger fraction of blocks in Ethereum than in Bitcoin, Ethereum uses an alternative protocol called "GHOST" to compute the consensus branch. It also uses a different proof of work. Currently, it's a mix of hash functions designed to be memory hard, though in the future Ethereum plans to switch to a proof-of-stake system.

This represents another major departure in philosophy from Bitcoin. The Ethereum project is stewarded by a nonprofit foundation and is relatively centralized in its planning and decision making. There is an announced schedule of future versions of the protocol that will introduce changes based on early Ethereum experience. These versions will be hard forks by design, and furthermore, every Ethereum contract will be destroyed in between versions. So Ethereum is still very much an experimental system with major changes planned. As of 2015, it's premature to invest too much in building real applications on top of Ethereum. But the system is very promising. Perhaps future versions of this book might even be called "Ethereum and Cryptocurrency Technologies."

To wrap up this chapter, we've talked about how Bitcoin is an important part of a much larger ecosystem of cryptocurrencies and altcoins. They compete, cooperate, and interact in various ways, some cooperative, some harmful. It's also possible that in the future, there will be technical ways for transactions in one block chain to explicitly refer to transactions in another block chain.

Several open questions remain. Will the altcoin ecosystem consolidate so that a small number of currencies dominate, or will it stay diversified? Will application-specific altcoins proliferate, or will the Ethereum model of a general-purpose platform come to dominate? Is Bitcoin itself eventually going to be overtaken by some other altcoin? Is it a good idea to encourage interaction between Bitcoin and altcoins? Or should each cryptocurrency be a separate system—for example, by using incompatible mining puzzles rather than merge mining? We can't answer these questions right now, but we've talked about all of the concepts you need to understand and appreciate their importance.

FURTHER READING

The sidechains white paper is:

Back, Adam, Matt Corallo, Luke Dashjr, Mark Friedenbach, Gregory Maxwell, Andrew Miller, Andrew Poelstra, Jorge Timón, and Pieter Wuille. "Enabling Blockchain Innovations with Pegged Sidechains." 2014. Available at https://blockstream.com/sidechains.pdf.

The following is a paper about Namecoin and alternate ways to design name/value stores using cryptocurrencies:

Kalodner, Harry, Miles Carlsten, Paul Ellenbogen, Joseph Bonneau, and Arvind Narayanan. "An Empirical Study of Namecoin and Lessons for Decentralized Namespace Design." Presented at the Workshop on the Economics of Information Security, 2015. Available at http://randomwalker.info/publications/namespaces.pdf.

The Ethereum white paper is:

Various authors. "A Next-Generation Smart Contract and Decentralized Application Platform." Available at https://github.com/ethereum/wiki/wiki/White-Paper.

This paper analyzes the incentive misalignment in Ethereum:

Luu, Loi, Jason Teutsch, Raghav Kulkarni, and Prateek Saxena. "Demystifying Incentives in the Consensus Computer." *Proceedings of the 22nd ACM SIGSAC Conference on Computer and Communications Security*, New York: ACM, 2015.

CHAPTER 11

Decentralized Institutions: The Future of Bitcoin?

So far in this book we've explored the state of Bitcoin and block chain technologies as of 2015. In this chapter, we consider what future possibilities may be realized by Bitcoin. We won't claim to know what might unfold, following the adage "never make predictions, especially about the future." Hence the question mark in the title.

Instead, we stick to the academic approach taken so far in this book, even when studying potential future technologies. Bitcoin's future is a subject that seems to muster enthusiastic and breathless visions of a true technological revolution. This chapter could be a manifesto. It is not. We identify notable proposals and take a clinical approach to categorizing them and critically evaluating their relative pros and cons.

Bitcoin is a broad subject that encompasses the protocol itself as well as its potential as a platform for new applications. The focus of this chapter is not the future of the Bitcoin protocol, although we recognize that many issues shaping the future of the protocol are important to study, including Bitcoin's governance, efficiency, scalability, and feature set.

Instead we focus on how Bitcoin's apparent success at decentralizing currency may cause a rethinking of other centralized institutions—ones dealing with stocks, bonds, property titles, and more. Can block chain technology be applied to decentralize them as well? And if decentralization is technically possible, is it also financially sensible and beneficial to society?

11.1. THE BLOCK CHAIN AS A VEHICLE FOR DECENTRALIZATION

There were numerous failed attempts at digital or electronic cash before Bitcoin (the Foreword touches on many of them). Bitcoin's key difference compared to most of these attempts is decentralization. The core innovation of Bitcoin that enables decentralization is the block chain.

In this section, we consider how block chain technology may enable decentralization in areas other than currency. Throughout this chapter, we use a running example of a car whose ownership is controlled through a block chain. This is a specific example of a more general idea of smart property, introduced in Chapter 9. Smart property, and digital contracts that govern them, were pioneered by Nick Szabo and others in the early 1990s, well before Bitcoin was proposed. However, with a block chain, the idea can be made concrete.

Motivating Example

Modern automobiles use two primary locking mechanisms: physical locks on the doors and a vehicle immobilizer, which electronically prevents the engine from starting. The owner is provided with a key fob that communicates wirelessly with the car to authorize the doors to unlock and the engine to start, based on the proximity of the fob to the car and potentially a user action, such as pushing a button.

To prevent an adversary from spoofing the car key, such unlocking mechanisms should use cryptography. While security researchers have found problems with many recently deployed locking protocols, it's possible to get it right. Typically, these algorithms employ symmetric key cryptography, but for the purposes of our example, consider one that uses a digital signature scheme, such as ECDSA, based on asymmetric cryptography.

In this example, the car might store a copy of the public key(s) of the fob(s) authorized to open the doors and start the engine. When a fob requests access, the car sends a random challenge and asks the fob to sign it with the private key that it stores. If and only if the fob can respond with a proper signature to this challenge, the car authorizes access. So far this is not much of a departure from how locking mechanisms actually work, except that it uses more asymmetric crypto that would be slightly more costly to deploy.

Get Smart

The next iteration of designing a smart car is to assume that the public key that verifies the key fob is not hardcoded by the manufacturer directly. Instead, the car has the technical capability to constantly, wirelessly receive new blocks from a block chain, such as Bitcoin's. When the car is manufactured, the public key in the key fob of its first user (e.g., a manager at the assembly plant) is added to the block chain in a special transaction, and the car is programmed with its transaction ID.

The core idea is that as the car changes possession—it might go from an assembly line, to quality control, to a delivery person, to a car dealership, and then to its first owner—updates to the block chain will authorize each transfer. It is important to note that in this model, the authorized key fob does not travel with the car. Each person or entity has a preexisting key fob (or carries/wears technology suitable for implementing the functions of a key fob) with a unique signing key that is activated or deactivated based on transactions that occur on the block chain. Such a transaction would take the car's most recent transaction ID as an input and designate a new public key as the output. It would be signed with the private key corresponding to the current owner.

This is similar to the idea of smart property discussed in Chapter 9, but with a key difference. The block chain transaction doesn't merely represent a change in ownership of the car: it additionally transfers actual physical control or possession of the car. When a car is transferred this way, the earlier owner's key fob stops working, and the new owner's key fob gains the ability to open the locks and start the engine. Equating ownership with possession in this way has profound implications. It enables a powerful kind of decentralization, but it is not obvious whether this is a good idea. We return to this question in Section 11.4.

Secure Exchange

Consider the situation where Alice owns a smart car and wants to sell it to Bob. The ability to transfer control digitally opens up interesting possibilities. For example, Alice might be traveling overseas, and to fund further travel expenses might want to sell her car, which is physically parked in her driveway back home. With an Internet connection, Bob could pay Alice for the car with Bitcoin, Alice can remotely transfer ownership to Bob with the block chain used by the car, and Bob can drive away with his new car.

However, such transactions carry a certain risk. If Bob sends payment first, Alice might keep the money and not transfer ownership. If Alice transfers ownership first, Bob might drive away without paying for the car. Even if Alice is physically present, one party might abort, and it could be difficult for a third party who was not present to mediate the dispute.

We've encountered this problem several times before, including when discussing CoinJoin (Chapter 6) and Namecoin (Chapter 10). The solution in all these cases uses the same principle. As long as the currency used for payment and the car ownership coexist on the same block chain, Alice and Bob can form a single atomic transaction that simultaneously transfers ownership of the car and the payment for the car. Specifically, the transaction would specify two inputs: Alice's ownership and Bob's payment; and specify two outputs: the ownership to Bob and the payment to Alice. The transaction requires both parties to sign, because both are providing inputs. If one signs and the other does not, the transaction is not valid. Once one party signs, the transaction details cannot be changed without invalidating the signature. Once the signed transaction is broadcast to the block chain, the car will wait for a preset number of confirmations (e.g., six) and then allow Bob access. Simultaneously, Bob's payment to Alice will be confirmed. One cannot happen without the other.

The diligent reader might notice a subtle problem. Bob could accept a transaction signed by Alice, sign it, but not actually broadcast it (yet). If the price of what Alice is selling changes, Bob can then broadcast the old transaction at the original price. More complicated atomic transactions have been proposed that include a time-out. Alice can also simply spend the coins to a new address she controls to invalidate the signed transaction she gave to Bob as a means of revoking it.

This is the first of many examples in this chapter that use block chain technologies to decentralize a variety of real-world protocols, and they achieve different types of decentralization. But this idea of *atomicity* is common to most of them, that is, coupling together the deliverables of each side of a transaction so they take place simultaneously (or not at all). Atomicity is an important security concept with applications beyond block chain technology.

11.2. ROUTES TO BLOCK CHAIN INTEGRATION

Because Bitcoin's block chain has been tailored for currency, it can be challenging to repurpose it to represent the semantics of other applications. In the Bitcoin community, you will find many people who are quite partial to either Bitcoin or alternative block chains as a platform for decentralization. We examine the two alternatives in this section.

Route 1: Directly on Bitcoin

The natural starting point for block chain integration is Bitcoin's block chain. This is the approach we used in the example of a smart car (Section 11.1). The main advantage to using Bitcoin directly is deployability: the code runs, the network has acquired significant mining power, and the consensus process appears sound. However, we were only able to use Bitcoin in the example application with some hacks, such as an equivalence between the crypto used to authorize Bitcoin transactions and that used to open car doors. Such hacks are not always possible. More fundamentally, if you have some arbitrarily complex contract between different parties, it may not be representable adequately on Bitcoin's block chain and executed atomically. To illustrate the perils of using Bitcoin's block chain, consider how we might implement a few natural applications of disintermediation.

First consider *crowd-funding services*. As of 2015, the most widely used such service is Kickstarter, which matches entrepreneurs with funders through a central website. If we liked the idea of Kickstarter but wanted to build a completely decentralized alternative, we would need to realize a system where entrepreneurs can request contributions but cannot spend the money until they collect a prespecified amount, all without the use of an intermediary.

A technical approach to achieve this using Bitcoin is to instruct entrepreneurs to create a single transaction with an arbitrary number of inputs (that can vary as the process continues) and a single output to themselves for a specified amount, say, 1,000 BTC. Such transactions will circulate among potential sponsors, where anyone can contribute by adding an input to the transaction for the amount of their contribution and digitally signing their own input, as well as the overall output. Such a transaction cannot be spent by the entrepreneur until the inputs are greater than or equal to the output (Figure 11.1). This method uses some little-known features of Bitcoin to spend the final

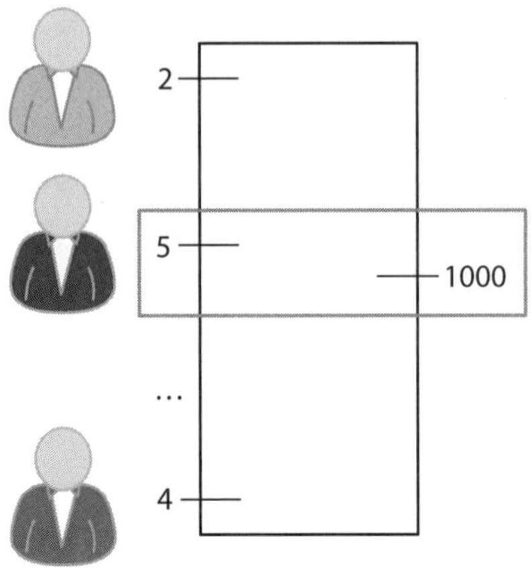

FIGURE 11.1. Crowd-funding via Bitcoin. A single transaction with numerous inputs contributed by different potential sponsors is shown. Each contributor signs her own input and the output, as shown. The transaction will be invalid unless the cumulative sum of input values matches or exceeds the output.

transaction, given only these signatures of limited form. While achievable today, we already have to delve into some little-known corners of Bitcoin. It is not an everyday standard Bitcoin transaction.

Now consider a second example: *paying for a proof*. This example may initially seem strange but has some important applications. To illustrate it, suppose there is a hash function H and a publicly known value y that is ostensibly an output value of H on some input value, or pre-image, x. Alice claims she knows this value x, and Bob would like to pay Alice to learn it as well. In general, H could instead be any computable program, and Bob would like to learn input values that produce certain outputs he is interested in. In a variant of this problem, Bob might pay for the input values to be published publicly on the block chain.

To securely realize this transaction, we must ensure atomicity: Alice should only get paid if she produces a correct input, and Bob must be committed to paying upon production of such an input. Recall that in the protocol for atomic cross-chain swaps in Chapter 10, we showed how to tie a payment with the revelation of the input value to a given hash output. A similar approach can be used here.

These examples illustrate an important limitation of the direct approach of using Bitcoin's block chain. In each case, we had to encode a complex transaction from the real world into Bitcoin's abstractions. This may not always be possible. In the example of the smart car, we conveniently assumed that the car uses ECDSA signatures for authenticating the car owner. That allowed us to use the same public/private key pair on the block chain and in a key fob to unlock and start the car. In the crowd-funding example, the way we have described it, entrepreneurs are able to collect only the exact amounts they requested, no more. If the contributions exceed that amount, that excess becomes a transaction fee. Finally, in the paying-for-proof example, linking the payment to the revelation of a value becomes tricky if the function H isn't one of the hash functions that Bitcoin's script supports.

If you can't—or don't want to—shoehorn your application into Bitcoin's transaction semantics, there is always the option of using an overlay currency, discussed in Chapter 9. This approach treats Bitcoin as a mere data store, so the expressiveness of Bitcoin's script becomes irrelevant. In addition to the ability to implement many more types of applications, this approach can also enable transparency. Consider the car sale example again. If the color of real-world objects (in the sense of colored coins) is known, anyone can examine the block chain to see when a car sale took place and how much was paid for it without necessarily knowing the identities of the buyer and seller. This may be useful in some circumstances, and the color can be kept private in situations where it is detrimental.

However, there are important drawbacks. Users of an overlay currency can't rely on Bitcoin miners to validate their transactions (since miners don't understand the transaction semantics of the overlay). So all users of the overlay must run their own full nodes, and SPV is not possible. Overlay currencies are also brittle if there are bugs in implementations that cause consensus protocol to fail. If two implementations of an overlay currency mutually disagree on whether a particular transaction is valid, it may fork the currency into two, with potentially disastrous consequences. In contrast, when miners are validating transactions, this is much less likely to happen, and if it does, it will be noticed quickly and is likely to be resolved without resulting in a fork.

An additional consideration—regardless of whether an overlay is used—is the issue of burdening or "polluting" the Bitcoin block chain with transactions that are outside its original scope. This is a divisive issue in the Bitcoin community. A way to mitigate this problem is by using Bitcoin as a mere timestamping service, as discussed in Section 9.1, and not even as a data store. As of 2015, there were nascent services that offer a separate block chain or data store, but one that is timestamped via the Bitcoin block chain. This is just like the method discussed in Chapter 9, but with hashes committed every 10 minutes to the Bitcoin block chain instead of every week in the newspaper. Using Bitcoin for timestamping requires only one transaction per block (for each such service or protocol). One drawback is that such external data stores are unlikely to be as widely replicated and available as Bitcoin's block chain. Additionally, it introduces a degree of centralization.

To summarize, whether using an embedding technique or not, Bitcoin's block chain does enable many novel applications. It comes with the benefit of wide-scale adoption, from both users and miners, which makes it a secure and readily deployable option.

Route 2: Alternative Block Chains

The other route to decentralization is to use an alternative block chain. Here again there are a few options. The most obvious one is to have a separate block chain with its own rules, functionality, and currency (i.e., an altcoin). A second option is sidechains, examined in Chapter 10. The main difference is that the currency represented by the sidechain would be pegged in a 1:1 fashion to Bitcoin. Sidechains with enhanced scripting capabilities could allow us to achieve complex contracts and enable disintermediation. However, supporting sidechains requires modifications to Bitcoin, and as of 2015, that hasn't yet happened.

The third option is to use an already-existing alternative block chain that supports the ability to create new applications on top of it. As of 2015, the most prominent project that seeks to be a platform for decentralized cryptocurrency-based applications is Ethereum, discussed in Chapter 10. Conceptually, it is a dream platform for decentralizing arbitrarily complex contracts. However, it also has some practical challenges: at least as of 2015, it does not have the maturity, adoption, or mining power of Bitcoin, nor has it received a comparable level of scrutiny. Nevertheless, it is a fascinating thought experiment for decentralizing powerful contracts, and either Ethereum or a similar system might become viable in the future.

11.3. TEMPLATE FOR DECENTRALIZATION

We have reviewed a number of avenues for achieving decentralization on a block chain. Next, it would be useful to establish a template for what decentralization looks like in terms of what is being decentralized, which type of block chain is appropriate, and what exactly decentralization means in terms of entities and security.

Levels of Decentralization

DECENTRALIZATION THROUGH DISINTERMEDIATION

Consider once again the example of the smart car. To understand it better, let us ask: what is the real-world process that this digital type of ownership transfer seeks to replace?

Sticking with cars as the example of property, in the United States ownership is determined by the title document. This is a centralized form of ownership. The title document only has meaning to the extent that the Department of Motor Vehicles (DMV) recognizes it. When a car is sold, it is not enough to physically transfer this document from the seller to the buyer. The transfer has to be registered in person with the DMV, which updates its central database. With block chain transfers, we move from a state-controlled centralized process to one without any intermediaries. It achieves decentralization through *disintermediation.*

DISPUTE MEDIATION: DECENTRALIZATION THROUGH COMPETITION

Now assume that there is a dispute about the sale of a car. Perhaps the seller sold a lemon car to the buyer, and the buyer is unhappy and wants to reverse the transaction.

In Chapter 3, we discussed 2-out-of-3 multisignature transactions, which can allow escrow if, in addition to the buyer and the seller, a judge or a mediator is involved. In this scenario, the buyer can transfer bitcoins in a separate transaction from the car, not directly to the seller, but instead to a 2-out-of-3 address, which is controlled jointly by the buyer, the seller, and the mediator. The mediator can either approve the transfer or revert it with the help of one or the other party, but cannot steal the money.

This is a good start to building a dispute-resolution mechanism, but many details still need to be sorted out. First, we lose the atomicity of the car sale that we relied on earlier. Second, it is not clear whether the car's ownership can be reverted with the money. Third, if the car is transacted to a 2-out-of-3 address as well, whose key fob should be authorized to unlock it while in this state? Our purpose here is not to iron out these issues but to use the example to carefully consider the role of the mediator. Specifically, let us compare this model of mediation to a more traditional model.

How would dispute mediation take place in the physical world? It would likely go through the court system, a centralized, state-controlled mediation process that is best navigated with the help of hired lawyers. In contrast, with a digital contract, the parties are free to choose any mediator they want. No longer mandated to work with the legal system, a private market for mediation could emerge where potential intermediaries can compete on perceived fairness, efficiency, and cost. Several challenges arise. The first is incentives: mediators might be bribed by either of the parties to a transaction. The second is that funds are locked up during the dispute-filing period. Finally, participants may be anonymous, which makes it difficult to ultimately involve the courts if internal dispute resolution fails. Even if the parties are identified, digital contracts are currently not recognized by courts.

Our point here, however, is that this is not decentralization through disintermediation—we are not completely removing the intermediary. Rather, it enables entities to choose who they trust. In other words, it is decentralization through *competition*. Thus there is a spectrum where on one side you have a single mandatory intermediary, and on the other, you remove the need for any intermediary at all—complete disintermediation. In the middle, you could have multiple competing intermediaries, as just discussed. In fact, we saw this earlier in Chapter 9, when discussing decentralized prediction markets. Instead of a single entity, like InTrade, running the market, participants are free to choose whom they trust from multiple competing arbitrators that perform the sensitive operations in the market.

How Security Is Achieved

We can make another observation about this example. The security of the dispute-mediation process does not rely on atomicity. Instead, it requires trusting the mediator. How do mediators become trustworthy? There could be a variety of ways, but an obvious one is reputation. Unlike atomicity, which is a technological security-enhancing mechanism, reputations are built up over time through inherently social mechanisms.

> **Trust**
>
> Some people in the Bitcoin community use such terms as "trust minimization" or "trustlessness" as a goal. This might sound backward—don't we want systems that we can trust to operate correctly?
>
> The word "trust" has different meanings, which might cause this confusion. When Alice lends Bob $10 and says she trusts him, she means that she thinks he's a trustworthy person, and that she has confidence that he'll pay her back. In the security context, a trusted component is one that you're forced to rely on. When people use the word "trusted" to describe certification authorities, they mean that online security guarantees would be void if such authorities misbehaved.
>
> "Trust minimization" is a worthwhile goal in the sense that, other things being equal, we want to build systems with fewer components that we're reliant on for security. But when you have a hammer, everything looks like a nail, and Bitcoin enthusiasts often get carried away with removing trusted components from systems. A trusted component is not always bad, and the existence of a real-world trust relationship is certainly not a problem by itself. Removing trusted components might also have other subtle drawbacks.
>
> We elaborate on these points in Section 11.4, but for now, having noted the complexity of the word "trust," we avoid it and instead talk about security, a less ambiguous word.

Reputation has a role to play in the absence of technological solutions or as a complement to them. However, it is not without drawbacks. Reputations are tied to identities, and if identities are not static or binding, reputation doesn't work well. For example, if a restaurant receives terrible reviews online and decides to close and reopen under the same management but a new name, its bad reputation is reset. In an anonymous environment, reputations cannot work at all, and in a pseudonymous environment where identities can be switched effortlessly, reputation-based systems face significant challenges. Reputation systems also struggle to validate the "he said/she said" assertions that impact one's reputation. In traditional systems like Yelp, businesses operate under their real names, and so do users to some extent. However, in a pseudonymous environment, it could be infeasible to sensibly sort out spurious accusations from facts.

Other security mechanisms, including secure hardware, are not elaborated on here. Regardless of the mechanism used, the lack of real-world enforcement ultimately makes security a big challenge. No punitive measures for misbehavior are available, and disputes cannot end up in court, especially if no one is using real-world identities. Offering debts is infeasible, as there is no enforcement to ensure that they will be repaid, and so transactions often require deposits, which lock up funds for the dispute period.

The Framework

To summarize the chapter to this point, we can characterize proposals for decentralizing a wide variety of things by asking four questions:

TABLE 11.1. CHARACTERISTICS OF PROPOSALS FOR BLOCK-CHAIN-BASED DECENTRALIZATION

	Proposal			
Characteristic	Smart property	Decentralized prediction markets	StorJ	Zerocoin
1. What is being decentralized?	Property ownership and trading	Prediction market	File storage and retrieval	Mixing of coins
2. What is the level of decentralization?	Disintermediation	Competition, disintermediation	Competition	Disintermediation
3. What block chain is deployed?	Bitcoin	Altcoin	Bitcoin	Altcoin
4. What security mechanism does it use?	Atomicity	Reputation, atomicity	Reputation	Atomicity

1. What is being decentralized?
2. What is the level of decentralization?
3. What block chain is deployed?
4. What security mechanism does it use?

With answers to these four questions, we can succinctly represent almost any of the proposals being mooted in the Bitcoin community for block-chain-based decentralization. Let's consider a few examples (Table 11.1).

SMART PROPERTY

As mentioned, smart property decentralizes the notion of property ownership and transfers of ownership. It achieves complete disintermediation—it eliminates the need for entities like the DMV or the state. We saw how to realize it using Bitcoin's block chain, but you could certainly use an alternative block chain. And finally, the key security principle used was atomicity in tying together the payment with the transfer of the car ownership.

DECENTRALIZED PREDICTION MARKETS

In a centralized prediction market, the centralized platform or exchange performs at least two crucial services: arbitrating the outcome of each event being wagered on, and selling shares to participants (or facilitating participants to securely trade with one another). The decentralized prediction market described in Chapter 9 does away with the need for a central authority for both of these features. It allows anyone to create a market for an event and be its arbiter by sending a simple transaction, lowering the barrier to entry for performing this function. Thus, intermediaries still exist, but users are free to choose from a set of competing intermediaries, and if a user is still unhappy, she can always perform this function herself. However, users directly trade shares with each other atomically, so this function of the central authority has been disintermediated.

Decentralized prediction markets require new functionality not present in Bitcoin itself and are thus naturally implemented through a customized altcoin with its own block chain.

STORJ

StorJ is a proposal by Greg Maxwell for file storage and retrieval. It has evolved over time, but we discuss a simple version of it. At a high level, StorJ deploys an "agent" that lives in the cloud and is programmed to make certain decisions on its own. For example, it can rent cloud computation and storage to give itself computational resources. Another feature it provides to users is the ability to store a file for a certain period, say, 24 hours, in exchange for payment in Bitcoin. It will keep hosting the file as long it keeps receiving payment. Beyond simple storage, it can do a number of interesting things not considered here. In our framework, StorJ decentralizes file storage and retrieval, which are the core features of centralized services like Dropbox. The agent is an intermediary; it doesn't matter for our purposes that it is automated. However, intermediaries can compete. Payment is done with Bitcoin, but there is no atomic link between the agent performing its services and the payments it receives, so security is a matter of the agent's reputation.

ZEROCOIN

Zerocoin, discussed in Chapter 6, is effectively a method for decentralizing the mixing of coins to achieve anonymity. Instead of using a centralized mixing service, Zerocoin realizes a cryptographic protocol that is functionally equivalent to using a mix but uses no intermediaries at all—only math and consensus. The relatively heavy cryptography needed in Zerocoin (and its successor, Zerocash) means that a separate block chain is the far more feasible route. As for the security mechanism, recall that the notion of burning a basecoin and getting a zerocoin in exchange for it are atomically coupled through the same transaction; and similarly for later redeeming a zerocoin. This is an example of atomicity.

11.4. WHEN IS DECENTRALIZATION A GOOD IDEA?

In this chapter so far, we have focused on the technical challenges of achieving decentralization. Now we delve into questions of motivation. These questions are nontechnical, but often they're just as difficult to answer: Is decentralization a good idea? Is it economically feasible? What are the social consequences of decentralization?

Until now, we have used the term "decentralization" as a technical concept without being explicit about the fact that it is politically charged. When we talk about replacing traditional systems fully or partly with technological alternatives, we are really talking about redistributing power from well-established legal, social, and financial institutions. Thus the idea of decentralization stems from Bitcoin's roots in the cypherpunk movement—a movement begun by nonconformists dreaming of cryptography's ability to empower individual autonomy (see the Foreword and Chapter 7). With the block chain, this ideal appears closer than ever. But is this ideal feasible or desirable?

Returning to our running example, the traditional institutions try to solve two problems for car owners. The first is enforcing ownership, or essentially preventing theft. The second is ensuring secure exchanges, or preventing someone from being ripped off during a sale. So to analyze how smart property fares compared to the existing system, we have to look at not just how efficient things are when everything goes right, but also, crucially, how bad things can get when something goes wrong.

The Challenge of Real-World Security

Defending against any form of theft—cars, art, money, and so forth—is an exercise of prevention, detection, and correction. Preventive security mechanisms try to stop theft before it happens, whereas detection mechanisms ensure theft is perceived so potential corrective measures can be taken to revert the damages of the theft and to punish the perpetrator (which could also serve as a deterrent to committing theft). Car locks and alarms are preventive mechanisms, while GPS tracing units (such as LoJack) can assist in detecting the theft and enabling law enforcement to recover the stolen car. The key insight is that the car lock is just one small piece of deterrence to car theft—one piece of a large, intricate system involving police, insurance companies, courts, and the like. If you lived in a lawless environment, a car lock by itself wouldn't be much of a deterrent to theft. Leaving your car locked on the street would ensure that it would be quickly stolen.

The model we have used for smart property relies heavily on preventive mechanisms. We were able to achieve decentralization only because we equated possession with ownership—owning a car is essentially equivalent to knowing the private key corresponding to a designated transaction on a block chain. But this control mechanism is a poor replacement for our current mosaic of institutional support.

If we reduce ownership to the problem of securing private keys, it raises the stakes for digital security—a difficult problem in which humans are a weak link. Programmers have endeavored to write bug-free code for decades, but the challenge remains elusive. Designers of cryptosystems have tried for decades to entice nontechnical users to use and manage private keys in a way that resists both theft and accidental loss of keys, also with little progress. If the model of decentralization relies excessively on private keys, cars might be stolen by malware or in phishing attacks, and the loss of a key might turn your car into a giant brick. While there could be fallback mechanisms to cover these types of events, inevitably such mechanisms tend to lead us back toward intermediaries and centralized systems, chipping away at the benefits of the decentralized model we were striving for.

Another area of property transfers that is fundamentally human oriented is dealing with disputes that might arise over the terms of sale or other aspects of the transfer. In the real world, if the participants cannot reach a resolution, the issue will end up in court, where a judge will methodically examine each bit of evidence, testimony, and written words to reach a nuanced ruling about the validity of the sale. It is tempting, particularly for technical people, to think of the law as a set of logical rules or algorithms that can produce a clear-cut ruling. However, the reality of the legal system is that not only are laws and contracts verbose, they are ultimately subject to human interpretation and discretion, which is further removed from the notion of clear-cut logical rules. This attribute is not a weakness. It allows for resolving situations that are far more complex than what was anticipated by the individuals writing the law.

To drive home the mismatch between the security properties derived from the decentralized model and the security properties that we actually want, let's revisit the earlier example of decentralized crowd-funding. We saw a technical mechanism to ensure an entrepreneur cannot cash out on investments until the contributions sum to some prespecified amount. However, this by no means prevents an entrepreneur who has successfully raised the funds from absconding with the money! In fact, even with the current centralized model, there have been numerous alleged scams on crowd-funding sites, resulting in several lawsuits. In a model where entrepreneurs are potentially anonymous and there is no deterrent effect from the threat of being sued, this problem is likely to be far worse. It is hard to imagine a technical solution to this problem. This is another case where the technology is only solving a small part of the problem, and frankly not even the interesting part of the problem.

To recap, the interesting problems with smart property seem to be social problems, issues that arise when something goes wrong. Technology can ensure an efficient transaction when all parties are satisfied, but it is not adept at solving thorny disputes.

Pros and Cons of Smart Property

As argued, smart property has difficulty decentralizing the aspects of a system that traditionally requires human intervention. In fact, automation may make it even more difficult by not composing well with mediation and other processes if the latter are layered on after the fact. Finally, it may create new categories of problems, such as requiring software security in addition to physical security in the case of a car.

These examples are, to a certain extent, cartoon versions of what a thorough proposal for smart property might look like. Many proposals in the Bitcoin community are more nuanced, but even in our simple setting, we can discern the advantages and disadvantages of smart property.

The main advantage of smart property is the efficiency of ownership transfer, which can be done from anywhere at any time. For sales of items less valuable than a car (e.g., a smartphone or computer), disputes are unlikely to end up in court, and so nothing is lost in that regard. For such items, atomic transactions are a useful security feature.

Smart property through block chains also provides greater privacy, and even anonymity. While we've argued that it complicates dispute resolution, privacy is also beneficial in a society where consumer data is used by companies in ways that are unseen and likely unintended by those making the purchases. In some cases, it might be important for the parties to a transaction not to disclose their identities, which is infeasible in a centralized intermediated model.

Finally, the decentralized model allows mediators to be chosen. Even if we are content with the legal system, often disputes are mediated by private companies like Visa or PayPal behind closed doors, using a method that is hard to scrutinize. By using an alternative model where such mediation is opened up to competition, we can potentially bring more transparency and public oversight to the process.

Crypto, the State, and the Big Opportunity

There is a striking parallel between the emergence of the modern state and the goals of the technology we have discussed in this chapter. In scaling society up from tribes and small groups, governments have had to confront precisely the problem of enabling secure commerce and other interactions among strangers. The methods may be very different, but the goal is a shared one.

Although a maximalist vision for decentralization might involve dismantling the state, this is not really a viable vision, especially when others who share our democracy want a state. However, decentralization through technology is not necessarily in opposition to the state at all. In fact, they can be mutually beneficial. For example, assuming well-identified parties, transfers of smart property can use the block chain for efficient transfers and still use the court system if a dispute arises. We think the big opportunity for block chain technology is implementing decentralization in a way that complements the functions of the state, rather than seeking to replace them.

It is tempting to think that certain processes will be decentralized simply because the technology exists. But in practice, there needs to be a compelling economic reason, such as government regulation that is particularly onerous or inefficient, or a power imbalance that could lead to abuse. As one illustration of this, people in various African countries have adopted cell phone minutes as an ad hoc currency that is outside of state control and less subject to abuses of power.

To summarize, we've described the technical blueprint for decentralization in this chapter and also critically examined the motivations behind decentralization. We encourage you to look for compelling use cases of decentralization, in particular ones that integrate into existing legal and regulatory practices.

Conclusion

Some people are excited about Bitcoin because of the underlying technology. Others are excited about its commercial possibilities, and yet others about its social and political implications. Reasonable people can disagree about the latter two, but we hope this book has convinced you that technologically, Bitcoin is deep, novel, interesting, and based on sound principles. Beyond Bitcoin is a fascinating world of alternative cryptocurrency designs that we're just starting to explore, some of which might one day be more important than Bitcoin itself.

We got into Bitcoin because we believe in the power of its technology, and we think it's deeply connected to the rest of computer science. While we've highlighted how seemingly amazing new technology can struggle to displace established institutions, we believe that in the long run people will continue to find new commercially and socially useful things to do with cryptocurrency technology. Even if your interest is primarily commercial, you'd do well to master the underlying technology—understanding its power and limitations will help you better weather the market's hype cycles.

Where should you go from here? One of the best things about decentralization is that it's a great platform for experimentation and learning. Anyone can download and analyze Bitcoin's block chain, or build their own applications on top of it; we hope you'll take advantage of these opportunities.

We've created online materials that complement this text. Our Coursera course (www.coursera.org/course/bitcointech) contains video lectures that mirror the contents of this book. It also has quizzes and a series of programming assignments (a link to the online materials can also be found at http://press.princeton.edu/titles/10908.html). Taking the course will also give you access to the forums where you'll find a community of like-minded learners.

Acknowledgments

We're immensely grateful to the students who helped develop programming assignments and to everyone who provided feedback on the drafts of this book. Princeton students Shivam Agarwal, Miles Carlsten, Paul Ellenbogen, Pranav Gokhale, Alex Iriza, Harry Kalodner, and Dillon Reisman, and Stanford students Allison Berke, Benedikt Bünz, and Alex Leishman deserve special praise. We're also thankful to Dan Boneh and Albert Szmigielski.

Arvind Narayanan gratefully acknowledges financial support from the National Science Foundation (grant number 1421689).

About the Authors

ARVIND NARAYANAN (PhD 2009) is an Assistant Professor of Computer Science at Princeton. Narayanan leads the Princeton Web Transparency and Accountability project that aims to uncover how companies are collecting and using our personal information. He also leads a research group studying the security, anonymity, and stability of Bitcoin and cryptocurrencies. His doctoral research showed that data anonymization is broken in fundamental ways, for which he jointly received the 2008 Privacy Enhancing Technologies Award.

JOSEPH BONNEAU is a Technology Fellow at the Electronic Frontier Foundation and Postdoctoral Researcher at Stanford. In addition to researching Bitcoin and cryptocurrencies he has worked on passwords and web authentication, secure messaging tools, and HTTPS for secure web browsing. Earlier he was a Postdoctoral Fellow at CITP, Princeton and he has previously worked at Google, Yahoo, and Cryptography Research Inc. He received a PhD from the University of Cambridge and an MS from Stanford.

EDWARD W. FELTEN is a Professor of Computer Science and Public Affairs at Princeton, and the founding Director of the Center for Information Technology Policy. In 2011–12 he served as the first Chief Technologist at the U.S. Federal Trade Commission. His research interests include computer security and privacy, and technology law and policy. He has published more than 100 papers in the research literature, and two books. His research on topics such as Internet security, privacy, copyright and copy protection, and electronic voting has been covered extensively in the popular press.

ANDREW MILLER is a computer science PhD student at the University of Maryland, and previously received his MS degree from the University of Central Florida. He has studied cryptocurrencies since 2011, and has authored scholarly papers on a wide range of original research, including new proof-of-work puzzle constructions, programming languages for block chain data structures, and peer-to-peer network measurement and simulation techniques. He is an Associate Director of the Initiative for Cryptocurrencies and Contracts (IC3) at Cornell and an advisor to the Zcash project.

STEVEN GOLDFEDER is a PhD student in the Department of Computer Science at Princeton University, advised by Arvind Narayanan. He is a member of the Security &

Privacy Research Group, a CITP Graduate Student Fellow, and a National Science Foundation Graduate Research Fellow. His research interests include cryptography, security, and privacy, especially decentralized digital currencies. His current work involves increasing the security of Bitcoin wallets.

JEREMY CLARK is an Assistant Professor at the Concordia Institute for Information Systems Engineering in Montreal. He received his PhD from the University of Waterloo in 2011, where he applied cryptography to designing and deploying verifiable voting systems, including Scantegrity—the first use of an end-to-end verifiable system in a public-sector election. He became interested in Bitcoin in 2010 and published one of the first academic papers in the area. Beyond research, he has worked with several municipalities on voting technology and testified to the Canadian Senate on Bitcoin.

Index

Italic page numbers refer to figures and tables.